Language Contact

Most societies in today's world are multilingual. 'Language contact' occurs when speakers of different languages interact and their languages influence each other. This book is an introduction to the subject, covering individual and societal multilingualism, the acquisition of two or more languages from birth, second-language acquisition in adulthood, language change, linguistic typology, language processing, and the structure of the language faculty. It explains the effects of multilingualism on society and language policy, as well as the consequences that long-term bilingualism within communities can have for the structure of languages. Drawing on the author's own first-hand observations of child and adult bilingualism, the book provides a clear analysis of such phenomena as language convergence, grammatical borrowing, and mixed languages.

YARON MATRAS is Professor of Linguistics in the School of Languages, Linguistics and Cultures at the University of Manchester. His recent publications include *Romani: A Linguistic Introduction* (Cambridge, 2002) and *Markedness and Language Change* (with Viktor Elšík, 2006).

Language Contact

In this series:

Language Contact

YARON MATRAS

University of Manchester

CAMBRIDGE
UNIVERSITY PRESS

CAMBRIDGE UNIVERSITY PRESS
Cambridge, New York, Melbourne, Madrid, Cape Town, Singapore, São Paulo, Delhi

Cambridge University Press
The Edinburgh Building, Cambridge CB2 8RU, UK

Published in the United States of America by Cambridge University Press, New York

www.cambridge.org
Information on this title: www.cambridge.org/9780521532211

First published 2009

Printed in the United Kingdom at the University Press, Cambridge

A catalogue record for this publication is available from the British Library

Library of Congress Cataloguing in Publication data
Matras, Yaron, 1963–
Language contact / Yaron Matras.
    p.   cm. – (Cambridge textbooks in linguistics)
Includes bibliographical references and index.
ISBN 978-0-521-82535-1 (hardback) – ISBN 978-0-521-53221-1 (pbk.)
1. Multilingualism.   2. Second language acquisition.   I. Title.   II. Series.
P115.M38   2009
306.44′6 – dc22   2009015836

ISBN 978-0-521-82535-1 hardback
ISBN 978-0-521-53221-1 paperback

Contents

Figures

Preface

In those very few societies in which monolingualism is the norm, bilinguals are sometimes asked which language they dream in. The answer is, of course, invariably: 'It depends what or whom we are dreaming about.' That tends to put monolinguals in their place: they show respect for the rhetoric. In fact, the correct answer is that as bilinguals we are unable to keep our languages entirely apart even in our dreams. We may associate certain expressions or phrases with particular events, gestures, or faces, but in our dreams as in our everyday conscious communication we strive for the absolute liberty to use our entire linguistic repertoire freely, with no constraints, and we adore those moments when we can converse with fellow bilinguals who understand and even encourage us to do so. Language contact is about the way we live with the expectation that even our dreams should be monolingual, about how we bypass these restrictions and mix our languages in actual conversation, and about the way in which even monolinguals sometimes end up enriching and re-shaping their own form of speech thanks to their interaction with bilingual individuals. This is essentially the idea that is presented, in somewhat more detail, in the following chapters.

I feel fortunate to have been raised in a multilingual environment and in a multilingual family, and I owe many of the insights that I am able to present here as my own to the stimulating and compelling circumstances that allowed me to participate, observe, and reflect on the way individuals and societies practice language contact. I am also privileged to have had the opportunity, over the years, to discuss issues of language contact at the professional level with many colleagues and friends, among them Greg Anderson, Peter Auer, Ad Backus, Peter Bakker, Giuliano Bernini, Walter Bisang, Simone Bol, David Bradley, Kate Burridge, Michael Clyne, Bernard Comrie, Bill Croft, Eva Csató, Guy Deutscher, Christina Eira, Viktor Elšík, Patty Epps, Marcel Erdal, Nick Evans, Dan Everett, Jonathan Fine, Victor Friedman, Friedel Frohwein, David Gil, Eitan Grossman, Dieter Halwachs, Ian Hancock, Martin Haspelmath, Bernd Heine, Peter Hendriks, Kees Hengeveld, Kristine Hildebrandt, Lars Johanson, František Kratochvíl, Masha Koptjevskaja-Tamm, Tanya Kuteva, Patrick McConvell, April McMahon, Felicity Meakins, Miriam Meyerhoff, Marianne Mithun, Pieter Muysken, Carol Myers-Scotton, Johana Nichols, Shana Poplack, Mark Post, Carmel O'Shannesy, Angelika Redder, Gertrud Reershemius, Jochen Rehbein, Jeanette Sakel, Eva Schultze-Berndt, Zdeněk Starý, Thomas Stolz, Uri Tadmor, Johan van der Auwera, Peter Wagner, and Debra Ziegeler; my thanks to all of them.

My students and collaborators in the Manchester Working Group on Language Contact have been a precious source of inspiration. For many hours of thought-provoking discussion I wish to thank Asma Al-Baluchi, Adele Chadwick, Claire Chen, Veliyana Chileva, Andrea Donakey, Francesco Goglia, Lucy Hottmann, Heveen Ali Kurdi, Sandy Lo, Mohamed Fathi Osman, Barbara Schrammel, Veronica Schulman, Maryam Shabibi, Ellen Smith, Declan Sweeney, Anton Tenser, Anne-Marie Thomson, and Şirin Tufan.

Some of the data included in this book and some of the ideas discussed here are, directly or indirectly, products of a series of externally funded projects carried out at the University of Manchester. I am grateful to the Arts and Humanities Research Council for funding some of my research on Mixed Languages and on Language Convergence and Linguistic Areas, to the Economic and Social Research Council, the Arts and Humanities Research Council, and the Open Society Institute for funding my research on Romani, to the British Academy for support for my research on Domari as well as the creation of a digital archive of recordings of endangered languages, and to the Special Research Area on Cultural and Linguistic Contacts in North Africa and Western Asia at the University of Mainz (SFB 295) for sponsoring my fieldwork on a number of languages. For technical support and assistance with the collection, processing, and archiving of data and data sources I thank Viktor Elšík, Barbara Schrammel, Jeanette Sakel, Christa Schubert, Charlotte Jones, Ruth Hill, Hazel Gardner, Chris White, Veronica Schulman, and Anthony Grant, who worked with me on these projects, as well as Martin Nissen, Dörte Hansen-Jaax, Dunja Rösteholm, Nellie Weiss, Mi'assar Sleem, Moshe Dafan, Greta Johansen, and many others who have provided interviews, shared data, or helped gloss and translate examples. I am deeply grateful to my colleagues in Linguistics and English Language at the School of Languages, Linguistics and Cultures of the University of Manchester for their support and enthusiasm, which allowed Manchester to become a thriving centre for discussions on language contact.

During the preparation of the book I benefited from audiences' comments in reaction to invited keynote addresses at the Annual Meeting of the Linguistics Association of Great Britain in Roehampton and at the Workshop on Language Variation and Contact-Induced Language Change at the Annual Meeting of the Association for Linguistic Typology in Paris, as well as from reactions to seminar presentations at the Max Planck Institute in Leipzig, at the universities of Cologne, Düsseldorf, Hamburg, York, Jerusalem, Prague, Melbourne, and Sydney, and at the Australian National University in Canberra and the Research Centre for Linguistic Typology at La Trobe University, Melbourne. I began writing the book during a research visit at the Max Planck Institute for Evolutionary Anthropology in Leipzig, in the spring of 2004, and I am grateful to Bernard Comrie and Martin Haspelmath for facilitating my stay there. I completed the manuscript in 2007 during my stay as International Linkage Fellow sponsored by the Australian Research Council and as Distinguished Fellow of the Institute for Advanced Studies at the Research Centre for Linguistic

Typology at La Trobe University, Melbourne, by invitation of Sasha Aikhenvald and Bob Dixon.

The ideas expressed in this book are grounded not just in the experience of language contact, but also in a general appreciation of what language is. I owe an immeasurable debt of gratitude to my teacher Jochen Rehbein, who, more than anyone, prompted me to reflect critically on the meaning of categorisations, labels, and models in linguistics, to search for the inner function of linguistic forms in the very purpose of linguistic activities, and to appreciate, unapologetically, the broad range of human communicative activities as an integrated whole and as the key to the study of the language faculty. I feel that his past years of guidance and inspiration have shaped my approach to the following chapters even more than they had influenced some of my earlier work, and I therefore dedicate this book to him.

Last but certainly not least, my love and very special thanks to Tom, for being the most wonderful 'Ben' that he is, and for always helping me see the world in full colour.

Abbreviations

1	First person	LOC	Locative
2	Second person	M	Masculine
3	Third person	NEG	Negation
ABL	Ablative	NEUTR	Neuter
ACC	Accusative	NOM	Nominative
AOR	Aorist	OBL	Oblique
ATT/R	Attributive	PART	Particle
COMP	Complementiser	PASS	Passive
CONSTR	Construct state	PAST	Past tense
COP	Copula	PL	Plural
DAT	Dative	POSS	Possessive
DEF	Definite (article)	PRED	Predication
DEIC	Deixis	PRES	Present tense
DET	Determiner	PROG	Progressive
F	Feminine	REL	Relativiser
GEN	Genitive	REM	Remote
IND	Indicative	SG	Singular
INSTR	Instrumental	SUBJ	Subjunctive
ITR	Intransitive	TR	Transitive

1 Introduction

1.1 The study of language contact

Manifestations of language contact are found in a great variety of domains, including language acquisition, language processing and production, conversation and discourse, social functions of language and language policy, typology and language change, and more. This makes it a special challenge to compile an overview of the subject. Most introductory works devoted to contact linguistics have hitherto chosen to specialise either in the individual-synchronic aspects of bilingualism, or in structural-diachronic aspects of contact-induced language change. This book introduces an integrated theory of language contact, within which the study of these various domains can be bound together.

Since the launch of modern contract linguistics through the works of Weinreich (1953) and Haugen (1953), the study of individual bilingualism and of societal multilingualism has occupied a centre-stage position in the field. A testimony to this position is provided by a series of introductory textbooks that focus on one or both these areas, covering topics such as the acquisition of two languages from birth, bilingual language processing, diglossia and societal bilingualism, and language policy in multilingual communities (see Grosjean 1982, Hamers and Blanc 1989, Romaine 1989, Hoffmann 1991). Appel and Muysken's (1987) textbook was one of the first introductory works to take into account diachronic aspects of contact-induced language change. It was soon followed by Thomason and Kaufman's (1988) monograph, which remains one of the most influential and frequently cited works on language contact in the context of historical linguistics. Both these books put a spotlight on grammatical borrowing, and on the emergence of areal language clusters and of new 'contact' languages. Two further domains of investigation within contact linguistics have received attention in specialised introductory textbooks: the study of pidgins and creoles (Holm 1988–89, Arends, Muysken, and Smith 1995), and the study of code switching (Muysken 2000a, Milroy and Muysken 1995).

In recent years, several valuable contributions have appeared that aim to provide a state-of-the-art description of the field of contact linguistics or parts of it. Thomason's (2001) introduction to language contact emphasises historical linguistic aspects, including linguistic areas, language maintenance and shift, and contact languages. Winford (2003) is one of the first to combine a discussion of codeswitching with an overview of historical aspects of contact, and Clyne (2003) combines a synthesis of other works on codeswitching and individual and societal bilingualism with a detailed discussion of the Melbourne corpus of immigrant languages. Myers-Scotton (2002b) outlines the Matrix Language Frame model of codeswitching and applies it to further phenomena such as language attrition, lexical borrowing, and the emergence of contact languages. The book is one of few attempts at a comprehensive discussion of contact phenomena within a specific theoretical framework. Further aspects of bilingualism, such as second-language acquisition and child bilingualism, societal multilingualism and language policy, and language processing and intercultural communication are covered in Myers-Scotton (2005).

1.2   Toward an integrated, functional approach to language contact

It is difficult to follow in the footsteps of the authors of these many insightful and inspiring works. My reason for wanting to add yet another book to the list of these fine introductions derives from a wish to strengthen the focus on a number of aspects in the discussion of language contact:

First, with the exception of Winford (2003) and Myers-Scotton (2002b), most textbooks continue to specialise in either synchronic (individual and societal) or diachronic aspects of language contact. Winford's book is an exception, as it devotes a chapter to a comprehensive and thorough discussion of codeswitching as well as accommodating a discussion of second-language acquisition. Missing from Winford's discussion are aspects of bilingual first-language acquisition and language processing, as well as an integrated theoretical approach that links the various domains. Myers-Scotton's (2002b) book is by contrast devoted entirely to introducing the Matrix Language Frame model, and does not pretend to cover the state-of-the-art in the individual fields to which the model is applied. The present book attempts to do both: To present the state-of-the-art in a wide range of sub-fields in contact linguistics, both synchronic and diachronic, and at the same time to offer a number of theoretical principles through which contact can be interpreted and appreciated in an integrated manner.

Second, it is my impression that much work has tended to focus on the implications of language contact to the inner coherence of language 'systems', while the perspective of the bilingual individual, which had stood so much in the foreground of Weinreich's (1953) work, seems to have been demoted. To be sure, this perspective is given much coverage in both conversation-analytical and 'rational choice' models of codeswitching (e.g. Auer 1984, Maschler 1994, Li Wei 2002, Myers-Scotton and Bolonyai 2001), in the recent direction in the study of child bilingualism (cf. Lanza 1997), and in some models of bilingual language processing (Grosjean 1998, Paradis 2004, Green 1998). But speakers' communicative goals and intentions, their discourse strategies, and their language processing capacities are at the core of any speech production and so also of the structural innovations that constitute the seeds of potential language change. They therefore merit consideration when we set out to interpret processes of contact-induced change. 'Contact' is, of course, a metaphor: language 'systems' do not genuinely touch or even influence one another. The relevant locus of contact is the language processing apparatus of the individual multilingual speaker and the employment of this apparatus in communicative interaction. It is therefore the multilingual speaker's interaction and the factors and motivations that shape it that deserve our attention in the study of language contact.

Third, while interest in language contact has been on the rise among language typologists, and while a series of generalisations on the structural outcomes of contact have been proposed, tested, and discussed in the past, a typologically oriented framework of contact is still missing. The discussion in this book is informed by recent sampling of cases of contact-induced change. Taking into account processes observed in other domains of contact such as second-language acquisition and bilingual language processing, I propose some generalisations about the degree to which different structural components of language and different grammatical categories are 'vulnerable' in contact situations. The underlying assumption is that the language faculty is stratified and that the hierarchical behaviour of categories will reflect this stratification. In this respect, the study of language contact is of value toward an understanding of the inner functions and the inner structure of 'grammar' and the language faculty itself.

Fourth, no integrated approach to language contact has yet been formulated from a functionalist perspective. Such a perspective rests on a view of language as social activity and of communication as goal-driven. Consequently, it views speakers as actors who use language in order to achieve goals, and it attributes the selection of entire codes and of individual structures of language – constructions, word-forms, intonation, and so on – to goal-oriented activity. Moreover, it regards the structures, categories, and forms of language as triggers of linguistic-mental processing tasks that engage the hearer in communication. The dimension of the 'hearer' is therefore crucial to our analysis of linguistic 'categories' and their function; and the function of 'categories' is in turn regarded as central to their fate in various processes, from acquisition to codemixing in conversation, and on to structural borrowing and deliberate manipulation of language.

The theory of contact that is explicated in the following chapters is not a 'Theory' in the sense of a formal, self-contained, finite set of rules and principles that label, and pretend to be able to predict, each and every outcome of language contact. Rather, it is a theoretical approach that seeks to make generalisations about various manifestations of language contact, informed by, and embedded within, a broader understanding of language and communication. Such an understanding draws on a variety of sources, ideas, and works in linguistics. It includes a view of communication as part of a repertoire of social activities (Labov 1972a and 1972b, Hymes 1974, Gumperz 1980, Schiffrin 1987, Saville-Troike 1989), of communicative interaction as a repetitive form of human behaviour (Sacks, Schegloff, and Jefferson 1974, Sperber and Wilson 1986, Ehlich and Rehbein 1986),[1] and of grammar as the packaging of information in discourse (Givón 1984, 1990). It is based on the assumption that speakers' linguistic repertoires consist not just of formal rules and a lexicon, but of constructions (Goldberg 1995, Croft 2001), that language change is the product of innovation by individuals (Labov 1994, Croft 2000), and that speakers are creative and able to exploit meanings in new contexts, leading to the formation of new categories through 'grammaticalisation' (Heine, Claudi, and Hünnemeyer 1991, Hopper and Traugott 1993). It is also guided by an appreciation of 'pragmatics' as a method to uncover the very purpose and the inner function of structural categories, and not just to describe their casual employment.

My principal assumption in this book is that bilingual (or multilingual) speakers have a complex repertoire of linguistic structures at their disposal. This repertoire is not organised in the form of 'languages' or 'language systems'; the latter is a meta-linguistic construct and a label which speakers learn to apply to their patterns of linguistic behaviour as part of a process of linguistic socialisation. Rather, elements of the repertoire (word-forms, phonological rules, constructions, and so on) gradually become associated, through a process of linguistic socialisation, with a range of social activities, including factors such as sets of interlocutors, topics, and institutional settings. Mature multilingual speakers face a constant challenge to maintain control over their complex repertoire of forms and structures and to select those forms that are context-appropriate. Context-appropriate selection does not necessarily conform to a separation of 'languages': In some contexts, certain types of cross-linguistic 'mixing' and 'inserting' may be socially acceptable and may constitute effective goal-oriented communication.

Speakers' awareness of, and ability to implement social norms on the selection of elements within the linguistic repertoire is a central aspect of communication in multilingual settings. Awareness and the ability to control the repertoire may receive support from institutions and overtly articulated social norms and values concerning language. On the other hand, the language faculty presents itself as uneven with respect to the ease of control and selection of structures, as some language processing operations may escape the speaker's control more easily than others.

Communication in a language contact setting is the product of the interplay of two primary factors (Figure 1.1): Loyalty to a set of norms that regulate the context-bound selection of elements from the repertoire, and a wish to be able to exploit the repertoire in its entirety irrespective of situational constraints. The balance between these two factors is determined by a need to remove hurdles that stand in the way of efficient communication.

When loyalty prevails in a strict manner, then 'interference' or compromises are likely to be minimal. But when the wish to exploit the full repertoire is given some leeway, then strict context-bound separation of repertoire components might be compromised. Individual words that are usually reserved for interaction

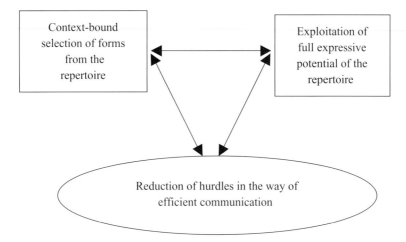

Figure 1.1 *The interplay of factors in communication in language contact settings.*

in Context set A might, for example, be employed ('inserted') also in interaction in Context set B. Second-language learners might draw on the phonology of their native language while communicating in a second language, bilingual children might employ constructions from one language that are not usually used in the chosen language of conversation, and adult bilinguals might insert discourse markers from one language when communicating in another. All this suggests that multilingual speakers do not 'block' or 'switch off' one of their languages when communicating in another, but that they have the full, complex linguistic repertoire at their disposal at all times.

The interplay of factors displayed in Figure 1.1 may lead to language change when a particular pattern of linguistic behaviour becomes widespread and accepted within a relevant sector of the speech community. Thus, an inserted word-form from another language may become a loanword, collective language-learning may show substrate influences in phonology (as well as in other domains of structure), the morpho-syntactic constructions of languages in bilingual communities may undergo convergence, and discourse markers from one language may be borrowed into another language. Contact-induced language change is thus ultimately the product of innovations that individual multilingual speakers introduce into discourse in a multilingual setting. Such innovations are, in turn, strategies that allow speakers to navigate between the two push-and-pull factors that we have identified: complying with social norms and expectations on context-appropriate selection of structures, on the one hand, and exploiting the full potential of the linguistic repertoire, on the other. From the point of view of their functionality, synchronic and diachronic manifestations of contact are therefore inseparable. Consequently, contact is not regarded here as an 'external' factor that triggers change, but as one that is internal to the processing and use of language itself in the multilingual speaker's repertoire of linguistic structures.

A final note is in order on the position of grammatical categories in the investigation of structural manifestations of contact. I follow a functionalist perspective that regards 'words' as more than just 'words': linguistic expressions and constructions – whether bound or unbound morphemes, or morpho-syntactic organisation patterns – trigger distinct types of mental processing operations. These operations may be organised and retrieved in different ways, allowing counterpart structures in the multilingual repertoire to be more or less easily distinguished from one another, selected and controlled. The inner function of grammatical categories therefore has a key role in explaining the behaviour of that category in language contact situations. In typological perspective, sampling reveals that there are some noteworthy differences between categories in respect of their likelihood to undergo change as a result of contact. Hierarchical differences among categories also appear in language acquisition and in language mixing in conversation. In line with explanatory accounts in linguistic typology, I take the view that re-occurring patterns of structural change and structural categorisation are not accidental, but that they are based in part on shared human conceptualisations of reality, and more specifically on the foundations of managing and engaging in human communicative interaction. I will be paying special attention to the role of categories and their functions, assigning similar outcomes of contact not just to similar social settings and similar processes of identity negotiation, but also to the role of categories in triggering and regulating distinct language processing operations. In this respect, I will be assuming that contact has not just a social dimension, but a communicative dimension, and that the structure of grammar and the changes that it undergoes are a reflection of this communicative dimension.

1.3   The structure of this book

Following from the interests and principles just described, this book is intended to deliver an integrated discussion of individual and social aspects of bilingualism as well as of processes of language change. As noted above, one of the aims of the book is to restore the centre-stage position of the bilingual speaker as a creative communicator in the perspective that we take when investigating language contact. I therefore open with a chapter that introduces the 'Preliminaries' of the emergence of a multilingual repertoire (Chapter 2). This chapter is a case study of the early acquisition of language in a trilingual child. Its main purpose is to illustrate how bilinguals develop a command of the repertoire along with the skills to manage the interplay of factors depicted in Figure 1.1: compliance with interlocutor expectations on the context-bound selection of elements from the repertoire, on the one hand, and exploitation of the full repertoire, on the other. Already at the early stages of language acquisition, the child speaker develops a sensitivity toward expectations on context-appropriateness of word-forms. At the same time, the compromises that are made are tightly connected to the referential and later to the language-processing function of the relevant word-form, and we obtain our first glimpse into the hierarchical nature of functional categories at work. As the child speaker matures, a balance between compliance with norms and exploitation of the full repertoire is struck through the application of a series of strategies, among them various types of language mixing as well as creative procedures such as the replication of constructions using context-appropriate word-forms. These strategies will accompany the speaker in adulthood and will constitute the core for individual innovations, which in turn constitute the foundation pool for potential processes of language change. On the whole, Chapter 2 thus gives us an overview of the potential effects of bilingualism in conversation, in language processing, and on language change.

Chapter 3 provides a brief examination of the principles by which components of the linguistic repertoire are mapped onto social activities, the triggers behind changes in this mapping arrangement, and the social and collective processes of intervention with the mapping of repertoire and activities. Chapter 4 returns to the principles of acquiring and maintaining a multilingual repertoire. I review current approaches to bilingual first-language acquisition, second-language acquisition, and bilingual aphasia, and discuss models of bilingual language processing and data on bilingual speech production errors. Three of the central themes of the book are strengthened in this chapter: The first is the proposal that multilingual speakers have at their disposal not 'language systems' that can be switched on and off, but an integrated repertoire from which elements are selected during each and every communicative task-schema. The second is the assumption that speakers are creative communicators, who will draw, if necessary, on the wide range of their repertoire in order to make communication more efficient. Evidence for this claim is found in the creative strategies employed by second-language learners. The third is the suggestion that the functional value of linguistic categories is a factor in speakers' ability to select structures within their repertoire; this makes certain categories more vulnerable during a failure of the 'selection mechanism' and so more likely to appear in non-voluntary language choices.

Chapter 5 examines the alternation of languages in conversation – codeswitching. We begin by interpreting the difference between codeswitching and borrowing as a gradient. Following a review of structural and conversational approaches to codeswitching, attention is paid again to the relevance of category affiliation to switching behaviour. The fact that speakers may exploit the contrast between languages or the complementary functions that they may have for a range of expression purposes is seen once again as confirmation that multilingual speakers have at their disposal an integrated, complex repertoire of linguistic structures.

Chapters 6, 7, 8, and 9 are all devoted to the effects of contact-induced language change that are most commonly known as 'borrowing'. In all four chapters, 'borrowing' is viewed as a form of levelling of structures across the multilingual repertoire, with the outcome that a single structure is employed, irrespective of interaction context and so irrespective of choice of 'language'. I start Chapter 6 by defining what I call the replication of linguistic Matter – concrete word-forms and morphs. I discuss the factors that motivate the replication of matter, and general statements that have been made in connection with the likelihood of borrowing to affect various grammatical categories. Chapter 7 discusses lexical borrowing and strategies to accommodate nouns, adjectives, and verbs, while Chapter 8 is devoted to the borrowing of grammatical structures and phonology. Chapter 9 focuses on the replication of linguistic Patterns – the arrangement, meaning, and combination of units of matter. I propose the model of 'pivot-matching' as an explanation for the creative procedure by which speakers avail themselves of a construction from within their repertoire, thereby exploiting the repertoire's full potential, and replicate it drawing on a constrained selection of linguistic matter or word-forms and morphs. Examples are discussed in a survey of categories and word classes, and space is given to the implications for language convergence and the formation of so-called linguistic areas.

Chapter 10, finally, is devoted to the emergence of new speech forms – 'contact languages' – in situations of language contact. I review current approaches to pidgins and creoles as well as mixed languages, and attempt to relate these products of language contact to the theme of multilinguals' creative use and exploitation of their repertoire: In the case of pidgins and resulting creoles, learners make efficient use of a variety of elements in a multilingual repertoire consisting of impressions of a target language, and a selection of structures from a substrate language, coupled with creative processes such as word-composition and grammaticalisation, in order to sustain communication in a new set of interaction contexts. Mixed languages are the product of a purpose-bound, conscious, and deliberate re-negotiation of the multilingual repertoire in a limited set of interaction contexts – usually those involving in-group re-affirmation of identity. The Outlook (Chapter 11) revisits the three central themes of the book: The constant availability and presence of a complex repertoire, the role of speakers as creative communicators and innovators, and the relevance of the inner stratification of the grammatical apparatus to processes of speech production and language change in language contact situations.

2   An emerging multilingual repertoire

2.1   A case study

The present chapter examines the emergence of the linguistic repertoire in an individual speaker in a multilingual setting. It traces the gradual development of constraints on the selection of structures within the repertoire and the acquisition of strategies to manage that repertoire. These strategies constitute the foundations on which bilinguals draw when alternating between languages. They also form the background and the pre-requisite for any contact-induced change. By surveying the bilingual child's strategies of managing the linguistic repertoire, we obtain a picture of the potential effects of language contact on speakers, on language use, and on the shape and structure of language.

I base this chapter on informal observations of the language acquisition process of a trilingual child, whom we shall call 'Ben'.[1] Born and raised in England in the late 1990s, Ben is exposed to two languages in the home: German, which he hears from his mother, and Hebrew, which he hears from his father. Both parents speak their respective languages consistently to Ben, consciously trying to avoid mixing. Between the ages of 0:4 and 4:4, input is balanced: During the first two years of his life Ben spends four days a week with an English-speaking child minder. He is cared for at home during roughly half of the working week primarily by his father, and during the other half primarily by his mother, while weekends are spent with both parents. At the age of 1:11, Ben's parents move into separate households, in separate towns. Ben stays primarily with his mother, spending three to four working days at an English-speaking nursery, while six days out of a fourteen-day cycle are spent with his father. Holiday time is spent equally with each of the parents. Most of the holiday time with the mother is spent in Germany, and around half the holiday time with the father is spent in Israel – in both countries with family and relations. On the whole, between the age of 0:4 and 4:4, Ben spends roughly equal amounts of time with each of the two parents (each speaking his/her language consistently) and at the English-speaking nursery, with exposure during holidays to monolingual contexts of German and Hebrew.

2.2   Lexical development

Ben's active language acquisition history begins at the age of 1:3. His first words are typically direct repetitions of words directed at him by a parent. For example, ['bada] follows the father's offer in Hebrew of *banána* 'banana', and ['ɛtɛ] follows the question in Hebrew *et-zé?* 'this one.ACC?' ('Do you want this one?'). At 1:4, words begin to appear on a more regular basis, and are no longer limited to direct repetitions. A number of onomatopoetic items are used, such as [baː] for 'sheep' and [ʔʊfʔʊf] for 'dog', [pək] for 'toaster' and ['tita] for 'clock' (*tick-tack*). Just like the lexical words, they too are introduced by the parents. While some of these sound-symbols – *tick-tack* for instance – might be regarded as universal, others actually differ from more conventional language-specific baby-talk, for instance from German *mäh* for 'sheep' or Hebrew *hau-hau* for 'dog'. The sound-symbol [baː] for 'sheep' in fact originates in direct imitation of sheep during a countryside holiday. Some forms, such as [pək] for 'toaster', are entirely improvised. The onomatopoetic set thus constitutes a kind of 'family speech'. Significantly, both parents continue to use the same onomatopoetic sound sequence once it is established for a particular referent. The 'multilingual' child is thus exposed at this early stage in the development of his linguistic resources to a set of labels – 'words' – that are used by both parents,[2] alongside another inventory of words that are specific to each of the parents (i.e. 'proper' words belonging to each of the two languages). The child's active repertoire of 'proper' words contains from the very beginning items from German – e.g. [da] for German *da* 'there', [bal] for *Ball* 'ball', ['bada] for *Badewanne* 'bathtub' – and from Hebrew – e.g. ['baji] for Hebrew *garbáyim* 'socks', ['ʔəxa] for *yaréax* 'moon', [bajt] for *naaléy báyit* 'slippers'. Significantly, at this stage, only a single word is used actively per referent/object. There are, in other words, no active 'bilingual synonyms' – different words, deriving from different languages, which are used alternately to represent the same referent/object. This is well in line with general observations on early stages in bilingual first-language acquisition (see Chapter 4), as well as with a more general assumption that infants show a 'mutual exclusivity bias' in acquiring labels for referents (cf. discussion in Bloom 2000).

At the age of 1:6, Ben's repertoire already consists of an active vocabulary of around 40 words that are used regularly. In addition, the child is familiar with some ten names of persons (three of which are mainly used to refer to persons that appear on photos contained in a family photo album). By and large, lexical tokens that have been 'acquired' – meaning that they have been used actively by the child in communicative interaction and not just as one-off, on-the-spot repetition of adult utterances – continue to be used consistently by the child, irrespective of the identity of the parent-interlocutor. The child's active use of vocabulary tokens in any given situation thus consists of a mixture of German- and Hebrew-derived items: we find for example [man] for German *Mann* 'man',

[kek] for *Keks* 'biscuit', [fau] for *Frau* 'woman', alongside [tik] for Hebrew *tik* 'bag', [ʔan] for *náal* 'shoe', ['kɔwa] for *kóva* 'hat'. The English child minder (who has no knowledge of either German or Hebrew) even learns the meanings of some of these words through her contact with the child. It is therefore clear that the child does not apply constraints on the selection of words, in any particular setting.

A significant number of tokens that form part of the child's repertoire tend to be used 'universally' by the child's adult interlocutors as well, at least so far as their speech is directed at the child. Thus, ['bagi] ('buggy') is used for 'pushchair' by both parents, as are the words for 'mommy' and 'daddy' – ['mama] from German *Mamma*, ['ʔaba] from Hebrew *ába* –, ['tedi] for 'teddy bear', ['baːj] for 'bye', as well as the names of individual persons, similarly an integral part of the child's modest active linguistic repertoire. Add to these several similar-sounding words such as those for 'bus' (German *Bus*, Hebrew *ótobus*), 'banana' (German *Banane*, Hebrew *banána*), and 'guitar' (German *Gitarre*, Hebrew *gitára*), all of which are part of the child's active vocabulary, and we can establish that, as the use of family-coined onomatopoetic formations declines, there is nevertheless a continuous presence of vocabulary tokens in the input directed at the child which are used indiscriminately of 'language'-context. In a sense, then, despite the fact that both parents are consistent in avoiding language mixing when communicating with the child (and the child-minder is monolingual), the child is, to some extent at least, confronted with 'mixed messages' as far as the situation-bound separation of sets of tokens is concerned: Some labels are exclusive to the interaction with a particular parent, others are not.

Both parents know all three languages. As hearers they can understand and react to the child's choice of vocabulary, irrespective of language. At the same time they each use their respective language very consistently with the child. In response to 'wrong' language choices made by the child, even at the very early stages, they generally adopt what Lanza (1997) refers to as the 'expressed guess strategy': confirming that they have understood the child's intention, but repeating the word in the 'correct' language, thereby prompting the child to conform to the expected rules on language selection. Gradually, the child's experience extends to cover a wider range of communicative situations: The language used among the parents is German, which is also the language used with a family friend who is a regular visitor, often several times a week. Both parents use English in the presence of the child when speaking to the child-minder as well as to most other visitors and in interaction in shops or other public places. At the age of 1:5, Ben's Hebrew-speaking grandmother arrives for a visit of several days, and at the age of 1:6 he spends a three-week holiday with the mother visiting the German-speaking grandparents in Germany, during which there is no exposure to either Hebrew or English. Parallel to the expanding repertoire of linguistic forms, the repertoire of communicative settings is thus undergoing expansion as well. The child develops the ability to associate clusters of lexical items with particular settings and groups of settings. The principal factor defining these settings remains, however, the presence of one of the three adults who play the principal roles in his life.

First signs of active attempts to use vocabulary tokens discriminately appear around the age of 1:8. In the 'English' context, i.e. with the child-minder, the tokens [kaː] 'car' and ['dɛdi] 'daddy' are used. Both words have equivalents that are used in the parental household, though interestingly there is, for both, only a single 'family' synonym that is used with both parents: ['ʔato] 'car' represents in all likelihood both German *Auto* and Hebrew *óto*, while ['baba] is used for 'daddy', based on both parents' use of Hebrew *ába* in the family context. By the age of 1:9, bilingual synonyms already cover a notable portion of Ben's active vocabulary. The child is clearly making some effort to select 'appropriate' items when communicating with the parents, and this effort is extended to other situations as well: During a three-week holiday in Israel at the age of 1:9, Ben is accompanied by both parents. But spending some hours on his own with local family members, he appears consistent in favouring Hebrew words. The exposure to new interaction settings, in which none of the three main adults is present, confronts the child with new challenges as far as selection from the linguistic repertoire is concerned. Maintaining demarcation boundaries between subsets of the repertoire becomes a more universal need, not just a task that is directed toward a particular individual.

The total number of active vocabulary items recorded at this age is 218.[3] Of those, 96 derive from German, 76 from Hebrew, 5 from English, and the rest represent items that can be assigned to more than one language.[4] Together they represent a total of 176 'concepts' or lexical meanings. Double or triple items – 'bilingual synonyms' – exist for only 46 concepts – roughly a quarter of the lexical 'concepts'. (Given that some items can be assigned to more than one language, the actual number of bilingual synonyms is potentially somewhat higher; see Figure 2.1.) The remaining lexical 'concepts' are each represented in the active vocabulary by just a single lexical item, from just one language. Despite the noted ability to associate settings with a particular subset of items from the repertoire, it is nevertheless clear that, for the bulk of the lexicon, the child continues to rely on the indiscriminate use of a single word per concept. This interim stage in the development of the child's multilingual repertoire therefore merits closer examination.

Let us first recapitulate: By the age of 1:9 the child has acquired an inventory of many dozen words in both languages, German and Hebrew, and at least a few words from English as well. A transition is ongoing between passive and active vocabulary use. This can be seen in the ability to activate vocabulary without explicit prompting, while on the other hand the child continues to repeat words and short phrases as situation-bound utterances. Aside from those, it is now possible to identify two different types of vocabulary items in the child's active repertoire. The first and larger group consists of words that are used by the child irrespective of addressee, and which therefore represent consistent preferences for the expression of certain concepts. The second type involves

Word class/ semantic domain	Number of referents for which active words exist	Number of referents for which bilingual synonyms exist	Number of referents for which words in two or more languages have similar shape	Proportion of referents for which bilingual synonyms exist	Proportion of referents with bilingual synonyms and same-shape words
Adjectives	13	7	0	61%	61%
Plants and nature	4	2	0	50%	50%
Animals	25	11	7	44%	72%
Misc. fiction-related	9	4	1	44%	55%
Vehicles	15	6	4	40%	66%
Locations	16	5	1	31%	38%
Adverbs and Particles	8	2	1	25%	38%
Persons	9	2	2	22%	44%
Food	17	2	11	12%	76%
Verbs	9	1	1	11%	22%
Household utensils and toys	37	3	7	8%	27%
Clothes and body utensils	14	1	2	7%	21%
Total	176	46	37	26%	47%

Figure 2.1 *Bilingual synonyms by semantic domains and word classes (age 1:9).*

word pairs (and in some cases triplets) that are used discriminately with each parent.

The lexical domain is enriched during this stage by the appearance of verbs, from both major languages: ['apibi] 'to wash up' from German *abwaschen*, ['kuken] 'to look' from German *gucken*, ['ʔɛdɛt] 'to descend' from Hebrew *larédet*, [kum] 'to stand up' from Hebrew *lakúm*, and more. Verbs are generally used in a modal sense, expressing the wish for an activity. They are

Form	Source word	Language	Meaning
'tiken	trinken	G	drink
ʔot	lištót	H	drink
kɔm	komm!	G and E	come!
ʔan	an (kommen -)	G	arrive
'ʔɛdɛ	larédet	H	go down
'kuken	gucken	G	look
maːən	malen	G	paint
kum	lakúm	H	stand up
'laːpə	laufen	G	walk, run
'ʔapibi	abwaschen	G	wash up

Figure 2.2 *Verbs (at age 1:9). Dark-shaded areas represent bilingual synonyms, faintly shaded areas represent words that have identical or similar shape in two or more languages.*

usually based on the infinitive form of the respective language, which in both languages is the form that accompanies modal verbs.[5] Some adjectives are also used. When accompanying nouns, they follow the word order rules of the respective languages: Adj-N with German [kajn 'ato] 'a small car' (*[ein] kleines Auto*), but N-Adj with Hebrew [buk tan] 'a small bottle' (*bakbúk katán*). Thus, some degree of 'language separation' appears in both lexicon and grammar. Nonetheless, the bulk of the vocabulary remains, as mentioned, undifferentiated for setting, context, or addressee.

A closer look at the breakdown of lexical items into word classes and semantic groups reveals something about the process through which the child is gradually learning to set demarcation boundaries within his linguistic repertoire (Figure 2.1). Ben has bilingual synonyms for most adjectives. Bilingual synonyms are also more frequent among concepts that relate to his physical environment, such as landscape and locations within and around the house, and among terms for animals and vehicles.

Terms for persons occupy a somewhat ambiguous position. They include a large proportion of proper names – 'grandma', 'grandpa', 'mommy' – which represent unique referents and are not differentiated for language in child-directed adult speech, either. The exception is the word for 'daddy'. Hebrew *ába* is the uniform term in the family context. But since it is usually the father who picks up the child from the child minder, the child is also exposed to the child minder's use of *daddy*. The word *baby* is common to both English and German. This leaves

Form	Source word	Language	Meaning
bal	Ball	G and E	ball
buːk	Buch	G and E	book
ˈbagiː	buggy	G, H, and E	buggy
ˈtaʁa	gitára	G, H, and E	guitar
ˈtedə	teddy	G, H, and E	teddy
tik	tik	H	bag
ˈbɔkala	Luftballon	G	balloon
pəχ, pak	pax	H	bin
ˈʔaɪma	Eimer	G	bucket
tuːl	Stuhl	G	chair
haːke	Hacke	G	hoe
ˈlampeˑ	Lampe	G	lamp
tav	mixtáv	H	letter
ton	itón	H	newspaper
ʔon	iparon	H	pencil
tɔp	Topf	G	pot
ziˑp	Sieb	G	sieve

Figure 2.3 *Selection among words for household utensils and toys (at age 1:9).*

only a single unambiguous bilingual synonym in this domain, namely [man] (German *Mann*) and [ʔit] (Hebrew *iš*) for 'man'.

By contrast, bilingual synonyms make up only a small proportion of the words for household utensils and toys, and for clothes. Verbs occupy a similar position. Among the relatively few verbs in the active vocabulary there is only one straightforward pair of synonyms – the words for 'drink' – and an additional form shared by German and English, for 'come' (Figure 2.2). This marginality of synonyms might just be a product of the marginal position of verbs in the vocabulary; but it could also indicate greater difficulty in separating *label* and *concept* in connection with modality (volition or manipulation), which is the primary function of the child's use of verbs at this stage. Among the nouns, terms for clothes, toys, and utensils represent objects that have a kind of 'institutionalised' role in the child's life and a continuous physical presence in his immediate world (see Figures 2.3 and 2.4). It appears that the child has a strong need to

Form	Source word	Language	Meaning
ˈloke	Socke	G	sock
ˈbaji(m)	garbájim	H	sock
ˈʔeme	Crème	G and H	créme
taɪts	tayts	H and E	tights
luk	xalúk	H	bathrobe
ˈtipe	Stiefel	G	boots
ˈkʊʊt	coat	E	coat
ˈnubə	Schnubbel	G	dummy
ˈbɪlə	Brille	G	glasses
ˈkɔwa	kóva	H	hat
ˈlake	Jacke	G	jacket
ʔit	karít	H	pillow
ʔip	tsa'íf	H	scarf
baɪt	(naayley) bayit	H	slippers
da	afudá	H	vest

Figure 2.4 *Words for clothes and body utensils (at age 1:9).*

continue to identify each of them as a unique and unambiguous referent. This need overrides the motivation to accommodate to adult expectations on the use of labels belonging to the appropriate subset of the lexicon – i.e. to choose the 'correct language' – in a given interaction setting. Animals and vehicles, which are largely the objects of fiction (e.g. pictures in storybooks), narration, and more remote observation, appear to be easier candidates for the separation of label and concept/referent, as are expressions of orientation (location) and evaluation (adjectives).[6]

The child's adoption and use of synonyms is motivated by the wish to comply with the communication norm set by adults. It is a pragmatic skill which the child acquires as he becomes more sensitive toward the reactions and expectations of his adult interlocutors. For the multilingual speaker, accommodating to interlocutors' expectations in regard to language choice will remain a lifelong pattern. We see, however, already at this early stage, that obstacles appear on the path toward complete control of the repertoire and the choices among repertoire items. These obstacles are inherently connected to the roles and functions that linguistic structures and categories assume in triggering mental processing operations. The semantic splits that we find in Ben's bilingual vocabulary at the age of 1:9 are indicators of a functional split between the processing of immediate and unique referents and the processing of more abstract, fictional, and remote entities. These word class splits represent different ways of handling orientation and evaluation on the one hand, and modality and manipulation of situations on the other. It is only with greater maturity that the child is able to overcome these obstacles, and the pragmatic motivation to accommodate to adult language-choice patterns takes over across the board. Within a few months, the child acquires a double set of lexical items for most concepts, and by the age of 2:0, single-language items have become the exception.

2.3   Controlling the selection mechanism

At the age of 1:11, Ben moves with his mother to a different house, in a different town, spending long weekends and several weeks during the summer holidays with his father. The separation gives rise to a more consistent separation of communicative settings. Each language is now used in a different location, in a different household, for a relatively intense period. German and Hebrew are now also associated with even wider contexts in each of the separate locations, as the mother and father each interact quite frequently with their respective fellow countrymen. English plays a role, to some extent, in both settings, as it continues to be associated with interactions in certain outdoor activities and during visits from friends and neighbours. Exposure to English is now also more intensive as the child spends four to five long days a week at nursery. The child is thus confronted even more strictly than before with monolingual settings and is experiencing even greater pressure to accommodate to them. His verbal communication with the parents becomes predominantly monolingual in the choice of vocabulary forms, with very few exceptions. Even his language of play when he is on his own tends to be monolingual: predominantly German when in the care of the mother, and predominantly Hebrew when staying with the father. Language selection has thus become not just addressee-oriented; it now helps define the child's environment and the setting of his activities, and it is even constitutive of the verbal organisation of his internal world. At 2:1, following a visit to an aircraft exhibition at the Science Museum, he expresses a metalinguistic awareness of the contextual separation of languages:[7]

(1)   mama   *Hübschrauber*,   ába   helikópter
       mommy   helicopter [German]   daddy   helicopter [Hebrew]
       'Mommy [says] *Hübschrauber*, daddy [says] *helikópter*'

Ben's functional repertoire of structures continues to expand, of course. At the age of 2:0 he is beginning to use finite verbs, first in German, then, within a couple of weeks, in Hebrew too. Definite articles and negation forms appear in both languages at 2:1, (Hebrew) pronominal endings at 2:3, and 3rd person pronouns as well as inflected past tense forms in both languages at 2:4. At this age, various clause-combining structures also emerge. During a weekend with the father, the child is inspecting the back garden in search for snails and makes the following remark:

(2)   mistakél   *ob*   xilazón *da*   *ist*
        look.SG.M whether [German] snail   there [German] is [German]
        'I am looking/ want to see *whether* [the/a] snail *is there*'

The chosen language of the utterance is Hebrew, in compliance with the setting, and the selection of the lexical items that are the principal carriers of the proposition follows this choice. But the clause-combining strategy expressing indirect condition or 'option' is German (*ob* 'whether'). The child has recently acquired this particular conjunction in German, along with its semantics and distribution rules. He is missing an equivalent construction in Hebrew. In fact, Hebrew lacks a specific construction for this function, as option clauses are formally grouped together with conditional clauses, both being introduced by the same conjunction, *im*.

With the acquisition of the German conjunction *ob*, the child's repertoire now contains an adequate construction to express a very specific semantic relation – that of indirect (embedded) condition or 'option'. Behind the mixing in (2) is a (non-reflected) motivation on the part of the child to make optimal use of his repertoire in order to express his thoughts as precisely and as effectively as possible. This motivation apparently overrides his attempt to remain within the constraints set by the interaction setting, which require selection from only a particular subset of the repertoire. This explains the insertion of *ob* into the Hebrew utterance. The mixture in the remaining part of the utterance is in a sense a mere by-product. The child does not simply select a German conjunction. Rather, he activates his knowledge of the only construction available in his repertoire for expressing the semantic relation of 'embedded options'. This includes the entire mode of anchoring the predication that is contained in the construction. Like other German subordinations, *ob*-clauses require the appearance of the finite verb in final position. Once again, replication of this rule in Hebrew is difficult, partly perhaps due to the absence in Hebrew of a present-tense finite copula. The selection of a German predication mode thus triggers the selection of the German predicate *da sein* 'to be present'. A remote parallel in Hebrew might be the uninflected, impersonal *yeš* 'there is'. But *yeš* denotes existence, normally of unspecified, newly introduced or indefinite entities. It is not equivalent to German *da sein* 'to be present [at a given location that is known to the interlocutor]'. Moreover, due to its co-appearance with subjects that have not been established in the preceding discourse, *yeš*, unlike normal Hebrew predicates, must always take the position preceding the subject. There is, thus, a Hebrew constraint disallowing its appearance in sentence-final position. All this adds to the motivation to select the German predicate once the overall blueprint of the subordinated construction has been adopted in the utterance. In line with German word-order rules, the predicate appears in the final position: . . . *da ist*.

Mixing of this kind is often regarded as motivated by 'gaps' in the child's competence in one of the languages – in this case Hebrew. The notion of a 'gap' somewhat obscures the fact that Hebrew does, in fact, possess a structure that can adequately render the intended semantic relation and that this structure is probably accessible in principle to the child (who knows how to form subordinate clauses in Hebrew, and who is familiar with Hebrew conditional clauses as well). The crucial factor is the recent addition of a highly specialised construction to the child's repertoire – the *ob*-clause as a unique expression of embedded options. The motivation to make use of this newly acquired structure illustrates that the child's verbal communication is serviced by an entire repertoire of linguistic forms and constructions, which the child has at his disposal.

Two motivations thus compete when the child is structuring his discourse: The first is to exploit all available elements of his repertoire in order to express himself as effectively as possible – and this includes using unique constructions wherever they are available for specific semantic relations. The other is to comply with expectations on appropriate choices in individual communication settings. Language mixing of the kind seen in (2) is a functionally motivated compromise between the two. A German construction is selected – the *ob*-clause – which triggers the use of not just one, but several features of German grammar and lexicon in the utterance. At the same time, we do not see a complete switch of convenience into German, but rather the selection of Hebrew *xilazón* to reinforce accommodation to the (Hebrew) speech setting. Mixing, by this stage at least, is thus not arbitrary, but functional to the pursuit of a range of communicative goals.

By the age of 2:4–2:6, Ben has a fairly fluent command of both his domestic/parental languages, German and Hebrew, with English lagging somewhat behind in active use. He is fully aware of the context-bound separation of languages, and pursues it consistently. Any lapses deserve careful consideration. In situations immediately following the transition from one parental household to another, i.e. within a few hours or on the first day, or in other situations in which the speech setting is ambiguous, notably when speaking on the phone to one parent while in the care of the other, insertions from the other language occasionally appear. The inserted material derives either from the language of the parent with whom the child had been spending the past few days prior to the transition, or, in the case of phone conversations, from the language of the parent at whose house the child is currently staying. I will, in the following, refer to these insertions as bilingual 'slips', or speech production errors because they are, quite clearly, unintentional. Nor are they motivated, as was the case in Example (2), by the need to supplement material from one language when communicating in another (i.e. by so-called 'gaps', or rather by an urge to fully exploit all possible constructions available within the entire linguistic repertoire regardless of the constraints imposed by the interaction setting). Indeed, sometimes the insertions are noticed and self-repaired by the child. Quite often, however, they remain unnoticed by the child, and usually uncommented on by the hearer.

The interesting aspect of these bilingual slips is the fact that they involve almost exclusively a particular class of functional elements: discourse particles, interjections, and connectivity markers. Frequently affected are the particles 'yes' (Hebrew *ken/* German *ja*) and 'no' (*lo/nein*), the conjunctions 'because' (*ki/weil*), 'and' (*ve/und*), 'or' (*o/oder*), and 'but' (*avál/aber*), fillers and tags, interjections, and occasionally focus particles such as 'too' (*gam/auch*), 'even' (*afílu/sogar*) or 'at all' (*bixlál/überhaupt*):

(3)   Hebrew; age 2:3, first few days in the father's care after the child's return from a 3-week holiday in Germany; inspecting the shell of a snail in the garden:
        báyit šel xilazón *aber*   éyn xilazón bifním
        house of   snail   but [German] is-no snail   inside
        'A snail-shell, *but* there is no snail inside'

(4)   German; age 7, on the phone to the mother while at the father's house, describing a collection of insects:
        dann gibt's Butterfly, *ve/*   und zwei Craneflies
        then   is   and [Hebrew] and two
        'Then there's a butterfly, *and/* and two craneflies'

(5)   Hebrew; age 7:2, on the phone to his father while on holiday in Germany, about a sports event shown on television there:
        Jan Ulrich hayá be'érex   mispár šéva *oder*   šmóne/ o šmóne
                     was approximately number seven or [German] eight or eight
        'Jan Ulrich was about number seven *or* eight/ or eight'

Language choice errors of the type illustrated in (1)–(4) occur in both directions – German connectors in Hebrew utterances and vice versa – especially during the age period 2:3–4:6, but, as seen in (4)–(5), also later. Of particular interest is the history of the adversative conjunction, Hebrew *avál*, German *aber*, at an earlier phase during this period. Both language forms of the conjunction (as well as the English form) had been acquired and used regularly in the individual languages before the age of 2:6. At 2:6, Ben spends a three-week holiday with his mother in Germany. Upon his return, and for the next three months, German *aber* consistently replaces the Hebrew adversative conjunction in Hebrew discourse. It appears as though the two languages have undergone a *fusion* of the structure expressing contrast between propositional units in discourse.[8] The demarcation line between the repertoire components collapses around the particular process-ing operation of contrast, allowing *aber* to function independently of context or setting and so independently of 'language' selection. This situation prevails until the age of 2:10, when Ben leaves for a three-week holiday with his father to Israel. Within a week of interacting in the monolingual Hebrew environment, Hebrew *avál* is reinstated in Hebrew discourse. Then, upon Ben's return home, and for the next two to three weeks, *avál* replaces *aber* in German discourse. A repetition of the process of fusion thus takes place, with the languages in reverse roles.

Recall that this kind of mixing accompanies the transition between settings. Such transitions require re-orientation between contradicting sets of constraints on the selection of particular elements within the linguistic repertoire. While the child is on the whole able to adapt and accommodate to the new setting very quickly and to control the selection of linguistic structures in communication, there is a class of items that frequently escapes that control. These are the elements mentioned above: connectors, discourse markers, focus particles, interjections, fillers, and tags. They all belong to the class of structures that help frame utterances and process the hearer's expectations and likely reactions to them. They are part of the monitoring-and-directing apparatus that is employed by the speaker to regulate the interaction. Why do these elements in particular escape the young bilingual speaker's control over language selection, even at the more mature age of 6–7?

However natural and intuitive the switch among languages in different settings has become for the child once his language skills are fully developed, it remains a strongly analytical mental task to maintain the demarcation boundaries within the linguistic repertoire. It seems, however, as though the elements on which the speaker relies in order to monitor and direct the hearer through the processing of the discourse are not processed exclusively at the analytical level. Discourse operators and the like are in some ways verbal gestures, the insertion of which carries with it certain aspects of a situational reflex (I shall return to this point in Chapter 4). Consider some of the other structures that are subject to language selection errors of this kind:

(6)   Hebrew; age 6:3, immediately after arrival at the father's home for the
       weekend; when asked what he did at school that day:
       Ach,   šum davár meyuxád
       oh [German] nothing   special
       '*Oh,* nothing special'

(7)   Hebrew; age 2:7, after returning from a three-week holiday in Germany;
       asking about an unidentified car that had been parked in front of the father's
       house.
       éyfo óto? *ich*   *mein*   lo óto šelánu, óto axér?
       where car I [German] mean [German] not car ours   car other
       'Where is [the] car? *I mean,* not our car, [the] other car?'

(8)   Hebrew; age 6:3, after returning from holiday in Germany; confronted with
        a request by the father, replies in German (the utterance is then followed by
        a self-repair in the form of a non-lexical filler – *eh* – and a head and face
        gesture):
        Wie bitte?
        'Pardon me?'

(9)   Hebrew; age 5:2, reaching to inspect his trousers while planning a game in
        which a toy is to be hidden in a pocket:
        yeš   li   *überhaupt*   kis?
        there.is to.1SG at all [German] pocket
        'Do I have a pocket *at all?*'

All the elements in question are essentially interaction-regulating gestures: In
Example (6), German *ach* indicates the speaker's self-prompting to provide a
reply. The German insertion appears to go unnoticed by the child, who quite
possibly does not identify *ach* as a 'word' in the conventional sense and so
does not consciously associate it with any particular set within the repertoire,
but treats it, rather, as a 'universal' device. The hearer does not comment on the
insertion.

The other examples show lexical material that is clearly attributed to a particular 'language'. In Example (7), German *ich mein* 'I mean' introduces a self-repair.
Despite the clear affiliation of the phrase to the German component of the repertoire, this insertion too appears to go unnoticed by the child, at this early age,
and is treated more like a gesture than a phrase. In (8), German *wie bitte* 'pardon
me?' prompts repetition of the hearer's utterance; it is in other words a device
that operates strictly at the level of the interaction management. The child notices
the wrong choice of language, and laughs in embarrassment after completing the
utterance. His reaction in (9) is similar. Here, German *überhaupt* 'at all' represents
a somewhat different class of items: The particle indicates the speaker's negative
expectation concerning the outlined state of affairs. Nevertheless, indirectly, it too
serves as a gesture, as it invites the hearer to share the speaker's sceptical attitude
surrounding the proposition. It thus assumes a role in processing the attitudes
of both participants in the interaction against a shared presuppositional basis.
This is not dissimilar to connectives, and especially to contrastive markers. The
latter alert the hearer to an upcoming difficulty in accepting a broken causal chain
(cf. Rudolph 1996), while at the same time reaching out to the hearer to accept the
speaker's proposition. This 'bear-with-me-effect', which the speaker is trying to
impress upon the hearer, is evidently a source of tension in the speaker's mental
planning of the utterance.

It is likely that this tension is a contributing factor in disturbing the speaker's
ability to control the selection mechanism and discriminate among the repertoire components that are socially acceptable in the current speech setting. The
behaviour of contrast is similar to, but more extreme, than that of the other connectivity markers. Contrastive markers are not only inserted from the 'wrong'

language, but, as we saw earlier, they even tend to replace an established marker, at least for a certain period. We thus see a connection between speech production at the synchronic, local level of discourse interaction, and the diachrony of, in this case, the child's idiosyncratic speech: Pressure on speech production may lead to language change.

It is important to note that the child's difficulty in maintaining separation between repertoire components in the domain of monitoring-and-directing operations is not due to the overall dominance of any single set of linguistic structures (i.e. one particular 'language'). Rather, 'dominance' or loyalty to a particular set of structures is variable and fluid. We see this in particular in the fate of the contrastive marker between the age of 2:6–2:11. It is, in a way, this changing loyalty, accompanying the accommodation to changing settings, that triggers the confusion in the first place. Re-directing his attention toward an alternate subset of his repertoire seems easier for the child in connection with some processing functions of language, more than for others. For the less analytical, more gesture-like functions, the pragmatic orientation toward a particular subset, arising from the previous setting, remains dominant for a while, until the child has become fully accustomed (in his mental processing of language) to the new setting. I refer to this phenomenon as the *pragmatically dominant language* – the language that has been the target of the speaker's accommodation efforts until shortly before the latest change of interaction setting (see Matras 1998a).

In this section we saw that even a bilingual child who is exposed to consistent domain separation between the languages, who has a high level of linguistic awareness, and who generally avoids mixing, encounters certain difficulties in keeping apart two of his languages around certain monitoring-and-directing functions of language. There is a difficulty, in situations of relative ambiguity which surround the transition between settings, in disassociating the relevant linguistic structures from the pragmatically dominant language – the language which communicative performance took place until the transition. This leads to an instantaneous or temporary *fusion* – i.e. non-separation – of the subsets within the repertoire around the structures that represent the relevant function.

2.4   Combining repertoire components

In the previous section I dealt with the variable selection of word-forms or linguistic 'matter' from the multilingual repertoire. In this section we examine how elements from both repertoire components are integrated by combining linguistic matter or word-forms belonging to one subset of the repertoire, with organisation patterns and meanings belonging to another. This is a strategy with which the child speaker creates hybrid constructions that do not exist in adult speech. Consider first the blending of German word order rules with Hebrew lexical items in the following example:

(10)   Hebrew; age 2:1, describing a museum exhibit that showed a wounded man
        lying down and a woman standing nearby:
        iš   ten,   išá   ten   lo
        man sleep woman sleep[9] no
        'The man is sleeping, the woman is not sleeping'

In (10), the Hebrew negator *lo* follows the verb (which in this instance, at this age, is both phonologically reduced, and lacks proper gender agreement with the subject noun). The rule in adult Hebrew is for the negator to precede the finite verb: *lo yašén* 'does not sleep/is not sleeping'. The structure is replicated from German, where the negator in main clauses follows the finite verb: *schläft nicht* 'is not sleeping'. What is the trigger for the hybrid construction? It is possible that the child is trying to implement a structure that he has recently acquired through communicative experience in the German setting as a unique way to express negation: placement of a negative particle after the finite verb. Conscious of the need to select appropriate matter in the Hebrew setting, he attempts to implement the new structure in the Hebrew setting by complying with the selection constraint, inserting a Hebrew negation particle in place of the German one. The separation of subsets of matter thus appears easier to maintain than the separation of the more abstract organisation patterns of the construction.

Postverbal negation continues to appear in the child's Hebrew sporadically even until the age of five. Particularly consistent is the child's negation of the possessive construction. In Hebrew, the possessive is expressed by impersonal *yeš* in the positive, and by its suppletive counterpart *eyn* in the negative, with the possessor appearing as a prepositional object: *yeš lánu* 'we have' (there.is to.us), *eyn lánu* 'we don't have' (there.is.not to.us). The child frequently uses *yeš lánu lo* by analogy to German *wir haben nicht/ wir haben kein-*. The irregular nature of the Hebrew possessive construction – the fact that it is both an impersonal construction, which is rare in a predication, and that it has a suppletive negative form – appears to prompt the child to create an alternative. This alternative is constructed by analogy to a negative possessive construction that already exists in his repertoire – the German *haben* + *nicht/kein* – drawing on lexical material that is available in Hebrew and is therefore permissible in the Hebrew-language setting.

Non-separation or fusion of sentence organisation patterns appears in various other constructions:

(11)   Hebrew; age 2:1, commenting on the father's remark during an activity:
        ába   "oops" amár
        daddy oops   said.3SG.M
        'Daddy said "oops"'

(12)   Hebrew; age 2:7, Ben tells a story that he made up. The father asks
              questions about the story, and the child replies:
              a. Father: lama hu amár   "ma"?
                         why   he said.3SG.M   what

              b. Child: ki   ha-migdál kol ha-zman "tralala" omér
                         because   the-tower all the-time tralala   says.SG.M

              a. Father: 'Why did he say "what"?'
              b. Child: 'Because the tower always says "tralala"'

In (11), the content verb 'said' is placed in final position, replicating the German
pattern for the use of the perfect tense (subject + auxiliary + object + lexical
verb; cf. *Aba hat 'oops' gesagt*). In (12b), word order features the German rule
on the placement of the finite verb in final sentence position in subordinate
clauses. Both examples show that in these instances, the child's planning of
the information structure of the utterance does not take into account the unique
rules that accompany each subset within the repertoire, despite the fact that the
selection of linguistic matter is consistent and complies with the constraints of
the context and setting.

   As the child grows older, especially after he starts attending school, and English
gradually becomes the dominant language for both play and verbal reasoning,
English construction patterns begin to appear in both German and Hebrew. In
(13)–(14), English preposition stranding is applied in *wh*-constructions in German
(13) and in Hebrew (14):

(13)   German; age 6:0, addressing both parents, commenting on their
              conversation (which is conducted in German):
              Was redet   ihr   über?
              what talk.2PL   you.PL   about
              'What are you talking about?'
              German: *Worüber/ Über was redet ihr?*

(14)   Hebrew; age 6:0, asking to see the content of a present bought for a friend:
              aní rocé   lir'ót   eyx ze nir'á   kmo
              I want.SG.M   see.INF   how this looks.SG.M like
              'I want to see what it looks like'
              Hebrew: *aní rocé lir'ót eyx ze nir'á*

Example (15) shows the child's usual expression, during this period, for 'I am
cold':

(15)   From around age 5:0, lasting until around age 8:0:
              a. Hebrew:
                 aní kar
                 I   cold.SG.M
                 'I am cold'

    b. German:
      ich bin kalt
      I   am   cold
      'I am cold'

Note that both languages have dative-experiencer constructions: Hebrew *kar li*, German *mir ist kalt* (both literally '[it] is cold to-me'). Here too, then, it is the abstract construction pattern that is generalised for the repertoire as a whole, or rather, the pattern of a construction that has been acquired and used in a particular set of contexts (i.e. the English-speaking settings) is activated in other contexts as well, but linguistic matter is selected in line with the constraints of those other contexts. Moreover, the replicated pattern itself is also adjusted to cater to the structural constraints of the selected language. Thus in Hebrew, no present-tense copula form appears, and the existential predication assumes the structure of a nominal sentence. It is therefore incorrect to speak of the 1:1 replication of an entire construction. Instead, it is the principal or pivotal feature of the construction that is selected; it is then matched with a structure representing a similar function in the other language. The process of 'pivot-matching' (see Chapter 9; cf. also Matras and Sakel 2007a) is subject to the constraints of the replica language. In (15), the selected pivotal feature is the use of the existential construction with the experiencer as subject.

    In many cases the child demonstrates creativity in assigning new functions and meanings to existing structures in order to reconstruct patterns drawing on linguistic matter from the 'appropriate' language. In (15) it is the distribution context of the existential construction that is extended, meeting one of the criteria for grammaticalisation as described for contact-induced change by Heine and Kuteva (2005). But meaning and indeed even category or class affiliation of words may be adjusted as well:

(16)   a. Hebrew; age 4:6, commenting on a drawing:
        ze   avál yafé!
        this but   nice
        'This is very nice indeed!'
     b. German model:
        Das ist aber   schön!
        this is PART nice
        'This is very nice indeed!'

In (16), the child has just recently begun to use German modal particles. The individual particle forms are identified by the child as belonging to the German subset of his repertoire. Nonetheless, the child treats the construction type 'modal particles' as part of his overall repertoire of modes of expression, not specifically bound to the German component. He attempts to implement the newly acquired construction in all possible contexts and interaction settings. Conscious of the constraints on matter-selection, and not having heard a (native) Hebrew representation of the construction which he can imitate, the child makes his own creative effort to accommodate the construction to the Hebrew setting by modifying the meanings of existing Hebrew word-forms. This process, which we might call 'replication' of the construction pattern in the Hebrew context, once again involves the selection of pivotal features and their mapping onto Hebrew items. The pivot in this case is German *aber*, which is a modal particle in the construction under scrutiny, but is identical in form to the German conjunction 'but'. Thus, polysemy is the key to the pivot-matching procedure. It inspires the child to select the translation equivalent in Hebrew, the conjunction *avál* 'but', and to assign to it the pivotal role in the modal particle construction. The process is reminiscent of what Heine and Kuteva (2005) refer to as 'replica grammaticalisation': the analogous promotion of an item up the grammaticalisation chain – in this case from conjunction to particle.

Pivot-matching does not, however, necessarily follow the grammaticalisation pathway, as can be seen from the following example (see also Matras and Sakel 2007a for a discussion). Around the age of four, the child acquires a new construction in German – the politeness term of address *Sie*. The German second-person polite form *Sie* is identical to the 3PL pronoun *sie*, and carries the same 3PL agreement marker on the verb. The context in which the child acquires this construction is a game which he plays with his mother, in which the child is a storekeeper and the mother is a customer coming to the shop, who addresses the shopkeeper in the polite form when enquiring about certain products (*haben Sie X?* 'do you.POLITE have X?'). The child's acquaintance with the German politeness form is, at this stage, limited to this particular context. Strictly speaking, he does not acquire a politeness marker as such, but a construction that is employed in a particular slot within the pre-defined pattern of speech activities that characterises the game 'shop'.

By acquiring this new construction, the child has extended his overall communicative repertoire. In this case, this is a more accurate description than to suggest that he has learned a new 'structure', since he is already familiar with the form of the 3PL pronoun and agreement marker, and it is only the use of the structure to refer to the addressee under strictly defined communicative circumstances that is novel to him. When the child is spending time with his father, a similar game is played in Hebrew. Note that the 'generic' shop-game, from the child's perspective, is played with the mother, and that it is in her household that the child has a range of accessories, including a toy counter and till, to facilitate the game. The shop-game in the father's household is thus a 'replica'. Having enriched his linguistic-communicative repertoire as part of mastering the shop-game, the child is eager to repeat the acquired pattern of activity associated with it. This includes the organisation of the question which he, now playing the role of the customer, puts to the storekeeper, this time the Hebrew-speaking father:

(17)   a. Hebrew; age 4:1, during role-play as a customer addressing a grocer:
               yeš lahem tapuxím?
               there.is to.3PL apples
               [Intended meaning]: 'Do you have apples?'
               [Actual meaning]: 'Do they have apples?'

            b. German model construction for polite form of address:
               haben   Sie   Äpfel?
               have.3PL you.POLITE/3PL apples
               'Do you have apples?'

Hebrew lacks a politeness pronoun. The child replicates the German construction
by employing a Hebrew possessive construction in the 3PL. Once again, the
child is picking up a single – albeit 'pivotal' – feature of the German construction,
namely the use of the 3PL. This is employed as a term of direct address, or listener-
deixis, and so in effect it is a case of de-grammaticalisation (from anaphora to
deixis).

   In Chapter 9 we will see how pattern replication through pivot-matching is a
common process in contact-induced language change. In the linguistic experience
of an individual speaker, such a process may occupy various positions on the
synchrony–diachrony continuum of the particular idiolect. The adoption of an
English-based pattern in (15) in both German and Hebrew is long-lasting in
the child's speech, and illustrates the potential contribution of pivot-matching to
language change – the only limitation here being the fact that we are dealing
with an individual's idiolect, and not with the collective speech form of a speech
community. The structure seen in (17) is a single occurrence, but this is due largely
to the fact that it is embedded into a particular slot in a fixed discourse pattern.
We might assume that frequent repetition of the role-play would in all likelihood
lead to a regularisation of the structure in this particular discourse organisation.
But the mechanism of pattern-matching itself is activated spontaneously as a
solution to on-the-spot, immediate, and local communicative needs. Consider the
following example:

(18)   Hebrew; age 7:3, while watching a football match broadcast (in English) on
            television:
            a. Child: *Penalty shot!*

            b. Father: me   ha-nekudá ha-levaná . . .
                       from the-spot   the-white.SG.F
                       'From the white spot . . . '

            c. Child: ze ma še   *penalty shot.*
                       that what REL
                       'That's what a *penalty shot* is.'

In his explanation of the term 'penalty shot' (replicated in English as a technical
term), in segment (c), the child uses a cleft construction. It is modelled structurally
on the Hebrew cleft construction, which assumes the form {this + what + COMP
+ verb}, as in *ze ma še aní amárti* 'that [is] what {COMP}I said'. In the absence
of a present-tense copula form, the Hebrew cleft construction is incompatible

with present-tense existential predications. The child attempts to reconcile the semantic function and distribution of an English cleft construction – 'that's what a penalty shot is' – with the structural features of Hebrew cleft constructions. The result is an ad hoc extension of the Hebrew structure. The construction used by the child in segment (c) does not exist in native adult Hebrew.

So far, we have seen how pattern replication is motivated by the need to employ a newly acquired semantic-pragmatic construction irrespective of interaction setting, adapting it to the relevant context through pivot-matching and the use of context-appropriate linguistic word-forms. The fact that the child is able to engage in such complex, creative procedures is a sign of growing linguistic maturity as well as of a strict awareness of the setting-bound constraints on the selection of overt linguistic matter. Pivot-matching is thus, essentially, an opportunistic strategy, which allows the speaker to make maximum use of his full linguistic-expressive resources while at the same time conform to the expectations on word-form selection in the particular conversational setting. With growing linguistic proficiency and expressive skills, especially at school age (after the age of five), when use of the individual languages becomes unbalanced and exposure to English takes on a leading role,[10] we see evidence of occasional difficulties in keeping apart repertoire components, particularly around certain types of constructions. While there is hardly any confusion at this stage around, for example, inflectional morphology or word order, vulnerable categories include the choice of prepositions modifying objects and adverbial modifications:

(19)   Hebrew; age 8:2, while the child is busy playing with a favourite jigsaw puzzle, in response to the father's suggestion that they should play music together:
        lo   sixákti   et   ze   kvar   le/ harbé zman
        NEG played.1SG ACC this already for much time
        'I haven't played this for a long time'

(20)   Hebrew; age 8:5:
        šaxáxti   al   ze
        forgot.1SG about this
        'I forgot about it'

In (19), the child begins to replicate the English model construction *for a long time*, by selecting, as a 'pivot match', the Hebrew benefactive object preposition *le*, though the construction is then interrupted by a self-repair (the proper Hebrew construction lacks a preposition here). It is the self-repair that provides an indication that pivot-matching in this case is motivated by a certain degree of insecurity in selecting appropriate constructions. One can assume a similar motivation in (20), resulting in the replication of the English prepositional object through the use of Hebrew *al* 'about, on' (instead of the expected Hebrew direct object preposition *et*). In this case, the replication goes unnoticed by the speaker (and uncommented on by the hearer). Lexical semantics are particularly prone to such processes:

(21)   German; age 5:8, offering the mother a taste of a dish he is having:
             Willst   du   schmecken?
             want.2SG   you   taste
             'Would you like to taste?'

(22)   Hebrew; age 6:4, in response to the father telling about an interesting film
             which he saw on television:
             lakáxta   et   ze/ hikláteta   et   ze?
             took.2SG   ACC   this recorded.2SG   ACC   this
             'Did you take it/ did you record it?'

In (21), German *schmecken* 'taste' (an intransitive verb meaning 'to be tasty') is used as a transitive-agentive verb in a meaning modelled on English 'taste' (both intransitive and transitive); the appropriate German verb would be *probieren*, lit. also 'to try out'. In (22), the start of the utterance reveals a plan toward the selection of a lexical construction modelled on the German *aufnehmen* 'to record', which is composed of the lexical item representing the concept 'to take' and an added component, a so-called 'verbal particle' *auf*, an aktionsart modifier derived from the preposition 'on, onto'. We see an attempt to match the meaning onto a similar component, integrating the Hebrew verb *lakáx–* 'to take'. The selection of the Hebrew past tense requires the insertion of finite verb inflection; the first part of the verbal construction having then been completed, once the direct object is inserted a search is presumably triggered for a match for the supplementary verbal particle *auf*.[11] When none is found, the speaker self-repairs and retrieves the relevant Hebrew lexical item, *hikláteta* 'you recorded'. These examples illustrate how word forms of the individual repertoire components are easily kept apart, but their semantic fields are sometimes fused, making accommodation to the setting (and so language choice) a straightforward, almost mechanical procedure of substituting one item by another, irrespective of any semantic-contextual constraints. Further examples are seen in (23)–(24), where replication targets an extended meaning of the respective lexical item:

(23)   a. German; age 4:6, addressing the mother, having made a witty comment
                that confused her:
                ich habe   dir   einen Trick gemacht
                I   have.1SG you.SG.DAT   a.ACC trick done
                'I played a trick on you'

             b. Hebrew model:
                asíti   lax   trik
                did.1SG   to.2.SG.F   trick
                'I played a trick on you'

(24)   a. Hebrew; age 4:6, in response to the father assuring him that a story he
                told him was true:
                ani xošév   lexá   et   ze
                I think.SG.M to.2SG.M   ACC this
                'I believe you'

  b. German model:
     Ich glaube   es dir
     I   think.1SG it you.SG.DAT
     'I believe you'

Once again, the process of accommodation testifies to the communicative maturity of the speaker: Replication of the construction is constrained in both examples by the morpho-syntactic rules of the accommodating language, represented by the selection of tense, case marking, and word order rules. It is once again the abstract organisation pattern of the construction that is replicated, and in both cases specifically the extension of the meaning of a lexical verb along with its argument structure: Hebrew {'to do' + benefactive + 'trick'}in (23), German {'to think' + direct object + benefactive}in the sense of 'to believe' in (24). In essence, a verb is identified as a match for the verb of the model construction, and inserted into an argument structure environment that similarly matches the model, resulting in an extension of meaning of the targeted verb.

Frequent candidates for such semantic extensions are verbs with a specification of local relations:

(25)   Hebrew; age 8:5, referring to the absence of the class teacher, in reply to the
         father's question why no merit certificates had been distributed to the
         child's classmates at that day's school assembly:
         ki   Miss Preston lo   haytá   šam
         because   NEG was.3SG.F there
         'Because Miss Preston wasn't there'

(26)   a. Hebrew; age 5:8, while taking a walk with the father, reaching the end
             of a path at the edge of a field:
             pašút   neléx   dérex
             simply go.1PL.FUT through
             'Let's simply cross [it]'
         b. German model:
             Gehen   wir einfach durch
             go.1PL we   simply   through
             'Let's simply cross [it]'

(27)   Hebrew; age 5:10, after playing outdoors for a while:
         aní rocé   laléxet le-tox
         I   want.SG.M go.INF   into
         'I want to go inside'

(28)   Hebrew; age 5:10, looking out of the window on a cloudy day:
         ha-šémeš bá'a   ha-xúca
         the-sun   came.3SG.F   outside
         'The sun came out'

In (25), a replica is sought for the English expression 'to be there', representing presence at a contextually identifiable location (also German *da sein*). In Hebrew, this function is simply covered by the plain copula (thus *lo haytá* 'she wasn't [there]'), with the location being contextually inferred rather than anaphorically specified. The Hebrew remote place deixis *šam* 'there' is employed to replicate the model construction and support the meaning extension of the main verb, *haytá* 'was'. In (26), the German composed verb meaning 'to cross', consisting of a main verb stem with the meaning 'to go' and a directional specification in the form of a verbal particle, is replicated by creating a Hebrew composition out of the verb 'to go' and the preposition 'through'. Both elements are recruited because they can serve as lexical translations of the respective German components of the construction when those appear in isolation.

The underlying assumption is therefore that the rules of combining separate forms into composite and derived meanings apply irrespective of the interaction setting and repertoire subset that is activated (i.e. independently of 'language'). The speaker is drawing on what is perceived as an integrated, universal inventory of rules of deriving lexical meanings in this fashion, exempting those rules from the otherwise stable demarcation boundaries separating subsets of linguistic forms and constructions. Similar procedures are documented in (27)–(28), where composites of verb + directional expression are used to convey meanings which in Hebrew are normally expressed by independent lexical stems – *lehikanés* 'to enter', *yac'á* 'came out'. While in (28) the use of the adverb *haxúca* 'outside' is at least permissible in such a context in Hebrew, in (27) the preposition *letóx*, which normally must precede a noun or carry a pronominal ending, is promoted to an adverbial directional expression or verbal particle modifying the lexical meaning of the verb.[12]

As we saw above, pattern-matching takes into account morpho-syntactic constraints of the replica language. This applies to the modification of lexical semantics as well:

(29)   Hebrew; age 6:2:
         ze osé   li   laxšóv   al ..
         it makes.SG.M to.1SG think.INF about
         'It makes me think of . . . '

(30)   Hebrew; age 6:2:
         nafálti   lišón
         fell.1SG sleep.INF
         'I fell asleep'

In (29), an analytical causative construction is modelled on English, filling the function of the Hebrew *ze mazkír li* 'it reminds me'. But note that the benefactive is expressed by the Hebrew prepositional object *li*. The child does not employ a Hebrew direct object pronoun (**otí* 'me'). In (30), the complex construction, modelled on English, substitutes Hebrew *nirdámti* 'I fell asleep', but the modifying component is not, as in English, an adverb, but the Hebrew infinitive 'to sleep'.

Finally, idiomatic expressions constitute a frequent target for pattern replication:

(31)   Hebrew; age 9:5, describing a family friend:
            hi   me'ód letóx kadurégel
            she very   into   football
            'She is very much into football'

(32)   Hebrew; age 9:7, reaching a footpath junction while taking a walk:
            éyze   dérex?
            which way
            'Which way?'

Once again, there is an underlying assumption on the part of the child-speaker that
pragmatically inferred meanings are universal, and not language-dependent. Thus
in (31) the Hebrew preposition *letóx* 'into' is used in its metaphorical extension
in the sense of 'interested in', while in Hebrew proper it has only a literal, spatial
meaning, and fondness is expressed by verbs such as *le'ehóv* 'to like'. In (32), the
request for instructions relating to the direction would be formulated differently,
e.g. *le-éyze kivún?* lit. 'to which direction?'

   Thus we still encounter, at an advanced age and linguistic maturity, conflicting
motivations in the child-speaker: on the one hand, the wish to comply with the
social expectations of the interlocutor and select only those items that are deemed
appropriate in the particular setting. Compliance with this 'selection constraint'
has become a badge of identity that defines the child's relationships with regular
interlocutors as well as with patterns of activities and situations. On the other
hand, there is a need to exploit as effectively as possible the full inventory of
linguistic-communicative resources that the child has at his disposal, in order to
maximise his ability to articulate intricate and highly differentiated meanings.
Pattern replication based on a pivot-matching procedure offers a possible resolu-
tion to these conflicting motivations. It enables the child to employ constructions
that represent a range of differentiated meanings without defying the 'selection
constraint'.

   The success of this strategy appears to depend on two conditions. The first is
comprehensibility of the child's creative constructions. In our case study, comprehensibility is guaranteed in most cases. Once English has become the dominant
language, creative pattern replication appears mainly in German and Hebrew;
the principal interlocutors for these languages – the parents – understand all
three languages. The child's innovative constructions are therefore seldom an
obstacle for effective communication. The second condition is acceptability of
the innovation. Once again, in what is in principle a supportive communicative environment, neither of the main interlocutors – the parents – will subject
the child to any sanctions, ridicule, or refusal of cooperation in the interaction
on the basis of the child's use of innovative constructions that do not comply
with the adult or monolingual norm. On the whole, then, such constructions
serve their communicative purposes and remain uncommented on by the parents. Occasionally, a parent might introduce the 'proper' construction, giving

the child support in acquiring an alternative to the improvised one. In the long run, the liberty to continue to replicate constructions will depend largely on the consistency of adult feedback and, later on, on the extent of exposure to other communicative settings, involving a larger range of interlocutors. Those would, one should assume, help the speaker extend the range of language-specific constructions at his disposal and consequently reduce his tendency to generalise just one construction pattern per communicative function, irrespective of setting. At the same time it would limit the acceptability and perhaps even the comprehensibility of such pattern replications, creating an incentive to avoid them.

2.5   Conscious exploitation of the full linguistic repertoire

In Sections 2.2 and 2.3 we saw that the child acquires the ability to activate elements within his repertoire selectively as a behavioural skill, which is part of the skill of accommodating to the interlocutor's expectations in particular interaction settings. The successful acquisition of this skill is to a considerable extent dependent on the behavioural model and the guidance that are provided by the parents (and where relevant by other interlocutors). The connection between domain or setting separation and language choice eventually becomes part of the child's identity and personality (see Chapter 3). As the child matures and his overall communicative confidence grows, he is able not only to control the selection of structures from his linguistic repertoire, but also to manipulate it. The stricter the expectations of his interlocutors become with regard to language separation, the more confidence is required on the part of the child in order to defy the selection constraints while winning over the hearer for the special effect that such defiance creates.[13]

In (33)–(34), the child is using events from school life as points of reference. The school is an English-speaking environment, key elements of which are institutionalised as unique referents. Although the child is in principle able to come up with translations or paraphrases for the relevant concepts in each of his other two languages, direct replication of the English form amounts to an activation in context of the world of associations represented by the original term. It is a discourse device that supports the transposition of the original scene or event into a specific setting; it has the effect of bringing to life the scene or event that the English term represents:

(33)   Hebrew; age 6:10, reporting on an event that took place at school:
         ze   hayá   be *assembly*
         that was.3.SG.M at
         'That was at *Assembly*'

(34)   German; age 7:6, when reminded of a past event:
            Da   war   ich noch in *year one*
            DEIC was.1SG I   still in
            'I was still in *Year one* then'

In order to take the liberty to defy the subset selection constraint and employ English terms in a setting defined as 'Hebrew' or 'German', the child must be able to anticipate his interlocutor's acceptance of the English insertion. In (33)–(34) the insertion of English terms activates a world of associations that is connected to the English-speaking school environment. *Assembly* can be regarded as a unique institution, since neither the child nor the parents have experience of an equivalent activity carried out in a language other than English. *Year one* similarly has the unique referential status of an institution term, since it can only be paralleled in the other languages by a system of counting grades, literally ('first year', etc.). However, any parental model for such constructions in the other languages is impeded by the lack of a one-to-one correspondence between what is, primarily in terms of age but also in terms of succession of years, considered the 'first' year of school in the English system and in the respective foreign systems. The English term is therefore the most accurate portrayal of the specific phase within the English school system, and hence uniquely referential.

The acceptance of insertions of this kind by the parent-interlocutors, and indeed the adoption of similar insertion patterns by the parents themselves, creates a general licence for the free selection of institutional terminology within the repertoire irrespective of the setting in which it was acquired and is normally used, i.e. irrespective of its 'source language'. In terms of the child's language development one might be tempted to speak of a wholesale 'borrowing' of English institutional terminology into the other languages. In practice, the relevant class of lexemes is simply exempt from the selection constraint.

A more complex issue is the insertion of phrases. Unlike institutional reference terms, phrases are less likely to establish a stable reference to an unambiguous, unique entity. Finer-tuned judgement on the part of the child-speaker is called for in respect of the contextual effects of phrase insertions:

(35)   Hebrew; age 6:10, addressing a somewhat younger bilingual (Hebrew-
            English) child, while walking on a low stone boundary on the edge of a
            footpath:
            káxa aní yexól   *to keep my balance*
            thus I   can.SG.M
            'This way I can *keep my balance*'

The switch into English is effectively a product of the child allowing himself to defy the selection constraint, anticipating that the special effect of the insertion will make the 'inappropriate' language choice acceptable to the hearer. Such choices are often a gamble on the part of the child. They require a careful assessment of the inferences that the interlocutor is likely to make about the tone and key of the message as a whole. In (35), the English insertion serves to activate associations with the play context among peers. The replication of the routine phrase comes more naturally than a cumbersome attempt at a translation. The child is evidently counting on the acceptance of his language choice by his younger interlocutor, who, however conscious of language separation herself, is similarly exposed to English in the school and peer settings and is likely to have a similar world of associations in respect of play and exercise routines of this kind.

When the interlocutor is an adult or parent, it is more difficult for the child to anticipate that a violation of the selection constraint will be accepted. An overt emphasis of the message key is crucial for the switch to be understood as stylistically motivated, rather than be interpreted as the child's communicative ineptness:

(36)   Hebrew; age 8:2, in a theatrical tone, in response to the father, who is
            cleaning the house and suggests to throw away a particular decorated
            cardboard box with which the child used to play at an earlier age:
            im atá   tizrók   otá,   *I shall make a complaint*
            if you.M throw.2.SG.M.FUT ACC.3SG.F
            to the government
            'If you throw it out, *I shall make a complaint to the government*'

The humour is evident in the mere content of the English phrase – notably the fact that the child pretends to be able to threaten the parent with sanctions of any kind. Note also the fact that by using *I shall* the child is mimicking a formal style that is entirely alien to the setting and indeed to any communicative interaction in which the child is likely to be involved. The entire utterance is thus a spontaneous, theatrical role-play. The choice of English as the language of the quasi 'threat' marks out the humour and shows that the child has learnt to manipulate language choice for stylistic-conversational effects such as humour or imitation of roles and styles. Once again, such manipulation – merely daring to issue an unrealistic threat knowing that the interlocutor will not take it literally, but will instead appreciate its entertainment value – requires a level of maturity and self-confidence in the overall handling of linguistic-communicative tasks.

Not only language choice, but also language itself can at this stage be used as an instrument for the creation of humour and conversational entertainment.

(37)   Hebrew; age 6:1, discussing an event that had happened over a year earlier:
            ze   hayá   kše   *fang*ti   *year one an.*
            that was.3.SG.M when began [German].1SG [Hebrew] PART [German]
            'That was when I *started year one*.'

(38)   (Hebrew-defined context and setting); age 8:6, calling to his father from the
            bathroom when washing his face before going to bed in the evening
            (insertions in segment (c) from German):

    a. Child: Aba!
    b. Father: Hmm.
    c. Child: Where do I get a *Lappen* so I can *wisch* my *Gesicht*?

    a. Child: Daddy!
    b. Father: Hmm.
    c. Child: Where do I get a *wash cloth* so I can *wipe* my *face*?

Examples (37)–(38) document more than just plain insertions or switches. This is deliberate and conscious language mixing. The child and his interlocutor are both aware that this kind of mixing is dysfunctional and unacceptable in everyday casual conversation. While the insertion of English *year one* in (37) is again an indication of how established or 'licensed' insertions of institutional terminology are (see Example (34)), the insertion of German *anfangen* 'to start' involves complex adjustment of the Hebrew sentence: the addition of suffixed person/tense inflection *-ti* to the main verb stem, complying with Hebrew morphology, the consequent isolation of the German verbal particle *an* (as in finite forms of German complex verbs) and its accommodation at the end of the clause, complying with its position in the German main clause containing a finite complex verb (cf. *ich fange an* 'I start'). The grammatical accommodation is, in all likelihood, spontaneous and not reflected, nor is the insertion of a German verb form pre-planned. Yet this pattern is entirely unknown in either the child's language use or in that of the parents.[14] It is safe to assume that the child was in this instance simply quicker to recall the German lexical item. But the confidence to produce an utterance that incorporates the German word, rather than delay the utterance until the Hebrew item is retrieved, indicates a willingness to engage in playful linguistic creativity.

    In (38), the choice of English (rather than Hebrew) in segment (c) as the language of the utterance directed at the Hebrew-speaking father already defies the normal setting constraint on language selection. The immediate effect is to highlight the utterance as distinct from an ordinary utterance, in this case to qualify the speech act as carrying a humorous key. In fact, the utterance contains a genuine request. The humour is an ornament, aimed at neutralising the possible alienating effect that a reading of the request as a complaint might have. The father has instructed the child to wash, but has failed to make the necessary arrangements and provide him with a cloth (which is the usual evening procedure). The choice of English as the carrier language for the utterance is thus in Myers-Scotton's (1993a) terms a 'marked' choice. The distance it creates neutralises possible dispreferred inferences. German too would have been a marked choice. However, being reserved to everyday household communication with the mother, German is an intimate language, unfit to convey distance. English, by contrast, is the default language of the outside world, fit for any purpose other than default communication with the parents or family relations. Moreover, in choosing English the child is also imitating both parents' (and especially the father's) occasional use of English to mark out phrases as humorous, presenting them as quasi-citations and thus creating the same kind of distance or demarcation between real-world communication and the special effect of the marked utterance. The child's own creative innovation is in going beyond the mere choice of English here. He inserts German content words into the English utterance, thus contributing further to lending the utterance an unreal appearance. Such conscious language mixing – deliberate manipulation of the demarcation boundaries within the multilingual repertoire – provides us with an illustration of the likely roots of community-level language mixtures of the type that will be discussed in Chapter 10.

2.6   Implications for the study of language contact

From the perspective of the individual multilingual speaker, 'language contact' is not about systems influencing one another. Rather, it is about the challenge of employing a repertoire of communicative resources, acquired in a range of different settings or from different interlocutors, in such a way that will comply with the expectations of audiences and interlocutors in various interaction settings. The bilingual speaker faces the task of maintaining strict demarcation boundaries among subsets of his or her linguistic repertoire in order to be able to communicate in monolingual settings. Failure to maintain such demarcation might inhibit communication in monolingual settings quite severely. Complying with the 'selection constraint' is therefore paramount, especially in environments in which languages have separate functions and separate social meanings.

The acquisition and maintenance of demarcations within the multilingual repertoire is motivated by the need to gain the approval of socially dominant interlocutors: initially the parents, and later also peers. But the ability to select context-appropriate structures depends not only on the input and expectations of the interlocutors. It is also sensitive to the function of individual linguistic structures, i.e. to the contribution that linguistic structures make to the mental processing and the organisation of discourse. Control over selection appears more difficult to maintain for some functions of language than for others. This suggests that language 'mixing' can be triggered not just by social factors such as language attitudes, or by material factors such as the presence of an object in one set of interaction settings but not in another. It is also triggered by cognitive factors. The infant acquiring bilingual synonyms, for example, appears to have greater difficulties applying the principle of multiple labels to salient objects and utensils of the immediate environment, which continue to be treated as unique referents for a longer period. The young child who has mastered the separation of languages shows lapses in the ability to control language selection around discourse markers and other structures belonging to the monitoring-and-directing apparatus especially in situations involving transitions between settings.

From the early stages of bilingualism onwards, the speaker has to balance potentially conflicting motivations on the way toward sustaining most effective communication. On the one hand there is a need to comply with the expectations of the interlocutors in selecting structures that are acceptable to them. On the other hand there is the need to exhaust the full resources of the linguistic repertoire in order to ensure maximum expressiveness. Early patterns of language mixing can be interpreted as attempts to exploit expressive resources, at the expense, sometimes, of compliance with hearer expectations. But as control and awareness of the structures and rules of language and of the social constraints on language choice increase, the speaker is in a position to try and bridge the two motivations. While linguistic matter – overt phonological representations – is more easily assigned to a particular subset, construction patterns and meanings are often treated as universal. The speaker will often try to employ constructions irrespective of the interaction setting, while still respecting the subset selection constraint with regard to matter (form or shape; including choice of lexemes, morphology, and morpho-syntactic rules).

Pattern replication through 'pivot-matching' thus rests on several preconditions. The first is a more rigid and conscious commitment on the part of the speaker to subset demarcation, greater social and audience sensitivity, and a greater fear to lose face in the event of violating hearer expectation on subset selection. In our case study, pattern replication emerges at a stage when the overall repertoire is expanding rapidly and new constructions are being acquired. But domain specialisation is also increasing, leading to an unequal expansion of the repertoire (both lexicon and grammar) in various settings. In other words, certain expressive skills are being developed in one language but not in the others. This gives rise to the need to 'import' constructions across languages. Finally, engaging in pivot-matching and pattern replication is a creative process, through which the young speaker produces forms that have not yet been heard. This requires skills in navigating through the rules of the language, obeying formal-grammatical constraints. It also requires self-confidence to confront the adult listener with structures that have not been 'tested' before; while on the other hand it presupposes a somewhat naïve appreciation of language separation according to which correct selection is manifested primarily through linguistic matter (and certain formal rules on conjoining matter), while abstract patterns and meanings assigned to matter may be flexible or even universal.

From the very beginning of the language acquisition process, the child-speaker learns that some linguistic items are 'universal', that is, they can be employed irrespective of setting or interlocutor. This principle of the existence of unique referents within the repertoire continues to accompany the bilingual speaker even in later stages. Even the more mature communicator entertains the notion that certain items are exempt from the need to select among repertoire subsets. In order to qualify for universal status, such items need to be both comprehended and accepted by key interlocutors as unique referents. Inevitably, acceptability is not evenly distributed among the different interaction settings and populations of interlocutors; only terms deriving from certain activity domains have a chance of becoming accepted, and then only among a certain circle of interlocutors who have potential access to the setting in which the terms are used. In our case study, English terms relating to certain institutions of school life, for example, may be used in conversation with the parents.

With even greater maturity and self-confidence, the young speaker is able to assess interlocutors' reactions and to try and exploit language mixing in conversation in order to win over the hearer for a special conversational effect or key. The motivation to manipulate language boundaries emerges along with greater complexity in the speaker's conversation and a need for a variety of forms of expression. The background against which the speaker may engage in language play or language manipulation of this kind is a strong enough social basis and intimate bond with an interlocutor audience to allow for mimicry and other theatrical acts of speech without alienating the hearer.

Against the background of the patterns of bilingual behaviour described in this chapter, we can understand a range of language contact phenomena: Bilingual first-language acquisition, domain separation of languages in individuals and in multilingual communities, 'accidental' language mixing and bilingual speech production errors, (stylistically motivated) conversational code switching, deliberate language mixing, language convergence, and the import of linguistic structures from one language into another ('borrowing'). Both the synchronic phenomena, and those that give rise to language change, arise from the conversational behaviour of bilinguals at different stages of their language-acquisition history – bilinguals who navigate between the need to maintain demarcation boundaries among subsets of their repertoire in order to satisfy social expectations on communicative behaviour, and the urge to make use of the full repertoire for maximum expressiveness.

3   Societal multilingualism

3.1   Linguistic repertoires and social activities: a micro-level approach

In Chapter 2 we observed how a multilingual child's linguistic social-isation involved the acquisition of the skill to select structures from the linguistic repertoire that match the expectations of his adult interlocutors. Already at an early stage in the acquisition process, individual words within the repertoire began to crystallise into coherent sets as a result of their association with the child's three principal adult interlocutors: the German-speaking mother, the Hebrew-speaking father, and the English-speaking child-minder. As the child's experience in social interaction grew, so did the inventory of cues associated with each set of struc-tures: a video in Hebrew, a family friend who speaks German, a shop where English is spoken and so on. This association between a set of interaction cues and a set of words leads to the gradual build-up of selection rules and mental demarcation lines among components within the linguistic repertoire. Later on, the child will learn to refer to these components as different 'languages'; but the separation of languages starts off as a differentiated mapping of sets of linguistic structures onto sets of social activities. This is the core of an individual's – or micro-level – management of a multilingual repertoire.

The same principle is followed as the range of social activities expands even further. In Ben's case, nursery attendance from the age of 1:11, and gradual expo-sure, from around that age onwards, to learning activities and learning materials primarily in English, followed by the beginning of school attendance at the age of 4:3, leads to the predominance of English in most intellectual activities outside the home as well as those stimulated by television, video, and most books within the home. From the early school years onwards English also becomes dominant in interaction with peers. Ben gradually develops a passion for reading and, by the age of 9–10, also for writing, and shows exceptional command of English vocabulary and style. German and Hebrew continue to play a role in learning, as the parents devote much time to stimulating and reviewing learning in the home. Ben is taught the basics of the German and Hebrew writing systems by his parents parallel to his learning to read in English. He becomes exposed more intensively to reading material in German around the age of 7:6 and eventually acquires the ability to read fluently in German. At the age of ten he maintains only a very basic familiarity with the Hebrew writing system, which helps him read signs when visiting in Israel and captions in Hebrew picture books and games. However, stimulated by the father he develops a routine of using the Roman script to read and write Hebrew, albeit in a somewhat makeshift manner, which he uses in occasional correspondence, including notes and email messages.

Ben's mapping of repertoire components onto a network of social activities is guided by several types of cues. The first and most obvious is the **differentiation of languages by addressee**. In Ben's specific case, there is absolute consistency in the choice of language used with each and every addressee, whether known to him or unknown. Parents, teachers, neighbours, schoolmates, family members, and friends are each individually associated with just one particular language. This association is stable and there are very few deviations from it. Exceptions are primarily situations in which a variety of addressees is present with whom different languages are usually spoken, and there is a need to address the entire group without excluding anybody. Most frequently, this kind of situation arises when Ben is in the company of one of the parents and an English-speaking non-family member. The language that is then selected is English, though side-comments targeting the parent are made in that parent's language. Ben usually spends no more than one evening a week with both parents together; Ben's parents understand one another's languages, and there is therefore never a need to avoid either German or Hebrew. Since the parents use German when speaking to one another, Ben tends to choose German when addressing both parents together. Thus, addressee-guided general principles of language selection are only overridden by changes within the addressee constellation itself.

Interaction settings constitute a further relevant dimension. Individual interlocutors can be grouped according to the place, mode, and purpose of interaction into settings such as school, neighbourhood, attractions, shops, visits abroad, family friends' households, and the two parental households. For each setting, there is a typical and almost invariably consistent choice of language. Within the parental households, a further differentiation into **interaction contexts** takes place: default interaction with the parent, interaction with visitors, telephone conversations with the other parent or with friends or relatives, telephone interactions with strangers (when answering the phone in English), radio and television, and so on. In effect, these constitute differentiated addressee constellations within a setting that is otherwise defined, by and large, by a stable and predictable choice of language. Thus, when Ben answers the doorbell to the postman he speaks English, and when his father's German-speaking colleague visits the father's household Ben speaks German.

To some extent, there is also an indirect mapping of languages to **topics of conversation**. In Ben's case this too is largely a product of the exclusivity of language use with different addressees. Domestic issues are negotiated in German or Hebrew, while learning and intellectual activities are carried out primarily in English. Gaps are bridged, however, through extensive reading and exposure to media and everyday conversation covering a wide range of subjects in English, on the one hand, and through the parents' own promotion of learning and intellectual activities in the homes, in German and Hebrew respectively, on the other. A balance in the association between languages with topics of conversation is enabled partly through the fact that relevant topical contexts are accessible at least in principle in each of the languages. Neither of his three languages is entirely absent from any interaction domain that plays a role in Ben's life; it is just that Ben's exposure to specific topics of interaction is not equal in all three languages. This results at times in unequal access to topic-specific vocabulary in the three languages, and so to a partial **dominance** of one language over the others in respect of certain domains. English is dominant in the domain of learning, problem-solving and argumentation, and sports, while use of German and Hebrew seems more spontaneous in the emotional domain and perhaps in relation to some domestic topics, especially those that are culture-specific, such as names of favourite dishes, festivities, and other customs.

A further product of the pattern of language separation by setting and activities is the differentiated mapping of **linguistic skills** onto the three languages in the repertoire. In addition to vocabulary, this pertains to the ability to read and write as well as to command different levels or registers of the languages. In this respect, at the age of ten, with Ben's pattern of language use for various activities having stabilised, the languages form a clear hierarchy: English is in the lead in writing, reading, the extent of vocabulary and error-free usage, and command of a formal style. German follows, but is weaker in respect of all of the above save perhaps phonology. Hebrew, though fluent, occupies the third position (including difficulties in understanding formal style, such as the language of formal broadcasting or printed media, and some interference in phonology).

Finally, Ben's mapping of repertoire components to social interaction is characterised by a differentiated set of **language demarcation rules**. These govern the liberty to mix and switch languages in different contexts. Once again, in Ben's particular case much of this is pre-determined by the choice of addressee. The majority of Ben's English-speaking addressees – peers, teachers, neighbours, shopkeepers, and other strangers in his home town – are monolingual. Settings defined by the presence of these addressees rule out any language mixing. Most interaction settings in Germany are also monolingual, though in the case of individual addressees occasional insertion of English concepts – mostly concepts relating to institutional terminology (see Chapter 2) – is 'permitted'; addressee identity thus overrides the constraints imposed by the setting. Interaction with Hebrew-speaking family members both in Israel and in the United States, by contrast, allows and even encourages English-language insertions for quotation and special effect. This is the case in most interaction with the parents, too, where the English-speaking environment is often referenced via direct replication of words and phrases, especially those pertaining to institutional activities.

Ben's differentiated use of his linguistic repertoire shows that several factors can be involved as cues in the choice of language in multilingual settings: among them are the addressee, the setting, the context, and the topic of conversation. Language specialisation for particular sets of activities may in addition shape the profile of an individual's linguistic skills in each of the languages. The overall patterns of addressee- and setting-based distribution of languages give rise to a variety of rules on language separation as well as possible options for mixed bilingual contexts. From all this we obtain a picture of languages that play distinct roles in the social interaction of a multilingual individual.

Naturally, the interplay of factors may differ from one individual to another. In Ben's case, we noted that the choice of addressee is normally the most important factor in determining language selection. Context-based language choice follows the addressee constellation, as does, in effect, setting-based language choice. The medium of active communication (e.g. writing or reading) is skills-dependent, but essentially language selection follows the cues provided by the setting, the context (e.g. watching English-language television in the parental household), and the addressee (e.g. writing a letter in German to a relative in Germany while on holiday in Australia). Changes of topic do not seem to influence the choice of language in any substantial way.

Among some bilinguals, however, addressee-based language selection might be less consistent than topic- or context-based language selection. A group of Kurdish émigrés from Turkey living in western Europe might, for example, switch to Turkish, the language in which they received their education, when discussing professional matters or current affairs. Topic-based language choice will in such a case override the factors addressee, context, and setting. An Akan-speaking student from the Ivory Coast living in the United States is likely to use French in a letter to his family, since French is the only written language used at home. The choice of medium and the presence of a language-specific skill thus overrides the choice of addressee in determining language selection. And an elderly Jewish couple born in Poland, who emigrated to Canada in the 1930s, might speak Yiddish at home, but use English in public, even if there are no other participants in their immediate conversation; here, setting overrides addressee in determining language choice.

3.2   Language–domain mapping at the macro-level

While Ben's multilingual profile comes about through circumstances that are particular to his biography and that of his emigrant parents, multilingualism is more often a community-wide phenomenon where entire sectors of a population share similar patterns of language use. In investigating the social roles of languages in multilingual contexts we are therefore concerned with the following questions: How are components of the linguistic repertoire mapped onto sets of social activities? What changes may affect this mapping pattern over time? And which actions do language users take, individually and via social institutions, in order to influence and intervene with these mapping patterns?

3.2.1   Role attributes of languages in multilingual societies

While addressee-based language choice is often central in micro-level (individual) management of the multilingual repertoire, when examining macro-level distribution of languages we are concerned with the interplay of setting, topic, goal, and mode (or medium) of interaction (e.g. face-to-face discourse, structured discourse, writing, broadcasting, etc.). This is often referred to as 'domains' of communication (Fishman 1965). It is assumed that in stable multilingual contexts, a domain will be associated with a preferred language of interaction, and that participants will accommodate to the expectations associated with each domain. The typical multilingual society is therefore according to Fishman (1967) one in which bilingualism combines with diglossia, where the languages have specialised and often complementary roles.

Discussions of multilingual societies tend to make use of a variety of attributes to describe the roles of languages used in a community. Many of these attributes are not mutually exclusive but define different aspects that are related to the diglossic setup. In the context of multilingual societies, the term 'dominant' serves as a kind of wholesale attribute for languages that constitute the default choice in a majority of interaction domains, especially in interaction in public and institutional domains. 'Dominant' represents the fact that some degree of proficiency in the relevant language is essential in order to participate in certain types of social activities, mostly those associated with public and institutional interaction: media, education, formal procedures such as correspondence with government agencies, and possibly any form of writing or even business transactions. The 'dominant' language at the societal level is sometimes referred to as a 'prestige' language. This term is somewhat misleading, as it is confined to so-called 'overt prestige' and disregards the value of other languages in speakers' private and community lives. 'Prestige' in this sense is more or less synonymous with institutional backing and dominance in the public domain, and in some cases with the default choice of language among individuals of different linguistic backgrounds.

The dominant or prestige language is often the domestic language of the numerical majority within the state (or a variety of that language) – the 'majority language'. 'Minority languages' by contrast are the property of a population that constitutes a numerical minority within a state. They tend to play a secondary role in the public domain. Indeed, they are often absent from the public domain altogether. When we speak of 'minority' languages, the reference framework is usually the nation-state and the choice of language largely within state institutions and state-controlled initiatives. The presence of linguistic minorities is often the result of historical circumstances that have led either to the inclusion of linguistically diverse populations within the boundaries of a single nation-state, or to population migrations into an existing nation-state.

'Dominant' need not always overlap with the 'majority language'. In post-colonial contexts, especially in Africa, the language of state institutions and the public domain is often not the everyday domestic language of the majority of the population. In such cases, there is an 'official' language, which enjoys institutional backing, while other languages are absent from most institutional domains. The official language is codified and its acquisition is supported and promoted by the state's education system and can therefore be described as a 'standard' language. Other languages may or may not be codified. In the absence of a standard, a language is described as a 'vernacular' whose primary function is to serve for oral communication in face-to-face, spontaneous (not pre-structured) interaction in 'informal' settings (settings in which the participants are familiar with one another, or where their roles are not regulated by an institution).

In the past decades there has been a growing tendency in many areas of the world to grant official recognition to languages that are not the languages of a numerical majority within a state and which have not enjoyed a position of dominance or prestige in state-backed institutions. 'Official recognition' in such cases usually entails both status and corpus planning (cf. Kaplan and Baldauf 1997), that is, the regulation of language use to include even a limited role in institutions, as well as codification and the emergence of some form of standard. The result is a standardised minority language with official status. Normally, a hierarchical configuration emerges in which certain roles remain the exclusive property of the 'national' language (typically the language of the majority or the former colonial language, or a selected indigenous language, e.g. Swahili in Tanzania or Hausa in Nigeria), while the official status assigned to the minority language is limited to a certain region, thus creating a 'regional' language (e.g. Welsh within the territory of Wales). Some states may have two or more national languages (e.g. French and Flemish in Belgium), or a national and several regional languages (Spanish, alongside Catalan, Galician, and Basque in the respective regions of Spain; English, alongside Hindi, Bengali, Gujarati, Tamil, and other official regional languages in India). States may also recognise and even promote the use of minority languages in specific domains, such as primary education, local and regional media, signposting, or printed information on local government services.

In this kind of linguistic pluralism, even vernaculars may play a role in the institutional use of language in the public domain. Luxemburgish, the native vernacular of the majority population of Luxemburg, is increasingly used in the press for advertising, in electronic media in informal programmes, and as a vehicle of oral communication in primary education, while French continues to serve as a national language. Moreover, status promotion of languages must no longer wait for state support and state intervention. Users of vernacular languages – Romani, colloquial Arabic, and Cypriot Greek are just some examples – are now able and willing to experiment with largely idiosyncratic, makeshift systems of writing especially in text-messaging and other computer-mediated communication.

Increased social and geographical mobility, widespread literacy, access to electronic media and communication, and devolution of various functions of government (both to regions and to multilateral organisations), all processes associated in some way or other with globalisation, have had an impact on the traditional dichotomies of majority/minority, standard/vernacular, national/regional languages, gradually turning them into a complex and multi-layered continuum (cf. Williams 2005: 22ff., Maurais 2003). Issues of 'dominance' and 'prestige' associated with individual languages are becoming less static and more of a dynamic process. Nonetheless, multilingual situations continue to show linguistic asymmetry in two respects. The first concerns the roles of the languages and their mapping onto sets of social activities. This division of labour among a multilingual individual's languages is what Fishman (1967) has referred to as 'bilingualism with diglossia'. It has since been regarded as a specialisation of languages for different activity 'domains'.

The other asymmetry is in the directionality of bilingualism. Some languages are spoken only by certain sectors or groups within a community as 'native' languages, while others are used more widely, frequently serving as 'target' languages for native speakers of other languages. This results in a hierarchy of distribution and use of languages in the community (where 'community' is defined in political, geographical, or socio-economic terms, e.g. a town, region, or state): Welsh, for instance, is a regional language, and nearly all speakers of Welsh also know English, which is the national language. Even within Wales, the majority of people whose first and primary everyday language is English do not, by contrast, learn Welsh. In Canada, both English and French are national languages, but bilingualism is to a large extent unidirectional: Speakers of French usually learn English, while only some English speakers learn French (at a level beyond a school subject).

Asymmetry in the social roles of languages and in the directionality of bilingualism is a crucial factor in determining the impact that contact is likely to have on the structures of the relevant languages. Languages that are used across a wide range of social activity domains by a population that is mainly monolingual, and which are highly regulated through standardisation and writing and through use within an institutional framework, will tend to absorb fewer influences from another language than those that are used as vernaculars in a limited set of interaction contexts by people who are all or mostly bilingual.

3.2.2　Types of domain specialisation

While an exhaustive survey of multilingual societies is far beyond the scope of this chapter, we can nevertheless outline a few examples of types of multilingualism along with typical patterns of domain-specialisation. A type that is rapidly vanishing from today's world is multilingualism among neighbouring

tribal communities in pre-urban, pre-industrialised societies. In the absence of
written historical records, it is not always obvious that we understand the precise
nature of the linguistic relations among such communities. Some authors believe
to have found evidence for prolonged reciprocal bilingualism among neighbouring communities. This appears to have been the case among some of the languages
of Arnhem Land in northern Australia (see Heath 1979), as well as among pairs or
groups of languages in the Amazon basin (Aikhenvald 2002). Other case studies
emphasise role divisions between an 'internal' and an 'external' language, with
the latter being the default language of communication among different tribal
groups (as well as being the language of a particular group) (see e.g. Ross 1996
on Melanesia).

Border-area multilingualism is common in industrialised societies, too. Where
foreign language learning is dependent on the institutional support of school
and media, border-area multilingualism is often unidirectional, favouring the
language of economic power. Along the borders of Germany with Denmark,
the Netherlands, Belgium, Poland, and the Czech Republic, it is German that
is being acquired by the neighbours, with little or no reciprocity. However, in
rural border areas and in ethnically mixed regions where languages are acquired
through face-to-face interaction, there is more frequently an equal incentive for
people from all communities to acquire each other's languages.

North Friesland, on the German side of the Danish–German border along the
North Sea coast, is a good example of a cross between border-type multilingualism and the presence of a minority language and a regional vernacular. The
older generation of farmers in the district is typically fluent in four or even five
languages. Frisian is the language of the home and the extended family. It is
also used with selected individuals in neighbouring villages. Due to considerable
differences among the dialects of Frisian in the region, the language is only used
within a relatively short distance of the home community, and nowadays almost
exclusively with people with whom the speaker is personally acquainted. The
language of everyday interaction with members of other rural communities in the
region as well as in the towns is the regional variety of Low German. Like Frisian,
Low German is primarily a vernacular, with only a very recent written tradition
that is largely limited to language activists. The regional dialect of Danish –
Jutland Danish, or 'Low Danish' as it is referred to locally – is the language most
commonly used at rural markets on the Danish side of the border. Both German
and Danish were used as a medium of instruction in local schools as a result of a
treaty between Germany and Denmark and the presence of a Danish minority in
the German state of Schleswig-Holstein, to which the district belongs. The choice
of Danish-medium schools was and is, however, voluntary. German remains the
principal language of writing, the only language of correspondence with authorities and the language of most media and formal transactions, including printed
information accompanying services and consumer goods, advertising, and more.

Colonial and former colonial settings constitute a further widespread
type of multilingual society (cf. Stroud 2007). Generally, they continue the

pre-industrialisation legacy, showing numerous village dialects or tribal languages. Each individual is usually a native speaker of a village-based, tribal
language, which is the main vehicle of oral communication in the domestic setting and of casual communication with neighbours and peers. Many individuals
may also acquire knowledge of a neighbouring tribal language as a result of
intermarriage between communities and family bonds, or through social or trade
contacts. A regional lingua franca (see Chapter 10) is often used for oral communication between speakers of different ethnic (tribal) languages. This may be
one of the indigenous languages that has acquired prestige as the language of a
politically powerful or economically dominant group, or even an indigenous language that has acquired official status in the post-colonial era, such as Swahili in
central and eastern Africa; or it may be a pidgin or a creole, a simplified language,
which in turn may be based either on an indigenous language, as in the case of
the Tupi-based *lingua geral* (or 'common language') of the Amazon region, or
on a colonial language, as in the case of English-based Tok Pisin in Papua New
Guinea. The language imposed during the colonial rule continues to serve as
the language of education, government, and media. It is usually the language of
institutions, the dominant language when discussing public affairs, the language
of business and national and international trade, and often the only language used
in writing. The colonial language may be a foreign language that is acquired
by all members of society, in the first instance via the education system, as in
the case of English in Nigeria or in India. Alternatively, it may be regarded as a
variety that is closely related to the dominant vernacular lingua franca, as in the
case of French in Haiti (where a French-based creole is spoken), or it may also be
the everyday native language of a sizeable part of the population, or indeed even
of the majority, as in the case of Portuguese in Brazil or of Spanish in most other
Latin American states. Countries like India and Algeria show features of both
the colonial and nation-state types: Each has indigenous languages that serve as
standard written languages in education and government (various state languages
in India, such as Gujarati, Hindi, and Tamil; Arabic in Algeria). Each also has
vernacular languages as well as linguistic minorities (e.g. Munda languages in
India, Berber or Kabyl in Algeria); and each has a former colonial language that
serves as a language of government, education, media, and commerce (English
in India, French in Algeria).

A type of multilingualism that is typical of the industrialised world is that
brought about through migration into urban centres (cf. Garcia and Fishman
2002, Extra and Yağmur 2004, Clyne and Kipp 2006a and 2006b). Immigrants
bring with them the language of their region of origin, for example Kurdish
among immigrants from northern Iraq, and, where it is different from their own
regional language, also the national language of their country of origin, in this
case Arabic. They acquire the national language of the country of immigration,
e.g Dutch in the Netherlands. The degree of support awarded to the background
languages via the media, the school system and community organisations, as well
as the extent of contact and cultural exchange with the country or region of origin

or with other diaspora communities of the same background, will determine the degree of successful maintenance of the immigrant languages beyond the first generation of migrants.

3.2.3   Domain stability and language maintenance

The domain-based analysis of language roles in multilingual contexts has been applied by Fishman (1964) and by others to investigate the maintenance of immigrant languages in urban centres. Fishman predicted that the economic and social integration of the second and third generation of immigrant families will necessarily lead to the growing importance of the majority language in most activity domains, until finally the background language will become limited to the domestic domain. The third generation, whose peer language was the majority language, would then in most cases shift to that language and abandon the immigrant language once they set up their own households. Bilingualism in the context of immigration into urban centres is therefore unstable.

But in the age of globalisation, frequent travel and cultural exchange with the country of origin, and the accessibility of media in the form of satellite broadcasts, films, and computer-mediated communication (chat rooms, websites and email), the survival prospects of linguistic-cultural diasporas – communities whose culture is not necessarily determined entirely by their geographical location but rather by their maintenance of traditions through a network of contacts – are arguably higher. While studies of urban immigrant minorities tend to agree that support is required if languages are to be maintained (cf. Clyne and Kipp 2006b), recent investigations in Manchester of the Cantonese-speaking community (Lo 2007) and of Arabic-speaking immigrants (Osman 2006) reveal that part-time primary and secondary school education in the heritage (immigrant) language, exposure to media including satellite television, tight-knit community structures, and the continuing absorption into the community of newly arrived immigrants all provide both incentives and opportunities for the British-born generation to maintain the language of their parents for use well beyond the domestic domain. Once language skills are recognised as valuable assets on the job market, the motivation to cultivate the background language is strengthened even further.

Nonetheless, alongside the emergence of diasporic language communities of this kind, numerous community languages are experiencing a shift toward national languages. This trend has been described for minority languages like Hungarian in the Austrian town of Oberwart (Gal 1979) and for regional languages such as Gaelic in Scotland (Dorian 1981) as a gradual retreat of the language from certain domains, coupled with the growing importance of new activities in which the national language is used exclusively, such as media or communication in the public domain. Reershemius (2002) reports on individuals' language preferences in a village in northern Germany where the regional vernacular is Low German (a dialect that is not mutually intelligible with Standard

In the home:

Age	LG	LG and SG	SG
15–30	2(15.4%)	6(46.2%)	5(38.4%)
30–40	4(14.8%)	16(59.3%)	7(25.9%)
40–50	1(5.6%)	15(83.3%)	2(11.1%)
50–60	12(48%)	6(24%)	7(28%)
over 60	22(57.9%)	11(28.9%)	5(13.2%)

At work:

Age	LG	LG and SG	SG
15–30	–	3(27.3%)	8(72.7%)
30–40	5(17.9%)	15(53.6%)	8(28.5%)
40–50	–	13(76.5%)	4(23.5%)
50–60	8(32%)	12(48%)	5(20%)
over 60	19(65.5%)	8(27.6%)	2(6.9%)

Figure 3.1 *Speakers' self-assessment of language use in a northern German village: Standard German (SG) and Low German (LG) (from Reershemius 2002).*

German). The differences among age groups illustrate the decline of Low German in the relevant domains of interaction (Figure 3.1). Although most parents in the village stopped speaking Low German to their children in the mid-1960s, the decline of Low German in the home is gradual, primarily due to the frequent co-habitation of three generations in the same household. More pronounced is the shift of languages in the workplace, due to the decline of agriculture and the growing importance of industrial work outside the village.

The differences among generations provide a picture of ongoing language abandonment or shift in apparent time: We can clearly predict the continuing retreat of Low German in the community in the next generation. The domain analysis – exemplified in Figure 3.1 by merely two domains, but just as applicable to a much more nuanced domain evaluation – provides a differentiated picture of language preferences of individuals and sectors within a multilingual community. It shows almost invariably that languages retreat as a result of two types of change: the extension of individuals' activity repertoire to include new interaction settings and contexts that are negotiated exclusively in another language, and the infiltration of that language into established activities that had previously been reserved for the 'older' language. Changes in the stability of bilingualism and language mapping are thus brought about by changes in speakers' activity constellations.

In the case of Low German, the expansion of employment opportunities outside the village-based agricultural economy created a change in the proportion of use of Standard and Low German at the work place. This in turn created an incentive to increase the role of Standard German in the domestic setting in order to provide stronger support for schoolchildren, who have now become more dependent on external employment opportunities and hence on good performance at school (where the language of instruction is exclusively Standard German). The extension of the range of potential activities and settings in which community members participate – new job prospects in the Standard German speaking, urban economy – triggers an infiltration of Standard German into the domestic domain of interaction.

The trend all around the globe is toward the growing dominance of those languages that enjoy firm anchoring in the public domain – as the languages of interaction settings such as educational institutions and government, of interaction contexts such as national and international commerce, and of interaction skills and media such as literacy and broadcasting. Command of these languages is the key to participation in modern institutions and the activities that they host and support. This comes at the expense of the majority of the world's languages, many of which are now endangered.

The tiny Domari-speaking community of Jerusalem, Israel/Palestine was engaged for generations in providing itinerant services, mostly as metalworkers and musicians, to the surrounding settled Arab-Palestinian population. The establishment of municipal services during the British rule in the 1920s opened up the opportunity for paid employment in municipal services such as waste removal, and by the 1940s the tent-dwelling smiths had abandoned their traditional trade and makeshift accommodation and had moved to rented, permanent housing. The next generation, born from the early 1950s onwards, was no longer familiar at all with the old lifestyle, and instead was the first to enjoy general school attendance – in Arabic. At this stage, parents began to speak Arabic to their children. By the 1990s, among the ca. 600 community members only around ten per cent – most of them born before 1940 – were fluent speakers of Domari, an archaic New Indo-Aryan language, which in this community can now be considered moribund (see Matras 1999a).

The fact that numerous languages around the world are in a state of obsolescence is due almost invariably to a cumulated retreat from the various domains in which they were once used. Typically, endangered languages are the property of very small societies with a limited range of social activities, few interaction settings, and a small and rather uniform set of participants (cf. Crystal 2000, Nettle and Romaine 2000, Tsunoda 2005). Once the community's set of interaction settings expands, the incentive to be able to participate in new activities may outweigh the emotional loyalty toward the original group language, leading to the abandonment of this language. Since individual management of the multilingual repertoire is based on mapping repertoire components to sets of activities, the stability of multilingualism depends on the stability of activity patterns. In some situations, participation in new activities will simply require the acquisition of a new language. In most parts of sub-Saharan Africa, the acquisition of literacy depends on the acquisition of the former colonial language, usually English or French. But the colonial language does not typically replace ethnic community languages in other domains, which remain stable.

3.3   Language management in multilingual settings

Above I referred to the individual bilingual speaker's skill to map languages onto addressee constellations and activity domains in a somewhat metaphorical sense as 'language management'. Genuine 'management' of languages is a collective procedure in which individuals and agents of institutions engage in order to regulate the use of language in various activity domains. In particular, language management is concerned with regulating possible competition between languages over activity domains, safeguarding the role that a language may have in society as well as ensuring the accessibility of social activities to a wide range of participants by promoting access to the languages that dominate those activity domains.

Language management usually becomes a political issue in response to a potential conflict. Language conflict can be defined as an overtly articulated dispute over the domain distribution of languages. Although a variety of strategies exist to regulate the role of languages and to try and resolve language conflict, we must bear in mind that in numerous cases disputes over the status of languages are merely an offshoot of other sources of tension. In such cases language is merely an arena on which political disputes over inter-ethnic relations are played out. The Soweto uprising in the second half of 1976 had been sparked by a government decision to enforce Afrikaans as the medium of school instruction. The policy did more than just create a need to learn another language. It represented the entire edifice of the white minority's Apartheid rule over a black majority in the country. The enacting of Bill 101 or the 'Charter of the French Language' by the Québec provincial government in August 1977 proclaimed French to be the sole language of government in Quebec as well as the 'normal and everyday language of work, instruction, communication, commerce and business'. More than just a means to regulate language use, it was a manifestation of the separatist agenda of the then ruling Parti Québécois and of the party's dissatisfaction with the traditional dominance of the Anglophone establishment in the province (cf. Coleman 1981).

Legislation is one of the means through which state institutions can attempt to regulate language use (cf. Turi 1995). As a language management tool, legislation can define and even prescribe a framework for mapping the languages in a community's macro-repertoire to activity domains. Turkey is an example of a state that is still engaged in a political discussion about the extent to which bans on languages other than the national language, Turkish, should be removed. For many years, Turkish was the only language permitted for use in the public domain, including state institutions, media, the education system and public rallies, and even distribution of printed material. Several minority languages, such as Greek and Armenian, were permitted for use in the context of minority religious institutions, while others, most notably Kurdish, were banned from use in any public or institutional domain. The early 1990s saw a gradual lifting of the ban and withdrawal of the state's threat to prosecute and penalise individuals for using Kurdish in this way. At the time of writing, instruction and broadcasting in Kurdish are permitted but limited to private initiatives.

Legislation will normally aim at taking the more constructive step to actively promote a language in the public domain. Official recognition of languages as second national languages, as in the case of Swedish (alongside Finnish) in Finland, of French (alongside English) in Canada, or of Arabic (alongside Hebrew) in Israel, or as regional languages, as in the case of Welsh in the United Kingdom (Wales), or of German in Italy (South Tirol), usually means at the very least that the state allows citizens to use this language for 'interaction' with the state itself – for example in court or in correspondence with government agencies – as well as to provide education and broadcasting opportunities in it. Sometimes, legislation will impose norms of bilingual labelling of services and products, or regulate the language qualifications that are expected from civil servants.

However, the legal status given to a language is usually just a part of the package which, if it is to be successful in regulating domain use, must usually also include the provision of resources (e.g. translation services, teacher training, media), incentives to use the language, and often a strategy to protect and promote it. One of the most comprehensive frameworks for the promotion of 'smaller' – minority and regional – languages is the European Charter for Minority or Regional Languages, drafted and monitored by the Council of Europe since 1992. At the time of writing, only around half the member states of the Council of Europe had signed the Charter, which is not legally binding, and which allows states to freely select the languages that they set out to protect. The Charter provides a catalogue of measures that governments are encouraged to take with respect of the minority languages that are granted protection. These range from raising awareness about the language, using it as a medium of instruction in pre-school education and as a subject in primary and secondary school, facilitating broadcasting and research on the language, and allowing use of the language in official documents.

In implementing language policy, states are often guided by one (or sometimes several) of the following principles. The **differentiation principle** is followed where state institutions are interested in promoting languages in order to enable individuals to participate in particular activity domains. Usually, the target

language is valued because of its association with a particular skill or context specialisation. As mentioned above, in sub-Saharan African countries the respective
colonial languages constitute an essential tool in order to participate in public
institutions. In the United Kingdom, by contrast, the study of foreign languages is
promoted primarily as an academic skill, with possible added long-term practical
benefits in terms of career opportunities in a limited set of domains, in some
public and economic sectors. In most Middle Eastern countries, English is, on
the other hand, a key skill and an essential pre-requisite for the entry into certain
sectors such as international trade, academia, management of large organisations,
and more.

Societies with an **equality principle** usually attribute to multilingualism a
key function in identity-formation and so in good citizenship. The expectation
imposed by state institutions and norms is that the relevant languages should have
balanced and legally equivalent roles in the running of institutional activities in
all sectors. Sometimes there is an expectation that every citizen, or at least those
in government service, should have full command of all relevant languages. The
language policy followed at the federal level in Canada in the 1970s, partly
in response to the French-only policy of Québec, was to require civil servants
to pass language tests in both French and English. In Belgium, where Flemish
and French are both national languages, higher-ranking soldiers in the armed
forces are expected to accommodate to the choice of language of lower-ranking
soldiers, thus linking greater responsibility and authority to an expectation toward
stronger bilingual proficiency. In Ireland, the civil service is bilingual in English
and Irish, which in practice is a minority language but which enjoys the status of
a national language, and broadcasting media and schools are offered incentives
in return for the inclusion of a certain proportion of Irish-language programmes
(broadcasting and teaching hours, respectively). Before it split into two separate
states, Czechoslovakia practiced a policy of equal hour broadcasting in its two
national languages, Czech and Slovak, encouraging citizens to acquire at least
passive fluency in the other language.

Both the practical implementation of equality between two or more national
languages, and especially the safeguarding and promotion of regional languages,
often follow a **territoriality principle** according to which certain languages
may be promoted within particular territorial boundaries. In Switzerland, most
Cantons or units of administration have only one of the three principal national
languages – German, French, and Italian – as a primary language of administration and public life. Belgium is divided into a French- and a Flemish-speaking
area, while Brussels is the only officially bilingual district. Regional languages
have, by definition, an official status primarily within their region. This is the
case with Welsh, Catalan, West Frisian (in the Netherlands), and numerous border minorities such as the Danes of Schleswig Holstein (Germany), the Germans
of South Tirol (Italy) or the Slovenes of Carinthia (Austria) in Europe, and with
individual official languages of various federal states in India. The territoriality
principle allows states to implement status-regulating measures within an area

in which the relevant language has a relatively high proportion of speakers, and thus to run the relevant measure both more effectively and with the backing of a larger population (see Nelde 1993). The **sector principle** operates in a similar way, but usually on the basis of local community demarcations rather than district boundaries. Palestinian Arab towns in Israel, for example, have Arabic as their principal language of public life, schools and other institutions, signposts and advertising, and follow the state-sponsored Arabic-language network of broadcasts in addition to broadcasts from neighbouring Arab states and the Palestinian Authority of the West Bank.

A different kind of principle operates in states in which access to language facilities are an **individual's right** and must be claimed by individuals in order to be realised (cf. Skutnabb-Kangas and Phillipson 1995). Provisions for immigrant languages typically fall under this category. The Australian LOTE ('Languages Other Than English') policy provides accredited school programmes that offer immigrant languages as subjects, while the public broadcasting network SBS accommodates programmes in several dozen languages, including productions by private community initiatives, and municipalities like Melbourne offer a free 24-hour telephone-based interpreting service. Sweden maintains a right to native language instruction at primary school level, which can be claimed by parents even on behalf of an individual child, which is then entitled to weekly tuition sessions by a specially appointed language tutor. In Manchester, England, the city council offers both leaflets and telephone advice on council services in a variety of languages, and public libraries are instructed to try and accommodate demand for book acquisitions in languages other than English. There is, however, no central planning of resources, nor a centralised procedure of identifying the languages in which services are to be offered, and the production or acquisition of materials in immigrant languages depends on the initiative of low-ranking officials, inspired by direct requests made to them by members of the public (cf. Donakey 2007).

Implementation of government support for multilingualism may thus also follow a bottom-up rather than a top-down approach: institutions and agencies react to demands for language support, but do not regulate the use of languages. Bottom-up approaches may aspire to extend the use of smaller languages beyond their traditional domains. This may be done in order to counteract the ongoing retreat of the language from its traditional domain, as a result of speakers favouring the dominant language of the public domain. But another goal is to use language as a token of empowerment. Since the early 1990s, Romani non-governmental organisations have been producing printed and electronic media in Romani and promoting the use of Romani in writing. These efforts have accompanied, and in some cases even created, entirely new activity domains such as NGO-sponsored media, websites, workshops, and conferences devoted to Romani political and cultural activism (see Halwachs 2005).

It is not uncommon for language maintenance and revitalisation efforts to forge such new activity domains, which then become the exclusive property of the minority language and a space in which it does not have to compete with the language that normally dominates public life. In parts of Australia, such as Victoria and New South Wales, Aboriginal languages that have been abandoned two or even three generations ago are being reconstructed with the help of linguists, often on the basis of fragmented documentation, and used to compose welcome speeches given by indigenous land custodians. Much of the activity promoting the use of Low German centres around local and regional theatre groups, while Gaelic in Scotland is promoted especially on signposts, restaurant menus, and in and around tourist attractions. In many such cases, language use takes on an **emblematic** function: it emphasises a group's ownership of its culture and language – quite often a compensatory reaction to the loss of key aspects of a community's heritage.

While the goal of language revitalisation is often thought of as a restoration of the language in activity domains in which it had once served for communicative interaction, the genuine success of revitalisation may in fact depend on the successful forging of new domains. Perhaps the most radical example is the creation of a new society of ideologically driven Jewish immigrants in Palestine from the 1880s onwards, whose need for both a symbol of national unity and a practical lingua franca enabled the revitalisation or rather the vernacularisation of Modern Hebrew (cf. Nahir 1998). Within the English Romani community, whose Romani speech was largely abandoned toward the end of the nineteenth century, a new Christian missionary movement with an orientation toward the international Romani community, and the integration of Romani-speaking immigrants from central and eastern Europe in connection with the EU enlargement between 2005 and 2008, have prompted widescale interest in acquiring European dialects of Romani. On the other hand, results of a recent survey in a small town in Ireland (Sweeney 2007) indicate that respondents value the presence of Irish in the media and state institutions even if they are unable to speak or understand much Irish themselves; the language serves a token function as a cherished identity badge.

3.4   Repertoire, activity domains, and language change

Two types of explanation have been offered in an attempt to link the roles that languages have in a community with the effect of multilingualism on structural change. The first distinguishes between structural influences that are gradually absorbed through prolonged contact in situations of language maintenance, and those that come about as a result of language shift and the carry-over of features from a substrate language into a target language – also called 'shift-induced interference' (cf. Thomason and Kaufman 1988, Thomason 2001, Winford 2003). The second kind of model distinguishes between situations of assumed socio-cultural equilibrium, where the relations between the two population groups are stable and equal in terms of social power relations and the absence of dominance, and where bilingualism is reciprocal, contrasting with situations in which one group dominates in vital domains of social activity and as a result language use is characterised by diglossia (cf. Aikhenvald 2002: 265ff.). It has been suggested that the borrowing of word-forms is typical for situations of language maintenance that are characterised by dominance and diglossia, whereas both shift-induced interference and linguistic equilibrium are likely to result in overall structural similarities but not in the concrete transfer of word-forms or morphs form one language to another.

It is worth examining the functionality of these distinctions somewhat more closely. During the acquisition of a target language, the learner's focus is on selecting context-appropriate word-forms. The organisational patterns that form phrases, sentences, and discourse-level presentation as well as phonology and especially phonetics and prosody are to some extent secondary both in learners' perception of what constitutes and symbolises the target language, and in regard to learners' ability to exercise conscious control over the selection of structures and features. Moreover, correct production of word-forms is essential for communication, while the production of prosody, phonetics, and often clause-level features such as morphological agreement or tense selection that deviate from the target norm do not always cause serious disruptions to communication. Second-language learners will therefore tend to concentrate on producing target-language word-forms consistently. Collective second-language learning followed by stabilisation is therefore likely to give rise to a form of the target language that is not substantially different from the target in lexicon, but may be different in its organisational patterns or constructions. We find this in cases of language shift (e.g. the Irish substrate in Hiberno-English; cf. Hickey 2006) as well as in ethnolects of minority groups (e.g. Czech as spoken by the Romani minority; cf. Bořkovcová 2006).

A contrasting scenario is a situation in which bilingualism is stable but largely unidirectional, i.e. group B acquires and uses the language of group A but not vice versa. Unidirectional bilingualism usually arises in circumstances where group A dominates certain activity domains to which group B members require access, but this relationship is not reciprocal. As a result, group B speakers will import into their own language word-forms acquired through interaction with group A in the relevant domains. However, it is not diglossia per se that is responsible for the type of structural changes that occur. This kind of scenario is typical of numerous linguistic minorities or speakers of smaller languages around the world – whether in border areas, in remote regions, in colonial and post-colonial settings, or in an immigrant context.

The word-forms that are imported by the minority language from the dominant language are not typically limited to domain-specific vocabulary that is associated with the domains in which language A is dominant, though this vocabulary is high on the list of likely borrowings (see Chapters 6–7). Borrowings may also occur in the domain of grammatical word-forms and even morphology. Items such as conjunctions and discourse markers, indefinite pronouns, agentive suffixes, superlative and comparative particles, numerals, and more are frequent borrowings in such situations (cf. Matras 2007b and see Chapter 8). Unlike institutional or technical terminology, we cannot account for such grammatical borrowings simply by attributing them to the pressure of diglossia and dominance of language A in the public or institutional domain. Rather, the pressure is attributable to the **unidirectionality of bilingualism** itself. Members of the weaker group are obliged to maintain tight control over their selection of word-forms whilst communicating in the dominant or majority language, since any carry-over of word-forms from their own native language would not be understood and might lead to a breakdown in communication. But when communicating with fellow speakers of the smaller language, most of whom are bilingual, control is lax; word-forms from the dominant language are understood, and their use during interaction in the minority language is generally tolerated.

Exceptions to this pattern may arise in situations in which the smaller or minority language is subjected to tight normative community attitudes, or to the intervention of institutions that seek to minimise the incorporation of recognisable foreign word-forms into community speech. Such values have been reported for a number of small communities, such as the Tariana of the Amazon (Aikhenvald 2002) and the Waskia of Papua (Ross 1996), and are commonplace in some national languages, such as French, Turkish, and Hebrew, where language academies are entrusted with minimising foreign influence.

Convergence of patterns or constructions, i.e. of structures that do not constitute overt word-forms, appears to be generally exempted from normative attitudes of this kind, as well as being subject to less awareness and overt control on the part of the speaker in spontaneous utterances. It is therefore found throughout the range of contact situations: in collective second-language acquisition and language shift (where patterns are imported from the substrate or native language), in contact situations involving diglossia and dominance (where patterns are imported from a dominant contact language), and in situations of bilingualism where there is resistance against the importation of overt word-forms. Clusters of languages that show primarily pattern-convergence of this kind – often referred to as 'linguistic areas' (see Chapter 9) – appear to be a product of such situations: communities are in prolonged and intense contact, and there is resistance toward the import of overt word-forms but tolerance toward drifts in the organisation patterns of phrases and utterances.

It is important to note that these principles and constraints do not apply to the actual speech production of bilingual speakers, but rather to the chances of propagation of any innovations that are a result of speakers' bilingualism. We saw in Chapter 2 that even a bilingual speaker at the beginning of the language socialisation process will make use of a wide range of strategies to manage and control the choices within the linguistic repertoire. These strategies are available to adult speakers too. They include word insertion or borrowing, codeswitching or meaningful language alternation, replication of linguistic matter (word-forms, morphemes), replication of sounds and sound patterns, replication of patterns (meaning, form–function mapping, constructions), and conscious language manipulation or play. The societal conditions of multilingualism and language attitudes will act as external constraints that will either allow innovative and creative use of language to spread within the community and become acceptable, leading to language change, or else they will block their propagation and so limit them to occasional occurrences in the discourse of individuals.

Alongside the two alternative scenarios discussed – second-language acquisition and unidirectional bilingualism – there exist numerous variants. For a start, some situations of language shift are characterised by the retention of considerable substrate vocabulary, as in the case of the Irish lexical substrate in Hiberno-English (Sweeney 2007) and the Frisian substrate in the eastern dialects of Low German (Scheuermann 2001). Many linguistic areas share word-forms as well as syntactic and semantic organisation patterns, as in eastern Anatolia and frequently also in East Asia. By contrast, the case of Takia and Waskia in Melanesia (Ross 1996) shows that word-forms may be filtered out even from the influence of a dominant language. On the other hand English, German, Hungarian, and Romanian all borrow loanwords from the stigmatised minority language Romani, which enjoys prestige among anti-establishment users of local slang (cf. Matras 2002: 249–250).

Where speakers must have quick resort to a common means of communication based on just superficial acquisition of a target language, a makeshift language or pidgin may emerge, which is characterised by replication of lexical material from the target language but simplification of grammar; other situations of bilingualism may give rise to deliberate language mixing and the stabilisation of mixed languages, especially in situations where ongoing language shift motivates speakers to hold on to mere components of a moribund community language, replicating mainly lexicon and selective grammatical word-forms (see Chapter 9). A characteristic feature that might be attributable to endangered languages is the proliferation of free variation as a result of the decline in normative awareness (cf. Dorian 1981, Tsunoda 2005: 76–116), while a further by-product of language shift, apart from substrate influence, can be, similarly, an increase in language-internal variation and processes of analogy and levelling brought about due to the absence of an established parental norm, as is the case in Modern Hebrew (see Matras and Schiff 2005).

4 Acquiring and maintaining a bilingual repertoire

4.1 Bilingual first-language acquisition

In Chapter 2 we followed the emergence of a bilingual repertoire. We witnessed a process of complex linguistic socialisation whereby the child speaker learns to comply with adult interlocutor expectations regarding the selection of structures in particular contexts. This process also gives rise to the more systematic and conventionalised mapping of sets of structures – the bilingual's 'languages' – onto sets of social activities, a mapping which in turn is anchored in the kind of multilingual reality as discussed in Chapter 3. The present section reviews key issues in the study of the acquisition of bilingual repertoires.

4.1.1 Definitions and methodological problems

The term 'bilingual' is often associated with the ability to use each language at a level of proficiency that equals that of monolingual speakers. This ability is sometimes captured more specifically in the notion of a 'balanced bilingual'. There is however consensus that bilinguals are not simply the sum of two monolinguals in one (cf. Grosjean 1989, De Houwer 1990: 339, Bauer, Hall, and Kruth 2002). Firstly, bilingual speakers may have certain preferences or patterns of dominance of one language over another in particular contexts. Second, bilinguals have, in addition to the ability to sustain monolingual conversations, also an important additional resource at their disposal, namely the ability to contrast languages in conversation. Interpreting the position and the functional value of language 'mixing' is crucial, as we shall see, in understanding the bilingual acquisition process.

The term Bilingual First-Language Acquisition is associated with the acquisition of two or more languages from birth. It captures situations in which the acquisition of language itself involves two (or more) languages. Researchers commonly distinguish between 'simultaneous' acquisition, where exposure to two languages begins immediately at birth, and 'successive' acquisition, where exposure to one of the languages begins later, though well within the period during which the child's basic linguistic skills are still developing. There is however little research comparing the two types systematically. Instead, the acquisition of full language capacity, typically by the age of three, is regarded as a clear borderline: up to this age, a child can acquire two languages as 'first' languages, a phenomenon referred to as 'early bilingualism'. Beyond this period, we are dealing with *second*-language acquisition or 'late bilingualism'.

Despite the existence of a wealth of individual case studies examining bilingual first-language acquisition, straightforward generalisations are often hampered by methodological difficulties and problems of comparability of datasets and findings.[1] Observing the acquisition process systematically requires a longitudinal study. This in turn presupposes long-term and continuous parental cooperation, which usually requires some degree of understanding on the part of the parents of the goals and benefits of a study which may infringe considerably on their family's privacy over a prolonged period. It also requires regular access on the part of the researcher to the subjects of the investigation, in an environment that is natural and yet controlled (since the presence of adult interlocutors is instrumental in defining the linguistic context for the child). All this results not surprisingly in the fact that the vast majority of child subjects considered so far in investigations reside in the proximity of major Western towns in which researchers are based. Most are children of academics, quite often the researcher's own children.

Moreover, the social environment in which most studies have been carried out is overwhelmingly a monolingual one, with the child's exposure to another language usually resulting from the fact that at least one of the parents is an immigrant. We must therefore acknowledge that most of our insights into the process of bilingual first-language acquisition derive from a very particular type of sector, one that is quite possibly not representative of the great majority of children around the world who grow up with more than one language in multiethnic communities.

Additional methodological issues affecting data comparability are the use of various methods of recording data – ranging from diary notes summarising the day's 'highlights', through audio recordings of closed experimental sessions, to video documentation of an entire interaction context. In addition, quantitative methods are often based on diverse and sometimes arbitrary criteria by which a form or structure are considered as 'acquired' (rather than just mimicked, for instance). We must also realise that the bilingual acquisition process, especially in the kind of situations that serve as settings for most investigations (urban, family-based input in a largely monolingual environment), is highly sensitive to changes in the balance of the interlocutor constellation as well as other aspects of the linguistic environment (cf. Grosjean 1998). Even two case studies carried out in two households with very similar background could differ substantially as a result of a relative – say a grandmother speaking the language which the child otherwise hears only from the father – spending a couple of months in the family home, or a video in one of the languages that is played over and over again. The emotional impact of persons, events, and other linguistic stimuli on the child can have a major effect on the development of language skills and language preferences. It is thus almost impossible to identify even two, let alone a whole series of case studies that are identical in all but one crucial variable, and it is therefore difficult to isolate the factors that determine different kinds of outcome in the bilingual acquisition process. This said, we can draw on case studies in order to highlight various relevant aspects of the bilingual acquisition process and the dilemmas that researchers face in interpreting data.

4.1.2   The separation of languages

As noted already, the research discussion of bilingual first-language acquisition is informed primarily by case studies based in Western, urban, monolingual environments, where exposure to a second language results from the foreign origin of at least one of the parents, sometimes of both (cf. e.g. Vihman 1985, Döpke 1992, Köppe 1996, Lanza 1997, Bolonyai 1998, Deuchar and Quay 2000, and more). This typically involves an activity constellation in which there is clear separation either between the language of the household and that of the community, or between the respective languages of the parents (one of which may or may not be the community language). Many studies have consequently focused on the factors that enable (or hinder) the child to acquire monolingual-level proficiency in each of the languages. From the onset of the study of bilingual first-language acquisition, then, investigations into the child's ability to *separate languages* have occupied a prominent position high on the research agenda in this field. The traditional view has been that consistency in the separation of languages by contexts facilitates the acquisition of native competence in each language. More recent literature, however, has begun to distance itself from this view (see e.g. Bhatia and Ritchie 1999: 589), regarding instead the acquisition process as one of *linguistic socialisation* that involves not just the acquisition of separate 'systems', but also of rules on where and how to mix and manipulate language use; or put in our terms, of the conventions and constraints on how to make use of the various structures and constructions that make up the bilingual's full linguistic repertoire.

The suggestion that bilingual children are unable to separate their two linguistic 'systems' at the early stage of acquisition goes back to one of the earliest case studies: Leopold (1949) observed that during the initial phase of acquisition, when the child's output consists of one-word utterances, the child lacks translation equivalents in the two languages and is therefore unable to respond in the appropriate language to the linguistic context as set by the adult interlocutor. Later on in the development, seemingly random mixing of languages within an utterance was regarded as further evidence of the child's inability to separate languages. This observation and the conclusions derived from it appear to have set the investigation agenda for many years to come around the question of when and how children acquire the ability to separate languages. The view that children lack the ability to distinguish their languages at an early stage of acquisition has become known as the Unitary Language System Hypothesis, the Fusion Hypothesis, or simply the One-System Hypothesis, while the opposing view is often referred to as the Differentiation Hypothesis, or the Two-System Hypothesis.

Before discussing the arguments for and against language separation, it is noteworthy that there is basic consensus that the language acquisition process in bilinguals resembles, in principle, that of monolinguals. Thus, speech output begins with one-word utterances, followed only later by the acquisition of morphosyntax. Pearson, Fernández, and Oller (1993) show that the total number of lexical types produced by bilinguals is roughly comparable to the total number produced by monolingual children, whereas in comprehension bilingual children tended to outscore monolingual children in both number of unique words and total of conceptual vocabulary. This suggests that the acquisition of conceptual vocabulary is not slowed down in bilinguals through the burden of learning two languages, even though the realisation of conceptual vocabulary is split among the two languages. De Houwer (1990) observes that the morpho-syntactic development of each of a bilingual's languages is fundamentally similar to the development patterns in monolingual speakers of the respective languages. She concludes that the morpho-syntactic development of each language proceeds independently, with no intersection (the 'Separate Development Hypothesis'). Meisel (2001: 40) even argues that the fact that bilinguals are ultimately able to achieve a level of competence in each language that is equivalent to that of monolinguals is evidence of a predisposition of individuals to becoming bilingual.

The One-System Hypothesis was first put forward by Volterra and Taeschner (1978), who suggested three stages in the bilingual acquisition process. At Stage I, the child shows a hybrid repertoire of words with no translation equivalents, indicating an inability to differentiate the two languages. Stage II then witnesses the gradual separation of the two lexicons, confirmed by the gradual acquisition of translation equivalents, but the same syntactic rules that are now emerging are being applied to both languages. Finally, Stage III sees the separation of the two languages in both vocabulary and syntax, with each language being used with a different person and thus context-dependent. By contrast, Redlinger and Park (1980) sought confirmation for the One-System Hypothesis in the observation that language mixing decreases as the acquisition process progresses, gradually giving way, in their interpretation, to the emergence of two linguistic systems.

The One-System Hypothesis has since drawn much criticism, on both methodological and general theoretical grounds, and it is fair to say that it is now rejected by the overwhelming majority of specialists in the field. Although an initial avoidance of translation equivalents is widely observed, it does not follow that the child lacks the cognitive ability to distinguish language 'systems', but rather that constraints on the separation of languages by context are still not fully acquired. In fact, translation equivalents are not uncommon, as noted already by Lindholm and Padilla (1978) in the earliest critical assessment of Volterra and Taeschner's work. In Chapter 2 we noted that Ben had numerous translation equivalents in

his active vocabulary by the age of 1:9, which had emerged gradually, both facilitated and constrained by particular functional domains. They were dispreferred,
for instance, with unique referents and expressions of modality. There is also
experimental evidence pointing out the enormous range of translation equivalents among individual bilingual children (Frank and Poulin-Dubois 2002).

In phonology, it has been suggested that bilingual children around the age of
two have separate but 'non-autonomous' phonological systems (Paradis 2001).
Suprasegmental features appear to be acquired earlier than segmental phonology
and are used to differentiate speech acts and contexts, with children applying
different systems of prosody to their respective languages (cf. Gut 2000). At the
same time, cross-linguistic interference may appear around ambiguous structures.
Johnson and Wilson (2002) observe that a young Japanese–English bilingual of
2:0 may be consistent in separating her two languages pragmatically and will
sound like a native speaker to adult speakers of each of the languages, but is
unable to differentiate voice onset timing in the two languages. By contrast, a
four-year-old is able to differentiate voice onset timing, but does not yet produce
the stops in quite the same way as they are produced by adults. They conclude
that children will do whatever they are physically capable of doing in order to
distinguish their languages.

As regards the argument for a syntactic fusion of languages (Volterra and
Taeschner's Stage II), Meisel (1989) argues that the pragmatic assembly of utterances precedes the acquisition of syntactic rules and thus obscures the ability
to tell whether the systems are distinguished, while on the other hand evidence
of early syntactic differentiation can in fact be found. Some similarities among
the bilingual's constructions in the two languages may however be due to transfer as a result of dominance of one language over the other. Müller (1998)
regards such transfer as a 'relief strategy' on which early bilinguals rely when the
input they receive in respect of a particular structure is ambiguous. Deuchar and
Quay (1998) favour an intermediate approach, proposing that prior to the actual
acquisition of syntax there is a period of 'rudimentary syntax' during which a
common predicate-argument structure is used for both languages. Discussing a
Spanish–English bilingual child, they argue that the acquisition of 'real' syntax begins only when morphology appears, and at this stage the languages are
differentiated.

One of the methodological criticisms of the One-System Hypothesis concerns the interpretation of mixed utterances in context. Deuchar and Quay (1998)
point out that mixing is a result of the lack of lexical resources rather than an
inability to distinguish between languages; and further, that not only are children able to distinguish lexical items by language, but that they in fact make
appropriate language choices in addressing and responding to adult interlocutors
(cf. Deuchar and Quay 2000: 64). These impressions are strengthened by experimental evidence that young children at the age of 2–3 are able to differentiate their
languages pragmatically and to accommodate to the context (Comeau, Genesee,
and Lapaquette 2003). Thus we can conclude that it is possible for a child to

make language choices before the age of two, both in one-word and in two-word utterances; but the child's choices might still be influenced by the complexity of changing interlocutors and contexts, resulting in lapses in reacting appropriately to relevant contextual constraints.

Rather than question the wholesale ability to differentiate languages, the challenging task is to identify whether there are any predictable impediments on the way toward full acquisition of the adult norms of negotiating linguistic contexts. One such constraint was described in Chapter 2, when we reported on Ben's repeated lapses in keeping his languages apart around discourse markers and certain types of connectors. Mixing around these and other function words, such as *yes*, *no*, *here*, *more*, and *again*, is observed in other studies as well (Vihman 1985, Köppe 1996). Deuchar (1999) even points out that a significant percentage of utterances identified in the literature on child bilingualism as 'mixed' in fact contained only a grammatical function word that was selected 'inappropriately', while lexical content words are much more likely to match the language context as defined by the adult interlocutors. Moreover, in many of the cases in which there is a mismatch between the language of the function word and the context, the child does in fact possess a translation equivalent (as indeed did Ben in the documented examples). This suggests that this kind of mixing is not motivated by vocabulary gaps and a consequent inability on the part of the child to accommodate to the established context. Rather, Deuchar concludes that function words might be treated as non-language-specific. While our own data (Chapter 2) might not enable us to carry the interpretation that far, they certainly do suggest that different functional classes of structures are sensitive in different ways to the emergence of form-separation by context (consider again the different treatment of labels for fictional entities and those for unique referents), and to the maintenance of form-separation (consider again lapses in the selection of discourse markers and connectors).

4.1.3   Linguistic socialisation and pragmatic competence

The fact that the bilingual behaviour of children can be accounted for in ways other than the denial of the ability to separate languages raises the general question whether language mixing in children is in fact significantly different from language mixing in adult bilinguals (cf. Bhatia and Ritchie 1999: 623). Nicoladis (1998), based on a six-month case-study of a Portuguese–English bilingual child, notes that lexical differentiation only appeared at the age of around 1:5 with a cumulative vocabulary of around 60 items, but that this was preceded by the ability to differentiate prosody. This in turn allows 'pragmatic differentiation', defined as the child's ability to identify the parents' choice of language (the factor which later on sets the context for language use). Nicoladis assumes that it is the child's ability to accommodate to this context that sets the scene for lexical differentiation. Crucially, the emergence of language differentiation is not regarded as a linear process, but reflecting the child's knowledge at given points in time, and as reflecting the child's sensitivity toward the surrounding social setting. Vihman (1985) attributes the decrease in mixing not plainly to the development of two systems, but to an emerging cognitive ability to reflect upon language use and adopt adult norms of language choice. This development tightly reflects the gradual emergence of self-awareness in the child. Köppe (1996) too highlights what she calls 'pragmatic competence' and argues that, since children can be shown to be able to identify language context, early mixing must be regarded not as evidence of language fusion, but instead as early use of codeswitching.

These and other studies represent an interactional perspective on bilingual language acquisition, which emphasises the fact that the child is not just acquiring two linguistic systems but also the rules of communicative competence (cf. e.g. Döpke 1992). As Lanza (1997: 7) puts it, learning when and when not to codeswitch is an essential part of the linguistic socialisation. Lanza takes issue with various studies that assume that mixing in early stages of acquisition, and codemixing, are separate phenomena. In her investigation of the language acquisition of two Norwegian–English bilingual children, Lanza observes that children as young as two are able to use their languages in a contextually sensitive way. However, the acquisition of communicative competence is a process during which the children's degree of separation of the languages has both formal and functional aspects. Thus, dominance in one of the languages may result in stronger mixing favouring that language. But the choice of the non-dominant language in interaction with the person with whom this language is associated is nevertheless evidence of the child's awareness of the functionality of language separation. Lanza emphasises language selection as a behavioural skill; like many other skills, it is acquired in direct relation to the model provided by the parents. More insistence on the part of the parents on maintaining a monolingual context will result in more consistent language choices on the part of the child, while parental negotiation of a situation as a bilingual context is likely to contribute to the child's expectation that the choice of either language in that situation would be appropriate.

The interaction-based approach to child bilingual speech receives support from Lanvers (2001), who analyses an early bilingual's mixed utterances as stages in the development of codeswitching competence. Language mixing is argued to be functional; while switches at an early stage (between 1:6 and 2:0) often derive from vocabulary gaps or retrieval difficulties, at a later age the pragmatic functions of switches include emphasis and appeal, change of topic, and accommodation to the adult interlocutor. Bauer, Hall, and Kruth (2002) even observe that switching languages may be used by the child during play as a tool to control the activities of the interlocutor. This further highlights the importance of taking into account roles in the interaction. Based on the highly nuanced, complex use of language choices, Bauer, Hall, and Kruth (2002: 72) argue against the notion of a 'balanced bilingual' and suggest instead that bilinguals should be viewed as users who possess multiple competencies in both languages.

4.1.4   Language systems vs. language repertoires

Pioneer writers on child bilingualism, such as Ronjat (1913) and Leopold (1949), were burdened by the need to tackle widespread prejudices about bilingualism as potentially harmful to the child's cognitive development. The modern research discussion was initially dominated by the question of system separation, gauging language use among bilinguals against formal, monolingual speech production competence and imposing an abstract, analytical notion of 'language system'. It has since moved on to assess the ways in which children acquire patterns of speech as modes of behaviour.

In this context, it seems worthwhile to abandon the notion of 'linguistic systems' and to devote our attention instead to the development of the child's linguistic repertoire. As the repertoire expands, so does the realisation that the use of word-forms (and later of constructions) is subject to situational and contextual constraints. Until such realisation is achieved, communication is a trial-and-error, experimental activity. The child tries to balance the benefits from exploiting the full repertoire for maximum effectiveness of expression against the need to maintain communicative harmony by complying with constraints on the appropriateness of the selection of word-forms and constructions. It is through this kind of prolonged process of linguistic socialisation that the repertoire is gradually shaped into subsets, or 'languages'.

4.2   Second-language acquisition

There is general consensus that the acquisition of a second language after a certain age follows a development process that is fundamentally different from the one described in the previous section. Two critical points in language development are the completion of the acquisition process of language, around the age of 3–4, and the considerable loss of learning flexibility that sets in with puberty. Accordingly, Klein (1986: 15) distinguishes three processes: First-language acquisition, either monolingual or multilingual, takes place during the child's first three years. Child second-language acquisition can take place between the age of 3–4 years and up to puberty, while adult second-language acquisition is the process that begins after puberty.

While our primary interest here are observations on the natural acquisition process rather than on methodology of second-language instruction, one must bear in mind that the study of second-language acquisition has always had a strong applied orientation. In its early phase, until the 1960s, much of the focus of research into second-language acquisition had been on contrastive analysis. This was based on an understanding that learners will encounter obstacles particularly around those structures that differ most strongly in their first and second languages. This direction gradually then gave way to error analysis, empirically recording the types of errors that learners make in order to be able to predict and pre-empt them through teaching materials. A subsequent development and one that still impacts on more recent work in the field is the interest in learner strategies and the investigation of natural acquisition sequences of forms and functions. This leads some recent works to emphasise the creative aspects of communicative interaction in a second language, and so away from the more traditional focus on the acquisition process as stretched in a linear way between a beginning and an end point.

4.2.1   Facilitating factors

The enormous range of variation among learners has prompted an interest in exploring factors that facilitate or constrain second-language acquisition. Among those we generally acknowledge resources such as memory, motivation and attitude, aptitude and attention, opportunity as well as the extent and nature of linguistic input (cf. Larsen-Freeman and Long 1991: 160ff.). A central factor already mentioned above is age – the principal key to defining second (by contrast to 'bilingual first') language acquisition. Age acts as a constraint to language learning at several different levels (cf. Hyltenstam and Abrahamsson 2003). On the social–psychological side, adults are more inhibited than children, and their identity is more firmly established in relation to their first language, or L1. From a cognitive perspective, adults can be seen to employ different learning strategies than children during L2 acquisition, drawing more strongly on problem-solving abilities.[2] Different patterns of cerebral lateralisation of language have been identified for early and later bilinguals, often with greater right hemispheric participation among late bilinguals, indicating that mature learners approach language learning as a different kind of task (cf. Vaid 1984: 176). This brings us to neurological aspects of age and language learning. Lateralisation, or the specialisation of the two brain sides, occurs in puberty, and it is assumed that the loss of cerebral plasticity has an adverse effect especially on the ability to control articulation.

The articulatory difficulties associated with second-language learning after puberty concern all aspects of phonology and phonetics, though prosody is especially affected. Why is it difficult to acquire the correct intonation or melody after puberty? Why is prosody one of the main contributing factors to what we normally recognise as a 'foreign accent'? In the acquisition of vocabulary and even of certain aspects of grammar, learners rely heavily on memory. By contrast, prosody is tightly associated with emotions and so with individuals' sense of identity. Professional actors are trained to perform roles that are not their own, and so are able to overcome the inhibition to adopt new prosody patterns and witness themselves in a role that is not a true reflection of their own sense of self. Learners find it easier to overcome difficulties in acquiring phonetic and phonemic features by making an analytical effort, than to acquire the target language's prosodic features. Paradoxically, it is precisely prosody that is sometimes adopted sub-consciously by bilinguals from their second language or from a different dialect and imported into their first language as a consequence of emotional identification with a new environment, a new circle of friends, or a partner with whom a second language is used. This confirms that prosody is not so much 'difficult' to learn as it is 'out of reach' of the conscious, analytical control effort.

Are some people more talented to learn languages than others? Aptitude in second-language learning is generally understood as a multidimensional composition of 'enduring characteristics' (Carroll 1981). Robinson (2003) discusses attention and memory as aptitude-related factors. These no doubt contribute to a learner's analytical ability to tackle the problem-solving tasks that present themselves in the acquisition of second languages. But emotional and personality-related factors are also key elements. Larsen-Freeman and Long (1991: 184ff.) list factors such as self-esteem, extroversion, risk-taking, empathy (and hence permeability of language ego boundaries), and tolerance of ambiguity as supporting the process of second-language development, contrasting with sensitivity to rejection, anxiety, and inhibition, which constrain the process. Clearly, pragmatic flexibility in the broader context of communicative interaction supports successful language learning. We shall return to this point when we examine language learners' communicative creativity in discourse in Section 4.2.4 below.

A central issue in second-language acquisition research has been the question of existence of a natural sequence of category acquisition. Pienemann (1998), for instance, draws on generative models of grammar in an attempt to predict which structures will be acquired by learners at which stage in their language development. Other works have explored the more 'objective', universal learnability of categories and category types as well as of communication modes. Klein (1986: 69ff.) relates the learnability of categories to prosodic features. Since content words are more likely to carry stress (loudness, pitch, duration) than function words or grammatical morphemes, they are more salient in conversation. This, in addition to the fact that they are more crucial to the delivery of content-meaning in communication, facilitates their acquisition early on in the process.

The acquisition of finiteness is characterised according to Klein (1986: 93ff.) initially by the use of non-inflected lexical units, organised by pragmatic principles of information-saliency. At a subsequent stage, two lexical units begin to show traces of inflection and assignment to word classes, in rough correspondence to the categories of the target language. Exceptions and overgeneralisations are common, however, and there is interference from the first language, until learners are finally able to build sentences that conform to the rules of the target language. In the acquisition of negation, learners tend to begin by using denials in response to questions, assertions, or requests (in the form of 'no'). They then proceed to use clause negations to deny the appropriateness of a predicate, using elements that correspond to 'not' as well as so-called 'negators with adverbial meaning' (or: negative indefinites) such as *never*, *nowhere*. Finally, they learn to use constituent-related negation, referring to just one constituent in the sentence ('it was not Henry who said that').

Klein (1986) follows Givón (1979) in distinguishing between two more general modes of communication. The pragmatic mode is the primary communication mode during the early stages of second-language acquisition. Its principle is to assemble components of the discourse and the utterance according to their information status, relying more strongly on 'crude' features such as position and intonation than on abstract and complex processing relations among elements (such as inflectional morphology). The pragmatic mode is characterised by a topic-comment structure, slow delivery rate, and the placement of given information before new information. Elements of functional value are placed in immediate proximity to corresponding elements of lexical value, orientational elements are placed at the beginning of the utterance, events are mentioned in natural temporal order, and modality is indicated primarily by intonation. Only in later stages does the learner gradually move on to the syntactic communicative mode, which is characterised by the presence of subordination, of word order as a reflection of syntactic relations, of elaborate use of grammatical morphology and a fast rate of delivery.

Finally, we come to the role of input in the second-language acquisition process. The effects of limited or constrained input especially on the informal, non-structured acquisition process have been debated intensively in connection with the immigration of industrial labourers into northwestern European countries such as Germany and the Netherlands in the 1960s. It has been suggested that the limited linguistic input, as a result of social isolation and only basic communication at the work place, often under unfavourable conditions of noise caused by heavy machinery and routine tasks the coordination of which depends on little more than gestures, restricts immigrant workers' chances of reaching proficiency in the target language (cf. Heidelberg Project 1975, Klein and Dittmar 1979). Moreover, the very fragments of the target language to which the generation of immigrant labourers was exposed often constitute a simplified register of the target language. Simplification strategies – referred to in the literature as 'foreigner talk' (cf. Ferguson 1977, Clyne 1982) – are common especially in situations where native speakers regard learners not as equals but as socially inferior. 'Simplified' talk is a way of talking down and asserting one's position of socio-political advantage and dominance. This is not always the case, however, and native speakers may sometimes adjust their speech either consciously or even intuitively simply in order to match their assumptions about a learner's ability to comprehend the target language. A catalogue of features of linguistic adjustment on the part of native speakers has been listed in the literature. These include a slower rate of delivery, exaggerated intonation, and the avoidance of contractions in phonology; shorter and less complex utterances, more retention of optional constituents, and more questions in morphosyntax; fewer idiomatic expressions, more overt marking of semantic relations, and a preference for full lexical material in semantics; and a narrower range of topics and more frequent confirmation checks, repetition, and expansions at the discourse level (cf. Ferguson 1977, Larsen-Freeman and Long 1991: 125–126).

4.2.2   Transfer and interference

Even very successful adult second-language learners are often distinguishable from native speakers by what we commonly call 'accent'. Weinreich (1953) was the first to offer a systematic analysis of the phenomenon. According to Weinreich, adult learners process their second language via their knowledge of their first language, at least initially. Their familiarity with the principles of complex expression of ideas in their first language often serves as a foundation on which they can build when acquiring the L2; indeed some structures of their L1 may even be helpful in understanding corresponding structures of L2, such as the divisions among tenses or aspects (if the two languages happen to have similar categories in these domains). Where modelling a structure on the L1 facilitates correct learning of the corresponding L2 structure, Weinreich speaks of 'positive transfer'. By contrast, an erroneous assumption that the structures are similar may according to Weinreich result in 'negative transfer', one where the L1 does not support, but rather *interferes* with the production of the correct structure of the target language.

A typical example of interference is **phone substitution**, such as the frequent use of the Hindi/Urdu retroflex [ṭ] as a substitute for the English apical [t] in *table*, pronounced [ṭe:bəl] by Indian learners of English. This may even take on a systematic form through re-interpretation of phonemic distinctions, as in the substitution of English /θ ð/ in *thing, that* by French learners through /s z/, giving /siŋ, zæt/. Other instances of interference may lead to **under-differentiation** of distinctions that are present in the target language, as in the merger of English *leave* and *live* as [liˑv] by Spanish learners, or else of **over-differentiation**, as in the split of Hebrew /e/ in /medabér/ 'speaks.м', pronounced [mɛdaˈbɛʀ], into two separate phonemes by learners with German as a first language: [mədaˈbɛɐ]. An erroneous assumption may even arise out of an awareness in principle of the differences between the languages, pre-empting negative transfer, albeit in the wrong position, a process known as **hyper-correction**. Consider for example the occasional pronunciation of English *adventure* as /adwentur/ by German learners. Conscious of the need to pre-empt a tendency to substitute the English phoneme /w/, which does not exist in German, through [v], the learner inserts the reverse substitution where in fact English /v/ would have been appropriate.

Interference is not limited to adult second-language learners, but can be encountered among child and adult bilinguals as well. An example of semantic interference is the case of a four-year-old Hebrew–Arabic bilingual, pointing to a snake and referring to it in Hebrew as *xayá*. The word means 'animal' in Hebrew, but is similar to (and an etymological cognate of) the Arabic *ħayye* 'snake'. Ben's speech also showed the occasional lexical interference, as in his use in Hebrew, at the age of 4:9, of *lidróš* in the meaning 'to thresh', modelled on German *dreschen*. The transfer process involves isolating the German root, re-interpreting it by analogy to Hebrew tri-consonantal word roots as *d.r.š* and inserting it into the infinitive derivation pattern, modelled on common Hebrew verbs, among them *likcór* 'to thresh', but also *lidróš* 'to demand', which may have existed in the child's repertoire and was confused with the German root. This kind of transfer is sometimes referred to as a 'contamination' of forms from both languages.

Another example is Ben's comment in Hebrew, at the age of 6:2, with reference to a puddle: *máyim šulím*, intended to mean 'shallow water'. The word *šulím* does not exist in Hebrew. Once again, it is constructed by recruiting the English word *shallow*, deriving from it an underlying, reduplicated consonantal root *š.l.l*, which is then inserted into the Hebrew derivational pattern *C.Cu.Cím*, modelled precisely on Hebrew *r(e)dudím* 'shallow.PL' (note that 'water' in Hebrew is plural, and requires plural adjective agreement). Moreover, the construction is with little doubt inspired by the Hebrew word for 'puddle', which happens to be *šulít*, equally possessing a reduplicated consonantal root.

This highly complex, creative process is guided by the correct identification of the context as Hebrew-speaking and thus the correct selection of Hebrew morphological derivational patterns and phonology, and of course the embedding of the word into a Hebrew utterance. The incorrect assumption that is made by the child pertains to the choice of lexical root, which in both cases is not Hebrew. In other words, what the child fails to do is maintain the correct demarcation boundary between components of the repertoire and exclude non-Hebrew lexical items from the Hebrew context. In both cases, and especially in the case of 'shallow water', it appears that the child is misguided by the availability in Hebrew of a similar root, in the second case one that is directly semantically related and is without a doubt activated through the reference context 'puddle'. Instead of keeping them separate, relevant elements of the child's full repertoire of linguistic structures are combined and re-arranged to produce structures with the intention of serving the child's communicative needs in the particular setting and context.

Let us examine just one more example: A seven-year-old German–English bilingual whose dominant language is English produced the German sentence *er ist grösser denn mir* in the intended meaning 'he is taller/bigger than me' (German *er ist grösser als ich*). The selection of *denn mir* for '... than me' in place of the German *als ich* (literally 'as I') is motivated in all likelihood by the sound similarity to the corresponding English words, as well as by their presence in German in somewhat related function. German *mir* is the dative 1SG pronoun, extended to this context replicating the (non-standard) use of the English oblique pronoun *me*. German *denn* is a particle expressing a range of meanings, among them modality and cause. The child is unlikely to be familiar with Standard German formal and literary constructions, where *denn* is employed to avoid repetition of the comparative preposition *als* in the meaning 'as' (cf. *er war erfolgreicher als Lehrer denn als Polizist* 'he was more successful as a teacher *than as* a police officer'). Thus, on the basis of vague similarities in phonology and even more vague similarities in meaning, the child licenses himself to 'transfer' an English meaning to two German word-forms, thereby once again transgressing the boundaries within the full, bilingual repertoire of structures.

We are now in a position to attribute a new interpretation to the process known as interference or transfer: it is a process by which the speaker makes or attempts to make creative communicative use of elements of the combined, full repertoire of linguistic structures in a context that requires selection from just a subset of that repertoire, i.e. from the appropriate 'language'. In the case of learners or bilinguals with a dominant language, the trigger behind the process is often lack of proficiency in the selected language of the context, or else a lapse in memory (retrieval difficulties) or in control over the selection mechanism of word-forms and other structures. Where articulatory interference among learners is concerned, social–psychological difficulties in overcoming physiological challenges to the familiar articulatory pattern may lead speakers to generalise this pattern and to assign it to the entire linguistic repertoire. Paradis (2004: 188) distinguishes two types of interference: the first, called 'static' interference, represents a speaker's implicit competence which differs from that of native speakers. The second, called 'dynamic' interference, is due to performance errors, or the inadvertent intrusion of an element from L1 into L2 (or vice versa). In both types, the motivation to communicate overrides the constraint on maintaining contextual separation between the subsets of the linguistic repertoire, or the bilingual's distinct 'languages'. Transfer and interference have traditionally been regarded as negative events in the learning process and as manifestations of failure to acquire the correct structures of the target language. But as long as they do not result in incomprehensibility and a breakdown of communication, one might instead view them as *enabling* factors that allow language users to create bridges among different subsets within their overall repertoire of linguistic forms, and to use these bridges to sustain communication.

4.2.3   Interlanguage and fossilisation

Inspired by the view that the learning process constitutes a linear development, from a starting point through to the acquisition of full proficiency in the L2, researchers have used the term *interlanguage* to refer to points on the learning continuum (cf. Larsen-Freeman and Long 1991: 60). An interlanguage is an individual learner's idiosyncratic use of target language structures, which may be variable in different contexts and of course subject to change as the learning process continues. While the traditional approach has been to view interlanguage as an incomplete or deficient version of the target language, an alternative approach defines interlanguage as a 'composite matrix language' that is a combination of three systems: the learner's previously acquired languages, a variety of the target language, and the developing learner variety (see Myers-Scotton and Jake 2000, Jake and Myers-Scotton 1997, Jake 1998). This enables a more positive definition of interlanguage, one that acknowledges both the communicative contribution of the L1-based structures on which learners draw in the interlanguage and learners' own creativity in adapting and re-shaping elements of the target language to their own communicative needs.

The notion of interlanguage usually presupposes some continuation of the acquisition process. But the reality of language learning is often characterised by learners failing to achieve full proficiency in the target language, yet still managing to sustain successful and effective communication in it. The term *fossilisation* was introduced to capture the phenomenon of a permanent adoption (regardless of age or amount of instruction) of idiosyncratic interlanguage features in a learner's L2. Selinker (1972) defined fossilisation as a cognitive mechanism that produces a non-target-like end-state. In effect, fossilisation can thus serve as an alternative to the notion of 'transfer'. Although fossilisation is normally viewed as the outermost limits of a learner's achievement potential, one must bear in mind that positive social factors may play a role in promoting fossilisation; thus, learners might lose the motivation to expand their knowledge of the L2 once they are satisfied with their own ability to communicate efficiently with others and once their speech is understood and accepted by listeners.

Long (2003) mentions as causes of fossilisation positive feedback on communication despite the occurrence of errors, absence of feedback, insensitivity to negative feedback, routine adoption of incorrect forms and rules, and unwillingness to risk re-structuring. Fossilisation is thus better described as stabilisation, brought about through a combination of input sensitivity with perceptual saliency, which together determine the speaker's ability to identify errors. One of the questions put forward in connection with the fossilisation discussion is whether there are any 'high risk categories' that can be predicted to be likely candidates for stabilisation. Long (2003: 518) identifies as more likely candidates for stabilisation morphology compared to syntax, inflectional morphology rather than free morphemes, as well as exceptional cases, which prove particularly problematic in the acquisition process. The cline seems to run again from the level of the utterance and phrase (syntax and free morphs), which is easier to accommodate to, to the level of the word (morphological inflection), which proves more difficult.[3]

The precise role of L1 as a factor in the stabilisation process remains controversial. Fossilisation is present only in L2 acquisition, and not in L1 acquisition (with the exception of special cases of impairment), suggesting that L2 acquisition is a fundamentally different cognitive process. Some researchers have taken this as an indication that L2 acquisition is modelled on L1, and that one might therefore expect learners to encounter difficulties when there is lack of congruency between the two languages. White (2003) for example suggests that there is evidence for a connection between L1 and L2 in the acquisition of morphology, as learners of a language with complex morphology such as Turkish can more easily acquire correct or near-correct use of English morphology than speakers of a language with hardly any morphology, such as Chinese. And yet considerable differences among language learners of similar backgrounds suggest that it is impossible to predict the degree of fossilisation.

Above we described fossilisation as idiosyncratic – the variable speech characteristics of an individual language learner. However, under certain socio-historical circumstances, an entire speech community or possibly a generation or a sector within a community may show similar stabilisation features. These would be the result of having the same first language and learning the same target language under the same or similar external circumstances such as input, opportunity, and feedback. Collective interlanguage features are extremely common in the speech of linguistic minorities with a more or less uniform type of exposure to the majority or national language. Typical features of the German spoken by members of the Romani-speaking community in Germany, for example, are the generalisation of the accusative case in determiners at the expense of the dative (*mit den Mann* instead of *mit dem Mann* 'with the man'), and the de-rounding of vowels (*Gerist* for *Gerüst* 'scaffold'). Clyne (2003: 152–157) reports on the emerging English ethnolects of immigrant groups in Australia. Such ethnolects may become a marker of identity, alongside the community's own traditional language, as indeed is the case with many creoles and pidgins. Collective interlanguage features are not restricted to minorities. The variety of English now accepted as standard in India, for example, shows clear phonetic interference features from Indian languages. Collective or community bilingualism may itself be a factor promoting interlanguage stabilisation, as each individual learner receives supporting feedback from fellow learners of a similar background. This social aspect of interlanguage is often overlooked in traditional approaches, which tend to focus on the individual's role in the second-language learning process.

Historical linguistics have paid more attention to collective interlanguage stabilisation, especially in cases of language shift. Thomason and Kaufman (1988: 38) identify what they call 'shift-induced interference' as a major type of contact-induced language change (see also Thomason 2001). It is argued that imperfect second-language learning by groups who then abandon their own language and shift to the second language results in the creation of a new variety or in structural re-shaping of that second language. This new, altered variety is then passed on to subsequent generations. The background language that is the source of transfer in such cases is referred to as the *substrate* language, while the target language to which a population shifts (and which is usually imposed on that population by a dominant elite or majority) is known as the *superstrate* language.

The problem with substrate-hypotheses (or: shift-induced interference) is the difficulty in finding concrete empirical evidence of underlying interference. A generation of historical linguists specialising in the Balkan languages had for many years accepted that the structural similarities among those languages (see Chapter 9) were a result of common substrate influence (see Solta 1980), despite the absence of any information about the structures of pre-historic languages of the region. Historically documented cases of language shift are often rather complex and not so straightforward. Some colloquial varieties of Hebrew, for example, show clear substrate traces of Arabic, the language of many Middle Eastern Jews who emigrated to Israel in the early 1950s. These include the neutralisation of the stative vs. directional opposition in location expressions (*yacáti ba-ħuc* rather than *yacáti ha-ħúca* 'I went out[side]') and the omission of prepositions with objects of state (*ʕavadeti pkidá* 'I worked [as] [a] secretary') (cf. Matras and Schiff 2005). Other features that resemble Arabic, such as the retention of etymological pharyngeals /ʕ/ and /ħ/ and the merger of the historical diphthong /ey/ with /e/, may well be a continuation of Middle Eastern reading traditions of liturgical Hebrew, and so only indirectly attributable to substrate influence. Most of the grammatical changes that are apparent in spoken Hebrew today can be attributed to internal levelling and analogies. There is little doubt, however, that the rapid pace of internal change in spoken Hebrew is due to the fact that the younger generation of native speakers, those born roughly between the 1950s and 1970s, consisted almost entirely of children of second-language learners who spoke an 'interlanguage' or learner varieties of Hebrew and so were unable to transmit a fully coherent and consistent linguistic system to the next generation.

Singapore English (or Singlish) is another useful example of the complexities of substrate influence. Arguably, Singlish is the product of Chinese and partly Malay substrate, and an English superstrate component. The language uses mainly English word-forms, but grammatical and lexical semantics are often based on the substrate languages. This can be clearly seen in the structuring of the aspectual system, where distinctions are carried out primarily with the help of particles (*it rain already*, *it ever rain*, *it never rain*, etc.), which are modelled on Chinese particles such as *le*, *guo*, *bù* (Bao 2005). Numerous lexical items are also direct translations from Chinese. Thus, the Singlish expression *eat salt* meaning 'to suffer a bitter or serious setback' is modelled on Mandarin Chinese *chī yán* (*chī* 'eat', *yán* 'salt'). But to speak of 'shift-induced interference' would not quite capture the reality of the situation in this case, either. Firstly, Singlish is often spoken alongside the substrate languages, and has not replaced them. Next, it is limited as a vehicle of communication to certain sociolinguistic contexts, while other varieties of English occupy acrolectal (public domain) functions. Users of Singlish are thus usually exposed to a continuum of English varieties, shaped to varying degrees by the substrate and superstrate languages.

Learners' interlanguage has long been considered a key factor in understanding the emergence of pidgins (see Chapter 9). Pidgins emerge in situations where language input is restricted as a result of non-immersion in the society that speaks the target language, and often due to exposure primarily to foreigner talk in interactions of limited scope (trade, work force). Véronique (2003) follows many other studies in describing structural similarities between early stages of non-guided acquisition of French, and French-lexifier creoles (which developed from pidgins). These include a mere rudimentary distinction between word classes, the absence of inflectional morphology, omission of determiners, an extended use of presentational constructions such as /jãna/ 'there is' and /se/ 'it is', and more.

Research into second-language acquisition in Germany during the late 1970s and early 1980s gave considerable attention to the suggestion that the learner interlanguage spoken by immigrant workers – termed *Gastarbeiterdeutsch* or 'guest workers' German' – had the potential of developing into a simplified variety of German, one that resembled a pidgin (see Clyne 1968, Ferguson 1977, Klein and Dittmar 1979). Note that substrate influence and interference were not in the centre of attention. Rather, the emphasis was on the collective fossilisation process, common to foreign workers of various linguistic backgrounds (Turkish, Portuguese, Italian, Greek), and resulting from shared factors that constrained the acquisition process: social isolation, limited input (often in the form of foreigner talk), lack of motivation, and lack of institutional support. Some common patterns could be observed throughout the population of immigrant workers. Different learner interlanguage varieties appeared to reinforce one another and thus contributed to stabilisation. Nevertheless, Gastarbeiterdeutsch remained part of a continuum of learner varieties stretching all the way to the target language. Despite the fact that not all learners had the motivation or opportunity to acquire full proficiency in German, exposure to German media and participation in German institutional life, including education, would ensure that the younger generation had, potentially at least, full access to the mainstream variety of German as spoken by the majority, and would thus be in a position to acquire full proficiency in the target language. Long-term stabilisation was therefore considered unlikely (cf. Meisel 1975). One generation later on, some features of the substrate languages nevertheless appear to have been retained at least among some groups of speakers. Queen (2001) for instance discusses the use of intonation patterns derived from Turkish as a pragmatic device in the German of young Turkish–German bilinguals. On the other hand, there is some evidence that the Turkish spoken by the younger generation of immigrants (those raised in Germany) is influenced by German, for instance in its use of interrogative elements as subordinators (Herkenrath, Karakoç, and Rehbein 2002).

Approaching the issue of interlanguage in terms of speakers' linguistic repertoires in multilingual constellations, we can note that speakers in situations of non-guided second-language acquisition generally do not wait until they have acquired full proficiency in the target language structures before communicating. Rather, their learning process is embedded into their efforts to engage in communicative interaction in contexts that are reserved for the target language. In order to sustain communication in these contexts they draw in a creative way on various components of their full linguistic repertoire, thereby often blurring the boundaries between 'languages' and over time conventionalising new structures. These innovations are nothing other than the product of learners' efforts to communicate effectively. In the next section we examine the process of learner creativity and communication efforts more closely.

4.2.4 Communicative creativity in L2 discourse

The view that second-language acquisition is a linear process, with a clear beginning and end point, is subject to growing criticism from researchers, who favour a more dynamic approach to second-language acquisition. De Bot, Lowie, and Verspoor (2007) for example have described the process as a dynamic iteration of simple procedures of learning that involve creative communicative behaviour. They argue that it is therefore impossible to make simplistic cause-and-effect predictions about the course of a learning process. Goglia (2006) pioneers the application of a communicative approach that focuses on the individual as effective-communication achiever in a situation where the target language is not easily accessible. Goglia examines the communicative behaviour of Igbo-Nigerian labour immigrants in northern Italy, whose linguistic repertoire typically consists of their native tribal or regional language Igbo, Nigerian Pidgin English, a continuum of mesolectal and acrolectal forms of English, and a learner variety of Italian, often influenced by the regional dialect spoken in and around Padua.

Goglia challenges the assumptions of traditional studies of second-language acquisition, which posit that language learners aim to achieve native speaker ability. He describes instead how speakers 'take inspiration' from the target-language input that is more or less at their disposal, while also drawing on knowledge of their previous languages and even trying out new linguistic forms, which may prove to be more or less effective in communication. In doing so, speakers appear to accept some resulting vagueness and ambiguity in their speech, on the assumption that meanings will be clarified if necessary by extra-linguistic factors such as the context or further explanation as the conversation proceeds (Goglia 2006: 60–64). Goglia describes three concrete strategies employed by the learners. The first is codeswitching into English, mainly in order to fill lexical gaps, on the assumption that the interlocutor will be able to understand the intended meaning (Goglia 2006: 124):

(1) a. Interviewer: Conosci anche nigeriani yoruba or hausa?
         know.2SG also Nigerian.PL Yoruba or Hausa

    b. Speaker: Sono conosce tanti di altre *tribes.*
         be.1SG know.3SG many.M.PL of other

    a. Interviewer: Do you also know Yoruba and Hausa Nigerians?
    b. Speaker: I know many from other *tribes.*

Quite often, English insertions of this kind are Italianised in an effort to integrate them into the context-language, Italian, and thereby to flag the speaker's commitment to the choice of Italian as the language of the ongoing interaction. Goglia (2006: 102, 143) documents the use of expressions such as *adressare the public* 'to address the public' (with an Italian infinitive ending), *leafo* 'leaf', and *businessa* 'business' (with Italian masculine and feminine nominal endings, respectively).

A further strategy is the generalisation or reanalysis of Italian markers. The Italian adversative conjunction *ma* for instance is also used to introduce relative clauses, quite possibly by analogy to a similar marker in Igbo (Goglia 2006: 168):

(2)   a. perché all'inizio   abitava   in via   Anelli,
              because at the beginning lived.3SG in street Anelli

        b. *ma* quartiere in Padova dove c'è   solo immigrati
              but district   in Padua where there.si only immigrant.PL

        a. because at the beginning I used to live in Anelli street,
        b. [which is] a district in Padua where there are only immigrants

Other phenomena include the generalisation of the preposition *per* 'for', as in *per adesso* 'for now', *per bicicletta* 'by bicycle', *per Jamaica* 'concerning Jamaica', *è difficile per prendere visa* 'it is difficult to get a visa'; and the use of reduplication, as in *caldo caldo* 'hot hot' = 'very hot', to express intensity (Goglia 2006: 173–175).

Finally, speakers' innovation and creativity in working with the input they receive is nicely exemplified by the common use, among the community of Igbo-Nigerian immigrants, of the Italian impersonal expression *c'e* 'there is' to express possession (avoiding the complex and irregular inflected verb 'to have'). The semantic relation between the topic-possessor, *c'e* as a predicate indicating possession, and the object of possession is indicated through plain juxtaposition (Goglia 2006: 193–194):

(3)   io c'è   tanti   amica
        I   there.is many.M.PL friend.F.SG
        'I had many friends'

(4)   anche io non c'è   soldi   per telefono.
        also   I NEG there.is money for telephone
        'and I do not have money to call'

Above we alluded to the discussion of 'Gastarbeiterdeutsch', the German inter-language of immigrant workers. The following two excerpts, recorded in southern Germany in 1984, illustrate some of the typical features of this interlanguage. The first speaker is of Turkish origin, and at the time of the recording had been living in Germany for eighteen years:

(5) a. So, meine Kollega   alles türkisch,
        so my   colleagues all   Turkish

     b. *ama* ich bin nix   zu viel   deutsch so sprecken.
        but   I am nothing too much German so speak

     c. immer türkisch sprecken immer türkisch sprecken.
        always Turkish speak   always Turkish speak

     d. meine Tochter   meine Sohn auf deutsch sprecken gut
        my   daughter my   son also German speak   well
        {Mm.}

     e. ah/ i keine Dolmetscher so mein/ oder so vielleichs am Arbeisamt oder so,
             I no   interpreter so my   or   so perhaps   at job office or   so

     f. so keine Dolmetscher.
        so no   interpreter

     g. immer meine Tochter   meine Sohn zusammen Dolmetscher so   sprecken.
        always my   daughter my   son together interpreter such speak
        {Mhm.}

     h. ich bin türkische/ türkisch sprecken, Kollega   deutsch/ sprech/ eh/
        I   am Turkish   Turkish speak   colleague German speak

     i. meine Sohn meine/ . . eh immer deutsch sprecken, Dolmetscher, jä?
        my   son my   always German speak   interpreter   yes

     j. ich bin nix   zu viel   deutsch sprechen.
        I   am nothing too much German speak

     k. achtzehn Jahre arbeiten *ama* keine . . .
        eighteen years work   but   none

     a. Well, my colleagues are all Turks.
     b. But I don't speak German very well.
     c. I always speak Turkish, I always speak Turkish.
     d. My daughter, my son also, [they] speak German well.
        {Mm.}
     e. ah/ I [don't need] an interpreter [or anything like that], my/ for example
        at the job office or something like that,
     f. [in such cases] I don't [need] an interpreter.
     g. My daughter and my son [are] always together [with me] and translate.
                                                        {Mhm.}
     h. I speak Turkish/ Turkish, the colleagues speak/ uh/
     i. my son and my/ .. uh always speaker German, they translate, yes?
     j. I don't speak Germany very well.
     k. Eighteen years I have been working [here], *but* [I don't] . . .

Rather than focus on the speaker's errors, we shall review his choice of structures and his ability to communicative effectively and creatively in a context that
is defined by the target language, German. The speaker tends to generalise the
German word *so* 'so, such, in this way' to indicate various connections to ideas
that have been expressed in the course of the conversation, beginning with 'well'
(in line (a)), 'or anything like that' and 'for example' (in line (e)), and on to 'in

such cases' (line (f)) and 'like this' (line (g)). The expression *so as well as oder so* is quite common in spoken German, but the speaker's over-generalisation of the word might be regarded as an attempt to reassure himself that the listener is following what he is saying and comprehends the various connections that he is making.

Words such as 'my' (possessive pronoun) and 'no' (negative determiner) generally carry inflection endings in German that agree with the following noun in gender and number. These agreement rules are not followed by this speaker, who instead generalises the ending *-e* (nominative feminine and plural): *meine* 'my', *keine* 'no(ne)'. The generalisation of this particular form is not surprising. It is the more frequent ending, since it appears in German both in the feminine singular and in the plural. Also, in the object case, the relevant forms tend to have two syllables (e.g. *keinen, keinem, keiner*), and so again they bear similarities to the form preferred by the speaker, *keine*. As a result of the generalisation of just one inflected form, we find grammatical errors where a feminine/plural form accompanies a masculine singular noun: *meine Sohn* 'my son' (lines (d), (g), (i)), *keine Dolmetscher* 'no interpreter' (lines (e), (f)).

German verb inflection is completely missing. The speaker uses the famous infinitive-style, a feature that is known to be characteristic of German 'foreigner talk'. All verbs appear in the infinitive form, with no marking for person, number, or tense. There is one exception: The speaker uses, as a fixed formula, the expression *ich bin* 'I am'. Although German does not have a progressive tense that uses the verb 'to be' as in English ('I am speaking'), the speaker extends the combination *ich bin*, inserting it along with various verbs as a way to compensate for the absence of person inflection: *ich bin nix zu viel deutsch sprecken* 'I don't speak very much German' (lines (b), (j)), *ich bin türkisch sprecken* 'I speak Turkish' (line (h)).

German word order rules are quite complex, and the position of constituents in the sentence varies according to the type of clause (e.g. main or subordinate) as well as the presence of elements at the beginning of a clause. Turkish word order on the other hand is much more rigid; the verb tends to appear in the final position, at least in simple sentences that lack special emphasis. The speaker tends to follow Turkish word order: *immer türkisch sprecken* '[I] always talk in Turkish' (line (c)), compare German *[ich] spreche immer türkisch*; or in line (k): *achtzehn Jahre arbeiten* '[I have been] working for eighteen years', German *[ich] arbeite [schon] achtzehn Jahre*'.

The speaker is creative in constructing vocabulary items for which he does not know the German expression. We see this with the verb 'to translate' or 'to interpret', which obviously plays an important role in what the speaker is trying to say in this excerpt. The speaker is not familiar with the German word for this verb. Instead, he uses a combination of the noun *Dolmetscher* 'interpreter' and the verb *sprechen* 'to speak' – literally: 'to speak interpreter'.

In phonology, the speaker has what we would normally refer to as a Turkish 'accent'. But notice some aspects of his pronunciation that are conspicuously different from German: The word *Kollega* has an *a* at the end, instead of *-e*. The word *nichts* 'nothing' is reduced to *nix* – this is no doubt influenced by colloquial and dialectal German. The sound /ch/ in *sprechen* changes to *sprecken* (lines (b), (c), (d) and more), and combinations of sounds at the end of words tend to be distorted: *vielleicht* 'maybe' becomes *vielleichs* (line (e)), *Arbeitsamt* 'job office' becomes *Arbeisamt* (line (e)).

Note that the speaker hardly uses any conjunctions. Connections are generally expressed by *so*, which, as discussed above, is generalised. When the speaker wishes to express contrast, he uses the Turkish conjunction *ama* 'but', which sounds somewhat similar to German *aber*: *ama ich bin nix zu viel deutsch sprecken* 'but I don't speak German very well' (line (b)), *ama keine...* 'but no...' (line (k)). Finally, verbs in German are negated by the particle *nicht* 'not', which normally follows the verb (though this depends on the overall word order in the sentence). The speaker uses the word for 'nothing', *nix*, as a generalised negator: *ich bin nix zu viel deutsch sprecken* 'I don't speak German very well' (line (l)). This too is a well-known feature of the German speech of foreign workers.

We thus find confirmation for the predominance of a pragmatic mode, with difficulties in acquiring proficiency in the use of target-language inflectional morphology, syntactic rules, complex operations such as conjunctions, and phonology. Instead we find extension of meaning and function of grammatical elements, generalisation of selected form to represent an entire paradigm (as in the case of possessors/determiners and the verbal infinitive), occasional reliance on first-language word order, conjunctions, and especially phonology, and some creative processes in lexicon. Note that throughout the excerpt the hearer gives positive feedback, and the speaker himself makes at least one overt attempt (in segment (i)) to reassure himself that the listener is following what he is saying. The interlanguage thus has communicative value and communicative effectiveness.

The following excerpt, also from a speaker of Turkish origin, further illustrates both the reliance on first-language structures and creativity processes based on the available input from the target language. The speaker describes the town in southern Germany in which he lives:

(6) a. Strasse ein bisse wenig aber/
        street a   bit few   but

     b. Autoparkplas auch wenig, Strassen.
        parking-space also few   streets

     c. immer so   schuldig parken schreiben, Geld sahlen.
        always such guilty   park   write   money pay

     d. aber nich gut, anderes besser, gell?
        but not good other   better right

     a. There aren't many streets but/

     b. There aren't many parking spaces either, on the streets.

      c. One always receives a parking ticket, and needs to pay a fine.
      d. But that's not good, something else would be better, right?

    In German, most nouns must be clearly identified, usually through their ending, as either singular or plural. Note that in line (a) the speaker is referring to 'streets' in the plural – arguing that there aren't many *streets*, but uses the German singular form: *Strasse* 'street'. By contrast, in line (b), he uses the German plural form *Strassen* 'streets'. Is this a question of not being certain about the plural ending? It may actually be a direct transfer from Turkish. In Turkish, one does not normally use the plural ending when the noun is determined by some kind of quantifier, such as 'a few' or even 'many', since the quantifier already specifies that the noun is plural. Thus, the Turkish equivalent of the sentence in line (a) would be: *sokak azdır*, literally 'street few.is'. On the other hand, when referring to a definite entity, the plural ending is obligatory (thus *sokaklar* '[the] streets'). Thus, when the speaker in line (b) refers back to the streets as the location of the (few) parking spaces, he is referring to a definite, known entity: 'the streets'. In Turkish, this would be *sokaklarda*, literally 'streets.on', 'on the streets'.

    Lexical creativity is found in this example too. The speaker improvises in order to create expressions for concepts that are not known to him in German. In line (c), he refers to the issuing of parking tickets. Not being familiar with the proper term in German, he puts together words whose meanings add up to represent the concept that he wishes to express: 'guilty' + 'park' + 'write' = 'parking ticket'. The concept of 'fine' is replaced by the more general 'money'.

    As in the previous example, few expressions are used to express connections between portions of what has been said. This speaker too uses *so* 'such, in this way'. In a sense, this serves as a signal to the listener to draw a connection between what is being said, and things that are generally known to be true: 'in this way' meaning 'you can imagine what I am saying'. But note how inexplicit the speaker is with regard to the connections to previous talk in line (d): What isn't good? What 'something' would be better? Much of the interpretation is left to the listener, and the speaker, for lack of vocabulary and especially for lack of command of grammatical vocabulary that can express connections or conditions, leaves quite a bit unexpressed, relying on the listener to do the work of contextual interpretation.

    The previous examples illustrated interference that results from lack of native-speaker proficiency in the target language – what Paradis (2004) calls 'static' interference. We turn now to an example of 'dynamic' interference, in the case of a German second-language user of English. Contrasting with the earlier examples of immigrant workers, the present speaker is an educated professional, who has enjoyed both some formal instruction of English at school level, and considerable immersion with English-speaking associates. One would certainly describe his English speech as 'fluent'. The excerpt is taken from an interview for a British television programme.[4] The context language is thus clearly defined and the setting is rather formal, permitting few hesitations and little improvisation:

(7)   a. At the border in England, *were* by the custom/
          b. They *have investigated* this car very very eh/ eh/ thoroughly and they
             have removed the panels from the doors, the panels from the *luggage
             room*,
          c. and they in/ investigated in the engine compartments *aber* they didn't
             find anything,
          d. but the/ they *have forgotten* to got *unten/* the/ [clears throat] they forgot
             to look under the car.

As an indication of the speaker's proficiency in English, note his use of some
rather elaborate vocabulary, such as the words *investigated*, *removed*, *thoroughly*,
and *compartments*. He also speaks fast, and in well-constructed sentences. But
notice nevertheless how his native German influences his English speech. In line
(a) the speaker follows German word order rules on the positioning of the finite
verb (*were*) in second constituent position, following the prepositional phrase *at
the border in England*. This verb is also used lexically in a way that resembles
German, to express existence, whereas the normal English equivalent would have
been *there were*. The speaker prefers the perfect tense to express past-tense events,
following German usage, whereas in English the more obvious choice for events
that have no direct bearing on the present situation is the simple past: *they have
investigated*, *they have removed* (line (b)), *they have forgotten* (line (d)). The
speaker refers to the boot of the car as the *luggage room* (line (b)), constructing
the expression following the German model: *Kofferraum*, where *-raum* (similar
to English *room*) actually means 'space'. This is a case of taking the pattern of
the German lexical construction, but the shape of corresponding words, or words
associated with the German model, from English.

Finally, under pressure to narrate the events, and approaching the climax of the
story, the speaker slips into German when uttering the contrastive conjunction
aber 'but'. (We know that he is familiar with the English expression *but*, which he
uses in the following line.) This is a case of a bilingual 'speech production error'
or slip of the tongue, where the choice of the correct form from the appropriate
language simply escapes the speaker's control (see below). Such slips are not
uncommon especially around discourse markers, interjections, and conjunctions.
But note that in line (d) something similar seems to happen: the speaker says
got but might have had the German word *gucken* 'to look' in mind, and this is
followed by German *unten* 'below'; note the speaker's embarrassment and slight
confusion after this slip, represented by the fact that he stops to clear his throat
before starting over again and re-phrasing.

4.2.5   Language learners and linguistic repertoires

We have seen in the preceding sections that learners do not simply
run through a checklist of target language items to be acquired. Rather, learners
are often innovators whose innovations constitute an attempt to sustain effective

communication. In some cases, idiosyncratic innovations may become stabilised, leading to interlanguage fossilisation. If shared with a wider community, and if the community has the chance to turn its collective interlanguage into the main vehicle of communication, then the innovation may lead to language change, that is, to the emergence of a variety of the language that is different from the target language. We saw however that the sociolinguistic complexity of modern societies – especially the register continuum to which speakers typically have access – puts many obstacles in the way of language change. The difficulty in finding unequivocal evidence for interference in the past makes it difficult to identify with certainty those cases where interlanguage may have led to language change in the past.

One of the pathways for learner innovation is to combine linguistic elements across the entire repertoire. This means that, pragmatically speaking, 'transfer' is not per se negative, but can act as a positive promoter of new communicative structures. It also means that speakers do not operate within closed linguistic systems; rather, they act pragmatically in drawing on flexible repertoires of linguistic structures when the need arises. In fact we can view the process of second-language acquisition as an expansion of the linguistic repertoire, with the goal of enabling the speaker/learner to communicate in a new set of contexts. As in bilingual first-language acquisition, the need to communicate sometimes overrides the desire to comply with the choice of context-language. In such instances, speakers will try to achieve both goals simultaneously: they will activate structures which they have at their disposal but are not necessarily part of the context-language, while making an attempt not to alienate their interlocutors by appearing incomprehensible. The results are the kind of communicative acts that are documented above, where speakers experiment and improvise creatively, or maintain structures that have proven effective in communication in the past.

4.3   Bilingualism and language processing

In his introduction to Weinreich's (1953: vii) monograph, André Martinet points out that a bilingual's alternative languages are not unlike the variants in a monolingual's repertoire. A similar point is made by Paradis (2004: 187), who states that 'interference and switching occur between languages as they occur between registers in a unilingual speaker. Translation between two languages corresponds to paraphrasing in a single language.' Paradis concludes from this that there is 'nothing in the bilingual brain that differs in nature from anything in the unilingual brain' (2004: 189). Yet numerous studies have been devoted to the special links between bilingualism and language processing.

One of the most well-cited models is Weinreich's distinction between compound, coordinate, and subordinate bilingualism. Weinreich imagined each type as a distinct way of accessing the bilingual lexicon. The compound bilingual has one single conceptual representation, but two word-forms that represent it. For the coordinate bilingual, translation equivalents in the two languages may be associated with different concepts. A frequent example is vocabulary representing culture-specific products or artefacts. Thus English *bread* may be a translation equivalent of French *pain*, but for the bilingual whose knowledge of the languages stems from interaction in both cultures, each word represents a distinct product, different in shape, in taste, and pattern of consumption. Weinreich's subordinate bilingual, finally, accesses the conceptual representation of an L2 word-form via its translation equivalent in L1. In Ervin and Osgood's (1954) revision of the model, 'subordinate' is subsumed under 'compound'. The remaining distinction between 'compound' and 'coordinate' is interpreted as reflecting uniform vs. separate contexts of acquisition, respectively. In this way, a connection was first proposed between the kind of activity tasks involved in the language acquisition process, and the resulting mode of language processing. Results of subsequent experimental testing were often interpreted as confirmation that the environment and mode of acquisition have an impact on the type of links that bilinguals create between translation equivalents (cf. for example Lambert, Havelka, and Crosby 1958).

4.3.1   Language separation in the brain

Weichreich's model launched a search for answers to the question whether bilingual storage of languages simply replicates the monolingual mode, or whether there are asymmetrical, non-equivalent modes of storing two (or more) languages. Empirical evidence in support of non-equivalence was cited from two domains: the fact that the ability to learn L2 is weakened after maturity, at least with respect to the non-analytical parts of language such as prosody; and asymmetric recovery patterns from aphasia among bilinguals. Aphasia – language disorders resulting from head and brain injuries – may lead to symptoms such as uncontrolled language mixing (among bilinguals), problems in turn taking, phonological and morphological deficiencies (agrammatism), and problems in lexicon selection. In most cases of aphasia in multilinguals, both languages are lost and recovered simultaneously and to the same extent. Treatment in one language generally results in recovery in the other languages as well (cf. Filiputti *et al.* 2002). Differential impairment or recovery is rare, but it has occupied the attention of researchers due to the difficulties in identifying the factors that are responsible for non-parallel developments (cf. Albert and Obler 1978, Paradis 1995, Goral, Levi, and Obler 2002).

Paradis (1995, 2004: 63ff.) names six possible recovery patterns among bilinguals: parallel (both languages recover together), differential (both languages recover to different extents), successive (one language recovers after the other), selective (only one language is recovered), antagonistic (recovery in one language is followed by regression, and only then by the recovery of the other language), and mixed (the patient's utterances show more mixture than before the illness). Among the earliest assumptions postulated in connection with bilingual aphasia, Ribot's (1881) idea that the first-learned language recovers first is supported only by some case studies while numerous others contradict it. Pitrès's (1895) suggestion that the most familiar or most used language recovers first is more widely accepted; at the very least, there is agreement that context of acquisition and degree of fluency and usage play a role for some patients, alongside the type of anatomical impairment. Kainz (1960) for instance generalises that the better recovered language is the one that is used consciously and not automatically, and that aphasia affects mainly the language that is used less consciously and automatically. Nevertheless, there is still no general causal account for the impairment patterns, nor is it clear which factors influence the patterns of recovery (Paradis 1995, Green and Price 2001).

While it is not believed that languages are separated anatomically in the sense that different areas of the brain are responsible for the storage of different linguistic systems,[5] selective recovery of only one language seems consistent with the notion that different languages are served by different neural systems, and that these separable systems can be selectively damaged (cf. Green and Price 2001: 197). Languages may thus serve different purposes, or be associated with different tasks or activities, and so be activated in asymmetrical ways.

It is assumed that the language system is generally lateralised to the left hemisphere, and that the right hemisphere contributes to the pragmatic aspects of language. Bilinguals show the same left-hemispheric dominance of language processing as monolinguals. But as Albert and Obler (1978) pointed out, late second-language speakers compensate for their lack of skill in their L2 by relying more on metalinguistic knowledge and pragmatic ability (resources that are also available to monolingual speakers but need not be activated as frequently) (see also Paradis 2004: 222–225). We witnessed the application of such skills in the examples in the previous section. Increased right-hemispheric participation is thus possible in the early stages of L2 learning, when learning is approached as a problem-solving task (cf. Filiputti *et al.* 2002). Vaid (1984: 190–191) had already suggested that differences in cerebral lateralisation of language among early and late bilinguals can be related to linguistic tasks and the demands on language processing. Specifically, early bilinguals appear to possess a semantic mode of processing linguistic input, a result of their early exposure to different forms conveying a single referent, while late bilinguals are more sensitive to surface features, which figure more prominently as markers of a particular input language. The greater potential for right-hemispheric participation among late L2 learners leads Green and Price (2001: 198) to suggest that antagonistic recovery of languages may derive from the degree of control. According to Filiputti *et al.* (2002), the overall impression from experimental situations using various neuroimaging techniques is that second-language processing may be organised more variably and individually across users; proficiency and frequency of use play a crucial role as variables (see also Abutalebi, Cappa, and Perani 2001).

Thus, the consensus seems to be that languages are not stored separately, but that different language functions may be accessed differently and may therefore be affected in different ways (or remain unaffected) by certain anatomical impairments. Bilinguals whose languages are specialised for different types of activities or were acquired in different ways may show asymmetrical impairment or recovery patterns.[6] Asymmetrical aphasia and late L2 acquisition are therefore intrinsically related as far as issues of lateralisation are concerned.

4.3.2 Models of bilingual language processing

With the rise of interest in theoretical models of speech production, some of the questions raised by Weinreich concerning the mode of accessing a bilingual lexicon have been revisited. In line with the influential model by Levelt, Roelofs, and Meyer (1999), most recent proposals recognise a conceptual level in speech production that is language-independent, alongside a language level that is subdivided into two (or more) subsystems. It is noteworthy that most models tend to focus just on the accessibility and production of the lexicon, and few address issues of grammar. Supporters of the Chomskyan minimalist programme have argued that bilinguals have separate lexicons and phonological systems for their languages, but a uniform syntactic system that generates the syntax for both languages (Macswan 2000). By contrast, Sharewood Smith's (1991) modular model of language processing separates linguistic subsystems and implies that such subsystem separation is applicable within each of the languages. Ullman (2001) points out that age of exposure to L2 has an adverse effect on the learning of grammar, but not vocabulary. Consequently, he argues for a neural separation of lexicon and grammar, which are organised in terms of two distinct memory sets, 'declarative' and 'procedural', respectively. The procedural memory is non-conscious. Ullman proposes that late L2 learners rely heavily on declarative memory rather than procedural memory to learn grammar.

A point of controversy is whether the speaker selects a language before selecting (content) lemmas and (phonological) word-forms, as suggested by Costa and Caramazza (1999), or whether lemmas and word-forms from both languages are candidates that compete with one another for selection as a means of representing an abstract (pre-linguistic or mental) concept, as advocated e.g. by Green (1998) and others. Hermans *et al.* (1998) provide experimental evidence that suggests that bilinguals are unable to suppress activation of their first language while carrying out naming tasks in their second language. Relying on subjects' reactions to interference stimuli in the form of words that are phonologically related to the translation equivalent of the target word, they show that Dutch–English bilinguals activate the Dutch name for a picture during the initial stages of preparation for the naming of the picture in the foreign language English. It appears that in the search for the correct word all lemmas that match the conceptual specification are activated. But if all possible lemmas are activated, how does the bilingual select the appropriate word-form?

Kroll and Sunderman (2003) propose that selection of an L2 form involves suppression of the selection mechanism for L1 words. This follows the selection of the conceptual representation in the first instance, which in turn is followed by the selection of a lemma at which level alternatives are still available in both languages. The suppression mechanism undergoes different stages of development during the acquisition process. At an early stage there is reliance on word-for-word translation, and so accessibility to the L2 word-form is via the word-form in L1. With increasing proficiency there is an increase in the ability to 'conceptually mediate' L2, in other words, to access a language-neutral concept, which in turn grants direct access to the L2 word-form. This follows Kroll and Stewart's (1994) proposal that different weighting is given to word-level and to conceptual mediation at different stages of the acquisition process. Green (1998; cf. also Green and Price 2001) offers a similar solution. He proposes a model according to which a conceptualiser is driven by a goal to achieve some effect through language (i.e. to communicate). The model assumes that the languages of an individual are subsets of the language system as a whole. The conceptualiser selects lemmas, which are tagged for language. An inhibition control mechanism is then applied to reject certain lemmas from proceeding into speech production based on the tags that are associated with them.

Inspired by a body of both experimental and naturally occurring evidence, many other researchers agree that bilinguals are unable to activate or de-activate languages on a wholesale basis. Gollan and Silverberg (2001) investigate tip-of-the-tongue states – a state of lexical activation that falls between knowing a word and being able to produce it without difficulty. Results with Hebrew–English bilinguals indicate that they have more retrieval failures compared to English monolinguals. This can be explained by the higher number of competitors that a word has in the bilingual lexicon, indicating in turn that bilinguals are unable to simply switch off one of their lexicons. Further support for a model of simultaneous activation of L1 and L2 lemmas is found in Poulisse's (1999) work on L1 substitution slips (where a speaker replaces an L2 item by a corresponding item from the L1).

Grosjean's (1998, 2001) model is considered a novel breakthrough especially in acknowledging that language separation is not necessarily the default option, and that for bilinguals language mixing is neither pathological nor exceptional. Grosjean suggests that bilinguals can select between various language modes; these are arranged on a continuum between monolingual and bilingual. Bilinguals enter the bilingual language mode when they communicate with or are listening to other bilinguals. They are typically in a monolingual mode when communicating with monolinguals. In the bilingual mode, both languages are active, but one is the primary language of processing. Thus, every mode will have a base language, but the degree of activation of the other language will vary across the modes. Modes can be selected according to interlocutor, purpose, or setting of the conversation.

Many of these ideas are integrated by Paradis (2004) into what he refers to as a comprehensive neurolinguistic model of bilingualism. In this model, the lexicon, which is part of the linguistic system, and the conceptual system are understood to be two separate neurofunctional entities (thus accounting for aphasia patients' ability to recognise a concept while they are unable to retrieve the word for it). A concept thus exists and is accessible independently of the lexical item that represents it in the language system. It is further proposed that bilinguals access each lexical item directly, and not via a filter for the appropriate language. Finally, it is assumed that each language is an independent neurofunctional module or subsystem within the language system. Activation of one language module results automatically in the inhibition of the other, unless the speaker is in a bilingual mode, in which case elements of the other module are integrated into a frame created by the base language. How then does the speaker select the language-correct target word? Paradis (2004: 207) does not object to the notion of a language 'tag' as a convenient abstraction, but insists that a lexical item's membership in a language subsystem Lx or Ly is a product of the general metalinguistic knowledge. The unconscious process that allows a bilingual speaker to recognise the language subsystem to which a word belongs is of the same kind as the process that allows a monolingual to determine whether a word is contextually appropriate. There is therefore according to Paradis no need to postulate a language tag that is specific to bilinguals.

Conclusions from recent experimental work by Kroll, Bobb, and Wodniecka (2006), based on picture-naming tasks administered to bilinguals, appear to be compatible with Paradis's model: they suggest that there is no single locus for language selection, but that instead language selection depends on a set of factors, including experience, the demands of the production task, and the degree of activity of the non-target language. Speakers thus appear to take a pragmatic rather than strictly modular approach to language selection. All this adds up to a growing trend to approach the bilingual repertoire as an integrated whole, rather than as a delineated combination of self-contained systems. As we saw in Chapter 2, the bilingual's development is marked by the gradual acquisition of the skill to identify the appropriateness of words and constructions in particular contexts and sets of interaction contexts. Language tags only account for part of the story. In certain contexts, it is both appropriate and effective for the bilingual to 'cross the demarcation boundary' and exploit elements of an L2 during interaction in L1.

4.3.3   Bilingual speech errors

Further evidence favouring flexibility in the processing of repertoire components comes from bilinguals' occasional failure to identify and select 'language-correct' items.

Consider first the case of a young but linguistically mature Hebrew–English bilingual, brought up partly in Israel and partly in the United States. At the age of around eight he is addressed, in Israel, by a monolingual Hebrew speaker of approximately the same age, who asks him a yes/no question (cf. Matras 2007a):

(8)   Hebrew; asked a yes-no question by Hebrew monolingual of same age group:
       S: uh-húh. [ʔʌ̃'hʌ̃]
          'Yes'.
       H: ((looks puzzled)) ma?
          'What'?

In his reply the speaker uses an affirmative signal, one which he does not attribute to either of the language-specific sectors of his linguistic repertoire – a kind of language-independent linguistic gesture. In other words, it is a communicative sign which in the speaker's experience and competence is not 'tagged' for any language-specific contexts. In reality, this sequence of segments is not understood in a Hebrew context/setting and is not familiar to the hearer with a monolingual Hebrew repertoire. Virtually the same kind of communicative breakdown occurs at a somewhat later age, in the United States, when the speaker is confronted with a question by an English monolingual adult:

(9)   English; having been asked a yes-no question by English monolingual adult:
       S: ts-. [ɹə]
          'No'.
       H: ((awaits response))

The click-related implosive sound indicating a negative reply is common in the eastern Mediterranean region, but meaningless to the English monolingual hearer, who continues to await a response. In both situations, the speaker mistook operators that help regulate the interaction for language-independent or universal pragmatic gestures. While the choice of these particular markers in these contexts allows us to infer that there are some gaps in the speaker's communicative competence, it is interesting to note that the selection errors pertain to elements that are both non-verbal and highly automated.

Consider now yet another excerpt from the television interview with a native speaker of German (cf. Example (7)). Here, he is being asked about his role in an arms smuggling scheme:

(10)   S: Well jus/ just the way ə ə the m/ the weapons ə brought ə/ I/ I have
          brought to London, nə, und I/ I have told them the truth, nə, that
          they were brought by car, nə and/ and ə . . .
       H: Were they very interested?
       S: Yes, they were very interested, nə, to know how, nə.

The excerpt is characterised by the frequent insertion of the (northern) German tag nə. Its consistent appearance suggests that it is not attributed by the speaker to any single component of his repertoire, but has the status of a subset-independent structure within the repertoire, a kind of universal communicative gesture, applicable with no setting-related constraints. In reality, of course, nə is completely foreign to English speakers and fails to achieve its communicative function when directed at a monolingual English addressee. But note also the insertion of German *und* 'and' in the first utterance. Although it is not clear whether the speaker noticed his error, as no self-repair is inserted, one can safely assume that he is aware of the German origin of the word and aware of its English equivalent. The selection of *und* is a kind of malfunction, a lapse in control over the selection of context-appropriate elements and the inhibition of those that are not appropriate. Significantly, both the gesture-like utterance-final *nə* and the connector *und* are part of the inventory of discourse-organising devices through which the speaker monitors and directs the hearer's processing of propositional content.

Example (11) documents a conversation that takes place at a wedding cele-bration in Germany. With the exception of the participants in this conversation, nearly all people at the event are German. BO and MA are native speakers of Polish, which they use among themselves; but they reside in Israel and are fluent in Hebrew. YA is a native speaker of Hebrew. All three are fluent in Ger-man. MA had just taken a photograph, and is confronted with the remarks by BO and YA:

(11)   a. BO lo   haya fleš.
                not was   flash
                'There was no flash.'

         b. YA lo   haya fleš.
                not was   flash
                'There was no flash.'

         c. MA lo   haya fleš?
                not was   flash
                'Was there no flash?'

         d. YA lo
                no
                'No.'

         e. MA *Doch*, haya fleš!
                yes   was   flash
                '*Yes*, there *was* a flash!'

German is not used habitually in this circle of speakers, and so we need not assume a conventionalisation of Hebrew–German switching habits along the lines of what Maschler (1997) calls an 'emergent bilingual grammar'. And yet it appears that the situative dominance of German as the language of interaction with virtually everybody present outside this circle of three speakers licenses the use of *doch* in segment (e); that is, the speaker considers it an appropriate insertion in the present context. It is noteworthy that Hebrew lacks a contrastive-affirmative marker that is equivalent in meaning to German *doch*, although there is a construction with equivalent function.[7] Inserting German *doch* may therefore indeed be a matter of 'convenience', though it is precisely this 'convenience' aspect that merits our attention: The speaker is utilising an element of her multilingual repertoire that appropriately captures the intention she wishes to convey during this particular speech act. She is doing this despite the fact that the language of the immediate context is Hebrew, backed quite possibly not just by the fact that all participants in the interaction know German, but also by the presence of German in the immediate surroundings. Thus, the speaker's selection of elements from the repertoire is pragmatic, and uninhibited by any abstract 'system'-affiliation of the relevant word-form. Note again, however, that we are dealing not with a content-lexeme, but with a discourse particle that regulates interactional roles.

The previous examples have shown that speakers may avail themselves of utterance-modifying elements in discourse in ignorance of their belonging to the non-selected language subsystem, or even despite their subsystem-affiliation. We now move on to a selection of examples that illustrates that speakers may at times suffer lapses in the control over the correct item for selection, and employ, inadvertently, equivalents from the non-selected language of the repertoire. In (12), a speaker of Judeo-Spanish (Ladino) born in Saloniki, Greece, and raised in Israel, describes the relations between the Greek Jewish community of his childhood and its neighbours (cf. Matras 1998a):

(12)   a. S: Los eh/ *mekomiyím*,   los lokales, eran relasiones midžores de
                 the uh locals [Hebrew] the locals   were relations better   from
                 los ɣrexos ke vinieron de la turkía.
                 the Greeks who came from Turkey
                 '[With] The uh/ locals, the locals, relations were better than [with] the
                 Greeks who came from Turkey.'

         b.   Por ke los   ke   vinieron de   Turkía eran ublixados de tomar
                 because those who came   from Turkey were obliged   to take
                 lavoros de   los eh/ sitadinos/ siudadinos, si.
                 jobs   from the uh citizens   citizens   yes
                 'Because those who came from Turkey were obliged to take jobs
                 from the citizens/ citizens, yes.'

         c. H: *Mhm, mhm.*

         d. S: Az/ *eh* es/ entonses empesó la/ la kel/ la enemistad la más grande.
                 so uh   then   began   the the the that the rivalry   the most great
                 '*So then*/ uh/ th/ then the/ uh/ the greatest rivalry emerged.'

The speaker spontaneously inserts the Hebrew sequential marker *az* in segment (d), but proceeds to a self-repair, eventually substituting it through the Spanish marker *entonses*. In the stages leading to production and articulation of the utterance, the speaker's selection of a connective device that adequately matches the language-processing task at hand (the need to express a sequence of events) remains uninhibited by any subsystem-affiliation constraint and uncontrolled by constraints of context-bound appropriateness. Nevertheless, contrary to the previous Example (11), the speaker in (12) is not licensing himself to utilise his spontaneous choice, but rather correcting himself, accommodating to the context-bound selection of Ladino as the interaction language.

With reference to Green's (1998) model of bilingual speech production we might argue that (12d) represents a malfunction of the inhibition and control mechanism which de-selects items that are not appropriate in the particular context since they do not belong to the selected language of the interaction. We might add that the mode selected for the interaction in (12) is not what Grosjean (2001) would term a 'bilingual mode', although both participants are bilingual; rather, it is an interview situation in which the speaker is asked explicitly to recall events of his childhood in his native language Ladino. To call the insertion of *az* a 'malfunction' therefore seems justified. In fact, Green's (1998: 77) model foresees an effect on language switching if the supervisory attention system that is responsible for carrying out communicative tasks has to monitor several tasks simultaneously. Green likens mental control of language to the control of action. Some action is routine, and requires a more shallow level of control. When a task has been previously carried out, the relevant schema can be retrieved from memory. The selection of task schemas to achieve communicative goals is otherwise mediated through the supervisory attention system.

How can we explain the malfunction of the selection mechanism around the connector *az*? In previous work (Matras 1998a, 2000b, 2007a) I suggested that connectors, discourse markers, interjections, tags, and other particles are part of an apparatus with which the speaker monitors and directs the hearer's processing of propositional content. Engaging the monitor-and-directing apparatus is necessary in order to guarantee that the speaker can maintain assertive authority and pre-empt any alienation of the listener (which may come about if the speaker asserts unrealistic event chains, for instance). The greater the likelihood that the listener might reject a propositional chain, the greater the mental effort that is required on the part of the speaker to pre-empt such rejection by preparing the hearer for that chain. The monitoring-and-directing apparatus is therefore costly in terms of the attention that it demands from the speaker.

We might associate the monitoring-and-directing apparatus with various sets of automated schemas in the sense of Green's (1998) model, and assume that engagement in monitoring-and-directing requires effort from the supervisory attentional system. Such effort is likely to distract from the system's ability to simultaneously select among meaning- or function-equivalent (or even near-equivalent) counterparts in the multilingual repertoire. This may result in malfunction of the selection mechanism, or specifically of what Green calls the 'inhibition mechanism' which de-selects those meaning-equivalents that are contextually inappropriate (since they do not belong to the repertoire-subset that is chosen for the interaction).

How can we predict which word-form will, and which will not, be selected? In (12) the speaker initially selects the word-form from the language that is the principal language of his environment, and which he has been speaking since his adolescence in most settings except for his parental household – Hebrew. Ladino is his native language and the language that he speaks with relatives of his own and the older generation, but not the language of most everyday interactions. In terms of regularity and frequency of use, Hebrew is clearly the dominant language. Let us examine a few more examples. In (13) a group of four Israelis – the speaker, her husband, and two friends – are having lunch at a Chinese restaurant in Manchester, England. While they are engaged in conversation in Hebrew, a waiter appears to take their order. The speaker's husband takes the active role in ordering most of the items. In (13) the speaker intervenes and adds:

(13)   . . . and one Won Ton soup *avál*/ eh/ the vegetarian one.
                                     but

The Hebrew contrastive conjunction *avál* appears here, rather than English *but*; it is possible, though not obvious, that the error was noticed by the speaker, for there is a pause and hesitation, but no explicit self-repair. It is nevertheless obvious that the use of the Hebrew conjunction is a result of a selection malfunction; neither is any special effect intended (or possible to achieve through *avál*), nor does the speaker lack the proficiency to be able in principle to use the English conjunction *but*, nor can the communicative goal be achieved effectively through an intentional insertion of a Hebrew element, since the Chinese waiter does not have any knowledge of Hebrew. Humorous or other stylistic effects can be ruled out, too. The speaker thus simply produces an error in her selection of the target word-form. The target of the error is Hebrew, which is the speaker's dominant language by all relevant measures: it is her native language, the language used in the context of her family, the language she knows best, and the language used in the ongoing interaction with her friends at the restaurant.

In (14), the Saudi Ambassador to the United Kingdom gives an interview on BBC television,[8] commenting on plans for municipal elections in Saudi Arabia. In response to a question challenging him about the authorities' ability to ensure fair elections, he says:

(14)   I would beg to say that *yaʕni*/ the Kingdom is a very big territory.

For a trained diplomat speaking on national television about matters of state, it is certain that the insertion of the Arabic filler/tag *yaʕni* constitutes a non-volitional, potentially embarrassing clash with his own and his audience's expectations in respect of the well-formedness of his discourse. We can safely assume that the insertion is not intentional nor strategic in any way, but that it represents a lapse in the speaker's control over the mechanism that governs selection over repertoire components. Once again the target of the error is the speaker's native language; and once again the error involves a member of the class of items that serve monitoring-and-directing operations, intervening with and guiding the listener's processing of the discourse.

Lapses in adult bilinguals' control of the language selection mechanism around connectors are common, but they do not always favour the speaker's native language. In (15), a Czech academic whose foreign working language is generally English gives a brief survey of her research activities at a German-speaking academic forum. Note the 'slip' into English for the coordinating conjunction 'and':

(15)   ... in Norwegen/ über diese zwei Sprachen, Bokmål *and* Nynorsk,
          '... in Norway/ about these two languages, Bokmål *and* Nynorsk,

          und so weiter.
          and so on.'

In (16), a native speaker of Polish who has been living in Germany for the past decade or so meets friends from Germany in London, where she has been attending an advanced English language course and living with an English family during the past two weeks. She crosses the street from the café where the party is sitting to inspect a restaurant which is said to be decorated in Polish style. Having returned and confirmed that the style is on the whole indeed Polish, she says:

(16)   ... bis auf/ bis auf   die Tischdecken, *because*/ eh weil   sie...
          '... except/ except for the tablecloth,   *because*/ uh because it...'

The error is noticed by the speaker, and a self-repair is inserted. Finally, in (17) a native speaker of German who has been living and working in Britain for the past three years is communicating in Hebrew, a language in which she is reasonably fluent but which requires some effort from her (commenting on an old church building that is being used as a warehouse):

(17)   ani xoševet   še ze lo   knesiya *anymore*
          I   think.SG.F that this NEG church
          'I think that this is no longer a church'

   Now, in (15)–(17), the selected item was not the word-form from the speaker's native language. In all three cases the target was a foreign language, in (16) even a language in which the speaker is not fully fluent. However, in all three cases the speakers are running through specific task schemas that they have generally or in the immediate past been operating routinely in the foreign language. Note that we must accept an enhanced definition of 'task schema' here, one that takes into account elements of the setting. In (16), the speaker has been directing her mental efforts over the past weeks toward learning English, and her routine task schemas run in English. This does not mean that she is unable to communicate in German; but it means that the automated task that is activated selects the English connector, and due to the high attention-load of the monitoring-and-directing mechanism operating around the connector, the selection mechanism fails to reject the more routine, automated schema that is retrieved from the shorter-term memory and to replace it by the more context-appropriate word-form. Similar circumstances apply in (15), where the task is associated with institutional communication at a professional conference abroad, for which the routine schema in English is selected; and in (17), where English is the routine mode of communication once the speaker's native language, German, is inhibited.

The selection of English in (17) suggests that the speaker is suppressing her native language, German, as a way of facilitating the selection of her second foreign language, Hebrew, but fails to inhibit the English form. Many multilinguals are familiar with this phenomenon; for instance, going on holiday from England to Spain, and ending up inadvertently making a request in French. It does not seem necessary to postulate a suppression or inhibition mechanism to explain this phenomenon, if one accepts (1) the principle of default selection of routine schemas, (2) the association of, for example, a foreign setting with a routine schema in which French is normally selected, and (3) the principle of malfunction of selection control under duress, which could mean tension, fatigue, or the diversion of attention for highly complex and challenging processing operations such as monitoring-and-directing.

Although in all these cases it is hard to argue for a general dominance of the 'successful', selected language in the lives of the respective speakers, given the particular settings one can speak of a 'pragmatically dominant' language (cf. Matras 1998a). The pragmatically dominant language is the language that the speaker associates most closely at the moment of interaction with the routine implementation of communicative tasks that are similar to the ongoing task. It is also the language in which the speaker feels compelled to perform appropriately, and which is therefore naturally and spontaneously prioritised unless overridden by the selection mechanism. To reformulate this statement once again in terms that are more congruent with our view of the linguistic repertoire as dynamic rather than divided into 'language systems': pragmatically dominant are those communicative schemas, word-forms, and constructions that, at a given time and setting, constitute the speaker's preferred, routine or default choice for the completion of a specific communicative task or sets of tasks. As seen in the previous three examples, the pragmatically dominant language can shift in different settings. On the other hand, speakers of a minority language who find themselves frequently having to interact with members of the majority language group in the majority language are likely to treat this majority language as pragmatically dominant in a stable way. This is because the tolerance level among monolingual interlocutors from the majority group toward slips into the minority language is likely to be low, while members of the bilingual minority are likely to (but will not always) be more tolerant toward use of the majority language. The suppression of the minority language in favour of the majority language will therefore be unidirectional.

A final note is in order concerning the functional class of items affected by selection malfunctions that favour the pragmatically dominant language. We have so far named two such classes: The first consisted of semi-lexical speech-act markers, such as the North-American English affirmative signal, the Eastern Mediterranean negative click, and the German tag. We identified them as likely candidates for erroneous selection since they escape the speaker's attention when it is directed exclusively or primarily at 'proper' lexical word-forms. The second class consisted of connectivity and interaction operators and included coordinating and subordinating conjunctions, sequential markers, and fillers (such as Arabic *yaʕni*). These items are clearly recognisable as language-particular; yet as argued above, they are prone to be affected by selection-malfunction due to their role in monitoring-and-directing operations. This role demands increased attention, which comes at the expense of firm control over the selection and inhibition mechanism. As a result, the default selection of the routine, pragmatically dominant schema is not overridden. (The case of *doch* in (11) is different, since it appears to be consciously licensed by the speaker.)[9] To which class does the phasal adverb in (17) – *anymore* – belong? I have proposed before (Matras 1998a) that phasal adverbs, focus particles, and numerous other grammatical function words (such as indefinites and comparative and superlative markers) are functionally related to the class of monitoring-and-directing operators, in that they process hearer-sided expectations and presuppositions. The 'discontinuative' (cf. van der Auwera 1998) phasal adverb *anymore* locates an event with reference to expectations concerning its duration, which the speaker and hearer are presumed to share. The presumption of consensus with the hearer entails, from the point of view of the speaker, a risk factor at the interaction level; for the hearer might reject the consensus and differ in respect of the expectation. This 'risk-factor' is the trigger of tension and hence increased attention, which in turn potentially weakens the selection mechanism. The 'risk-factor' may be predicted to increase the greater the potential clash between hearer-sided and speaker expectations, which is why expressions of 'contrast' can be expected to be particularly vulnerable to a malfunction of the selection mechanism.

4.4   Conclusion

In this chapter we examined the cognitive background for what Weinreich (1953) correctly defined as the only true locus of language contact – the bilingual speaker. We noted that in all three fields of investigation examined here – bilingual first-language acquisition, second-language acquisition, and models of bilingual language processing – a trend has gradually emerged to look beyond the confinements of a two-language-system approach to bilingualism, and to adopt a more dynamic and pragmatic understanding of bilingualism as a complex repertoire of linguistic schemas, word-forms, and constructions, accompanied by complex, context-sensitive social conventions on their appropriate selection. In this respect, the bilingual repertoire is not fundamentally different from the monolingual repertoire; both consist of a continuum of speech modes. The major difference is the presence, potentially, at the respective ends of the multilingual continuum of speech modes that are not mutually comprehensible (though even speakers of entirely different languages might find a rudimentary form of communication through gestures and spontaneous accommodation; while the monolingual continuum can similarly hold registers at its opposite ends that are barely mutually intelligible).

This general perspective on bilingualism has implications for our understanding of all the three areas: in bilingual first-language acquisition it calls for a focus on the way infants gradually acquire the rules of linguistic behaviour enabling them to become competent multilinguals (rather than to separate abstract language systems). In second-language acquisition it requires us to give attention to the creative strategies that learners adopt in order to communicate and to the enabling role that interference and transfer can have. In language processing we are challenged to explore models that account for the availability in principle of the entire repertoire of structures during speech production, allowing experienced bilinguals to incorporate contextual knowledge into the selection procedure of appropriate elements.

We devoted some attention in this chapter to malfunctions of the selection mechanism among experienced as well as relatively experienced bilinguals, and it is useful to recapitulate the main points here again. We identified one cause of mal-selection in inadequate pragmatic competence and neglect on the part of relatively experienced bilinguals to suppress communicative routines that are semi-lexical and gesture-like, and so are erroneously treated as universally appropriate, irrespective of language-context. Another cause is the competition for supervisory attention of the speech production mechanism as a whole. This is triggered by language processing operations that rely intensively on a presuppositional basis and so seek to pre-empt possible clashes between hearer and speaker expectations, and are therefore high-risk operations in the interaction-pragmatic sense. Malfunction will tend to result in performance of the routine, pragmatically dominant schema for the particular communicative task. In Chapter 5 we shall return to cognitive processing mechanisms and malfunctions in particular and explore their connection to contact-induced language change.

5 Crossing the boundaries: codeswitching in conversation

5.1 Defining codeswitching

Codeswitching is the term that is normally applied to the alternation of languages within a conversation. Some authors use 'codemixing' to refer to language mixing within the phrase or utterance, reserving 'codeswitching' for the alternation of languages in-between utterances or phrases (inter-sentential switching). Others employ 'codemixing' to denote the structures that are the product of language mixing and do not occur in the speech of monolinguals. Yet another use of 'codemixing' is as a cover term for various types of language mixing phenomena. In the absence of a general consensus, I shall be using the two terms – 'codeswitching' and 'codemixing' – interchangeably.

A distinction is commonly made between 'alternational' codeswitching – alternating languages between utterances or sentences –, and 'insertional' codeswitching – the insertion of a word or phrase into an utterance or sentence formed in a particular base or frame language (Muysken 2000a). As we shall see, the two phenomena are frequently, if not indeed generally, motivated by different functional goals. (Recall that in Chapter 2 we discussed the contrast between the insertional switch in Examples (33)–(35), and the alternational switch in Example (36).)

5.1.1 Language mixing in the bilingual mode

The study of codeswitching elevated a phenomenon that had been traditionally viewed by normative grammarians as 'language corruption' to an investigation field in its own right. The underlying assumption in the literature devoted to this field is that codeswitching is not arbitrary, but that it follows various regularities (cf. Fishman 1965, Clyne 1967, Pfaff 1979, Poplack 1980). Researchers have since been focusing on situational and contextual motivations for switching as well as on the structural characteristics of codeswitching, aiming to identify general patterns. Switching is considered functional in the sense that speakers are motivated by various factors to switch at particular points in the discourse. At the same time it is clear that language mixing is multilayered and that it can serve various different purposes even in the same conversation. The

following extract from the narrative of a speaker of the Kelderaš/Lovari variety
of Romani, who was raised and resides in Hamburg in northern Germany, provides an illustration of the complexity and multilayered nature of conversational
codeswitching in bilingual settings:

(1)   Lovari Romani/German:
          a. S: Amende akana te merel   varekon,   naj   konik   kothe
                 1PL.LOC now   if die.3SG somebody is.not somebody there

                 bešel   amensa.
                 sit.3SG 1PL.INSTR

          b.   Amen   korkore si te   bešas, ke   naj   konik.
                 1PL.NOM   alone   is COMP sit.1PL because is.not somebody

          c.   Var/
                 some

          d. H: Feri e   familja.
                 only the family

          e. S: Feri e   familja si.
                 only the family is

          f. H: Hm.

          g. S: Aj varekana kana merelas   varekon   anda kaver foruri
                 and sometime when die.3SG.REM somebody from other towns

                 avenas,   ta   kidilas   pe   po šela   Rom.
                 come.3PL.REM and collect.3SG.REM REFL at hundreds Roms

          h.   Taj bešenas   kodole   njamonsa   kodola trin račja,
                 and sit.3PL.REM those.OBL relatives.INSTR those three nights

                 te   les/   te   na s/ vorbinas   lenca,   te
                 COMP take.2SG COMP NEG speak.3PL.REM 3PL.INSTR COMP

                 len   le   tele pa gindo   pa kodo hačares   sa.
                 take.3PL 3PL.OBL down on thought on this understand.2SG all

          i.   E familja či   trobulas   te   del   pe   gindo sar
                 the family NEG must.3SG.REM COMP give.3SG REFL tought how

                 te   praxov   les   si te   žav   kudka te   kerav
                 COMP bury.1SG 3SG.OBL is COMP go.1SG there COMP do.1SG

                 kuko *formularo* kothe.
                 that form   there

          j. H: Ja, mhm, mhm.

          k. S: Kodo nas   la familjako   bajo, kodo či kerelas   e
                 this was.not the family.GEN thing this NEG do.3SG.REM the

                 familja, kodo e   sterine Rom kerenas.
                 family this the strange Roms do.3PL.REM

          l.   Aj akana, *obwohl* kadka meres   ke   muljas   tuke
                 and now   although here die.2SG because died.3SG 2SG.DAT

varekon,   hačares,   *du bist total fertig*,   tu   si
somebody   understand.2SG   you are totally devastated 2SG is

te   žas   inke te   des   tu   gindo kaj   te
COMP   go.2SG   still COMP give.2SG 2SG thought where COMP

praxov   les,   kudka si   te   žav,   *Bestattungsinstitut*,
bury.1SG 3SG.OBL   here   is   COMP go.1SG funeral home

ehm/ pa/ pa/ pa *Meldeamt*,   eh   *Geb/ Sterbeurkunde*,
on   on   on registration office bir   death certificate

m. H: Mhm.

n. S: Hačares,   *es ist weg*.
        understand.2SG   it is gone

o.   *Beispiel* akana feri phendem tuke,   hačares.
        example   now   only said.1SG 2SG.DAT   understand.2SG

p. H: Mm.

q. S: *Es sind   so   alles, alles verschiedene Sachen*.
        it be.PL such all   all   different   things

r.   Kaj   trobul   tu   kaver manuš, čiro   manuš, kaj
        where need.3SG 2SG.OBL other person 2SG.POSS person REL

        hačarel   tu,   kaj vi vov sa kade hačarel   sar
        understand.3SG you   REL too he all such understand.3SG how

        tu,   naj,   *ist weg*.
        you   is.not is gone

s.   Ke   vi   amari   doš si, *wir haben uns   isoliert...*
        because too 1PL.POSS.F fault is we have   REFL.1PL isolated

t. H: Mm.

u. S: ...katar e   kaver Rom.
        from   the other Roms

v.   Ame bešas   ando Hamburg.
        we live.1PL in

w.   Ame naj   ame   *kontakto* kavre   Romensa   ke
        we is.not 1PL.OBL   contact   other.OBL roms.INSTR because

        naj   ame   vrama akana.
        is.not 1PL.OBL   time now

x.   Dikh o ( ): Me či   dikhav les kurkensa,   šonensa.
        see the   I NEG   see.1SG him weeks.INSTR months.INSTR

        manchmal
        sometimes

y.   *Er hat seine Sache zu tun, ich hab meine Sache zu tun*.
        he has his   thing to do I   have my   thing to do

z.   Muro   phral pale, mure   dad   mure
        1SG.POSS.M   brother again 1SG.POSS.PL father 1SG.POSS.PL

<table>
<tr><td></td><td>phralen</td><td>či</td><td>dikhav</td><td>po duj-trin</td><td>kurke.</td></tr>
<tr><td></td><td>brothers.OBL</td><td>NEG</td><td>see.1SG</td><td>on two three</td><td>weeks</td></tr>
</table>

aa.   *Und das find ich das ist krank.*
and that find I   that is sick

a. S: Nowadays, when somebody dies in our community, there is nobody who mourns with us.

b.   We have to mourn alone, because there is nobody.

c.   Some/

d. H: Just the family.

e. S: There's just the family.

f. H: Hm.

g. S: And there used to be times when somebody died they came over from other towns and hundreds of Roma got together.

h.   And they sat with the relatives for the three nights, to take/ so that they won't/ they talked to them in order to distract their thoughts away from it all, you understand.

i.   The family didn't have to think about how should I bury him, I have to go there, I have to fill in this form there.

j. H: Yes, mhm, mhm.

k. S: It wasn't the family's problem, the family didn't have to do it, strangers did it.

l.   And now, *although* you're dying here because one of your people died, you understand, *you're totally devastated*, you still have to go and think about where should I bury him, I have to go there, *funeral home*, ehm/ to/ to/ to the *registration office*, eh *birth/death certificate*,

m. H: Mhm.

n. S: You understand, *it's gone*.

o.   I just gave you an *example* now, you understand.

p. H: Mm.

q. S: *It's all, all these different things.*

r.   When you need another person, your own person, who understands you, who sees everything just like you do, there isn't anyone, *it's gone*.

s.   Because, it's our own fault too, *we've isolated ourselves . . .*

t. H: Mm.

u. S: . . . from the other Roms.

v.   We live in Hamburg.

w.   We don't have any contact to the other Roms, because we don't have time now.

x.   Look at ( ): I don't see him for weeks, for months *sometimes*.

y.   *He has his things to do, I have my things to do.*

z.   My brother too, my father, my brothers, I don't see them for two three weeks.

aa.   *And I find it sick.*

Example (1) is a nice illustration of the way bilinguals speak in what Grosjean (2001) calls the 'bilingual mode'. Arguably, most interactions in Romani occur by default in a 'bilingual mode', since all Roms are bilingual from a very young age and since Romani is almost always the language of informal interactions. Possible exceptions to this generalisation are conversations among Roms from different countries who do not share a second language, especially speech of a more ceremonial nature in such international encounters, as well as the recently emerging institutional discourse in Romani, such as radio broadcasts. In the present example, the context is that of an informal but tape-recorded interview, the topic of which is life within the Romani community. Romani is the selected language of the interaction, and this choice is respected for the duration of most of the conversation. But the speaker frequently inserts German words, phrases, and utterances.

In interpreting codeswitches, we assume that language alternation is not entirely arbitrary, but that it is driven by various levels of control over language-processing. Both insertional and alternational switches may be motivated by difficulties of retrievability of adequate means of expression in one of the languages, by stylistic effects and the creative structuring of the discourse, or by language-specific associations evoked during the conversation. Following Clyne (1967), the motivation for the switch is usually referred to as the 'trigger'.

Word retrievability as a trigger for switching is seen in segment (s). The switch into German in *wir haben uns isoliert* 'we've isolated ourselves' is triggered by the availability in German of a particular expression – 'isolated' – that is not readily available in Romani. Although the depiction of separation of the family from other Roms might also have been delivered in Romani, the specific concept of isolation as captured by the German expression offers the speaker an opportunity to represent the state of affairs more precisely. We witness here the dynamic and flexible nature of the bilingual repertoire, especially when used in the bilingual mode, free or relatively free of situation-bound constraints on the choice of individual expressions. The speaker is able to begin her argument in Romani (*Ke vi amari doš si* 'because it's also our own fault'), insert a German verb phrase that captures the events and justifies her argument (*wir haben uns isoliert* 'we have isolated ourselves'), and then complete the very same sentence in Romani (*katar e kaver Rom* 'from the other Roms').

Alternational switches in Example (1) can be divided into two classes, based on their discourse-related function. The first group includes phrase-level paraphrases and reiterations. These are often used to repeat a point that has just been made in Romani, often adding a special nuance by employing an idiomatic expression (i.e. one that exists in German and is appropriate for capturing the content intended, but is difficult to translate). In segment (l) the speaker describes the state of a bereaved family member in Romani, only to reiterate using the German idiom *du bist total fertig* 'you are totally devastated [lit. 'completed']'; in lines (n) and (r) she uses the phrase *ist weg* 'it's gone' to paraphrase a point that had just been made concerning the disappearance of earlier customs, with the second occurrence immediately following the Romani *naj* 'there isn't' almost as a literal translation. These reiterations are stylistic choices made by the speaker to emphasise a point of view and thereby to evoke the hearer's identification with her viewpoint.

The second type of alternational switch appears at the utterance-level. It is used in the excerpt to mark out side-comments, explanations, and evaluations that are external to the main narration line. Here too, codeswitching supports the structure of the presentation. Sometimes the switch into German serves to highlight a summary of ideas that have been presented earlier, as in segment (q), *es sind alles, alles verschiedee Sachen* 'It's all, all these different things', and in segment (aa), *Und das finde ich das ist krank* 'And I find this is sick'. In segment (y) the switch into *Er hat seine Sache zu tun, ich habe meine Sache zu tun* 'He has his things to do, I have my things to do' serves as both illustration and clarification of the immediately preceding statement. The contrast between the two languages is used here to set apart different speech acts as discrete moves within the interaction, each pursuing a different goal; we shall return to the conversational functions of codeswitching below.

5.1.2   Single-word insertions and their integration

Considerable attention has been given in the research literature to the distinction between single-word insertions and 'borrowing'. In the broader context of general linguistics, 'borrowing' usually refers to the diachronic process by which languages enhance their vocabulary (or other domains of structure), while 'codeswitching' is reserved for instances of spontaneous language mixing in the conversation of bilinguals. This raises the issue of the precise criteria by which to distinguish established borrowings from spontaneous insertions in the speech of bilinguals. Some studies have relied on frequency measures, but comparability among them is impaired due to the absence of any uniform standard according to which a form's frequency of occurrence could be assessed.

A further distinction criterion is the degree of integration of the item. Poplack, Sankoff, and Miller (1988) propose that lexical insertions fall into two groups: those that are structurally integrated from the onset, and those that are not. Structural integration can occur in the speech of bilinguals independently of frequency of use. It is therefore not necessarily the product of a prolonged, diachronic process. Poplack, Sankoff, and Miller conclude that borrowing and codeswitching are separate phenomena from the onset. They introduce the term 'nonce borrowing' as a designation for on-the-spot borrowings that are structurally integrated but have not necessarily reached a wide level of propagation within the speech community or even within a corpus (see already Poplack 1980).

In Chapter 4 we saw that second-language learners employ insertional codeswitching as a way to compensate for lexical gaps in the target language. An effort is sometimes made to integrate such insertions spontaneously into the structure of the target language, as was the case with *leaf-o* and *business-a* in the speech of Igbo-Nigerian in Italy (Goglia 2006). This integration effort is a pragmatic attempt to reconcile the need to import English words into the conversation with the wish to comply with the choice of Italian as the language of the interaction. Speakers allow themselves discretion as to the extent to which they pursue such strategies. The choices that they make will depend on a variety of factors, among them their confidence in the two languages, their relation to the interlocutor, and their assessment of the interlocutor's expectations concerning language use, as well as any constraints imposed by the interaction setting, by the goals of language mixing, and by the type of structures that it involves.

In Example (1), a frequent target for insertions from German is institutional terminology, including names for institutions and institutional procedures. We find several of those in segment (l): *Bestattungsinstitut* 'funeral home', *Meldeamt* 'registration office', and *Sterbeurkunde* 'death certificate'. There is perhaps a double motivation to use these German terms. First, in the absence of Romani institutions there is no obvious Romani terminology; translating the terms requires effort that would not be well invested since the terms are not used frequently enough and since a monolingual Romani context is virtually non-existent. Second, institutions and their procedures constitute unique referents, much like proper nouns. The use of the original name evokes associations with the original setting and allows the speaker to import the image of that setting directly into the context of the ongoing conversation. Use of the German terms thus supports the authenticity of the description.

We've already encountered specific behaviour around terms for unique referents in Chapter 2. Translation equivalents for unique referents were acquired at a slower rate compared to other lexemes; and at a later stage insertional switches were used to refer to institutional concepts. We see here that the latter strategy continues to be at the disposal of the adult, experienced bilingual. Backus (1996) describes two distinct factors that promote insertional switches. The first is 'specificity', which favours the insertion of names of specific or unique referents such as proper nouns. The second is 'awareness', which supports the insertion of words with more transparent meanings that are clearly distinguishable from possible translation equivalents in the receiving language. Names of institutions neatly satisfy both criteria: They designate unique and specific referents, and the fact that they belong to the world of associations of the second language is transparent.

Further German nominal insertions are *Beispiel* 'example' in segment (o), *formularo* '(application) form' in segment (i) (German *Formular*), and *kontakto* 'contact' in segment (w) (German *Kontakt*). Note that the latter two are integrated phonologically into Romani – a trilled /r/ is used, and the vowels are short – and that they carry the inflectional ending *-o*.[1] This integration process resembles very much the one observed for diachronic loans – borrowings from other languages with which the speaker is not familiar, which have entered the language in previous generations – such as *gindo* 'thought', from Romanian, or *vrjama* 'time', from Slovak/Polish. It appears then that some spontaneous insertions of German nouns are integrated to sound and inflect like Romani words, while with others the speaker prefers to activate the original German form.

There are no obvious semantic or formal triggers for the integration process. Instead, we must attribute the difference to distinct pragmatic strategies employed by the speaker to make use of her full vocabulary repertoire. The first of those strategies consists of creatively extending the vocabulary that is marked as Romani. The structural integration of words like *kontakto* and *formularo* is a token of the speaker's judgement that such concepts can or should be accepted as part of any regular Romani-speaking context. The speaker thus acts as language innovator (much like the Igbo-Nigerian learners cited in Chapter 4). The alternative strategy is to make use of the bilingual mode to activate the world of concepts and associations of the second language as part of the ongoing interaction. This is the preferred strategy when mentioning unique referents, such as names of institutions, or when for some other reason the intended effect is to activate images that are associated with the German interaction context of the original concept. Thus, the use of *Beispiel* 'example' might indicate that a possible Romani word exists that is not retrievable at the present moment, or alternatively that providing an 'example' is treated as a discourse mode that is associated with a type of interaction setting such as analytical argumentation, in which German dominates.

It is noteworthy that structural criteria do not appear to be at work here. Unlike German *Kontákt* and *Formulár*,[2] the word *Béispiel* carries initial stress, and its integration into Romani would require a change of the stress position. But elsewhere in the conversation we find *feléro* 'error', based on German *Féhler*, a common loan in the Romani speech of this speaker's family, indicating that stress patterns do not constrain integration. Moreover, institutional and administrative terms may undergo structural integration if they deserve attention as pragmatically integrated concepts. Thus, during the period in which the recording of Example (1) took place, in 1989–1990, the German word *Áufenthalt* 'stay, sojourn', representing the administrative term *Aufenthaltserlaubnis* 'residence permit', was taken over regularly in Romani as *aufentálo*, in connection with the involvement of local Romani activists in Hamburg in a campaign to secure the residence status of immigrant Romani families from eastern Europe. It seems, then, that members of this particular speech community have a choice between adopting an insertion and flagging it as an integrated part of their expanded Romani vocabulary, and merely activating an insertion's meaning and the pragmatic context-associations that it evokes in the source language.

Not all bilingual constellations offer speakers such strategic choices. Some languages may lack any formal means of integration due to minimal use of inflectional morphology, as is the case with Chinese loans in Vietnamese; and some language pairs may have identical or near-identical phonologies so that no nativisation adjustment will be audible, as is the case with Kurdish insertions in Neo-Aramaic, or with Kriol insertions into the Australian language Jaminjung (cf. Schultze-Berndt 2007). Some bilingual communities might avoid any integration, either phonological or morphological, simply as part of their conventionalised language mixing patterns. This is often the case when there is stable access to monolingual contexts in both languages. The codeswitching patterns of American–Israeli Hebrew–English bilinguals are a good example (cf. Olshtain and Blum-Kulka 1989, Maschler 1998). In such settings, codeswitching is primarily a strategy to create bridges between the respective contexts, to activate images that are normally associated with the other language, or to exploit the contrast between the languages; it is not typically a strategy of extending the language-specific lexicon.

Contrasting with the type of insertions that we have seen so far, there is another type, consisting of items that have grammatical rather than lexical function. In Example (1) this type includes the concessive connector *obwohl* 'although' in segment (l) and the indefinite expression *manchmal* 'sometimes' in segment (x). They satisfy neither Backus's (1996) specificity criterion, being general grammatical operators rather than terms for unique referents, nor his awareness criterion, being routine processing markers with highly abstract rather than transparent semantic content. Both, however, are reminiscent of the type of operators that were discussed in Chapter 4 as frequent candidates for selection malfunctions or bilingual 'slips'.

In the present example it seems less likely that we are dealing with a production error and more likely that the speaker is taking the liberty to insert these items irrespective of their 'language tag'. Alongside other switches, this is one of the manifestations of the bilingual mode. Nonetheless, the choice of operators reveals that the motivation for switching here is not unrelated to the background for malfunction around the same class of elements, as described in Chapter 4. Here too, the operators represent a high degree of monitoring and intervention with hearer-sided processing. The contrastive-concessive 'although' pre-empts hearer-sided disapproval, while the indefinite 'sometimes' leaves the temporal specification open to hearer-sided interpretation. This intense monitoring of hearer-sided processing puts a high demand on the speaker's 'supervisory attention system' (Green 1998). This can be said to tempt the speaker into disengaging the selection mechanism (or the inhibition mechanism that de-selects candidate word-forms) altogether, leading to a fall-back to routine, automated task schemas in the 'pragmatically dominant' language.

The outcome of this procedure is the production of some relevant operators in German, embedded into Romani discourse. Romani, as a minority language, is normally spoken in the bilingual mode, whereas German is frequently used in monolingual contexts. Moreover, Romani is used in informal settings, mainly in the family domain or with close friends, whereas German occupies institutional domains and most business transactions and conversations with strangers. The Romani context is thus generally more tolerant toward linguistic variability, whereas in the German context social acceptance depends on adequate adherence to tightly defined linguistic norms. All this makes German the 'pragmatically dominant' language and the default language for routine and automated task schemas. We shall return to switching around discourse-level elements such as these in the final section of this chapter.

5.1.3   The codeswitching–borrowing continuum

Our discussion of Example (1) has shown that there are different levels of language mixing in conversation with different strategies employed in pursuit of different communicative goals, resulting in a variety of structural outcomes. The structural integration of lexical insertions is one of those pragmatic strategies. How, then, do we distinguish between insertions or one-word codeswitches, and borrowings?

Since we can assume that contact-induced language change begins with the use of items from another language in conversation by people who are either bilingual or have at least some exposure to another language, it seems useful to view the two phenomena as related points on a continuum. Myers-Scotton (1993b: 163ff.) distinguishes two semantic types of borrowed word-forms. The first are so-called Cultural forms (also: cultural loans). These are concepts that are new to the matrix language (or recipient language) culture. They include, for instance, institutional terminology. Such concepts are more easily adopted by monolinguals since they accompany new concepts or objects for which an earlier, established word does not yet exist. The second type are called Core forms and encompass those items that have equivalents in the recipient or matrix language. The use of core forms from another language presupposes bilingualism and so codeswitching, at least initially. The connection between codeswitching and borrowing is thus essentially a diachronic one. It involves an increase in the usage frequency of new word-forms and their potential adoption by monolinguals (cf. Myers-Scotton 1993b: 182–207).

Myers-Scotton's motivation to distinguish between borrowings and codeswitches stems at least in part from a need to satisfy the internal mechanics of her Matrix Language Frame model. The core of the model is a distinction between the Matrix Language (ML) and the Embedded Language (EL) (see Section 5.3), and it therefore also requires a mechanism to distinguish between ML and EL lexemes. If, however, we take a more pragmatic approach to the multilingual repertoire, then such a two-way distinction can conceivably be replaced by a continuum, where some lexemes enjoy greater variability of distribution in different interaction settings compared to others. Thus, for the German–English bilingual, the word *Internet* can be interpreted as a single concept, represented by a single word-form, equally employable in English and in German-speaking interaction contexts subject to the respective rules on morpho-syntactic formation within the sentence. Other English words may only be appropriate in a subset of German-language interaction contexts, perhaps for special effects, or only in the presence of bilingual interlocutors. Such a continuum would thus be dynamic, rather than strictly linear: It represents not just the length of time during which a

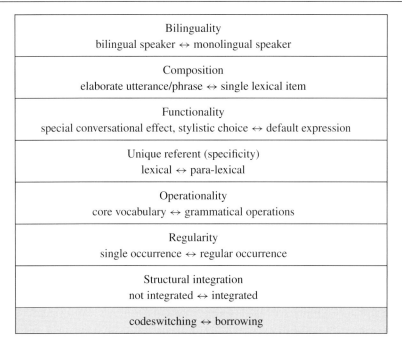

| Bilinguality |
| bilingual speaker ↔ monolingual speaker |
| **Composition** |
| elaborate utterance/phrase ↔ single lexical item |
| **Functionality** |
| special conversational effect, stylistic choice ↔ default expression |
| **Unique referent (specificity)** |
| lexical ↔ para-lexical |
| **Operationality** |
| core vocabulary ↔ grammatical operations |
| **Regularity** |
| single occurrence ↔ regular occurrence |
| **Structural integration** |
| not integrated ↔ integrated |
| codeswitching ↔ borrowing |

Figure 5.1 *Dimensions of the codeswitching–borrowing continuum.*

lexical item has been in use, but various constraints and preferences conditioning its employment in a variety of interaction contexts and settings.

It is therefore useful to identify several different dimensions that join together to determine the status of a word-form in a language contact constellation (Figure 5.1).

The first of those is the bilinguality continuum. Naturally, it makes sense to refer to 'codeswitching' only in connection with speakers who are able to maintain some kind of consistent separation between subsets of their linguistic repertoire – their 'languages' – and to use them, if necessary, in separate contexts. This said, we must acknowledge that bilingualism may manifest itself in a minimal way in speakers who have just rudimentary knowledge of another language, perhaps even only a small inventory of foreign words. A good example is the English spoken by taxi drivers in Beijing, often amounting to just a few basic expressions, among them numbers used to quote the fare. This small inventory of English structures is reserved almost exclusively for interaction with foreign passengers. When one Beijing taxi driver shares stories with a colleague, he might codeswitch into this form of 'English' when quoting verbatim what he had said to one of his passengers. In this way codeswitching can occur even in situations of superficial or minimal bilingualism. By contrast, there are situations in which bilingualism is the norm, and the bilingual mode is the default mode of conversation, as discussed above for Romani. Since the full vocabulary of the second language is available to Romani speakers in almost any interaction in their first language, the potential for codeswitching is virtually unlimited. At the other end of the bilinguality continuum we find the monolingual speaker, who is unable to activate any word-forms from another code. In the strictly monolingual setting, imported word-forms are foreign by etymology only. There are no codeswitches, only borrowings, established through a diachronic process of propagation throughout the monolingual speech community.

The next relevant measure is the compositional continuum, which captures the complexity as well as the uniqueness and context-dependency of the structure that is derived from the other language. Alternational switches at the utterance level, and creative phrases constructed in the immediate context of the interaction, demand full competence in both languages, and, unlike single lexical items, they are not likely to become established loans. Complex insertions require not only high proficiency in the second language (hence they correlate with bilinguality), they also demand more self-confidence on the part of the speaker to re-negotiate the language of the interaction even if only for the duration of a brief utterance. They also attract greater attention on the part of the listener, and so they have a greater potential to flag special conversational effects (and so are likely to correlate with the functional continuum, below). Exceptions are formulaic expressions of the kind represented by Latin-derived judicial terms in European languages, such as *ipso facto* or *prima facie*, or Arabic-derived greetings and exclamations in various Asian and African languages, such as *as-salāmu aleykum* or *ma šaa-llah*.

The functional continuum has insertions for special conversational effect, on the one side, and default expressions for the relevant concept, on the other. Codeswitches are more likely to fulfil the first function, while established borrowings are often the only expression in the language representing the particular concept. The functional continuum treats prototypical instances of codeswitching as conscious and discourse-strategic, at least in the sense that they are triggered in a non-random way by situational or contextual factors and that they constitute an alternative to a default formulation of the same propositional content. Exceptions occur here as well; we have seen how bilinguals in the bilingual mode regularly draw on their second language in order to name concepts and institutions that are particular to interaction in that language. On the other hand, a borrowing might have inherited synonyms in the language, as in Hebrew *tikšóret* and *komunikacija*, both 'communication', and these may be stylistically specialised, as in German *Fernsprecher* and *Telefon*, both 'telephone', the former normally reserved for official or institutional, written style, such as letterheads or business cards.

Unique referents were discussed above, and reference was made to Backus's (1996) Specificity hierarchy. I have dubbed them 'para-lexical', since they entail a referencing procedure that is beyond the mere generic labelling of concepts or objects and resembles or indeed equals the assignment of word-forms as individualised identity-badges. Above we discussed the use of institution names and institutional terminology. Inserting the original word-forms allows bilinguals to activate the precise image that is associated with the particular institution as an activity setting. For this reason, bilinguals will often not bother to translate names even if they are easily translatable; Turkish immigrants in Germany for example usually prefer the German word *Bahnhof* 'train station' to its Turkish translation. Terms of affection and kin terms used as terms of address often belong to this class, too. British-born Cantonese speakers often address their mothers as *mami* (Lo 2007) but speak to them in Cantonese; and the daughter of a Syrian family living in Germany is reported to address her Syrian grandmother as *Oma* (German for 'grandmother') but speaks to her in Arabic.[3] The preference for these 'original' labels as designations for 'original' objects reduces the choice-effect that bilinguals exercise in selecting their expressions. By contrast, 'genuine' lexical items – Core lexicon, in the terminology used by Myers-Scotton (2006) – are often inserted by choice in order to create a special conversational effect. Based on these considerations, para-lexical items are closer to the Borrowing side of the continuum.

The operationality continuum singles out those grammatical elements as closer to the Borrowing end of the cline that are produced non-consciously in order to reduce the processing effort associated with the selection/inhibition mechanism. The assumption is that it is in most cases easier for the bilingual to retrieve core lexical expressions and to make appropriate choices between translation equivalents in the core vocabulary than it is to maintain consistent control over the selection mechanism around automated, non-referential operational elements such as discourse markers, indefinites, comparative/superlative markers, and more. Once again, the absence of the element of 'choice' in the production of L2-operators of this type brings them close on the continuum to Borrowings.

The final two criteria are regularity of occurrence and structural integration, both of which were already discussed in the previous section. Regularity is not necessarily to be measured in terms of frequency. Rather, it means that the item in question is independent of any contextual selection constraints and so it is deemed appropriate in whichever language context that is being activated. The criterion of integration presupposes that there are identifiable procedures of structural integration. Above we already mentioned the problems associated with structural integration in languages that assign little inflectional morphology, or when languages are in contact that barely differ in their phonological systems. Conversely, in some languages certain phonemes or morphemes will appear only in loanwords, e.g. Hebrew initial /f/ as in *fibrék* 'fabricate', or the English plural in *-a* as in *phenomena*, suggesting that integration is in fact incomplete and therefore itself subject to degree. Finally, integration conventions may vary across bilingual communities or even among individual bilingual speakers.

All this underlines the fact that the distinction between borrowing and codeswitching is not a simple one, but involves a bundle of criteria, each arranged on a continuum. The prototypical, least controversial kind of borrowing thus involves the regular occurrence of a structurally integrated, single lexical item that is used as a default expression, often a designation for a unique referent or a grammatical marker, in a monolingual context. The least controversial codeswitch is an alternational switch at the utterance level, produced by a bilingual consciously and by choice, as a single occurrence, for special stylistic effects. In-between the two we encounter fuzzy ground. Note, however, that the potential for fuzziness is largely limited to bilinguals. Bilinguals may use a word regularly but still maintain its original phonological shape, or vice versa – they may integrate a word that is only used once. A considerable degree of ambiguity will therefore always remain in respect of the language mixing patterns of bilinguals and of any single bilingual corpus.

5.2   Situational and conversational codeswitching

5.2.1   Code selection: social norms and identity

Early works such as Clyne (1967) noted that switching often occurs in response to 'triggers' in the interaction. Insertions of the type discussed above have been noted to serve as frequent triggers for an alternational switch, that is, for the continuation of the turn in the other language to which the insertion itself belongs. The switch in this case might be seen as a two-stage procedure: First, the speaker is motivated to insert a word from the other language, either in response to a problem in retrieving an appropriate word in the current language of the utterance, or for one of the effects described above. Next, the insertion itself prompts a switch for the remainder of the utterance or a portion thereof. Ambiguous words or constructions that happen to be identical or similar in both languages may also serve as triggers, in which case the triggering procedure is even more direct (cf. Clyne 1987; see also Broersma and De Bot 2006).[4]

Changes in the discourse setting constitute another type of trigger that was identified at an early stage of codeswitching research (Fishman 1965, Blom and Gumperz 1972). Termed 'situational switching', this kind of language alternation can be directly related to the roles that each language has and the rules on appropriateness of language choice in specific sets or domains of social activity. Changing activity constellations will thus trigger a change in the language of the interaction. Such changes may be subtle, such as shifts in topics, the wish to include or exclude other participants (even bilingual participants), or the presence of bystanders.

Clyne's (1967, 1987) notion of 'trigger' thus helped describe codeswitching as *responsive* to events surrounding the communicative interaction: the appearance of certain words, topics, participants or settings. With research in sociolinguistics expanding into the exploration of the role of style and accommodation as *constructive* processes, a new direction emerged in the interpretation of codeswitching, attributing it to a process of active negotiation of social roles, obligations, and identities. Elaborating on an earlier model by Blom and Gumperz (1972), Gumperz (1982) emphasises the role of codeswitching in helping the speaker to re-define the conversational context. Speakers *initiate* switches in order to construct and to broadcast a particular relationship between what is said and aspects of the conversation context. Switches are, in this respect, meaningful devices that help contextualise information – 'contextualisation cues'. The contrast effect that is achieved through switching is a 'meaningful juxtaposition'. The choices between languages that speakers make in conversation are determined not just by situational factors and the roles that the languages have in social domains, but by dynamic and creative factors that support expressivity. Expanding this idea in the methodological context of Conversation Analysis, Auer's (1984) investigation of codeswitching behaviour among second-generation Italian immigrants in southern Germany provides a landmark in the study of conversational switches as devices that serve a variety of discourse-structuring functions. Auer interprets the 'meaningfulness' of switches at the local level of the immediate conversation, emphasising their function in establishing sequences or demarcations between individual acts of speech. We shall return to the role of codeswitching as discourse strategy below.

The emphasis on micro-level interaction, rather than domain alternation, as the scene of language choice, raises the question of how to deal with the relationship between code choice at the local level and the social meanings that languages have in activity routines. Gardner-Chloros (1991) surveys choices that speakers make among French and Alsatian in a series of institutional interaction settings (shops, offices) and private conversations in Strasbourg. She concludes that switching is constrained by the social situation – the identity of the interlocutors and the relations between them, the formality of the setting, and the roles that the languages play in the lives of individuals. At the same time it is motivated by a need to negotiate an adequate mode of communication that takes into account personal preferences and competence, accommodation to notions of the interlocutor's expectations, terminological issues, as well as conversational effects (such as topic change, constellation change, and inclusion or exclusion of interlocutors). Each language may thus represent a whole array of functions and symbolisms at a given moment in conversation. Motivations to choose one language over another are therefore multiple and complex.

The reliance on local interpretations of switching is criticised by Myers-Scotton (1993a), who suggests instead that speakers' language choices are not random but predictable via a set of indicators that are associated with each of the languages in their repertoire. She proposes a model of markedness, which makes predictions about the choices that are available to speakers in a given interaction context.[5] According to this model, in every multilingual community there is always a language that can be considered the unmarked choice in a specific interaction type. 'Unmarked' is defined as an index of the default relations among participants – their set of 'Rights and Obligations' – in that specific interaction context. This indexicality is the product of repetitive use in particular types of conversations and settings, leading to the regularity of choices in these settings. Knowledge of this regularity in turn forms part of speakers' communicative competence. 'Unmarked' is thus understood both as the 'default' choice, and as the most frequent choice. Codeswitching itself can constitute an unmarked choice, if speakers choose to use language mixing to symbolise their social identity and social relationships in certain settings. Marked choices are choices that are not expected; speakers make such choices in order to signal dis-identification with interlocutors or another aspect of the conversation.

In this way, the choice of language is indexical not just of social values and rules, but of a speaker's acceptance or non-acceptance of those values and rules in any given moment in conversation. But if unmarked code choice is predictable through a set of social conventions, why do speakers defy these very same conventions and make marked choices? Myers-Scotton (1993a: 100–106) suggests that speakers act rationally, calculating risks and gains, while using the contrast between languages strategically (see also Myers-Scotton and Bolonyai 2001). In this way, speakers exploit the social meanings associated with their languages.

5.2.2   Discourse functions of codeswitching

The use of language alternation to signal contrast between the contents of portions of speech is what makes codeswitching according to Gumperz (1982) 'metaphorical'. Consider language alternation in the following narration:

(2)   Cypriot Greek/English (Christodoulou 1991: 92):
    a. Kápote   káthume če miló   tis   Eliniká, alá léxis
       sometimes sit.1PL and speak.1SG 3SG.F.DAT Greek   but words

       pu   δen tes   ikséro   laló   sta Englézika.
       REL NEG 3PL.ACC know.1SG say.1SG in English

    b. *And then I start talking in English for a little while,*
    c. če ístera pao   píso sta Eliniká.
      and then   go.1SG back in Greek

    a. Sometimes I sit and talk to her in Greek, but words that I don't
      know I say in English.
    b. *And then I start talking in English for a little while,*
    c. and then I go back to Greek.

The switch into English in segment (b), as well as that back into Greek in segment (c), is 'metaphorical' in the sense that there is a direct association between the language into which the switch takes place, and the meaning or propositional content conveyed by the portion of the utterance that contains the switch. In this case, the choice of language demonstrates literally the kind of events that the speaker is describing.

But discourse-functional codeswitching is not limited to metaphorical uses of this kind. Auer (1984, 1995) distinguishes participant-related functions of codeswitching from conversation-oriented functions. The first include a change in the participant constellation, addressee selection, and inclusion or exclusion of bystanders. The latter include the highlighting of reported speech, parentheses or side-comments, reiterations or quasi translations for emphasis, change of mode (for instance, from formal interview to informal conversation), language play, and topicalisation (focus or contrast). This means that codeswitching can signal a transition between various levels or layers of the discourse. Consider the following example from an interview with a schoolteacher in the northern German town of Niebüll. The speaker belongs to the North Frisian linguistic minority of the region and teaches her native language at a local school. She is asked by an investigator – a linguist studying activities to promote Frisian – to describe, in Frisian, the instruction methods and the teaching materials that she employs:

(3)   North Frisian/German:
    a. S: Än wat   da mååste jungse gåns hål   mooge, as heer da
           and what the most   kids   very much like.PL is here the

           latje/ suk latje seetinge tu leesen ooder suk latje
           little such little sentences to read   or   such little

           gedichte heer tu leesen.
           poems   here to read

    b. H: Mhm.

    c. S: Deer jeeft't   gåns, gåns njütie for jungse uk, da   mååge
           there give.3SG-it very very nice for kids   too these make.1PL

           we dan uk *immer* iinjsen tubai.
           we then also always once   privately

    d.   *Das ist also   ganz/ Dieses Buch hier ist ganz toll, können*
           this is PART very this   book here is very nice can.2POL

           Sie ganz bestimmt kaufen im Nordfriisk Instituut oder auch hier,
           you very certainly buy   in   or   also here

           in jeder Buchhandlung hier bei uns hier oben.
           in every bookshop   here at us   here above

    e. H: Aha.   Aha.

    f. S: Än dän hääw   ik uk   nuch en bök 'Max än Moritz' aw
           and then have.1SG I also still a book   in

           frasch,
           Frisian

    g. H: Ah ja, mhm, mhm.

    h. S: Dåt hääw   ik fort   treed schöljiir, än dän hääw   ik
           that have.1SG I for.the third schoolyear and then have.1SG I

           nuch: 'We bjarne foon Bullerbü' fort   fiird   schöljiir.
           still we children from   for.the fourth schoolyear

    a. S: And what most kids really like is here to read the little/ these little
           sentences, or to read these little poems.

    b. H: Mhm.

   c. S: There are many nice ones, for kids too, we *always* produce them
            ourselves, in our spare time.

   d.   *And this is a very/ This book is very nice, you can certainly purchase*
            it at the North Frisian Institute or even here, in every bookshop in
            our area up here.

   e. H: Aha.   Aha.

   f. S: And then I have another book, 'Max and Moritz' in Frisian,

   g. H: Oh yes, mhm, mhm.

   h. S: I have that one for year three, and then I also have 'We Children
            from Bullerby', for year four.'

Note that the listener understands Frisian, but does not speak it. He puts his
questions in German, but provides listener feedback while listening to the Frisian
narrative and is able to reassure the speaker that he follows the full content of her
talk. The switch is therefore not intended as a clarification of anything that might
not have been understood by the listener. Rather, it marks out a turn in the content
and purpose of a particular portion of the narrative: For the main topic of her
narration – the description of Frisian teaching materials – the speaker uses Frisian.
In segment (d) she departs from this topic to make a side-comment, directed at
the listener, praising a particular book, recommending it to the listener and even
volunteering information on where it can be purchased. The speaker returns
to the main topic of her narrative – a survey and description of Frisian teaching
materials – in segment (f), switching back to Frisian. Codeswitching in this extract
thus helps structure the conversation by highlighting a side-comment against the
background of the more general narration line. Note that there is no change during
this extract in either the interpersonal relations between the participants, or in
the setting, the participant constellation, the overall topic of the conversation,
or the mode or key (attitudes or emotional content) of the interaction. Rather,
the contrast of languages marks out a very local shift between more topical and
less topical information, between a more 'global' statement given in response to
the question of the interview and so directed potentially at other, future listeners
(the interview is not necessarily intended for broadcasting or publication, but
is being tape-recorded), and a more 'private' recommendation to the individual
listener/ investigator. The switches do not occur in response to structural triggers,
either. For the identification of the functionality of the switch we rely therefore
on an interpretation of the organisation and event structuring within the narrative
(Labov 1972b). The next example provides a further illustration:

(4)   Lovari Romani/German:

     a. Taj či   žanav,   varesar areslas   ando phanglipe, phandadi
         and NEG know.1SG somehow arrived.3SG in   prison   locked.F

         sas.
         was.3SG

     b. But   berš bešlas,
         many year sat.3SG

c. ta   jekh džes angla kodo kana sas   te   mekhen la avri,
   and one day before that when was.3SG COMP let.3PL her out

d. voj či žanelas   kodo,
   she NEG know.3SG.REM that

e. kamelas   te   kerel varesar te   šaj žal   ande
   want.3SG.REM COMP do.3SG somehow COMP can go.3SG in

   špital, žanes,   te   šaj len   la te   ingren   la
   hospital know.2SG COMP can take.3PL her COMP bring.3PL her

   ande špital.
   in   hospital

f. Numa voj či žanelas   ke   voj po kaver džes avri žal.
   but she NEG know.3SG.REM COMP she on other day out go.3SG

g. Ta las   jekh roj,
   and took.3SG a   spoon

h. *und das stimmt*,
   and that is.true

i. ekh roj   las,   roj,
   a   spoon took3SG spoon

j. *Löffel*,
   spoon

k. Las   ekh roj, aj kamelas   te   phagel
   took.3SG a   spoon and want.3SG.REM COMP break.3SG

   pesko   dand.
   REFL.POSS tooth

l. Ta sar zumadas kodo nakhadas   e   roj, aj mulas.
   and how tried.3SG that swallowed.3SG the spoon and died.3SG

m. *Das war   Tragödie.*
   that was.3SG tragedy

n. Ale či žanelas,   po kaver džes *war sie frei.*
   but NEG know.3SG.REM on other day was.3SG she free

o. *Mhm . . . gibt's 'n paar Sachen.*
                   give.3SG-it few things

a. And I don't know, somehow she ended up in jail, she was locked up.

b. She sat for many years,

c. and one day before she was supposed to be released,

d. she didn't know it,

e. she somehow wanted to do something so that she could go to the hospital,
   you know, so that they would take her and bring her to the hospital.

f. But she didn't know that she was coming out the next day.

g. And she took a spoon,

h. *And this is true*,

i. She took a spoon, spoon,

    j. *Spoon,*
    k. She took a spoon, and she wanted to pull out her tooth.
    l. And as she tried to do it, she swallowed the spoon, and she died.
    m. *It was a tragedy.*
    n. But she didn't know, the next day *she was free.*
    o. *Mhm . . . things happen.*

The topic of the narration is the tragic story of a distant family relative. This too is a tape-recorded interview situation, though in this case the speaker and the listener are work colleagues. For the purpose of the interview, the speaker is asked questions about her life history and that of her family and relations. The chosen language for the interview is Romani, though the everyday language of interaction among the participants tends to be German. Note that here too, not unlike the previous example (3), the main narration line is delivered in Romani, the selected language of the requested narration activity (the 'narrative interview'). Here too, the speaker switches to German when she departs from the main narrative line.

In segment (h) she uses German to confirm the truth of her story. This is done at the immediate level of interaction between speaker and listener. The comment is directed at the listener, ensuring him of the speaker's 'qualification' as a narrator of true events. Indirectly, the side-comment also contributes to the build-up of suspense in preparation of the complicating event that is about to be introduced. Another switch appears in segment (j). It follows the repetition and emphasis, beginning in segment (g), three times already, of the fact that the character took a spoon, the instrument that was to have a crucial role in the story. It is possible that the translation into German is also intended to ensure that the listener understood the meaning of the Romani word *roj*, in the absence of any positive listener feedback. The next switch comes in segment (m), giving an evaluation of the event in the context in which it was received by those affected by it, namely as a tragedy.

The next segment is something of a hybrid. Its purpose is to justify the evaluation offered in (m); the need for justification arises from the fact that the speaker has now reached the phase of the narration at which establishment of common ground and a common attitude with the listener are sought. This kind of act belongs to the level of interaction between speaker and listener, and not to the narration line. However, in order to justify her evaluation, the speaker needs to return to the narration line and emphasise the part of the chain of events that justifies the categorisation as 'tragic': The tragic aspect is the contrast between the protagonist's desperate action with fatal consequence, and the fact that her upcoming release was unknown to her. The contrast of languages in segment (n) is a metaphorical expression of this contrast of events. The final move, segment (o) in German, provides yet another evaluative commentary on the entire narrated episode and at the same time a sign off, bringing the narration turn to an end. It too, like the other segments delivered in German, operates as a side-comment at the level of interaction-management. The distribution of languages along positions in the interaction is plotted in Figure 5.2.

Segment	Language	Position	Categorisation
a.	Romani	background	story-line
b.	Romani	cont.	
c.	Romani	complication	
d.	Romani	clarification	
e.	Romani	cont. complication	
f.	Romani	cont.	
g.	Romani	build-up for climax	
h.	German	reassurance/commentary	side-comment
i.	Romani	reiteration	story-line
j.	German	clarification/emphasis	side-comment
k.	Romani	reiteration of i.	story-line
l.	Romani	climax	
m.	German	evaluation	side-comment
n.	Romani→ German	justification of m.	[story-line/side-comment]
o.	German	sign-off	side-comment

Figure 5.2 *Distribution of languages over positions in Example (4).*

The language choices that the speakers make in Examples (3)–(4) are not directly connected with the overall social roles that the languages have, or with the values that the participants attribute to those languages. Rather, language alternation is an instrument that is employed by the speakers to achieve a local goal, that goal being to guide the listener to distinguish between the content of a narration line and the departure from that line to convey evaluations, attitudes, and justifications in the form of side-comments. Codeswitching is, in other words, an instrument used by the speaker to structure and organise a prolonged narrative in a single, multi-utterance, complex turn.

Li Wei and Milroy (1995) demonstrate how codeswitching can equally be used as an instrument to organise the *sequentiality* of discourse, marking out special effects in intra-turn sequences of speech. The analysis draws on the identification of adjacency pairs in the Conversation Analytical approach. It is argued that a contrast effect is achieved when the language used in the second turn in an adjacency pair contrasts with that used in the first part of the pair. Typical functions of switching in such environments are to express disagreement, to refuse an offer, or to initiate a repair on the part of the listener. Consider the following example from Li Wei and Milroy's work in the Tyneside Chinese community in Britain:

(5)   Cantonese/English (Li Wei and Milroy 1995: 287–288):
           a. A: Oy-m-oy faan a?
                  'Want some rice?'
           b. B: (no response)
           c. A: Chaaufan a, oy-m-oy?
                  'Fried rice. Want or not?'
           d. B: (2.0) *I'll have some shrimps.*
           e. A: Mut-ye? (1) Chaaufan a.
                  'What?   Fried rice'
           f. B: Hai a.
                  'O.k.'

A's offer of rice receives no reply from B at first. The repeated offer (segment (c)) receives no reply either, initially, then after a delay of two seconds it is indirectly declined by the request for something else (segment (d)). B's reaction is, in Conversation Analysis terms, a dispreferred second turn in an adjacency pair (the preferred reply would have been acceptance of the offer; cf. Sacks, Schegloff, and Jefferson 1974). It is marked as such through the switch of languages, which highlights the contrast to A's expectations. Note that B's acceptance of the offer of rice in segment (f) is rendered in Cantonese, like the offer itself.

In the Conversation Analysis approach to codeswitching, explanations that focus on the local level of the immediate interaction are preferred over rationalisations that relate the choice of code to its overall societal function. It is argued that speakers act locally in order to achieve goals within the ongoing interaction (see Li Wei 2005, 1998). Against the Rational Choice model proposed by Myers-Scotton (1993a: 100–106; also Myers-Scotton and Bolonyai 2001), it is argued that it is not possible for the analyst to know the social value of a code (unless the analyst is a member of the community or is closely familiar with the participants), and yet it is still possible for the analyst to interpret the interpersonal goal-oriented significance of code choice by analysing interactions such as those presented in the above examples. This is taken as confirmation that the local level of interaction provides the crucial driving force behind the choices that speakers make, while social value may be an added bonus to the effects created by a code. Conversation analysts therefore doubt the ability of any analysis to predict conversation choices that are not a response to situational constraints but are aimed at the internal structuring of the conversation (cf. Auer 1995, Li Wei 2005).

In fact, the difference between the Rational Choice model and the Conversation Analytical approach is not very substantial in what concerns the actual interpretation of the motivations behind switches and the goals that they serve. It is rather more pronounced in the kind of evidence that the two methods are prepared to take into account. The Rational Choice model stresses that social knowledge is incorporated into participants' choices. It suggests that speakers rationally exploit the social meaning of a code in order to achieve their immediate conversational goal. But while reiterating the rational choice hypothesis, Myers-Scotton (2002a: 206) emphasises that markedness can be an individual property of code choice, and not just a social property: 'Speakers almost always have multiple identities. A linguistic choice reflects the presentation of one identity rather than the other.' Myers-Scotton (2002a) speaks of three 'filters': An external filter gauges language choice against the social meanings of the code and the social conventions of code choice (by domains of social activity). An internal filter draws on the individual speaker's experience, and helps assess priorities and code choice meaning at the local level. Finally, a rationality filter helps the speaker decide how to act most effectively in order to achieve particular goals.

This obscures the differences between the models even more: if individual speakers have individual code preferences, and if these preferences are the key to understanding the choices that speakers make in pursuit of certain goals in communication, then any analysis must take into account the participants' full range of social networks and social activities. Consider again our Examples (3) and (4), above. Taking a conversation analytical approach, we may interpret the switches as marking transitions between neighbouring speech acts that achieve different goals, such as presentation of a 'generally applicable' narration line and the marking out of individualised side-comments directed at the specific listener. We do not need to know anything about the participants' language preferences. However, if we do take those preferences into account, then this adds meaning to the choice. Thus in Example (3) the North Frisian teacher switches into German for the side-comment because that is the default or unmarked language that she would normally use with the listener/interviewer. In this respect, the choice of German for a personal recommendation directed at the listener is socially meaningful. At the same time, however, German is arguably a marked choice in the particular interview setting, since interviewee and interviewer had agreed to choose Frisian as the default language of the interview. If frequency of choice within the particular interaction context is a criterion, then Frisian is the unmarked choice in this particular interaction. The teacher's use of German in segment (d) of Example (3) is marked against the background of Frisian as the default interview language, but unmarked against the background of German as the expected and more effective language of interaction with the listener outside of the interview context. Similarly, in Example (4), German is arguably a marked choice against the background of Romani as the default language of narration of family events in this particular setting, but at the same time the unmarked choice in everyday interaction involving the same participants. Given the fact that both participants are in this case bilingual, one might speculate that, had German been chosen at the request of the interviewer instead of Romani as the language of narration, then any side-remarks directed at the listener might have been highlighted in Romani; the markedness relationship between the languages as used by the very same participants in the same setting might have been reversed.

This suggests that the markedness of code selection is itself context-dependent, and is potentially created and negotiated by the participants as part of the setup of the interaction. The meanings that codes acquire can be multidimensional and can draw on their macro-social functions, on their significance for individuals, and on the choices that have already been made earlier in the same interaction. These may then be put to use in pursuit of the various goals that speakers wish to achieve at the local level of the conversation. The debate between the Rational Choice approach and the Conversation Analytical method is at least in part an issue of the chosen style of reasoning: the Markedness Model is in some aspects of its reasoning and presentation style inspired by modular theories, and assumes a deductive approach to the issue of code choice. This contrasts with the approach of the Conversation Analysts whose reasoning is mainly inductive – a bottom-up approach that moves from local observations towards the building of a theory.

Two recent works on codeswitching corpora demonstrate how the Conversation Analytical approach can be supplemented by taking into account relevant aspects of the social meanings behind code choice. Chen (2007) distinguishes several different levels of functionality in a corpus of Taiwanese/Mandarin switches in the context of television talkshows. Discourse-related switching contributes to the organisation and structuring of the discourse, for purposes such as bracketing side-comments, reported speech, or self-repair, within turns, and for side-sequences, obtaining of the floor, and repair/reformulation, between turns. Content-related switching is a means of amplification, metaphorical contrasting, or shifting; it can be used to express uncertainty, disagreement, irony or ridicule, or topic change. Participant-related codeswitching supports exclusion and inclusion of particants, role-change, perspective-taking, and symbolic side-switching. Finally, some switches are directly code-related in that they exploit the inherent social functions associated with each of the codes. These include ethnic solidarity, symbolic opposition, expression of authority and emotiveness, and the flagging of social style.

While this typology attempts to identify distinct functions and environments of switches, Chen emphasises that the negotiation of codes in conversation is a dynamic process that can be driven my multiple factors. A good example is the following use of Taiwanese for 'metalanguaging' purposes[6] – in others words, to present a commentary on the discourse itself:

(6)   Taiwanese (italics)/Mandarin (Chen 2007: 130–131):
        a. Z: *m-si*   *la,*   *gua si*   *kong a//*   *gua si*   *kong* neixian
                NEG-COP PART 1SG COP say   PART 1SG COP say internal.line

            chedao ruguo la   *honn* dou shi   gei   chaoche yong, chaoche
            lane   if   PART PART all COP COV overtake use   overtake

cai   neng yong ma,   qita dou yao zai bijiao waimian
so.that can use   PART other all need LOC COMP outside

zhe liang ge chedao, zhe liang ge chedao hui   biande
this two CL lane   this two CL lane   AUX become

hen sai   ma,   ni   zhe bian shi   kongde ma (.)
very packed PART 2SG this side COP empty PART

→ b.   *gua cit-ma be   hisu si   kong..., ce..=*
        1SG now   want mean COP say   this

→ c. Y: =zhezhong zhifa   you-mei-you   keneng la
         this.kind law.enforcement have-NEG-have possible PART

   d. Z: zhezhong zhifa   *honn* dou   mei you kaolü
         this.kind law.enforcement PART all/both NEG have consider

        dao   sianshi de   wenti   la,
        PREP reality NOM problem PART

   e.   {addresses L with eye contact} *li   thiann   u   bo?*
                                         2SG hear/listen have Q

   a. Z: '*No, I mean/I mean* if the internal lane is only used for overtaking,
          only if you want to cut in, and except for that you have to drive in
          two of the outer lanes, these two lanes will then become
          very packed as this side (i.e. the internal lane) is empty.
   b.   *What I want to say is that. . . , this..=*
   c. Y: =Is this kind of enforcement possible or not?
   d. Z: This kind of enforcement does not at all take the real problems
          into consideration.
          {addresses L with eye contact}*Do you understand?*'

In Example (6), Z has two interlocutors, Y and L, as well as a spectator audience. His turn in segment (a) begins with a metalinguistic introduction ('No, I mean/I mean') in Taiwanese, followed by the presentation of his argument in Mandarin. Once the argument has been presented, he begins a further metalinguistic comment, in segment (b) ('What I want to say. . .'). Note the switch back to Taiwanese for the purpose of metalanguaging. His hesitation at the end of this utterance is then interrupted by Y, who helps Z complete his argument. Note Y's choice of Mandarin, the language in which Z had presented his original argument in segment (a). Z then accommodates to Y's choice of language, and returns to Mandarin when taking the floor again in segment (d) to continue his argument. He then directs a question to L, for which he chooses Taiwanese – once again, metalanguaging the content presented in the preceding utterances. While Mandarin has enjoyed an uninterrupted status as the language of the public domain, use of Taiwanese in media and institutional discourse is recent, and this language is still associated by many with more intimate or informal discourse. These social meanings may play a role in the choice of codes – Mandarin for the presentation of the argument, Taiwanese for personal side-comments. However, no prediction can be made to this effect since it is the contrast of languages itself that is being exploited for the purposes of local management of the discourse.

In another recent work, Lo (2007) discusses an example from the Chinese community in Manchester. The conversation involves the Singaporean-born mother (M), the Hong Kong-born father (F), and their British-born daughter (D). Mother and daughter had just been looking at promotion brochures, discussing the colours of paint with which they would like to decorate their house.

(7)   Cantonese/English (Lo 2007: 93–94):
  a. D: maami   aa, *when are you next going again?*
        mammy PRT

  b. M: nei man nei dedi   laa
        you ask you daddy PRT

  c. D: dedi   nei geisi zoi   heoi aa?
        daddy you when again go   PRT

  d. F: heoi bindou aa?
        go   where PRT

  e. D: B&Q.

  f.   *I need to get some of these.*

  g. F: *Get what?*

  h. D: *This one.*

  i.   *I need to get the pink one*

  j. F: ngo
        I see

  k. D: *I need it.*
        (5 sec)

  l. F: dai   jat aa
        another day PRT

  a. D: Mammy, *when are you next going again?*

  b. M: You ask your daddy.

  c. D: Daddy, when will you go there again?

  d. F: Go where?

  e. D: B&Q.[7]

  f.   *I need to get some of these.*

  g. F: *Get what?*

  h. D: *This one.*

  i.   *I need to get the pink one.*

  j. F: I see.

  k. D: *I need it.*
        (5 sec)

  l. F: Another day.

Lo (2007) presents the following interpretation of the extract: in segment (a), the daughter addresses her mother in English, their preferred common language. She enquires about the mother's intentions to visit the shop whose promotion brochures they have been looking at. The mother interprets the daughter's utterance as a request, not a question, and instead of either granting or rejecting her request, she refers her to her father. The mother's reaction is a dispreferred second in the adjacency pair, marked out by Cantonese, a marked choice in the context of her interaction with her daughter (segment (b)). The daughter follows her mother's instruction and turns to her father, now accommodating her language choice to the father's preferred language, Cantonese, in an attempt to obtain a positive reaction to her request from the father (segment (c)).

Note that the father does not comply with the request, but delays a decision, asking for clarification (segment (d)). The daughter complies with the request for clarification (segment (d)–(e)), but returns to her preferred language, English, not having obtained the desired result from her initial accommodation to the father. Conscious of the daughter's return to English and quite possibly interpreting it as a possible signal of her disappointment at failing to obtain an immediate promise to go to B&Q, the father then accommodates to the daughter's choice, English (segment (g)). However, having listened to the daughter's repetition of the request in segments (h)–(i), the father stalls, returning to his preferred language, Cantonese, signalling that he might not comply with the request (a dispreferred second). The daughter repeats the request, standing her ground in her preferred language, English (segment (k)). The father's rejection of the request is finally delivered again in Cantonese. Lo (2007) emphasises how both mother and father avoid a direct reply to the daughter's request, using the contrast of languages to mark these dispreferred seconds in the adjacency pair. A summary of the language choices used and their distribution along speech acts in the extract is presented in Figure 5.3.

Language alternation does not always constitute a meaningful juxtaposition that is symbolic, reinforcing the contrast between points in the conversation. What Grosjean (2001) refers to as the 'bilingual mode', and what Myers-Scotton (1993a) identifies as 'unmarked codeswitching', may itself constitute a default option that is meaningful as a signal of shared, multilingual identity. Meeuwis and Blommaert (1998) for instance describe Lingala–French language mixing patterns among Zairians in Belgium as a kind of 'monolectal codeswitching' – a mixture of structures that is perceived by speakers not as the product of the blending of two languages, but as one code in its own right, the default choice in in-group communication. This is not an isolated approach to codeswitching. Maschler (1997, 1998, 2000) too speaks of certain patterns of Hebrew–English switches among American Israelis as an 'emergent code', and Auer (1999) proposes the notion of a 'fused lect' to denote a mixture-by-default, where the combination of structures from different language sources no longer has any particular conversation-structuring function, but is instead meaningful as a wholesale token of group identity and mode of conversation.[8] Discussing

Segment	Language	Speech act	Choice
a.	English	Question 1	D's default
b.	Cantonese	Request to ask the dad	M's marked
c.	Cantonese	Question 1	D's respect
d.	Cantonese	Request for clarification	F's default
e.	English	Clarification	D's default/opposition
f.	English	Explanation for the request	(cont.)
g.	English	Request for clarification	F reaching out
h.	English	Clarification	D's default
i.	English	Request	(cont.)
j.	Cantonese	Understanding	F's default, non-compliance
k.	English	Request again	D's default, insistence
	Silence		
l.	Cantonese	Answer to Question 1	F's default, rejection

Figure 5.3 *Language choices, their meanings, and speech act distribution in Example (7) (adapted from Lo 2007: 93–94).*

three sets of data – Kinyarwanda/French, Catalan/Castilian, and Catalan and Castilian/English – Garafanga and Torras (2002) similarly note that bilinguals may combine elements of their languages as if they were speaking one single language, using a bilingual medium as the default choice. Meaningful switches can still occur when the speaker suspends the bilingual medium and switches to a monolingual one.

These views on codeswitching strengthen our position that a multilingual individual's 'languages' are better understood as an overall repertoire of linguistic structures, from which speakers choose according to the needs of communication and the constraints of the situation and context. Complete separation of repertoire subsets in 'monolingual' contexts is an extreme mode of communication in most multilingual situations, whereas some degree of mixing – that is, of drawing on elements of the full repertoire regardless of subset-affiliation – is common. In some cases speakers allow themselves considerable freedom of choice and combination, drawing on a bilingual medium as the default choice. Where the choice of structure partly answers to situational and contextual constraints, codemixing can be functional at various levels: it can evoke meanings associated with the social and cultural context in which the inserted words or structures are normally used, it can trigger associations with the more general social meaning associated on a wholesale basis with one of the languages, it can be used strictly metaphorically to mark out boundaries in the organisation of the talk, or in a combination of any of these factors. Codeswitching is thus an instrument that bilinguals have at their disposal. It shows us that, given the opportunity, bilinguals are often tempted to exploit their full linguistic repertoire in order to have at their disposal both a full range of meanings and an array of conversational strategies and effects.

5.3 Structural aspects of codeswitching

The realisation that codeswitching is not a corrupt form of speech, a semi-lingualism impairing bilinguals had prompted the search for structural generalisations with a predictive power that could prove the non-randomness of codeswitching. Among the earliest proposed regularities was Poplack's (1980) 'Free Morpheme Constraint', which suggested that possible points of switching are restricted to the position of free morphemes. Formulated with reference to inflectional languages (an English/Spanish corpus, later extended to Engish/French and subsequently to other pairs of languages), it implied that utterances are somehow grammatically anchored in one language, and that grammatical morphology from the other language can not be freely inserted. Excluded therefore are occurrences such as English–Spanish *run-eando* 'running', since 'run' is 'unambiguously English' (as a result of the phonological realisation of the /r/), while occurrences such as *flipeando* 'flipping' are permitted since here the root is phonologically integrated and therefore not considered a case of codeswitching (cf. Sankoff and Poplack 1981: 5). Thus, bound morphemes can accompany loanwords, but not switches.

A further generalisation concerned the congruence between the languages. It was suggested that speakers will produce sentences or parts of sentences that are grammatical in both their languages, and so they will avoid violating the word order rules of either of the participating languages (Pfaff 1979, Poplack 1980). This principle, which became known as the 'Equivalence Constraint', can be illustrated by the following, well-cited English/Spanish switch (from Poplack 1981: 170):

(8)   You didn't have to worry *que* somebody *te*   iba   *a*
                      COMP   you.OBL go.3SG.PROG.PAST to
        tirar con cerveza o una botella or something like that.
        throw with beer   or a.F bottle
        'You didn't have to worry that somebody was going to throw beer
        or a bottle or something like that at you'

Sankoff and Poplack's (1981) proposal of a 'formal grammar for code-switching' essentially continues this approach, basing its predictions upon a review of the likely points of switches with reference to constituent types or word class. Critique of the formal models has centred around testing the predictive power of these generalisations. Violations of the Equivalence Constraint, for instance, have since been cited quite frequently in the literature (e.g. Berk-Seligson 1986). While some works have since adopted the viewpoint that generalisation ought to be made with reference to just a specific language pair (cf. Bentahila and Davies 1983), there is still interest in identifying universal features of a 'grammar' of codeswitching (cf. Sankoff 1998).

Myers-Scotton's (1993b, 2002b) Matrix Language Frame (MLF) model has had a very strong impact on the field of codeswitching research during the mid and late 1990s. Its popularity is with little doubt due to the fact that it sets out to accommodate different types of language contact phenomena within a single framework and to relate them to a more general model of speech production and the structure of grammar. In part, its appeal will also have been a result of the model's tendency to imitate the style of generative models of grammar by formulating a fixed set of basic principles, accompanied by a further set of more particular rules that explain seeming deviations from the general patterns, by the occasional use of tree-diagrams, and especially through the focus on hierarchies within the structure of the isolated sentence; this, despite the fact that the underlying empirical data derive from transcribed recordings of natural discourse. Many students and researchers welcomed the introduction of a formalist style of description into contact studies.

The MLF model revolves around the description of sentences that contain codeswitches. It views these sentences as frames and seeks to describe the hierarchies that apply within the frame (Myers-Scotton 1993b: 75ff.). The main operating principle of the MLF model is the distinction between the Matrix Language, which is the exclusive supplier of system morphemes in sentences but can also supply content morphs, and the Embedded Language, whose role is limited to supplying content morphs. This distinction is based in turn on a division between system morphs, which are roughly equivalent to 'grammar', and content morphs, which are roughly equivalent to 'lexicon'. The precise definition of the two kinds of morphs rests on their relation to what is called 'Thematic Roles' (roughly equivalent to semantic case-roles). Content morphs assign and receive thematic roles while system morphs do not.

The model's interest is in sentences that contain codeswitches, and those are expected to show ML system morphs and EL content morphs, as illustrated by the following example of Turkish (ML)–Dutch (EL) switching (Backus 1996: 232):

(9)   *ennvoudig*-ti   *foto*-yu   onlar dört ayda   yaptı
        simple-3SG.PAST x-ray-ACC they four month.LOC did.3SG
        'It was *simple*, they could take an *X-ray* after four months'

Since the ML can also supply content morphs, so-called 'ML islands' – portions of sentences that contain only material from the ML – are expected, too. The model also acknowledges the occurrence of 'EL islands' – portions that are entirely made up of EL material. It is hypothesised that formulaic expressions such as idioms are at the top of the hierarchy of EL islands, followed by other time and manner expressions, quantifier expressions, verb phrase complements, agent noun phrases, and lastly thematic role and case assigners (i.e. verbs) (cf. Myers-Scotton 1993b: 144). Consider the following example of English–Hebrew switching:

(10)   It's a very complex *yeri'á* that he *porés*
                          sheet   spreads.3SG.M
            'He is providing a very complex account'

The speaker is reporting on an academic book and referring to the complexity of the account provided by the author. He chooses the Hebrew idiom *p.r.s yeri'á* lit. 'to spread a sheet', meaning 'to provide a complex account'. Note however that the idiom is not presented in one coherent block within the utterance. It is not an 'island', but rather a kind of *archipelago*, its components spread out within the frame of the matrix language, English. What makes the insertion of the Hebrew idiom an 'island' is the fact that it contains system morphemes, in the form of the finite verb inflection in *porés* 'spreads'. In all other features, the two Hebrew constituents are 'legitimate' EL constituents: This can be seen in the fact that the Hebrew noun *yeri'á* 'sheet' is preceded by the English adjective *complex*. The sentence also follows the word order rules of the Matrix Language, which is another principle guiding the identification of the ML (called the 'Morpheme-Order-Principle of the ML-Hypothesis' in the model-internal terminology).

Finally, the MLF model makes formal predictions about the points at which switches are likely to occur. Dubbed the 'Blocking Hypothesis', the expectation is that EL's can only occur if they are congruent with the corresponding ML morphs. 'Congruence' is taken to mean adherence to a similar category (content or system morph), similar assignment of thematic roles, and discourse or pragmatic functions. The congruence constraint still allows speakers considerable creativity. Consider the following example, also from an English–Hebrew bilingual:

(11)   Get rid of that *paxad-elohím tústus!*
                          fear.of.God   motorbike

In colloquial Hebrew, *paxad-elohím* lit. 'fear-of-God' can stand as a predicate meaning 'terrifying' in a copula predication (*ze hayá paxad-elohím!* 'it was terrifying!'), but it cannot be used as an attribute (**tústus paxad-elohím* '*a terrifying motorbike'). It is the pragmatic extension of the noun with predicational capacity in Hebrew to a predicate with attributive qualities that licenses its insertion as an adjective into the English matrix, in line with English word order rules.

In a further development of the MLF model, Myers-Scotton and Jake (2000) propose the Four-Morpheme (or: 4-M) Model (see also Myers-Scotton

2002b: 73ff.). The model replaces the juxtaposition of content and system morphs by altogether four layers. Content morphemes remain one of those entities. System morphemes are now divided into 'early system morphs', 'bridge late system morphemes', and 'late system morphemes'. The justification for the division is formulated in part with reference to formal generative syntax, in part with reference to thematic roles. The inspiration comes from the distinct behaviour of the relevant categories in a variety of circumstances, including language impairment (aphasia), second-language acquisition, codeswitching and borrowing. The metaphors 'early' and 'late' are used with reference to suggested stages in the speech production procedure in which each of the morpheme types acquires its position in the sentence prior to its articulation.

Examples of early system morphemes are determiners (definite articles, possessive expressions) and plural marking. They are 'closest' to the content morphemes in that they are, like content morphemes, conceptually activated, i.e they are directly elected by their head content morpheme as part of its representation in the mental lexicon. Late system morphemes are, by contrast, not conceptually activated. Two sub-types are distinguished. 'Bridge' system morphemes connect content morphemes with each other without reference to the properties of those morphemes; English *of* or French *de* are cited as examples (Myers-Scotton 2002b: 75). 'Outsider' late system morphemes depend on information outside the head; examples are subject-agreement morphemes and case affixes.

The 4-M model gives rise to various hypotheses about the differentiated behaviour of classes of morphemes in codeswitching. It is anticipated, for instance, that early system morphemes (such as plural endings) will sometimes be doubled in codeswitching (Myers-Scotton 2002b: 92). Domari for instance adds its own plural to the Arabic plural morpheme of Arabic word-forms, as in *zálame* 'man', plural *zlām-é* (Arabic singular *zálame*, plural *zlām*), and a Hebrew/English bilingual refers to the 'Alps' in Hebrew as *ha-Alps-im* 'the Alps-PL'. We also find diachronic evidence for the doubling of early system morphemes, for example in the use of definite articles with Arabic loans in Spanish: *el Alcalde* 'the mayor' (Arabic *al-qāḍī* 'the magistrate'), *el arroz* 'the rice' (Arabic *ar-ruzz* 'the rice'). It is also hypothesised that non-finite verb forms are more likely to participate in switches than finite verb forms, since the morphology of non-finite forms (infinitives, participles) consists of early system morphemes that are selected by the head (i.e. the particular verb, in some languages by inflection class), rather than by the relation between the head and the outside environment, as is the case with finite verb morphology (person agreement and tense/aspect marking).

The role and relevance of grammatical category and word class membership in codeswitching has been given attention in other frameworks as well. Muysken (2000a: 154ff.) devotes a chapter to the discussion of function words, defined broadly as syn-semantic (whose meaning depends on a combination with other elements), closed-class elements, which often have a role in structuring the clause, are organised paradigmatically, and tend to be phonologically weak (often monosyllabic). Two principal factors inhibit switching around function words: the first is the fact that function words score low on Backus's (1996) specificity continuum (see above). The second is related to equivalence or congruence: the greater variability among languages in the structural realisation of 'functions' results in a greater likelihood of incongruence around functional elements compared with semantically autonomous content words.

Muysken's discussion of the likely distribution of switches over grammatical categories takes into account different investigations of codeswitching corpora by several different authors (cf. survey in Muysken 2000a: 232–239). An in-depth comparison of datasets is not always possible, since data are often tabled in different ways, not all categories are considered in each and every survey, and even the definitions of some categories may vary. Moreover, some studies have found differences among the direction of switches (e.g. Spanish to English vs. English to Spanish) in the absolute numbers and proportions of switches around certain categories. Nonetheless, the following generalisations based on the data presented in several different studies (including some of those cited by Muysken, as well as others) provide a tentative picture of the relevance of category affiliation. The hierarchies convey the relevant frequency of switches around the relevant category:

(12)   Relative frequency of categories affected by codeswitching
     a. Backus (1996): Turkish/Dutch
          nouns > verbs > adverbs > adjectives, prepositional
          phrases > conjunctions > pronouns

     b. Nortier (1990): Moroccan Arabic/Dutch
          nouns > adverbs > adjectives > conjunctions > verbs >
          prepositions > pronouns > numerals

     c. Myers-Scotton (1993b): Swahili/English
          nouns > verbs > adjectives > adverbs > interjections >
          conjunctions

     d. Gardner-Chloros (1991): Alsatian/French
          nouns > greetings, interjections, tags, phatic markers >
          adverbs > verbs > adjectives > conjunctions

     e. Berk-Seligson (1986): (Judeo-)Spanish/Hebrew
          nouns > adverbs > adjectives > conjunctions > verb
          phrases > prepositional phrases > pronouns, interrogatives >
          verbs

     f. Pfaff (1979): Spanish/English
          noun phrases > verb phrases > adjectives

     g. Poplack (1980): Spanish/English
          noun phrases > verb phrases, conjunctions > adverbs >
          adjectives

     h. Bentahila and Davies (1995): Moroccan Arabic/French,
          nouns > adjectives > verbs > pronouns, adpositions

The consistent position of nouns at the very top of the hierarchy stands out. This position can be easily explained: nouns are more likely than any other word class to appear at the top of the specificity and awareness hierarchies (Backus 1996), as labels for unique referents or for new products, artefacts or concepts. Since the bilingual contexts surveyed in the cited studies all involve cultural contacts, the transferability of cultural concepts and terms for cultural objects and institutions from one context of speech to another is easily accounted for. Conversely, pronouns figure consistently low on the hierarchy. There is no semantic motivation to switch around pronouns, since they are rarely associated with any specific interaction context and since they perform roughly the same grammatical operations in all the languages involved.[9] Moreover, pronouns operate on the firm assumption of the presence of an established deictic/anaphoric field that is shared by the participants (see Bühler 1934). There is therefore no pressure on the speaker to monitor and direct the listener's participation in the processing of the discourse and therefore no high risk of malfunctions of the mechanism that selects the contextually appropriate word-form from the repertoire and inhibits the selection of non-appropriate equivalents (see Chapter 4). Pronoun switching is therefore rare by comparison.

Elsewhere, the general picture becomes a bit fuzzy. It is possible that the different status of conjunctions in different corpora is in part due to differences in the definition. The category may include coordinating and subordinating conjunctions and perhaps other discourse markers. Adverbs and adjectives tend to occupy adjoining positions, somewhere lower on the hierarchy than nouns, which reflects their status as content words that are less likely to denote specific or unique referents than nouns. The most irregular and unpredictable position seems to be that of verbs. The behaviour of verbs seems to depend both on the combination of languages, and the switching habits of speakers. Note for instance that in combinations with the two agglutinating languages, Turkish and Swahili, verbs occupy the highest possible position after nouns. In the other cases, verb phrases tend to appear higher on the hierarchy than plain verbs.

Apart from their structural complexity, which no doubt plays a role in the degree of convenience with which verbs can or cannot be integrated into a wide range of sentence structures in bilingual discourse, verbs occupy a crucial position in functional perspective. We have seen that bilinguals may claim considerable freedom in selecting items from their multilingual repertoire in contexts where use of the bilingual mode is appropriate. Yet even in those contexts, it is accepted that every utterance has an identifiable base-language, or in the terms of the MLF model, a Matrix language. Moreover, it is assumed by most approaches that the choice of a base language in a given context is not accidental, be it for the duration of the entire speech event or even just for individual moves, turns, or speech acts. In a functional perspective, the core of the utterance is the predication; the base language is therefore the language in which the speaker chooses to anchor and initiate the predication. In an effort to comply even with lax norms on the selection of word-forms and constructions, bilinguals seem to want to avoid ambiguity in the choice of the language of the predication. The insertion of finite verbs may, in some cases, result in such ambiguity.

Example (10) illustrates how ambiguity may at times be tolerated. In this particular case, the main, focused clause in the cleft construction has English as its base- or predication-language, while the subordinated, relative clause containing given information (the second part of a known idiom) has Hebrew as its predication-language. The idiomatic character of the predication and the fact that we have a complex clause with not just one, but two, predications no doubt helps license this switch of predication languages within a single utterance. In other types of utterances, however, speakers may feel more reluctant to compromise the predication. This creates a conflict between the efficiency of expression, which at times will call on bilinguals to draw on their full repertoire and insert lexical items, including descriptions of events, states, and actions, in other words including verbs, into the utterance, irrespective of the subset or 'language' affiliation of these items; and the need for a coherent predication that is compliant with the underlying basic language-choice that is relevant for the utterance.

One way to resolve the conflict is by stripping the imported verb of its function as the anchor of the predication and treating it merely as a lexical root, that is as the mere depiction of the state, event or action to be portrayed. This is facilitated when the language pair involved allows on the one hand to isolate a lexical root of the verb, and on the other hand a straightforward integration of that lexical root into a regular morphological template that is responsible for the predicate-initiation function. This is the case when Swahili is the base language and an English verb is inserted: consider *mu-no-criticize* [2PL-HABIT-criticise] 'you criticise' (Myers-Scotton 1993b: 184). An alternative, in the event that it is not convenient to isolate the lexical root of the verb, is to simply disregard its predicate-initiating function and to treat an inflected form of the verb as a mere lexical entry. This is the case with Dutch verbal insertions into Turkish: *beheers-en yap-ıyor-ken* [control-INF make-PROG-CONV] 'while he controls . . .' (Backus 1996: 232). Here, the Dutch infinitive *beheersen* 'to control' is adopted in a non-finite form as a token for the mere lexical meaning of the verb, neutralising its 'verbality' in the sense of an inherent predication-anchoring function. That function is instead carried by the so-called 'light verb' or integration auxiliary, for which purpose speakers of Turkish use the verb *yap-* 'to do'.

Muysken (2000a: 184) identifies four main types of structural integration of switched verbs: (a) The new verb is inserted into a position corresponding to the native verb (as in the Swahili/English example above); (b) the new verb is adjoined to a helping verb; Muysken cites Hungarian, Navaho, and other examples. A further example is Domari, where Arabic loan verbs are augmented by either the native suffix -k- deriving from the verb 'to do', or the native suffix -(h)o- deriving from the verb 'to be/to become': *štrī-k-ami* [buy-AUG-1SG] 'I buy', *skunn-ho-ndi* [reside-AUG-3PL] 'they reside'; (c) the new verb is a nominalised complement in a verbal compound (as in the Turkish/Dutch example above); and (d) the new verb is an infinitive and the complement of a native auxiliary.[10]

For the latter strategy, see the following two examples, both for the language pair English/Hebrew, both from bilingual children. Although the language combination is the same, as is the age group and the kind of linguistic input that the children are and have been exposed to, there appear to be different personal preferences for verb integration:

(13)   Ben; Hebrew; age 6:10, addressing a somewhat younger bilingual Hebrew–
          (English) child, while walking on a low stone boundary on the edge of a
          footpath:
                káxa aní yexól   *to keep my balance*
                thus I   can.SG.M
                'This way I can *keep my balance*'

(14)   Ben's Israeli-American cousin; age 5:7, addressing her uncle in the family
          language, Hebrew, while giving him a picture she had drawn:
                atá yexól laasót   *keep it*
                you can   do.INF
                'You can keep it'

The first child (13) chooses the complement + infinitive strategy, while the second (14) uses a supporting verb. Note however how in both cases the insertion of English *keep* triggers a switch into English for the remainder of the verb phrase. In (13), the motivation is the preservation of a collocation as well as the reproduction, in all likelihood, of the original context of the playful challenge in the English-speaking school. In (14), it would appear that the switch into English helps avoid the ambiguity of positioning a Hebrew direct object between the supporting verb *laasót* and the inserted English verb *keep*. This would be an unnatural construction in Hebrew, which does not have compound verbs. It also helps avoid placing a Hebrew object after the English verb, in a position isolated from the Hebrew part of the sentence. At any rate, the employment of two distinct integration strategies under comparable circumstances – both linguistic and social – indicates that some structural constraints are fairly open to speakers' choices and personal preferences. This is not altogether a surprising finding; despite efforts to describe its formal regularities, codeswitching remains to a considerable extent the creative, improvised composition of individual speakers wishing to take advantage of the enormous assortment of nuances that their complex, multilingual repertoire affords.

5.4   Codeswitching and utterance modifiers

In example (1) we noted the insertion of two German word-forms into Romani discourse that do not comply with Backus's (1996) specificity or awareness criteria, and would hence not be predicted, according to that model, as likely candidates for switching: The concessive subordinating conjunction *obwohl* 'although', and the temporal indefinite *manchmal* 'sometimes'. We noted that both forms represent what we might refer to, in terms relating to language processing in communicative interaction, as 'high-risk' operators: They either instigate a potential clash with hearer expectations, as is the case with the contrastive-concessive; or they leave crucial semantic content unspecified thereby abandoning typical speaker-sided guidance of the hearer, as is the case with the indefinite. We noted that operators of this kind run the risk of alienating the hearer and are therefore points in the formulation of the utterance at which increased attention and monitoring activity of the hearer's reaction is demanded from the speaker. This in turn, it was argued, weakens the selection mechanism for context-appropriate (i.e. language-particular) word-forms and increases the likelihood of a fall-back onto the most recently activated routine option in the pragmatically dominant language.

Common candidates for such processes are discourse markers, in the sense defined by Schiffrin (1987), Fraser (1990), and Blakemore (2002), but also in a broader definition, one that includes focus and modal particles (see König 1991), interjections and tags or so-called 'expeditive' procedures and 'speech act enhancers' (Ehlich 1986, Rehbein 1979), as well as, due to their role in directly processing events in relation to expectations, phasal adverbs such as 'already' or 'no longer' (Van der Auwera 1998). I have proposed the term 'utterance modifiers' to capture this somewhat extended group of operators that are responsible for monitoring and directing the hearer's processing of propositional content (Matras 1998a). We encountered this group of markers in the context of multilingual first-language acquisition in Chapter 2, where we saw that they are particularly prone to selection malfunctions and so to bilingual speech production errors.

There is widespread agreement in the literature on bilingual speech concerning the high frequency of L2-insertion of discourse markers and related operators. Some recent studies include Brody (1987) on Spanish markers in Mayan languages, Savić (1995) on English markers in the speech of Serbian immigrants, De Rooij (2000) on French markers in Shaba Swahili, Fuller (2001) on English forms in Pennsylvania German, Torres (2002) on English markers in New York Puerto Rican Spanish, Sakel (2007) on Spanish markers in Mosetén, Stolz (2007) on Italian discourse markers in neighbouring languages including Maltese, and many more.

Already Weinreich (1953: 30), commenting on American Yiddish utterances like *nit er bʌt ix* 'not he but I', had suggested that 'forms belonging to some classes [may be] more subject to transfer than others'. Poplack (1980: 602) reported that discourse markers, tags, interjections, and fillers accounted for 29% of all codeswitches in the corpus of Puerto Rican Spanish–English bilinguals in New York City. Poplack's (1980: 605–608) explanation for the phenomenon was that these elements require less proficiency in English and are therefore used opportunistically by Spanish-dominant speakers to flag their bilingual competence. Stolz and Stolz (1996) provide a similar explanation for the use of Spanish discourse markers in a large sample of Mesoamerican languages, interpreting them as signals of prestige and a 'Spanish flavour' of the discourse.

Maschler (1994) interprets Hebrew discourse markers in Israeli–English discourse as a strategy applied in order to 'metalanguage' discourse boundaries. This notion of a discourse strategy differs from Poplack's (1980) idea of 'emblematic' switches. It focuses not on the mere bilingual flavour achieved by inserting switched items, nor on the overall social effects which this creates, but on the connection between switching and the internal, communicative function of the items themselves: Language alternation is seen as a way of highlighting the function of discourse markers in framing units of talk (cf. Schiffrin 1987). De Rooij (1996: 168–171, 2000) follows Maschler in arguing in favour of a strategic usage of French discourse markers in Shaba Swahili. Nortier (1990) mentions how in Moroccan Arabic/Dutch codeswitching, it is usually Dutch elements that are inserted into Arabic, but that discourse markers such as Arabic *walakin* 'but', *wella* 'or', *u/wa* 'and', and the tag *fhemti?* 'you understand?' are the exception.

Myers-Scotton (1993b: 201–203) discusses the use of English *because* and *but* in Shona discourse, which amounts to 7% and 8% of occurrence of the respective function-words in the corpus. She emphasises that both words have structural and functional equivalents in Shona and are therefore not 'gap fillers', and adds that their occurrence in Shona discourse is not triggered by any English items in the immediate environment. Myers-Scotton concludes that, like other discourse markers, *because* and *but* in Shona are borrowings, not codeswitches, and that their borrowing is facilitated by their function, which is to combine propositions, and by the fact that they are free forms. Muysken (2000a: 106–114) rejects gap-related explanations, pointing out the frequent 'doubling' of discourse markers – a Spanish word-form co-occurring with a native word-form – in various South American languages, such as Otomi, Quechua, and Popoloca (for a similar phenomenon in other South and Central American languages, see Brody 1987, Campbell 1993, Stolz and Stolz 1996, Sakel 2007a). The 'gap hypothesis' has been rejected by others as well because it is known that borrowed markers have replaced, over time, markers that had been their structural and functional equivalents (Matras 1998a, Dal Negro 2005).

It is noteworthy that some authors discuss bilingual discourse markers as codeswitches, attributing to their use special conversational effects such as competence- or identity-flagging or the highlighting of discourse boundaries, while others treat them as borrowings or indications of ongoing language change. It appears that we are dealing with an area in which frequent insertional switching has the potential and the tendency to become stabilised and over time to lead to language change. Thus, the full continuum between 'switching' and 'borrowing' as discussed earlier in this chapter appears visible not just by comparing different case studies, but even when focusing on individual bilingual communities. Discussing the use of English discourse markers by immigrants to Australia within their ethnic-language discourse, Clyne (2003: 225–233) for instance notes that they are more prolific among the second generation. Among speakers of Hungarian and German, the use of English discourse markers comes at the expense of the gradual abandonment of modal particles in these languages. Clyne interprets these parallel developments as a token of the speakers' cultural adaptation to Australian communicative norms.

Hlavac (2006) describes how English discourse markers co-occur with their Croatian counterparts in the speech of Croatian immigrants, though English forms that enjoy a high frequency in English and are also poly-functional occur in the corpus with a higher frequency than their Croatian counterparts. This helps shed some light on the nature of the development, which in some cases at least may lead toward a wholesale abandonment, over time, of the native system of discourse markers, and its replacement by that of the contact languages.

In an influential study on the use of English discourse markers among speakers of German in Texas, Salmons (1990) notes that the wholesale adoption of the English system of discourse marking coincides with the loss of the German system of modal particles. He concludes that the systems of discourse-regulating functions in the two languages have undergone convergence, and relates this structural convergence to the mutual adaptation of general communicative patterns in language contact situations. The gradual introduction of discourse operators from a contact language has been documented for the Wallser German dialects of Switzerland by Dal Negro (2005). Drawing on older documentation of the dialects, she traces the introduction of Italian *ma* 'but', which now figures alongside German *aber* 'but' in most locations, and has even replaced the original German word-form in one of the locations. Chen (2007) points out the regularity of use of Taiwanese sentence particles in the Mandarin as spoken in Taiwan for just over two generations.

Bilingual speech provides us with an opportunity to examine the fate of discourse operators in what often turns out to be a transition stage between the occasional, accidental selection of a word-form from the other language, to the sedimentation of such forms, leading ultimately to their long-term borrowing and propagation throughout the speech community (see also Matras 1998a, 2000b, 2007a). Consider first two more examples from Lovari Romani as spoken in Hamburg; the speaker was born in Poland, but immigrated to Germany at a young age. Her principal second language is German:

(15)   Laki familija sas   *also*   kesave sar   te   phenav, artisturi, *nə*?
        her family   were PART   such   how COMP say.1SG artists   PART
        Her family were *like* such how shall I say, showpeople, *right*?

(16)   Taj žasas   ande veša   taj rodasas,   taj dikhasas, khelasas
        and went.1PL in   woods and searched.1PL and saw.1PL   played.1PL

        ame *halt*,   *nə*.
        we   PART PART
        'And we used to go into the woods and search, and look around, we *like*
        used to play, *right*.'

The German discourse particles *also*, *halt*, *nə* are treated as an integral part of the Romani discourse. They are not regarded as foreign, and they do not disturb the subjective (from the speaker's point of view) well-formedness of the Romani discourse. It is important to note that they do not cause either loss of face or barriers to comprehensibility within the extended family, which is where Romani is mainly used. On the other hand, there is nothing to suggest that acceptance of German culture, or flagging of German-language competence, are motivating triggers behind the insertion of German particles. Bilingualism is the reality in Romani communities, and, as we mentioned earlier, the bilingual mode is the default mode for most Romani conversations. At the same time, members of the Romani community are very proud of their ethnicity and community pressure disfavours assimilation. There is therefore no obvious advantage to flagging any form of cultural or emotional accommodation to the outside, non-Romani world.

Examples (15)–(16) therefore do not show any symbolic token of cultural adaptation per se, but rather an emerging acceptance of a uniform system of utterance-management devices that apply to the speaker's full linguistic repertoire, irrespective of language-particular context. Naturally, the expansion of word-forms is one-sided: German operators are accepted and used in Romani discourse, but not vice versa. This is a consequence of the acceptance of the bilingual mode in the context of Romani interaction. What is the reason behind this acceptance specifically of discourse operators? There are, I suggest, two principal motivations, which are interconnected. The first is the vulnerability of discourse operators to selection malfunctions, as discussed above and in Chapter 4. This leads to a relatively high frequency of 'slips' or fallbacks into the pragmatically dominant language – German, in this case – and so to acceptance of the occasional or perhaps even regular occurrence of German discourse operators in Romani discourse, which in turn may license the general use of German discourse operators. The second reason has to do with the fact that discourse operators or utterance modifiers carry out highly automated routine tasks, for which routine schemas appear to exist. Their role in managing the interaction and in mentally reaching out to the hearer gives them a gesture-like function. As such, they are less identifiable with just a particular subset of the repertoire and its permissible usage contexts – i.e. less attributable to a particular 'language' – and are instead accepted as more universal. They are, in other words, 'pragmatically detachable' from their source language (see Matras 1998a; cf. also Fuller 2001).

The acceptance of majority-language discourse operators as a routine part of minority-language discourse is attested from other contexts too. The following examples (17)–(18) stem from a corpus of recordings among the Volga Germans of Russia (Anders 1993: II/8 and I/6–7):

(17)   Und auch in einer Brigade, wo   mer hat (2.0) *etot*   (A)/ (1.0)
         and also in a   brigade   where one has   this uh

         war ich auch wie der Helfer   zum Brigadier.
         was I   also like the assistant to-the brigadier
         'And also in a brigade, where we had (2.0) *what-do-you-call-it* (uh)/ (1.0) I
         was also like an assistant to the brigadier.'

(18)   a. Und die hat doch lauter/ die Katarina hat lauter so (3.0)
            and she has PART all   the Katarina has all   such

            specialisty, die   wo (2.0) baue hän kenne. Die, wo   des alles
            specialists those REL   build have could those REL that all

            hän   kenne mache.
            have could do

        b. Und so weiter und weiter und/ wie wir dort sin
            and so on   and on   and as we there are

            niberkomme (1.0) alle.
            come-over   all

        c. *Potom* (1.0) *nu*   die Wolgarepublik, *potom/ nu*   so is
            then   PART the Volga Republic then   PART so is

            weiter und weiter/(1.0) die ganze *istorija*!
            on   and on   the entire history

        a. And she had all those/ Katarina had all those (3.0) specialists, who
            (2.0) were able to build. Those who were able to do everything.
        b. And so on and on and/ when we all came there,
        c. *And then* (1.0) *well*, the Volga Republic, *then/ well* it went on and
            on like this/ (1.0) the whole *story*!

Alongside Russian lexical insertions the extracts also contain Russian utterance
modifiers: The hesitation marker/filler in *etot* in (17), the sequential marker *potom*
'and then' in (18a), and the filler *nu*. They are used with relatively high frequency,
and, much like the German utterance modifiers in Romani speech, they are not
followed by any self-repair, indicating that the speaker fully accepts their role in
the utterance.

In both the Romani and the Volga German example sets, discourse markers are
integrated that do not have exact native equivalents, alongside some that do, such
as *potom* 'and then' (German: *und dann*). It is possible that the need to manage
the interaction in a similar way while conversing in both languages motivates
the adoption at first of those forms and functions that are missing in the native,
minority or in-group language (cf. also Hlavac 2006). But the fact that it may also
lead to a substitution of native forms by L2-equivalents suggests that the process
is not limited to the creation of harmony in functions across the two languages,
but extends to harmony of the form inventory as well.

The following examples are from conversations with two native speakers of
Low German. Born and raised in Schleswig-Holstein in northern Germany, they
emigrated to the United States as teenagers in the mid 1950s. The recordings,
carried out in the early 1990s,[11] document their speech after some 35 years in a
predominantly English-speaking environment:

(19)   dat weer'n Ünnericht för süstein Stunnen, *but* ik hef   bloos
            that was a lesson   for sixteen hours   but I have only

acht Stunnen måkt, åber dor   hef   ik uk   nix   leert.
eight hours   made but   there have I   also nothing learned
'That was a sixteen-hour class, but I only did eight, but I also didn't
learn anything there.'

(20)   a. *And* as   ik in Clinton ankeem, den haa'k fiif Dåler   nåå, und
               and when I in Clinton arrived then had I five dollars left and

               den hef ik se   dat jüst wiist,   ob he mi nåå dedore Adres
               then have I them that just showed if he me to   that   address

               dor   för fiif Dåler hen dee.
               there for five dollars to   does

            b. Den is de gude Man nåå't *telephone* gåån *and* het de   anropen
               then is the good man to-the telephone gone and has him called

               and secht, dat ik hiir weer und dat he mi bringen dee.
               and says   that I here was and that he me bring   does

            c. Dat *normally* wor   fillicht foftein Dåler kossen, *but* he dee dat
               that normally would maybe   fifteen dollars cost   but he did that

               för fiif.
               for five

            a. '*And* when arrived in Clinton I had five dollars left, and then I just
               showed it to them, if he would bring me to that address for five dollars.

            b. So the good man went to the *telephone and* he called him *and* said that
               I was there and that he would bring me.

            c. That would *normally* cost maybe fifteen dollars, *but* he did it for five.'

Both speakers use the English conjunctions *and, but*, interchangeably with
their Low German counterparts, indicating their acceptance despite the existence
of equivalent native word-forms. The adoption of forms in this way can lead
ultimately to a loss of any inherited inventory of utterance modifiers and to the
wholesale adoption instead of the inventory of the contact language – a process which I described as 'fusion' (Matras 1998a, 2000b). This is demonstrated
by the following extract from Domari, which draws entirely on the discourse-
marking and utterance-modifying instruments of its main contact language,
Arabic:

(21)   a. *ū   daʔiman/ yaʕnī/ kunt   ama kury-a-m-ēk   wala*
               and always   that.is was.1SG I   house-OBL-LOC-PRED.F and.not

               kil-šami wala   aw-ami. wala   waddik-ar-m-i   maḥall-ak
               exit-1SG and.not come-1SG and.not bring-3SG-1SG-PRES place-INDEF

            b. *ya par-ar-m-i   wāš-īs   kamk-am,   ū*
               or take-3SG-1SG-PRES with-3SG work-1SG.SUBJ and

               par-ar-i   plē-m.
               take-3SG-PRES money-1SG

c. *ū* gištanē-san *kānu*   *yaʕnī* ʕamilk-ad-m-a   *mišš* ghāy
  and all-3pl   was.3PL that.is treat-3PL-1SG-REM NEG good

  kury-am-a
  house-OBL-LOC

d. *bass* kānat   dāy-os   ḥayyat-ē-ki   ghāy wāš-īm.
  but was.3SG.F mother-NOM.3SG   OBL-ABL good with-1SG

e. pandži rabbik-ed-os-im.   *yaʕnī lamma kānat*
  she   bring.up-PERF-NOM.3SG-OBL.1SG that.is when   was.3SG.F

  ḥayyāt far-m-a   *wila ʾiši*   *kānat*   ḥazzirk-ar-s-a.
      hit-1SG-REM or   something was.3SG.F warn-3SG-3SG-REM

a. *'And I was always/ I mean/* at home, *not* going out *nor* coming *nor*
  would she take me *anywhere.*

b. *Or* she takes me with her to work, *and* she takes my money.

c. *And* they all *used to* treat me badly at home.

d. *But* Hayyat's mother was nice to me.

e. She brought me up. *I mean, whenever* Hayyat *used to* beat me *or
  anything* she *used to* tell her off.'

I do not challenge either the interpretation of bilingual discourse markers as
strategies of reinforcing contrast in discourse, as proposed by Maschler (1994),
or the notion that discourse markers can be used to flag proficiency in the second language or even adaptation to the majority culture, as proposed by various
authors. However, I do not believe that these factors on their own are powerful
enough to lead to the long-term adoption of key operators such as coordinating conjunctions, fillers, or tags, or even to the wholesale substitution of the
entire system of discourse markers. The mere structural character of discourse
operators is not, in my view, a sufficient explanation for their vulnerability and
borrowability, either.

The contrastive or metalinguistic function of bilingual discourse markers as
discussed by Maschler (1994) relies on the contrast between the discourse marker
systems of the two languages. Once the systems converge, the contrast effect is
lost. As for the need to flag bilingual competence, it fails to explain the adoption
of foreign discourse markers in situations where bilingualism is taken for granted
and there is little to be gained by flagging acculturation. Note that two, almost
opposite views have been expressed in the literature with regard to the symbolic
effect of bilingual discourse markers. Poplack (1980) explained frequent use of
English operators as an almost compensatory strategy employed by those whose
English proficiency was potentially in doubt and so needed to be flagged. Clyne
(2003) on the other hand observes that foreign discourse markers are used more
frequently by those who are more acculturated and so can be expected to be
more proficient bilinguals.

Acculturation suggests more frequent and more intense involvement in activity
contexts in which the L2 is used, and a considerable strengthening of the L2

as the pragmatically dominant language. Speakers who are, by this definition, 'acculturated', will require greater mental effort in keeping apart their utterance modifying systems, are more prone to performing selection errors, and so more likely over time to license themselves to simply adopt the set of foreign markers and, social attitudes permitting, to use them regularly irrespective of the context of interaction (and so irrespective of language choice).

Finally, the structural argument posits that L2-discourse markers are easily integrated because they tend to be uninflected and phonologically simple, and because they appear in utterance-peripheral positions. Again, it is certainly possible that these typical structural characteristics of discourse markers, at least in some languages, support their generalisation within a bilingual individual's repertoire. However, the structural 'simplicity' of discourse markers itself does not offer an explanation for the motivation to generalise just one set within the bilingual repertoire in the first place. The structural argument seems to be predicated on the assumption that *some* borrowing or interference among the systems will take place due to the social pressures of a dominant language, and that, once that social process is put in motion, the first candidates for borrowing are those that are structurally easiest to integrate. This argument ignores the actual function of discourse markers as well as the fact that there are other potential candidates that fit a similar structural profile, such as place adverbs 'here' and 'there', or adpositions in some languages, which are not subject to prolific codeswitching or borrowing. The argument also ignores the proneness of discourse markers to bilingual selection errors, treating it as a mere coincidence.

In earlier work (Matras 1998a, 2000b, 2007a, 2007b) I made the case for a functional, language-processing related motivation for the frequent insertion of foreign utterance modifiers or discourse markers. This case was further developed in Chapters 2 and 4 of this book, and will be sketched briefly once more here, as a summary. I return first of all to the speaker perspective on bilingual speech: communicative interaction does not involve the activation or disengagement of 'systems', but rather constant choices among components of the full repertoire of linguistic structures (word-forms, constructions, phonetic realisations, and so on). In selecting among items, bilingual speakers are guided, naturally, by the meaning and function of those items, but also by their context-appropriateness. This involves assessing the immediate communicative interaction and classifying it as more or less strict in respect of expectations on code choice, as well as negotiating the integration of meanings and associations from other activity contexts, special effects and metalanguaging, authenticity, and so on. Control over the selection mechanism is a necessary pre-requisite for all these processes.

But control may be vulnerable around certain types of language-processing operations, as discussed in Chapter 4. They include monitoring-and-directing hearer-sided participation in the interaction and the hearer's processing of propositional content – functions carried out by the broader class of discourse operators which we call 'utterance modifiers': conjunctions, tags, fillers, interjections, focus particles, and others. This may lead to frequent malfunctions and the production of selection errors, as we saw in Chapter 4. At stake is, of course, compliance with the norms on context-appropriate choices within the linguistic repertoire. But in a community in which bilingualism is accepted, and attitudes do not necessarily inhibit some degree of flexibility in the selection of word-forms, speakers may over time opt for just one set of markers, thus eliminating or at least reducing the need to select among competing word-forms around discourse regulating operations. In reducing the choice, one set is typically abandoned, while the other prevails. By necessity, if there is asymmetry in the opportunities to use a bilingual mode in conversation – if speakers of one language are bilingual, but speakers of the other language are not – and if one of the languages dominates in institutional contexts, where lax control over appropriate word-form selection is not permissible, then speakers will generalise the one set of markers that cannot be compromised, and abandon the other. The outcome can be described as a 'fusion' of the set of discourse marking operations, or the prevalence of just one system in the bilingual repertoire, which is employed irrespective of interaction context. In this way, individual aspects of the bilinguals' speech production and performance are inherently and tightly linked to the social aspects of bilingualism, which determine the extent to which individual innovations may be propagated throughout the speech community and adopted, eventually, by most speakers, or at least by entire sectors within the group.

6   The replication of linguistic 'matter'

6.1   Defining 'borrowings'

One of the outcomes of language contact is a change in the structural inventory of at least one of the languages involved, and sometimes of both. This is often viewed as a kind of import of a structure or form from one language system into another. The process is best known as 'borrowing' (cf. Haugen 1950); items affected by it are called 'borrowings', 'loans', or 'transfers', and the languages involved are frequently labelled, according to their roles, 'donor' and 'recipient' (Weinreich 1953).

Though well-established, the term 'borrowing' is sometimes criticised. Like any metaphor, it lacks accuracy. For a start, borrowing typically leads to the long-term incorporation of an item into the inventory of the recipient language. Bilingual speakers may well be aware of the origin of a word or morpheme in a particular 'donor' language, but this awareness may be blurred over time, especially if active bilingualism declines, or when use of the item spreads to monolingual sectors of the speech community. Not only is there no intention to return the 'borrowed' item to its rightful 'owner', but for most speakers its original 'ownership' may not always be traceable. As Johanson (2002: 8) states, the term 'borrowing' may also be misleading in that it implies that the donor language is being 'robbed' of an element that belongs to it.

One might thus contend that 'borrowing' emphasises too much the aspect of ownership and the boundaries between the linguistic systems involved, and that this diverts attention away from the dynamic process of sharing a structure or word-form, adopting, applying, and using it. Johanson (2002) therefore favours the term 'copying', which emphasises the creative use of an item within the 'recipient' language. I will use the term *replication* to capture even more closely the fact that we are dealing not with issues of ownership or even direct imitation or duplication, but rather with the activity of employing an item, in context, in order to achieve a communicative goal. For fear of contributing further to an unnecessary proliferation of terminology, I shall not abandon the term 'borrowing', but simply clarify here that I use the term to refer to the *replication* of a linguistic structure, of any kind, in a new, extended set of contexts, understood to be negotiated in a different 'language'.

It is widely accepted that the seeds of borrowing are found in the occasional use of second-language insertions in the speech of bilinguals. In Chapter 5 I described the codeswitching–borrowing continuum and criteria for distinguishing between the two phenomena. It was argued that bilinguals generally assess the immediate interaction context and the appropriateness of foreign insertions, and that they tend to give themselves considerable freedom in this respect when interacting in what Grosjean (2001) calls the 'bilingual mode'. From the perspective of the speaker, borrowing involves a long-term or permanent licence to lift selection constraints on the use of a word-form or structure. Rather than serve in just a limited set of contexts, that word-form or structure now becomes available in a wider set of interaction contexts, perhaps with no limitation at all. As discussed in Chapter 5, one of the important criteria for distinguishing codeswitching from borrowing is the replication of the item by monolingual speakers, if there are any, and in monolingual contexts.

In distinguishing bilingual and monolingual contexts, it is advantageous to accept a continuum of 'bilingualism', as discussed in Chapter 5. At the far end of this continuum is the rudimentary ability to interact in 'foreign' contexts. According to Sakel (2007b), members of the isolated Pirahã tribe in the Brazilian Amazon region, despite being monolingual, have adopted the word *topagahai*, their replication of the English word 'tape-recorder' used by American missionary-linguists who frequented their villages, as well as a longer list of Portuguese words used in occasional contacts with other visitors, such as *bobói* 'candy' (Portuguese *bombom*), *pága* 'pay' (Portuguese *paga*), and *kai* 'house' (Portuguese *casa*). Their interactions with these visitors, in which new words occurred that were not otherwise used among the Pirahã in group-internal communication, are perhaps the most basic manifestation of a bilingual interaction context. As soon as speakers begin to interact in new contexts and use new word-forms to accommodate specifically to those contexts, we can speak of the emergence of some notion of 'bilingualism', however basic.

Young Kurdish children in the outskirts of Diyarbakir in eastern Anatolia (Turkey) provide another example. In the mid 1980s, they used to address Western tourists with the word *okay!* In the absence of opportunities to learn European languages or to intensify their contacts with foreigners, the word had a token function. It was used as a kind of greeting, symbolising an attitude favourable in principle toward communication in a foreign, Western tongue. This was, in a way, an even more basic bilingual context than the rudimentary verbal interaction between the Pirahã and their visitors. Thomason's (2001: 67–68) definition of 'borrowing' as 'the kind of interference that occurs when the process does not involve any effects of imperfect learning' might therefore be modified to cover, at least at the extreme end of the continuum, superficial communication of this kind. Such situations only offer limited communicative opportunities, but they nevertheless constitute distinct and identifiable interaction contexts. Word-forms that are initially reserved for these contexts of interaction with outsiders, but are later replicated in interaction with insiders, may count as borrowings.

Consider a German–English bilingual's use of the terms *internet, download, computer*. With slight variation in phonological/phonetic realisation and morpho-syntactic integration into the sentence (as well as in spelling, where nouns are concerned),[1] the same word-forms can be used irrespective of context of inter-action – whether the context is one in which German is spoken, or whether the language is English. This means that for each of these particular concepts, bilin-guals will only have a single word-form in their repertoire of linguistic structures, with no need to select the appropriate form according to 'language' – the set-ting or context of the conversation. Moreover, even monolinguals might be able to recognise and comprehend the respective equivalent in the other language. Bulgarians shopping for fish at a Turkish market, for example, will have little difficulty identifying their choices by name even if they are unable to speak any Turkish at all; names for fish and other natural foods are often shared across the contiguous languages Turkish, Bulgarian, and Greek as a result of centuries-old cultural and trade contacts.

In Chapters 2, 4, and 5 we examined different motivations for the failure to keep apart subsets of the linguistic repertoire around specific forms or structures. They range from the wish to maintain consistent labelling for unique referents such as institutions, through the wish to make use of the full expressive repertoire, to special conversational effects, and on to lapses in the speaker's control over the selection of word-forms. We saw that different constructions, categories, and word classes may be susceptible in different ways both to strategic exploitation of the full repertoire, and to lapses in control over the selection mechanism. We might therefore expect that different word classes will also show different degrees of susceptibility to long-term adoption or borrowing. Much of this and the following two chapters will survey the borrowability of various linguistic categories. I devote Chapters 6–8 specifically to the replication of what I call linguistic *matter*: concrete, identifiable sound-shapes of words and morphs. Linguistic matter has certain properties that distinguish it from the mode of organising units of speech, or *patterns*. Perhaps the most relevant property is that matter-units are concrete phonological units and as such are more easily identifiable as belonging to certain subsets of the repertoire. When it comes to matter units, speakers seem to be on the whole more conscious of their selection.

A matter-item is a complex unit. It has a phonological form, a meaning (whether lexical or grammatical), and a distinct status as an item in the lex-icon, with implications for inflectional potential and positioning within the sentence. The process of replication may affect any one of these dimensions: phonology, meaning, or morphology and morpho-syntactic status. For exam-ple, only those acquainted with the Pirahã will be able to recognise the word-form *topagahai* as a replication of English 'tape-recorder'. With no contextual cues, quite a bit of imagination would also be needed in order to recognise the origin of the Palestinian/Jordanian Arabic word *banšer* as deriving from English 'puncture'. The phonological adaptation of these words illustrates the potential implications of a process of context-bound *replication*: far from entailing just plain 'copying', it is open to modifications, adaptations, and changes.

Here are some further examples: the Romani word *tajśa* is a replication of the (medieval and dialectal) Greek word *taixiá* meaning 'tomorrow', but in Romani it can mean both 'tomorrow' and 'yesterday'. The Greek loan had replaced the original Romani *kal(iko)*, still attested in some dialects of the language, which is cognate with the modern Indo-Aryan word *kal* meaning both 'tomorrow' and 'yesterday'. Here we see that not all components of the original word are in fact copied in Romani. The borrowing process entails in this case only a partial replication of the phonological form and a partial replication of meaning, while at the same time the word acquires new meanings through its association with a concept represented by an inherited Romani word-form. The Hindi/Urdu local relation expression *bād* 'after' occurs after its head (cf. *is-ke bād* 'after this'). It replicates the word-shape and meaning of the Persian–Arabic prepositional model (Persian *baad*, Arabic *baʕd*), but not its position in the phrase.

The Hebrew word *fiksés* 'he sent a fax' is associated only in its abstract, consonantal root form with its model, English/European *fax*, following integration into a Hebrew word-formation template of what is, for this purpose, identified as the underlying word stem (*f.k.s—*); it is this abstract phonological representation, reduplicated in the integration process from *f.k.s* to *f.k.s.s.*, that is replicated, along with its semantic meaning, even though such an abstract entity arguably does not exist in a monolingual form of English. Finally, the Swahili word *vitabu* 'books' bears only partial resemblance to its model Arabic word *kitāb* 'book'. The first syllable of the Arabic model word-form *ki-*is reinterpreted as the Swahili singular nominal prefix *ki-*. The counterpart plural marker for the same Swahili nominal class is *vi-*, which alternates with *ki-* at the beginning of the word, giving the plural form *vitabu*. The final segment *-u* is used generically to accommodate Arabic loan nouns into Swahili.

6.2   Generalisations on borrowing

6.2.1   Motivations for borrowing

What motivates the borrowing of linguistic matter? The two most frequently cited motivations for structural borrowing are *gaps* in the structural inventory of the recipient language, and the *prestige* enjoyed by the donor language. The 'gap' hypothesis assumes that bilingual or semi-bilingual speakers notice that one language is in possession of expressive means that do not exist in the other. In an effort to extend the range of expressive choices when communicating in the other, the supposedly 'poorly equipped' language, they replicate the structure that is available in the 'better-equipped' language. What the gap hypothesis essentially implies is that speakers are sometimes willing to compromise the maintenance of clear demarcation boundaries among subsets within their linguistic repertoire in the interest of availing themselves of the full range of expressive means that their repertoire offers, irrespective of the setting of the conversation and the linguistic choices that normally go with it. 'Gaps' are therefore not to be interepreted as deficiencies in the recipient system, but rather as speakers' attempt to avail themselves of their full inventory of linguistic resources, at all times and in all contexts of interaction.

Typical 'gap'-fillers are so-called 'cultural loans'. Cultural loans are labels that accompany new social activities and cultural acquisitions. They often refer to community functions and institutions, e.g. Spanish *al-calde* 'mayor', from Arabic *al-qāḍī* 'magistrate', or *jubilee*, from Latin *jubilaeus annus* 'jubilee year', from (Classical) Hebrew *(šənat) yōbel*; to agricultural and food products, such as *coffee*, via French *café* and Turkish *kahve*, from Arabic *qahwe*; and to technological innovations, as in German *Internet* from English. Generally speaking, cultural loans may be regarded as items that enrich the lexicon of a language.

The 'prestige' hypothesis assumes that speakers imitate elements of the speech of a socially more powerful, dominant community in order to gain approval and social status. What this means in practice is that bilingual speakers associate certain elements within their repertoire with a particular set of contexts in which these elements are normally used. By using those elements in other settings, speakers seek to activate those associations. Unlike cultural loans or 'gap-fillers', 'prestige' loans often have parallel expressions in the recipient language. However, these parallel expressions are not full equivalents in the pragmatic sense, since they lack the special conversational effect that is evoked by the loanword. English terms such as mutton, poultry, pork, and beef are frequently cited examples. They were originally French equivalents of the Anglo-Saxon-derived words lamb, chicken, pig, and ox. The association of sophisticated cuisine with the French-speaking aristocracy motivated the use of the French expressions with reference specifically to meat and the preparation of dishes, giving rise to a semantic differentiation between the native words, which continue to denote animals, and the borrowed terms, which denote their culinary products.

Like 'gap-fillers', prestige loans can in this way enrich the lexical inventory of the recipient language. But they may also replace native expressions, as in the case of French-derived *uncle* which replaced Anglo-Saxon *eam*. Here too, the role of what is generally referred to as '(social) prestige' is to be found more specifically in the special conversational effects evoked by the use of a term that is associated with a particular set of contexts and interaction settings. Recall, from Chapter 2, Ben's use of English *year one* rather than its translation equivalent in his conversation in German, and the contextual associations of the English-speaking school environment that are activated along with the term.

The notion of 'prestige' in fact covers a wide range of possible motivations. Colloquial English *pal* (a 'friend, companion') and (British English) *chav* 'rogue youth', for instance, come from Angloromani – the Romani-derived vocabulary used by English and Welsh Gypsies. The first is Angloromani *pal* (from Romani *phral*) 'brother', the second is *chavvy* (Romani *čhavo*) 'boy'. Despite the fact that Romani was neither a dominant nor a powerful language in Britain, it was attractive to certain social circles as the speech of a population that distanced itself from the establishment and it became a target for imitation in certain styles of speech that signalled non-conformity with the ruling order. By contrast, Judeo-Spanish *día del-xad* 'Sunday', literally 'day one', containing the Aramaic element *xad* 'one' adopted from religious scriptures, is used as a marker of distance from the Christian associations of the Spanish equivalent *domingo*, literally 'day of the Lord'.

Neither 'gaps' nor 'prestige' therefore necessarily imply that the donor language is the language of a politically powerful social elite and that the recipient language is the speech-form of the subordinated population. Although this is often the case, since the social elite runs societal institutions, imports technological innovations, and is often the target for imitation of fashion and general attitudes, products and innovations are sometimes introduced through contacts with small, less powerful, and even remote population groups; consider English words for tropical fruit, for instance, such as *mango* via Portuguese *manga*, based on Malay *mangga*, from Tamil *mankay*. Fashionable words can also come, as we saw, from the speech of marginalised and minority groups. The goals that speakers pursue when integrating foreign vocabulary items in conversation are oriented toward the communicative interaction and the effect that language use will have on the interlocutor. Those are shaped by the range of speakers' associations with each of the languages involved, and these associations in turn are determined by the roles and functions that the languages have in the social routines of the speech community. It is in this somewhat indirect and mediated way that social factors are involved in borrowing.

So far we have discussed motivations to use lexical vocabulary in a way that allows speakers to avail themselves of full forms of expression at all times (i.e. to fill 'gaps'), and to convey (or to avoid) specific social meanings that are associated with particular terms (i.e. to acquire 'prestige'). A third and quite distinct motivation for structural borrowing is related to the cognitive side of language processing. As discussed in Chapter 4, the bilingual speaker faces the challenge of maintaining control over the language processing mechanism that enables selection of context-appropriate structures within the repertoire and inhibition of those that are not appropriate. There is pressure on the bilingual to simplify the selection procedure by reducing the degree of separation between the subsets of the repertoire, allowing the two 'languages' to converge. Focusing for the moment on word-forms or linguistic matter, reduction of choices for selection may be less of a priority around lexical items, where the choice is more conscious and the meaning more transparent. It is more relevant in connection with grammatical operators, whose meaning is more abstract and whose employment is more gesture-like and routine-driven and less subject to reflection.

In Chapter 5 we saw how bilinguals license themselves to freely use foreign discourse markers in their bilingual mode. In speech communities in which the native language is always or nearly always spoken in a bilingual mode, since everyone is bilingual, the permanent license to integrate foreign grammatical operators can lead to long-term integration of such operators into the recipient language. We will see in the following discussion that there is evidence from cross-linguistic sampling of grammatical borrowing that points to the higher susceptibility to borrowing of grammatical markers that involve complex language processing, are therefore costly in terms of demanding processing effort from the speaker, and are therefore more likely to be affected by malfunctions of the selection mechanism. This leads to 'wrong' choices among functionally equivalent repertoire elements, or to a malfunction of the inhibition mechanism that normally filters out non-appropriate structures even if they do not have appropriate equivalents. There is, in other words, a direct link between borrowing and the control over the selection of context-appropriate structures in bilingual speech.

Underlying all the different motivations for borrowing is the bilingual's need to negotiate a complex repertoire of linguistic structures and to balance effectiveness and precision of expression against the social demand on complying with the norm to select only context-appropriate structures. There are three types of conflict that can arise between effectiveness of expression and compliance with context-appropriateness: (a) when certain meanings can be expressed in one language or set of contexts, but not in another ('gaps'); (b) when the social associations of one set of contexts need to be replicated ('prestige'); and (c) when it is inconvenient to maintain the separation of the two languages ('cognitive pressure').

An illustration of how various motivations for borrowing may combine is provided by the following examples. In Khuzistani Arabic (the Arabic dialect spoken as a minority language in the Iranian province of Khuzistan), the word for 'bus' is *bāṣ*, a loanword from English that is common in Arabic dialects in regions that were under British colonial rule during the earlier part of the twentieth century. The plural, however, is *otobūshā*, borrowed from the majority language, Persian (itself a European loanword, 'autobus'). The singular is borrowed from a language previously associated with technological innovations, English, to fill a 'gap'. The plural form is borrowed from a 'prestige' language associated with institutions and public life. Why, however, is borrowing from Persian limited to the plural form? It appears that cognitive factors are at work here too. The singular is used more frequently in connection with the individual's own activities: taking a bus, stepping into and off a bus, waiting for the bus, and so on. The plural belongs more frequently to the domain of institutional discourse: the provision of buses, the traffic of buses, etc. In this way, the prevailing diglossia influences the retrievability of certain lexical items and so ultimately the composition of the lexicon.

By contrast, colloquial Modern Hebrew has a European loanword for the singular of 'car', *óto* (from 'auto'), but in the plural speakers use the neologism *mexoniyót*, singular *mexonít* (inspired by European *machina/machine*), while the plural **ótoim* is normally reserved for designating toy cars in child speech. Here too, the sociolinguistic roles of the languages come into play in the cognitive retrievability of lexical elements: being a revitalised language and so a foreign tongue to its first generation of speakers in the 1920s–1930s, Hebrew filled lexical 'gaps' by drawing on languages associated with technical innovations, in the casual, informal reference to the singular (one's own car, the car of one's neighbour, one's preferred model, etc.). Lexical renewal in Hebrew is associated with the efforts of the Hebrew Language Academy, and neologisms are hence associated primarily with institutional domains of discourse. The plural 'cars', used more frequently in association with formal or technical contexts (regulating traffic, licensing issues, etc.), is associated with the formal language, and occupied by a neologism. Thus, the associations of singular with casual and of plural with formal interaction domains, when it comes to vehicles, are identical in Khuzistani Arabic and in colloquial Hebrew. The mapping of formal and informal functions onto the native or nativised language and the foreign language is, however, in effect reversed in the two languages, due to their very different historical roles as an established native but minority language, in the case of Khuzistani Arabic, and as a revitalised language promoted by institutions, in the case of Modern Hebrew.

6.2.2   Borrowing hierarchies

Explanations of borrowing are usually based on one of the following assumptions: (1) The degree of borrowing is related to the extent of exposure to the contact language, (2) The outcome of language contact is a product of the structural similarities and differences (congruence) among the languages concerned, and (3) Borrowability is conditioned by the inherent semantic-pragmatic or structural properties of the affected categories. Issues such as prestige and domain-specialisation of the languages typically fall under (1), while conjectures about functional 'gaps' as motivating factors fall under (2). An important question that has often been raised in discussions of borrowing is whether there are inherent differences in the likelihood of different word classes, categories, or types of morphemes to be affected by borrowing.

This question is relevant in addressing at least two separate issues: the first is the motivation for borrowing. Exploring general trends, including possible limitations on borrowing, can help illuminate the mechanisms and the factors that bring about and shape borrowing in the first place. The second is the value of insights from contact linguistics to a general theory of grammar. Here, language contact can act as a kind of external 'shock-factor' which brings to light connections among categories which are otherwise less apparent. Assuming that general trends in the borrowability of categories can be established and that these trends are not random but are somehow anchored in the functionality of categories and their position within the generic language faculty, borrowing hierarchies might serve as a further clue toward an understanding of the layered structure of the language faculty (cf. Matras 2007a, Myers-Scotton and Jake 2000).

One of the difficulties in providing a conclusive answer to the question of the borrowability of categories is the reliance on sampling. Language typologists rely on samples in order to make generalisations about human languages without having to study each and every individual language. Since Greenberg (1966) it has been accepted that samples should try and reflect at least the present-day diversity of languages, and avoid areal or genetic biases (cf. Rijkhoff *et al.* 1993, Haspelmath *et al.* 2005). Most linguistic samples have been used in order to study a particular structural phenomenon or the structural representation of a functional category.

The study of borrowing presents special challenges (cf. Matras and Sakel 2007b). Borrowing may affect various different categories, and so a comparative study of borrowing must take into account not just the diversity of sample languages, but also that of structural categories that are potentially affected by contact. Moreover, since borrowing is measured mostly in diachronic terms, information is required about the history of contact of the languages that are examined. This can bias the corpus, since secure diachronic information and so the ability to determine with confidence what has been borrowed is lacking with respect to the languages of entire regions. In addition, we assume that borrowing depends on extralinguistic factors such as the duration and intensity of cultural contact, the roles and status of the participating languages, language attitudes, and the degree of institutional support enjoyed by the languages (e.g. the presence of literacy). These factors must therefore be taken into account as well when comparing the borrowability of a certain functional category in one contact situation, as compared with another. Finally, sampling for contact phenomena is made difficult by the fact that information on borrowing is not always included in descriptive grammars of languages. However much information can be derived from the many excellent, specialised discussions of contact phenomena, each study naturally has its own points of focus, which makes it difficult to draw comparisons among different languages.

It is therefore not surprising that most attempts to arrive at cross-linguistic generalisations about contact-induced change have been based on casual observations rather than on systematic sampling. There exists nonetheless a large corpus of observations on borrowing in particular contact situations. Many approaches to borrowability are based on the frequency of borrowed categories (cf. Haugen 1950, Heath 1984, Thomason and Kaufman 1988, van Hout and Muysken 1994, Stolz and Stolz 1996 and 1997, Winford 2003, Aikhenvald 2006). It is assumed that a category is 'more likely' to be borrowed, relative to other categories, if it is borrowed more frequently in cross-linguistic comparison. Corpus-internal frequencies are generally not an adequate measure of borrowability due to the difficulties in distinguishing frequency of borrowing from frequency of usage (cf. van Hout and Muysken 1994: 42–43, Matras 2007b: 32–33). Implicational hierarchies go beyond frequency counts in suggesting that the process of contact-induced change follows, to some extent at least, a predictable pathway, with one stage leading as a pre-requisite to another (cf. Moravcsik 1978, Stolz 1996, Matras 1998 and 2007b, Field 2002, Elšík and Matras 2006).

Weinreich (1953: 35) summarises his own and earlier observations on the borrowability of grammatical elements in the statement 'the fuller the integration of the morpheme, the less likelihood of transfer'. This notion partly resurfaces in Moravcsik's (1978) implicational constraints, interpreted in (1):

(1)   Constraints on borrowing (after Moravcsik 1978):
            a. lexical > non-lexical (= lexical item > non-lexical grammatical
               property such as linear order)
            b. free morphemes > bound morphemes
            c. nouns > non-nouns
            d. derivational morphology > inflectional morphology
            e. the rules of linear ordering which apply in the donor language will
               accompany grammatical elements borrowed from that language
            f. a lexical item whose meaning is verbal cannot be borrowed

The general theme in (1) as regards morphological forms and categories is that both greater referential transparency and morpho-syntactic autonomy are factors that facilitate borrowing. Thus, nouns have greater referential stability than other word classes, derivational morphology is semantically more transparent than inflectional morphology, and lexical elements are both semantically transparent and usually more independent than grammatical operators.

Moravcsik's generalisations have been the subject of critique in the literature (cf. Thomason and Kaufman 1988: 11–34, Campbell 1993, Harris and Campbell 1995: 122–136). Campbell (1993) categorically rejects two of Moravcsik's statements: the claim that no verbs are borrowed as verbs, and the claim that borrowing of derivation is a pre-condition for the borrowing of inflection. Campbell also dismisses the observation that non-lexical (grammatical) properties will not be borrowed without lexical borrowings as 'theoretically insignificant' (1993: 101), arguing that there is no conditioning relation between the two. The fact that prepositions from Arabic and Persian can be used as postpositions in Urdu *bād* 'after' and Turkish *rağmen* 'in spite of' seems to contradict Moravcsik's claim on the retention of linear ordering rules from the donor language.

Nonetheless, some of Moravcsik's constraints receive support in the literature. They are in line with Winter's (1973) claim that the paradigmatic part of morphology is the most stable component of grammar and is less likely to be affected by borrowing, while the lexical and stylistic sides of language appear at the opposite end of the scale. This impression that borrowing begins at the level of the clause, and gradually makes its way to the phrase and finally to paradigms at the word level has since been expressed in a number of other studies (cf. van Hout and Muysken 1994, Stolz and Stolz 1996, Ross 2001). Johanson (2002: 44ff.) proposes the idea of 'attractive features' as a factor in borrowing. Such features include transparency of meaning and easily recognisable relations between form and content. Field (2002) also provides support for some of the structural constraints formulated and implied by Moravcsik (1978). He begins by combining two sub-hierarchies (Field 2002: 36–38, 117). The first (2) pertains to word classes:

(2)   nouns > adjectives, verbs

The second hierarchy (3) focuses on grammatical morphology:

(3)   function word > agglutinating affix > fusional affix

The two are then combined into a single, general hierarchy, which is said to capture the likelihood of borrowing for the relevant categories:

(4)   content item > function word > agglutinating affix > fusional affix

The prediction of the combined hierarchy in (4) entails both a quantitative and a temporal claim. The quantitative claim is that in any contact situation more content items will be borrowed than function words, more function words will be borrowed than agglutinating affixes, and so on. The temporal claim is that content words are more likely to be borrowed through superficial (less prolonged or less intensive) socio-cultural contacts. This is justified by the fact that forms that provide labels, and thus have visible, tangible referents, are more salient and transparent and so are easiest to learn, and therefore will be borrowed more quickly (Field 2002: 46–47). Field regards this prediction as confirmed in the borrowing of Spanish elements into Nahautl (Mexicano).

The frequently cited borrowing scale proposed by Thomason and Kaufman (1988: 74–75) is an attempt to relate the likelihood of structural borrowing to the intensity of contact, though unlike Field's (2002) hierarchy it does not identify a structural common denominator for the hierarchical ordering of elements. Instead, the scale is divided into categories, each representing a more intense degree of cultural contacts between the two speaker communities. Grammatical categories are arranged on this continuum according to the relative intensity of contact that is required before they can be borrowed:

(5)   Thomason and Kaufman's (1988) borrowing scale
            Casual contact Category 1: content words
                            Category 2: function words, minor phonological features,
                                         lexical semantic features
                            Category 3: adpositions, derivational suffixes, phonemes
                            Category 4: word order, distinctive features in phonology,
                                         inflectional morphology
            Intense contact Category 5: significant typological disruption, phonetic
                                         changes

Intensity of contact is interpreted in the model in terms of cultural pressure, though the model does not specify indicators for cultural pressure. One of the difficulties in applying the model to concrete language contact situations arises from the fact that intensity of contacts and cultural pressure are not strictly linear. A number of different factors are involved, including the degree of bilingualism and the roles that the languages have in various domains of social interaction, the degree of institutional support afforded to the languages (e.g. literacy, school instruction, media, language planning), and community attitudes. These factors may interact in different ways. Thus, the centuries-old contact between Irish and English, intensive bilingualism, and widespread dominance of English in most domains is counteracted by the institutional support given to Irish and the sense of pride in Irish as a national language. Some of the category definitions in the model remain unclear. The label 'function words' can cover categories as different in their contact behaviour as discourse markers and definite articles – the first are extremely prone to borrowing, the latter are fairly resistant. Finally, the model does not offer any explanation as to the reasons why some categories are borrowed more easily through shallow, casual contacts, while others require prolonged and intense cultural pressure.

Other observations on the borrowability of word classes based on individual case studies have tended to confirm the greater likelihood of open-class items to be borrowed compared to closed-class items:

(6)   Haugen (1950: 224), on Norwegian and Swedish immigrant speech in the US: nouns > verbs > adjectives > adverbs, prepositions, interjections

(7)   Muysken (1981), on Spanish in Quechua (repeated by Winford 2003: 51): nouns > adjectives > verbs > prepositions > coordinating conjunctions > quantifiers > determiners > free pronouns > clitic pronouns > subordinating conjunctions

These hierarchies both represent a quantitative cline: more borrowed types are attested for higher-ranking categories than for lower-ranking categories. As already mentioned above, such hierarchies are partly pre-conditioned by the greater availability of types belonging to open-class categories. A comparative evaluation of first-hand observations on a sample of 27 languages in contact from different parts of the world (Matras 2007b) gives the following, frequency-based hierarchy:

(8)   nouns, conjunctions > verbs > discourse markers > adjectives > interjections > adverbs > other particles, adpositions > numerals > pronouns > derivational affixes > inflectional affixes

This hierarchy is not based on the quantity of tokens or types, but rather on the number of languages in the sample that show borrowings belonging to the relevant categories. Thus, all languages in the sample display borrowing of nouns and conjunctions, while the borrowing of inflectional affixes is attested in the smallest number of languages, and pronouns are the least-frequently borrowed word class.

While such hierarchies provide a rough indication of possible predictions on borrowing, their meaningfulness is debatable as far as an explanatory account of the borrowability of categories is concerned. On a word-class hierarchy, there is not always an obvious link between any two categories that occupy any

two positions, whether they are adjacent or not. Unlike the hierarchies proposed by Moravcsik (1978) and by Field (2002), word class and structural
feature hierarchies of the kind presented in (5)–(8) are generally not implicational. The borrowing of a higher-ranking item is not a pre-requisite for the
borrowing of a lower-ranking item; their co-occurrence is rather only a likely
prediction.

More recent sample-based studies devote attention to implicational relationships, as related to borrowing, among individual paradigm values within discrete
functional categories. Such values are usually distinguished by a specific semantic feature. One of the first studies of a cross-linguistic sample of borrowing
with reference to a consistent set of categories and category values is Stolz
and Stolz's (1996, 1997; cf. also Stolz 1996) discussion of Spanish borrowings
into Central American and Pacific languages. Their frequency count shows tendencies that favour the borrowing of *pero* 'but', *o* 'or', *porque* 'because', and
antes 'before'. Stolz (1996: 150–152) formulates this in terms of the following
implications:

(9)   Implications for the borrowing of Spanish function words in Central
      American and Oceanic languages (Stolz 1996):
      a. If a language has borrowed *porque* 'because', than it will always have
         borrowed *pero* 'but'
      b. If a language has borrowed more than two function words [from
         Spanish], then *pero* 'but' is among them.

Stolz (1996) does not provide an explanation for the prominence of contrastive
pero 'but' among the borrowed function words, though in Stolz and Stolz (1996)
reference is made to the particular vulnerability of the discourse-organisation
domain to language convergence in contact situations.

In Matras (1998a, 2000c) I examined a sample consisting of various dialects of
Romani in contact with different languages (such as French, Hungarian, Romanian, Turkish, and Greek), a sample of languages under the historical sphere
of influence of Arabic, either directly or mediated via other languages such as
Turkish or Persian (including Hausa, Swahili, Kurdish, Neo-Aramaic, Turkish,
Lezgian, Macedonian, Persian, Urdu, and more), and Stolz and Stolz's (1996)
sample of some 40 Central American languages in contact with Spanish. The
combined samples showed, among other hierarchies, an implicational borrowing
hierarchy for coordinating conjunctions:

(10)   but > or > and

This confirms Stolz's observations. Moreover, it places the borrowing of 'but' in
the functional context of the borrowing of functionally related elements. Since we
are dealing here with values of the same word class and the same functional sub-
category, namely coordinating conjunctions, it is possible to reduce the opposition
between the values to a single semantic-pragmatic feature, namely the expression

of 'contrast'. On this basis we can postulate a link between the expression of contrast and the likelihood of borrowing; we can thus isolate the semantic-pragmatics of contrast as a factor motivating borrowing.[2] The explanation offered in Matras (1998a) for the high susceptibility of contrast to borrowing is the interaction-level tension surrounding the act of contradicting shared presupposition. This tension may at times interfere with the 'language-correct' selection of an item, leading to bilingual speech production errors, which, if allowed to stabilise, may lead to language change. The explanation offered for the overall tendency to borrow connectors is much the same, attributing to connectors a position in the speaker's monitoring-and-directing apparatus, which demands an exceptional amount of supervisory control during language processing.

This kind of method of analysis has since been applied in the evaluation of two more samples. Elšík and Matras (2006) investigate the borrowing behaviour of some 75 dialects of Romani in contact with some 25 languages as diverse as Finnish, Bulgarian, Turkish, Italian, German, and Hungarian;[3] and in Matras (2007b), I evaluate a sample of some 30 first-hand descriptions of diverse contact situations from around the world, contained in the edited collection by Matras and Sakel (2007) and an accompanying database.[4]

Both investigations consider a diverse set of functional categories. For the Romani sample, Elšík and Matras (2006: 370ff.) identify two types of patterns, which are related to two separate motivations for borrowing. In the first pattern, values that represent greater intensity of language processing are more likely to be borrowed. This involves, among others, higher cardinal numerals, non-positive degree (comparative and superlative), expressions of contrast and separation, and peripheral local relations. The first set of borrowing hierarchies (Figure 6.1) thus reflects the tendency of languages in the bilingual's repertoire to converge around those semantic-pragmatic functions that demand greater processing effort and around which it is more difficult to maintain control over the separation of subsets in the linguistic repertoire.

Elšík and Matras conclude that borrowing is a strategy that supports the bilingual speaker in successfully managing language choices in interaction. It reduces the need for choices to be made among word-forms or morphemes of equivalent function, and so it increases communicative efficiency without compromising the separation of languages and language contexts and the potential for flagging identity that this separation entails.

A second set of hierarchies (Figure 6.1) represents value types in which a word-form is more likely to be borrowed. Thus 3SG inflectional endings are more borrowable than other endings, nouns are more borrowable in the nominative form than in other case forms, inflected verb-forms are more likely to be borrowed in the realis than in irrealis, etc. Here, more frequent, simplex, accessible, and transparent forms have an advantage in terms of ease of replication.

One might refer to the first set as 'marked' category values, and to the second as 'unmarked'. Clyne (2003: 98) points out the difficulties in defining 'markedness', and the contradictory claims that have been made about the relation between

Borrowing	Polarity for complexity	Polarity for differentiation	Borrowable value
plural > singular	+	−	marked
high cardinal > low cardinal	+	−	
(superlative > comparative) > positive	+	−	
local relations: peripheral > core	+	−	
separative (source) > directive > stative	+	−	
content lexeme > auxiliary	+	−	
contrast/restriction > addition/continuation	+	−	
low ordinal > high ordinal	−	+	unmarked
non-remote tense > future > remote tense	−	+	
affirmative > negative	−	+	
realis > potentialis > irrealis	−	+	
nominative > oblique	−	+	

Figure 6.1 *Borrowing and 'markedness' in dialects of Romani (adapted from Elšík and Matras 2006: 371).*

markedness and borrowing.[5] Elšík and Matras's findings show that the two sets correlate in different ways with formal criteria for markedness, such as structural complexity or differentiation potential (see Figure 6.1). The left-hand column in Figure 6.1 lists the implicational borrowing hierarchies as evidenced by the sample of Romani dialects. The other two columns indicate the polarity direction of the hierarchy with respect to the features 'complexity' and 'differentiation', respectively. Thus, the hierarchy 'plural > singular' indicates that the value 'plural' is more prone to borrowing than the value 'singular'. The symbol '+' for the feature 'complexity' indicates that the same polarity holds for complexity (i.e plurality is more complex than singularity), whereas the symbol '−' for 'differentiation' indicates that the opposite polarity holds for this feature (i.e. plurality is less differentiated than singularity).

The Markedness hypothesis generally treats those category values as 'marked' that show greater complexity and lower differentiation, and those that show lower complexity but greater differentiation as 'unmarked'. Figure 6.1 illustrates that borrowing does not correlate with markedness in a uniform way. Rather, each of the two motivations for borrowing targets a different set of values. Borrowing as a replication of routine forms targets 'unmarked' values, which tend to show greater frequency. Borrowing as a strategy to reduce processing load tends to target more 'marked' values.

The evaluation of the cross-linguistic borrowing sample (Matras 2007b) also showed different motivations for borrowing. A first group of hierarchies show a 'utilitarian' motivation for borrowing. Here, the more borrowable element is associated more strongly with interaction contexts in the donor language:

(11)   Utilitarian hierarchies (context specialisation of donor language):
        a. unique referents > general/core vocabulary
        b. nouns > non-nouns
        c. numerals in formal contexts > numerals in informal contexts
        d. higher cardinal numerals > lower cardinal numerals
        e. days of week > times of day

'Unique referents' are specific terms for institutions, procedures or other concepts that are tightly bound to the activities carried out in a particular context domain and so they are associated with a particular language. They are more likely to be represented by nouns, hence the higher position of nouns over non-nouns on the hierarchy. In some languages, borrowed numerals are reserved for formal or institutional interactions. Higher cardinal numbers and reference to days of the week are more tightly associated with interaction in institutional contexts, where the donor language prevails.

A second set of hierarchies can be related to the reduction of processing load. Under (12) we find those in which the more borrowable element represents a semantically less accessible domain (by comparison), while the less borrowable value is protected by frequency, routine, and casualness of usage:

(12)   Hierarchies of accessibility (as well as frequency):
        a. more remote kin > close kin
        b. peripheral local relations > core local relations

Under (13) we see that values that represent greater intervention with, or greater reliance on, the presupposition domain also show a higher degree of borrowability. The superlative, for example, contrasts an item against a presupposed set; indefinites ('somewhere', 'somebody', etc.) fail to specify the item of reference and so they rely on the hearer's mental supplementation of information; focus and modal particles process expectations and attitudes. Phasal adverbs like 'already' and focus particles like 'only' limit a set of events or objects in relation to assumptions about it.

(13)   Speaker's intervention with or overt reference to presupposition domain:
        a. but > or > and
        b. superlative > comparative > (positive)
        c. indefinites > interrogatives > (other) deixis, anaphora
        d. focus and modal particles > other particles
        e. already > still; only > too

The hierarchies grouped under (14) represent degrees of the speaker's secure knowledge and control. Weaker control, as in the case of modality, or an external force acting on the speaker (obligation as opposed to ability or desire), or the linking of independent events through factual complementation, may put the speaker's assertive authority at risk. This may trigger tension that interferes with the control over the selection and inhibition mechanism. Under (15) we find hierarchies that relate directly to the monitoring-and-directing apparatus:

(14)   Speaker's secure knowledge and control, external force and semantic integration:
    a. modality > aspect/aktionsart > future tense > (other tenses)
    b. obligation > necessity > possibility > ability > desire
    c. concessive, conditional, causal, purpose > other subordinators
    d. factual complementisers > non-factual complementisers

(15)   Speaker's monitoring and directing of the interaction:
    a. discourse markers, fillers, tags, interjections, greetings > other function words
    b. prosody > segmental phonology

Note that some hierarchies may meet the criteria for more than one group. Thus, connectors can be said to relate to presuppositions and at the same time serve as 'discourse markers' and direct the participation at the level of the interaction (cf. Schiffrin 1987); concessive conjunctions connect independent events but also express contrast and unexpectedness, while causal subordinators also provide a justification at the interaction level; and so on. The sub-grouping of hierarchies in (12)–(15) is thus chiefly a matter of convenience. The recurring theme is the potential clash between hearer-sided and speaker-sided attitudes and expectations, a consequent relative rise in interactional tension and intensity of speaker-sided processing, and greater likelihood to lose control over the selection and inhibition mechanism.

Significantly, the hierarchies of the cross-linguistic sample (Matras 2007b) appear to be fully compatible with those identified by Elšík and Matras (2006) for the Romani sample. This suggests that the structural features of the recipient and donor languages are not of uppermost relevance to the borrowing process. It also reduces the likelihood that specific cultural or sociolinguistic factors are influential in the process, for such factors are unlikely to replicate themselves throughout the cross-linguistic sample in a way that would provide a coherent pattern. Although most situations in the sample represent a division of roles between an informal, primarily oral, in-group language of a minority or colonised population, and an official, majority, literary language with institutional support, not all cases conform strictly to this type, and we also find contiguous languages with comparable roles (e.g. Neo-Aramaic and Kurdish; Hup and Tukano), languages in contact with an oral lingua franca (Jaminjung with Kriol, Likpe with Ewe), minority languages with a past history of institutional support and a literary tradition (Khuzistani Arabic, Yiddish, Macedonian Turkish), languages that have undergone changes through the impact of a literary language (Indonesian, Vietnamese), and others.

To be sure, not all languages in the sample show borrowings in all categories. Social factors such as language attitudes and institutional support certainly play a role in determining both the *extent* of borrowing within individual category groups, and the degree to which borrowing spreads to various domains of grammar. To cite just one example, languages that enjoy or have enjoyed institutional support in the form of literacy in the native language or a closely related variety, such as Macedonian Turkish (Ottoman Turkish has been the language of administration and education in the Balkans), Khuzistani Arabic (religious education entails reading or memorising Classical Arabic texts from the Quran), or Yiddish (where modern, everyday native-language literacy was widespread at least in some parts of the speech community), as a rule do not borrow numerals.

Nonetheless, even if in a given language contact situation borrowing does not extend to all category domains, and even if in some domains only higher-ranking category values are affected, the sample still shows borrowing patterns that are consistent with the hierarchies presented above. This is significant in two ways. First, it means that that we can make predictions about the general course that borrowing is likely to take and use these hierarchical predictions as a clue to interpret the motivations behind borrowing. Second, it reveals that the motivation to borrow is anchored in the intrinsic semantic-pragmatic function of the affected categories and in the contribution they make toward the mental processing of utterances in discourse. This in turn suggests that the motivation to borrow is typically triggered by the language-processing mechanism itself, not by the convenience or inconvenience offered by the formal shape of the structure, nor by social or cultural attitudes. The latter contribute to the propagation of borrowed forms throughout the speech community, but they are not responsible for an individual speaker's motivation to introduce them into the discourse in the first place.

It would otherwise not be possible to explain hierarchies such as {but>or>and}, or any of the other, function-based hierarchies: there is no reason why 'but' should be culturally more attractive than 'and' as a way of flagging bilingual competence or the prestige of the donor language, nor is there a reason why the propagation of borrowed 'but' should be favoured by social attitudes over that of 'and'. Even if such attitudes could be identified for the culture of a particular speech community, they are unlikely to be replicated across the diverse contact situations considered in the samples, and so they cannot explain the recurring pattern. Similarly, we cannot take for granted that 'but' is universally more or less structurally complex than 'and'. Thus, we are left with the internal semantic-pragmatic function of the form as the only clue toward understanding the motivation for borrowing. We must then identify a connection between this internal function, and the processing of language by bilinguals in discourse interaction, one which is likely to prompt the insertion of a foreign form into native-language discourse.

In Chapters 4 and 5 we examined how bilingual speakers license themselves to reduce the inventory of structures in their linguistic repertoire around certain processing functions in order to eliminate the need to activate the selection and inhibition mechanism, and so to avoid malfunctions of that selection mechanism. The motivation for 'fusion' of this kind arises, we saw, around those operations that place a high demand on the speaker's supervisory control of the discourse, and so run the risk of interfering with the control over selection of context-appropriate items. 'Risk' situations of this kind arise when the speaker is making a direct effort to monitor and direct hearer-sided participation in the discourse, as well as when there is a potential clash between the attitudes of speaker and listener, such as when the domain of shared presupposition is called into question.

The hierarchies depicted under (12)–(15) match precisely this characterisation. They show a correlation between greater likelihood of borrowing, and operations around which the speaker's assertive authority is at stake and a special effort is needed in order to win over the hearer's confidence.

In conclusion, we must distinguish between factors that facilitate borrowing, and factors that motivate borrowing. Language-internal factors that facilitate borrowing are the referential autonomy or semantic discreteness and so the semantic accessibility of a structure; this is often linked to morpho-syntactic independence, though this link is dependent on the morphological typology of an individual language. Thus, nouns in most languages are unbound morphemes, but verbs in some languages may be bound and inseparable from synthetic derivational/inflectional morphology. This connection between word-form independence and language-particular features explains the variation among certain word classes in postulated formal hierarchies of borrowing. A further language-internal factor that participates in facilitating or inhibiting borrowing is the degree of 'defaultness' of a form. High familiarity, usually correlating with high frequency of use, appears to 'protect' expressions from being borrowed by counteracting the pressure to associate referents primarily with contexts of interaction that are dominated by the donor language.

Alongside these language-internal facilitating factors, we can identify factors that motivate borrowing, in the sense that they trigger a need on the part of the speaker to employ linguistic matter from the donor language in interaction contexts that are normally reserved for the recipient language. One such motivation is the wish to replicate the specific contextual associations triggered by the donor-language word-form. This applies to linguistic matter which typically represents domains of activity that are negotiated primarily in the donor language, whether abstract reasoning, technical work, or institutional activities of various kinds. A different kind of motivation affects grammatical operations that are responsible for language processing in discourse. Here we have seen that the hierarchical arrangement of category values points clearly to the high susceptibility to borrowing of operators that represent 'high-risk' points in the communicative interaction, i.e. points of a potential clash between the expectations of the speaker and the listener. These operations demand an intensified processing effort, which is more likely to compete with the effort required in order to control the selection and inhibition mechanism that regulates choices within the linguistic repertoire.

The need to pre-empt selection malfunctions or to prevent them from disturbing the flow of communication leads to the acceptance and gradual stabilisation of donor-language elements.

Both motivations for borrowing must be facilitated by language-external factors, most importantly by attitudes permitting and favouring the employment of donor-language material in recipient-language discourse interaction. This condition is likely to be met if interaction in the recipient language tends to be by default in a bilingual mode, as is the case with many linguistic minorities. Institutional regulation of language use in some domains of interaction and insistence on monolingual communication modes is likely to slow down the process of borrowing of linguistic matter, as are community attitudes that regard the selection of context-appropriate linguistic matter as a display of loyalty to the community. In cases where part of the speech community is monolingual, the chances of successful borrowing will depend on the social position of the bilingual innovators acting as the principal agents of potential language change.

A final note is in order on the relevance of exceptions to postulated hierarchies. Some works on borrowing have tended to emphasise the lack of predictability, and the fact that no absolute constraints on borrowing can be formulated for which no counter example could be found (cf. Thomason and Kaufman 1988, Campbell 1993). Our present discussion aims at understanding the factors that facilitate structural borrowing among languages. It would be counter-productive to ignore tendencies that are followed by a substantial group of languages within a sample only because they are not followed by all, or indeed because they might be contradicted in one or two instances. Quite often, it is the counter-example that can be explained as resulting from a local, language-particular constraint that impedes the realisation of common patterns in a particular instance. Where general trends appear and can be associated with a motivation showing that they are beyond pure coincidence, then these trends deserve our attention.

7   Lexical borrowing

7.1   Content words and the position of nouns

It is often assumed that there is a core vocabulary that is to some extent at least resistant to borrowing. This assumption is yet to be verified empirically on the basis of a systematic analysis of a cross-linguistic sample.[1] It is perhaps most closely associated with the name of Morris Swadesh, whose list of 207 items of supposed basic vocabulary has been widely used by linguists as the basis for the so-called 'lexico-statistic' method (see Swadesh 1952). This method in turn has formed the foundation for comparisons among languages and often for the postulation of language families and sub-families, as well as for calculations of the time depth of splits into sub-groups – a procedure referred to as 'glottochronology'.

At the heart of Swadesh's list is the prediction that some concepts are 'generic', in the sense that they represent objects or ideas that accompany human beings independently of their specific environment. Names of body-parts, close kin, body-related activities, pronouns, interrogatives, and basic concepts for nature and geography[2] have all been considered a part of this generic lexical inventory. Since these concepts exist, according to the assumption, in every human community, there would be no need to borrow the relevant labels from languages of neighbouring communities.

Clearly, such a view of borrowing is oriented almost entirely toward the 'gap' hypothesis. The list's intended role as a reliable indicator of genetic relatedness, rather than as a tool to verify the stability of vocabulary in situations of contact, is evident through numerous attempts to design formulae that would help eliminate loanwords from calculations based on it (e.g. Minett and Wang 2003). English shows around 13% loans among the items on the list – 14 from Scandinavian languages and 13 from French (Ogura and Wang 1996: 320), including *animal*, *mountain*, *forest*, and *fruit*. Domari borrows a massive 43–47% (taking into account variation of words as well as variation among speakers) of the list items, primarily from its contemporary contact language, Arabic. The loans include, as in English, the words for 'animal' (*ḥaywān*), 'mountain' (*žbāl*), 'forest' (*yēba*), and 'fruit' (*fawākēni*), but also those for 'grass', 'leaf', 'tree', 'bird', 'fish', 'ice', 'sky', 'star', 'moon', 'child', and more. Given that the list is rather short,

Word class	Otomi	Quechua	Guarani
Noun	40.7	54.0	37.2
Verb	4.8	17.7	18.3
Adverb	4.5	3.4	2.3
Adjective	1.9	8.5	7.4
Total	51.9	83.6	65.2

Figure 7.1 *Proportion of content-lexical word classes among Spanish borrowings (from Hekking and Bakker 2007) (remaining borrowed items are grammatical function words).*

it is difficult to use it as a basis for statements about the stability of either individual semantic domains or word classes. Stolz (2003: 289–291) cites a figure of 26–39% for Spanish loans in Chamorro for a slightly modified 203-item list (again taking variation into consideration), and around 27% for Italian loans in Maltese. The latter is remarkably close to the figure of 25.5–28.5% given by Krier (1980) as an estimate for the total proportion of loanwords in the entire Maltese vocabulary. My own count for Maltese based on the 207-list provided by Borg and Azzopardi-Alexander (1997: 353–357), however, shows only between 5–8% Italian loans.[3] Among the indisputable Italian loans in Maltese we encounter once again the words for 'animal' (*annimal*), 'mountain' (*muntanja*), 'forest' (*foresta*), and 'fruit' (*frott*), casting doubt on their reliability as indicators of non-borrowable vocabulary.

The prominence of nouns among borrowed lexical word classes is documented in most studies that contain borrowing statistics. Hekking and Bakker (2007: 444) compare the borrowing of Spanish word classes into three indigenous languages of South America (Figure 7.1).

Field (2002: 153, 206–228) gives a survey of word-forms and morphemes that are borrowed from Spanish into Nahautl. Of some 552 borrowed nouns, 221 represent institutional agents and names of organisations or institutions, 142 are abstract nouns including religious, legal, and cultural concepts, 121 are animates (persons, kinship terms, animals), and 75 are materials, artefacts, and buildings. Nouns constitute, by far, the largest group of loans. They are followed by some 80 verbs, some 75 adjectives, and some 45 adverbs (including location expressions).

These figures give some insights into what seems to be, statistically at least, the high borrowability of nouns. In cross-cultural contact, integrating the appropriate labels allows reference to second-language interaction contexts and activation of knowledge and associations from those contexts during native-language conversations; we have seen this demonstrated in discourse by Ben's inclusion of the English terms *assembly* and *Year One* when referring to the English-speaking school context (Chapter 2), and by the inclusion of German institutional and administrative terminology into Romani discourse (Chapter 5). Note the prominence of 'unique referents' among the Spanish borrowings in Nahuatl.

Rebuck (2002) attributes the borrowing of English words into Japanese not just to the need to fill lexical gaps, but also to a need for 'special effects', imitation of fashions and trends, and euphemism. According to Loveday (1996: 79, 101–117), English loans make up to 7.3% of the Japanese lexicon; 94% of the 7,045 English loans recorded in Japanese are nouns. The distribution of English loans in some domains is shown in (1):

(1)   Percentage of English loans in Japanese by selected, specialised semantic
        domains (from Loveday 1996):
        computer (99%) > broadcasting (82%) > journalism, marketing (75%) >
        engineering (67%)> flowers (52%) > vegetables (35%) > animals
        (24%) > colours (9%)

The high borrowability of nouns is thus primarily a product of their referential functions: nouns cover the most differentiated domain for labelling concepts, objects, and roles. This includes industrial and agricultural products, artefacts, institutions and institutional agents, procedures, conceptual innovations, as well as technical innovations and instruments. It is not a coincidence that institutional, social, and technological innovations are often expressed by loanwords in the languages of cultures that absorb foreign influences, as can be seen from the Japanese data, as well as through the token display of terms for just three concepts in Figure 7.2.

Brown (1999) devotes a lengthy investigation exclusive to the borrowing of nouns from European languages into Native American languages. Correlating such factors as frequency of use in the original language and the presence of a semantic equivalent in the recipient language, he concludes that even words for objects and concepts introduced by Europeans vary considerably with respect to their borrowability. Pragmatic saliency appears to determine the hierarchy here, with terms for living things outranking those for artefacts, and terms for animals outranking those for plants.

Elšík (in press) lists loanwords in the Romani dialect of Selice (southern Slovakia), based on the Loanword Typology sample list of 1430 lexemes. An impressive 63% of the lexemes are loanwords, though they entered the language in different phases, some of them already as loans into earlier, pre-European stages of Romani. Nonetheless, some 53% of the words on the list (and 84% of all loanwords) are from Hungarian, the principal contact language of Selice Romani in recent generations. Hungarian loans constitute 63% of all nouns on the list, 41% of verbs, 42% of adjectives, 50% of adverbs, and 23% of function words.[4] Arranged by semantic domains, roughly the following hierarchy can be postulated for loanwords from Hungarian and Slovak, the two contemporary contact languages:

English	university	democracy	television
Albanian	universitet	demokraci	televizion
Maltese	università	demokrazija	televizjoni
Turkish	üniversite	demokrasi	televizyon
Hebrew	univérsita	demokrátya	televízya
Malay	universiti	demokrasi	televisyen
Japanese	yunibashiti	minsei	terebijon
Hausa	jami'a	dimokurad'iyya	telebijin
Arabic	džāmiʕa	dimoqraṭiyya	tilfizyon
Farsi	dānešgāh	demokrasi	televizyon
Swahili	chuo kikuu	kidemokrasi	televisheni

Figure 7.2 *Loanwords for three concepts in several languages (inherited terms are shaded).*

(2)   Percentage of loanwords by semantic domain in Selice Romani (Elšík in press):
household, modern world, agriculture (over 90%) > clothing, warfare (over 80%) > animals, social and political relations, the physical world (over 70%) > religion and belief, speech and language, law, technology, food and drink (over 60%) > time, the body, motion, perception, emotion, cognition, values (over 50%) > spatial relations (over 40%) > quantity, kinship (over 30%)

Little can be said at this stage about just how representative the Selice Romani data are. Nonetheless, the pattern that arises appears to confirm the greater stability of concepts pertaining to the immediate surroundings: orientation in space, time and quantity, the private domain of mental and physical activity, and the nearest human environment (body and close kin). Concepts that involve negotiation of activity with others are, by contrast, more prone to borrowing (for similar generalisations on loanwords in Romani, see already Matras 2002: 30).

This 'proximity' constraint receives further support from the specific semantic domain of kinship terms. Kin terms are of course representative of the private, personal domain; at the same time, however, extended kin can serve in some societies as a window to interaction with outsiders, while in others more remote kin does not figure prominently at all in the perception of family relations. Kinship terms are therefore an interesting case study for a possible semantic continuum of borrowing. Consider the background of consanguineal kin terms in

	grand-(parents)			
aunt	mother		father	uncle
cousin	sister	*EGO*	brother	cousin
niece	daughter		son	nephew
	grand-(children)			

Figure 7.3 *Close kin and remote kin in English (shaded cells represent borrowed terms).*

	nanna 'grandmother'		*nannu* 'grandfather'	
aunt	*omm* 'mother'		*missier* 'father'	*ziju* 'uncle'
kuġina 'cousin'	*oħt* 'sister'	*EGO*	*ħu-* 'brother'	*kuġin* 'cousin'
neputija 'niece'	*bint* 'daughter'		*(i)bn-* 'son'	*neputi* 'nephew'
	neputija 'granddaughter'		*neputi* 'grandson'	

Figure 7.4 *Close kin and remote kin in Maltese (shaded cells represent borrowed terms).*

English (Figure 7.3). English retains inherited Germanic terminology for kin that are closest to the speaker in age as well as degree of relatedness, i.e. members of the nuclear family (in either childhood or adulthood). For those that are removed (related via a third or fourth person), English borrows French terms. The borrowing process was not motivated by the need to fill gaps or introduce new types of relations, for Old English already possessed equivalent terms such as *eam* 'uncle' and *nydmæag* 'cousin'. In fact, Old French *neveu* 'nephew' even replaced a very similar, etymologically cognate Old English term, *nefa*. But the use of French words for family relations will have been fashionable in Medieval English due to its association with the terms used by the French-speaking social elite. Why then was this fashion not extended to closer kin? There appears to be some reluctance on the part of speakers to compromise certain familiar, intimate terms of everyday life. This reluctance competes with, and counteracts, the prestige-driven trend to use fashionable, new terms, thus 'protecting' the more intimate terms from replacement through loans. We might interpret this competition as reflecting a tension between the cognitive need for stability in one's immediate surroundings, and the social aspiration to partake in fashionable new activities.

A remarkably similar pattern is found in Maltese (Figure 7.4) (data from Borg and Azzopardi-Alexander 1997: 339–340). The principal difference is the

džīd 'great grandfather'				
dādī 'grandmother'			*bād* 'grandfather'	
xāl/xālī 'maternal uncle/aunt'	*day* 'mother'	**EGO**	*båy* 'father'	*mām/māmī* 'paternal uncle/aunt'
xāl dīr/putur 'maternal cousin'	*bēn* 'sister'		*bar* 'brother'	*mām dīr/putur* 'paternal cousin'
	dīr 'daughter'		*putur* 'son'	

Figure 7.5 *Consanguineal kinship terms in Domari (shaded cells represent borrowed terms).*

borrowing of *missier*, literally 'Sir', for 'father', quite obviously deriving from the form of a direct, respectful term of address.

Figure 7.5 shows a somewhat more extended table of terms for consanguineal kin in Domari, which has been in close contact with Arabic for the past few centuries, and with Kurdish before that. Despite an enormous amount of lexical loans, Domari is somewhat more conservative than English in retaining inherited (Indo-Aryan) terms for grandparents. The term for 'great-grandfather' however is an Arabic loan. Domari borrows its terms for 'aunt'/'uncle' from Kurdish, along with the system that distinguishes maternal from paternal relations (at this and the next generation level). This system is common in other languages of the region; in fact, the Kurdish term for maternal uncle, *xāl*, is itself an Arabic loan. It is therefore possible that the motivation to borrow terms in this domain results from a need to adopt a new referential system. Either way, we notice again the relative conservatism of words belonging to the closer, more intimate domains of reference.

It appears that cognitive proximity, familiarity, routine, intimacy, and frequency are all features that may compete with social motivations to borrow word-forms. Some motivations for borrowing may, however, override even the proximity constraint. Comrie (2000) discusses the case of Haruai, a Papuan (i.e. non-Austronesian) language of Papua New Guinea. In Haruai society, there is a taboo against saying the name of relatives of a certain degree, such as in-laws or cousins. Since most personal names are also ordinary words, the taboo affects the articulation of everyday vocabulary. The need thus arises to replace certain vocabulary items, and they are usually replaced by words from the surrounding languages with which the Haruai are familiar, such as genetically unrelated

Kobon or the lingua franca Tok Pisin. In fact, in order to be prepared for changes in family relations arising through marriage, the Haruai maintain an entire inventory of double lexemes that can be used interchangeably, one typically an inherited Haruai word, the other typically a loan from Kobon (Comrie 2000: 81–82). Even beyond the taboos, Haruai is reported to borrow many basic vocabulary items from Kobon, including kinship terms and words like *ram* 'house' (Kobon *ram*), *rmj* 'ear' (Kobon *rɨmɨd*), and *hödal* 'wind (breeze)' (Kobon *hadal*) (Comrie 2000: 84).

Even within the lexical domain, borrowing can result from an array of different motivations. Yiddish, for instance, employs Hebrew-derived terms for religious institutions, practices, and festivals, and social organisation, such as *broxe* 'blessing' (Hebrew *bəraxa*), *xejdər* 'primary school' (Hebrew *xeder*), and *yešive* 'religious secondary/higher education school' (Hebrew *yešiva*). While it retains Germanic terms for some animals, such as *fert* 'horse', *hint* 'dog', *fejgalə* 'small bird', the word for 'pig' is *xázər* (Hebrew *xazir*) and for 'cattle' *behéjmə* (Hebrew *beheyma* 'large mammal, beast'), both evoking culture-specific associations – with pigs as unclean animals whose meat is forbidden for consumption, and with cattle as untamed beasts; 'duck' in turn is *kačkə*, a Polish borrowing (*kaczka*) with no apparent association other than the likely context of acquisition or frequent use, its relatively low prominence relative to the household environment making it vulnerable to replacement in the bilingual environment of central-eastern Europe.

7.2   The structural integration of nouns

We have noted the special position of nouns in the borrowing of lexical content words, as representing the most differentiated inventory of labels for concepts, practices, artefacts, products, human agents, and more. It is the function of nouns – their particular, specific referentiality – that makes them borrowable, rather than just structural features such as supposed ease of integration. In principle, languages have a finite number of options for the morphological integration of nouns: (1) To treat borrowed nouns just like native nouns, and integrate them into native inflection patterns. (2) To avoid integration and maintain just a simplified representation of borrowed nouns. (3) To integrate nouns along with their original inflection in the source language. (4) To apply a special integration strategy that marks out borrowed nouns as loans. A combination of strategies is not excluded, either.

Identifying strategies for the integration of loans brings us back to the discussion of the codeswitching–borrowing continuum. We saw in Chapter 5 that bilinguals may choose to integrate some insertions but not to integrate others. This flexibility is largely limited, however, to active bilinguals; once a word

has spread into the repertoire of monolinguals, it will tend to follow a fixed
morpho-syntactic integration pattern. Although a comprehensive comparative
survey is yet to be undertaken, it appears that languages that show case, possessive inflection, and other forms of nominal inflection tend to apply them to
loanwords as well:

(3)   Inflectional integration of borrowed nouns
        a. Turkish: *dünya* 'world', from Arabic/Persian
           dünya-'nın geleceğ-i
           world-GEN future-3SG
           'the future of the world'
        b. Domari: *kart* 'postcard', via Arabic *kart* from English *card*
           ktib-k-ed-a   aha *kart-ás*
           write-LOAN.TR-PAST-3SG.M this card-ACC
           'He wrote this card'
        c. Japanese (Loveday 1996: 117): *kyatto-fūdo* 'cat-food', *baransu*
           'balance'
           kyatto-fūdo wa   eiyō-*baransu*   ni ...
           cat.food   TOP nutrition.balance DAT
           'As for cat-food in its balance of nutrition ...'
        d. Adyghe (Höhlig 1997: 255): *mutfaq* 'kitchen' from Turkish *mutfak*
           qı-ze-kᴵo-jı-m   se sı-q-iç'ığ   *mutfaq*-ım
           DIR-ANAPH-come-back-ANAPH I 1SG-DIR-exit kitchen-OBL
           'When he arrived, I came out into the kitchen'
        e. Kurdish: *tarîx* 'history' from Arabic *taʔrīx*
           tarîx-a   kurd-an
           history-ATTR.F kurd-OBL.PL
           'The history of the Kurds'

The import of productive nominal inflection markers accompanying borrowed
nouns is rare. A notable exception are Mixed Languages, discussed in Chapter 10;
but since these languages emerge under very particular circumstances, I do not
consider them a case of borrowing in the sense defined here. Case endings may
be retained in replicated adverbial phrases, such as the Latin terms *ex officio*, *ipso
facto* or *prima facie*. The proper noun *Jesus*, when used in non-nominative cases
in some European languages, may retain its Latin case form (which in turn is
based on Greek); thus German *die Geschichte Jesu* 'the story of Jesus'.

Romani is probably a rather exceptional case in its productive use of borrowed
nominal inflection endings. Early (Medieval) Romani borrowed Greek nouns
along with their nominative inflection markers, thus *for-os* 'town' (from the
Greek word for 'market'), plural *for-i*, *kokal-o* 'bone', pl. *kokal-a* (note that pre-
European Romani nouns end either in a consonant in the singular, carrying *-a*
in the plural, or else in a vocalic inflectional ending, masculine *-o*, feminine *-i*,
plural *-e*). These Greek-derived inflectional endings continue to be productive
in the European dialects of Romani and serve as the basis for the integration

of further loanwords from later, contemporary contact languages: e.g. *president-os* 'president', *doktor-is* 'doctor', *šeft-o* 'deal' (German *Geschäft* 'business'). In Romani non-nominative cases, however, there is a tendency to assimilate inflection to the inherited system. The same agglutinating case endings are used throughout the whole vocabulary. The oblique ending, which mediates between the noun stem and agglutinating case endings, is based either on the Greek-derived nominative endings, as in *president-os-ke* 'for the president' (in masculine nouns, where the ending *-s* resembles the oblique ending for inherited nouns in *-es*), or it assimilates completely or partly to the inherited forms (thus in the plural either the completely assimilated *president-en-sa* 'with the presidents', compare with inherited *čhavor-en-sa* 'with the boys', or the hybrid form *president-on-sa*).

As far as can be ascertained, languages that assign gender or class and overt definiteness or indefiniteness to inherited nouns also assign them to borrowed nouns. Gender identity may or may not be retained, even between languages with similar gender systems. Thus, *taʔrīx* 'history' is masculine in Arabic, but in Kurdish the loanword *tarîx* is feminine. Factors involved in gender assignment to new loans include natural gender (but note that German *Baby* 'baby' is neuter), the gender of the word in the donor language, and the gender of an existing equivalent or near-equivalent in the recipient language. Thus German *Mail* 'email message' is often feminine, possibly by analogy to German *Post* 'post, mail', and/or *Nachricht* 'message'.

A further factor may be the morphological and phonological shape of the word and the correlation of gender with phonological shapes in the inherited vocabulary. In Hebrew, European abstract nouns ending in *-átsya*, such as *komunikátsya* 'communication', which normally derive from Polish or Russian, are classified as feminine on the basis of their original gender, but this is facilitated further by the fact that Hebrew nouns ending in /-a/ are generally feminine. In Swahili, the first syllable in the loanword *kitabu* 'book', from Arabic *kitāb*, is reinterpreted as a classifier *ki-*, giving rise to the inflection paradigm SG *kitabu*, PL *vitabu*. The same process is followed in the English pseudo-loan *kipilefti* 'roundabout' (from 'keep left'), PL *vipilefti*. Gender may also be introduced into a language along with borrowed forms. Tadmor (2007: 311) reports how Malay-Indonesian, which lacks grammatical gender, adopts a gender distinction with Sanskrit loanwords that come in gendered pairs, as in *putra* 'son' and *putri* 'daughter', *wartawan* '(male) journalist' and *wartawati* '(female) journalist'.

Another aspect of nominal grammatical marking that might be said to be carried over from the donor language with some degree of frequency are plural markers and definite articles – a fact that inspires Myers-Scotton and Jake (2000) to define them as 'early system morphemes' (see Chapter 5). Nonetheless, replicated plural markers, and especially definite articles, are often not productive, and are frequently 'doubled' through native morphology; consider once again the examples cited in Chapter 5, Domari *zálame* 'man', plural *zlām-é* (from Arabic *zálame* 'man', plural *zlām*), and Spanish *el arroz* 'the rice' (Arabic *ar-ruzz* 'the rice'). Simango (2000: 494) even notes the use of English plural forms accompanied by native plural affixes in Chichewa – *ma-refugee-s* 'refugees' – for plural meaning, while English plurals that are unaccompanied by Chichewa class/number affixes are interpreted as singulars: *apples i-modzi* 'one apple'. The integration into the plural inflection patterns of the recipient language may involve a rather radical structural integration; thus in Arabic, inanimate loans are generally assigned the 'full' or 'regular' feminine plural suffix – *trāk* 'truck, lorry', plural *trāk-āt* – while masculine animates are often assigned the so-called 'broken plural', which entails insertion of the consonantal root into an inflectional template: *daktōr* 'doctor', plural *dakātra*.

A final note on integration concerns the construction of 'pseudo-loans' in some languages. I mention this phenomenon under integration, although it does not concern the grammatical or morphological integration of elements, since, much like the processes discussed so far in this section, it involves the activation of creative, dynamic processes of accommodation in the recipient language. The issue is statistically perhaps of marginal relevance. It concerns the emergence of words such as German *Handy* 'a mobile phone, cell-phone', and *Beamer* 'a projector linked to a computer'. Both words are widely perceived in a monolingual and semi-bilingual environment in Germany as English loanwords due to their spelling and pronunciation. As technical innovations they also fit into the semantic category in which one would expect to find loans. But while they do constitute replications of English-derived word-forms, the meanings associated with them are entirely the product of internal, German-context based creations that do not exist in an English-speaking context. While these two words are widely cited, there are other examples. Swahili *kipilefti* 'roundabout' (from 'keep left') is one such example; Hebrew military slang *áfter*, denoting a short-term, evening leave following a day's training, is another, based on an extension of English *after*. Despite constituting, in all likelihood, a minority among loans, such semi-borrowed word-forms are valuable in illuminating the mechanisms of lexical borrowing. They indicate to us that bilingual speakers are not just 'copiers' of forms, but that they can also act as creative replicators of raw material which they recruit in the context of interaction in the 'donor' language, but shape and re-model functionally within the context of the 'recipient' language.

7.3   The borrowing of verbs

Verbs clearly figure among the word classes that are borrowed among languages; consider English borrowings like *to demand* from French, German *downloaden* 'to download' from English, Polish Romani *trafineł* 'to meet' from Polish *trafiać* which in turn derives from German *treffen*, and Maltese *jimmodifik* 'to modify'. Nonetheless, there appears to be a near-consensus view that the borrowing of verbs is made more cumbersome in some languages due to the widespread tendency of verbs to be morphologically more complex (see Winford

2003: 52). Moravcsik (1975) had drawn attention to the frequent use of incorporation strategies to accommodate borrowed verbs. The typological discussion of verb borrowability has recently been revived by online discussions (Huttar 2002). Wichmann and Wohlgemuth (2007) hypothesise that the following hierarchy might be identified for the structural integration of loan verbs:

(4)   Hypothesised hierarchy of loan verb integration (Wichmann and
            Wohlgemuth 2007):
        light verbs > indirect insertions > direct insertion > paradigm transfer

In the absence of a comprehensive survey or even a systematic sample of languages that borrow verbs, it is difficult to either confirm or refute the existence of a hierarchy. It is nevertheless noteworthy that Wichmann and Wohlgemuth name four different types of strategies, some of which resemble the integration types listed by Muysken (2000: 184; see Chapter 5) for bilingual conversation. It seems useful to list these types once again, without a hierarchy, but to rename them slightly and interpret the actual strategy involved:

(5)   Types of loan verb integration:
        a. No modification of the original form of the verb ('direct insertion')
        b. Morphological modification of the original form of the verb ('indirect
           insertion')
        c. Insertion of the original form of the verb into a compound construction
           where it is accompanied by an inherited verb ('light verb')
        d. Import of the original verb along with its original inflection
           ('paradigm transfer')

As we shall see, the types may in fact present a continuum, rather than segregated strategies. Some languages will not overtly modify the original verb form (thus 'direct insertion'), but will assign it to a specific inherited inflection class, either one that is reserved exclusively for loans, thus flagging it as a loan verb, or perhaps one that is used for intensification of actions; in either case, the original verb, while remaining unmodified, is treated like a non-verb and so in a way that resembles the modification (so-called 'indirect insertion') strategy. The continuum may also have an historical dimension. A light verb (a verb whose function is to integrate a borrowed verb-form) may in time undergo grammaticalisation and develop into a morphological integration marker. There is even some evidence to suggest that borrowed inflection markers may also develop into morphological integration markers. Quite often, morphological integration markers are verbalising affixes that are used to derive verbs from non-verbs within the inherited vocabulary (see already Moravcsik 1975, 1978). The same is true of light verbs in some languages. This presents us with a rather close functional affinity between the so-called 'indirect insertion' strategy and the 'light verb' strategy.

A further, cross-cutting strategy is the choice of form that is replicated from the donor language. This can be a verbal root, if one can be isolated. It is often a default, though sometimes complex (bi-morphic) form, such as an infinitive or a 3SG finite form, in which latter case selection for tense and aspect may also take place. In identifying a bare root speakers might be guided by the typology of both the donor and the recipient language, and adjustments may have to be made to resolve conflicts among the two. All this makes it interesting to examine how various strategies are distributed among languages, what might motivate the choice of one strategy over another, and especially why the integration of verbs appears to be so complex in so many languages.

As seen above, some languages borrow verbs without any formal adaptation. Plain forms of the verb are carried over into Vietnamese from Chinese, where there is no morphology in either the recipient or the donor language (Alves 2007), as well as in Likpe (Ameka 2007: 113), where isolating Ewe contributes verb roots into an agglutinative structure. Imbabura Quechua is another example of plain insertion. Spanish verbs are borrowed as 'bare' forms (i.e. as stems without the Spanish infinitive marker) and Quechua verbal inflection is added directly to this form: *balura-ni* 'I value' from Spanish *valora-r* (Rendón 2007: 497). In Tasawaq, Tuareg verbs are integrated either without any reflex of the Tuareg verb inflection, as in *gílìllìt* 'to be round', or based on the Tuareg 3SG Perfective form in *y-*, as in *yízmàm* 'to press' from Tuareg *y-ǝʒmǎm* 'he pressed' (Kossmann 2007: 82).

Hayward and Orwin (1991) report on the interesting case of the East-Cushitic variety of Qafar-Saho in Ethiopia and Eritrea. The language has two co-existing inflection classes. The younger and more widespread class has the suffixed person markers: 3SG *fak-e* 2SG *fek-te* 'open'. The more archaic inflection class features prefixed person markers: 3SG *y-eḥet-e* 2SG *t-eḥet-e* 'chew'. These are direct descendants of the Afro-Asiatic conjugation markers, found in Semitic, Berber, and elsewhere in Cushitic (e.g. with a small number of verbs in Somali). Verbal loans from Tigrinya, a neighbouring South Semitic language, are integrated into the old, prefixed conjugation: 3SG *y-idgim-e*, 2SG *t-idgim-e* 'repeat', from Tigrinya *dägäm-*. It appears that the presence in (Semitic) Tigrinya of a prefixed conjugation, which strongly resembles (and is historically related to) the archaic Cushitic one, lends support to the selection of the prefixed conjugation as the accommodating pattern. It might be argued that speakers exploit the similarities between the 'old' native class and the inflection patterns of the donor language to lend authenticity to the verbal loans.

Romani too assigns loan-verbs into a special inflection class. The history of loan-verb adaptation markers in Romani goes back to the replication of Greek-derived inflectional markers, which accompanied Greek loan verbs in Early Romani, when Greek was the principal contact language, during the late Byzantine period (see Matras 2002, Chapter 6; see also Bakker 1997b). Once contact with Greek was lost, following the decline of the Byzantine Empire as well as the dispersal of Romani-speaking populations throughout Europe from the late fourteenth century onwards, the Greek inflection class markers lost their significance as indicators of the specific class affiliation of Greek verbs, but were retained, albeit selectively and in a somewhat simplified form, and assigned to all new verbal loans from subsequent contact languages. The markers concerned are the verbal augments, which in Greek also indicate tense/aspect. Their original tense/aspect opposition remains partly productive in Romani, but they are doubled by the inherited Romani markers. Thus, Romani dialects in central-eastern and southeastern Europe have either *ir-in-av* or *ir-iz-av* 'I return' (Greek *jir-íz-o*), past-tense *ir-is-ájlom* 'I returned' (Greek *jír-is-a*). The same affixes are assigned to new verbal loans: *misl-in-av*, *misl-iz-av* 'I think', from Slavic *misl-*.

Northern Vlax (Transylvanian and Moldovan) Romani dialects tend to simplify the inherited Greek morphemes into a new vocalic inflection class, which continues to distinguish inherited, pre-European verbs from borrowed, European verbs: Compare the inherited verbs *mang-av* 'I ask', *phen-av* 'I say', *asa-v* 'I laugh', with the borrowed *gind-i-v* 'I think' from Romanian *gândi*, *vorb-i-v* 'I speak' from Romanian *vorbi*, *ažut-i-v* 'I help' from Romanian *ajuta*. Thus, the Greek endings have been lost, but the principle of assignment of loan verbs to a new class has been retained. This shows us altogether three stages in a historical process involving firstly the partial replication of donor-language morphology (indicating class affiliation and tense/aspect), then the continuing, albeit selective replication of that same morphology and its application to new verbs from new contact languages, and finally the abandonment of the original morphology but retention of the principle of class-segregation of loan verbs. German has, in a way, undergone a development in the opposite direction. It had once required an augmenting suffix *-ier-* to be added to the root of French-derived verbs: *telefonieren* 'to telephone', French *téléphoner*. As we saw above, this is no longer a requirement for the contemporary integration of loan verbs from English.

Modern Hebrew inserts loan verbs into an inflectional template past *CiCCéC*, infinitive *leCaCCéC*, based on the isolation of a four-consonantal root. Inherited Semitic roots are normally tri-consonantal. The four-consonantal template is thus already an inflectional oddity in the morphological typology of the language. Apart from loans, it is also used for composite neologisms, such as *ʔidkén* 'update, renew', based on the inherited roots *ʔ.(w).d* 'to return' and *k.(w).n* 'to be'. The origin of the template is in a replication of an Aramaic template, used initially for intensification of an action: *šixpél* 'multiply', from *š+k.f.l.*, i.e. a grammatical prefix followed by the root meaning 'double', *šidrég* 'upgrade', from *š+d.r.g.* 'step, grade', or *tifʕél* 'operate a machine', from *t+p.ʕ.l.* 'do, act'. With loan verbs, where a four-consonantal root is retrievable, it is inserted into the template, ignoring any vowels in the original word: *firgén* 'grant, allow' from Yiddish *fargenen*, *tilfén* 'telephone', *diskés* 'discuss'. Where no four-consonantal root is retrievable, the final consonant identified as a root consonant is reduplicated in order to match the template: *fiksés* 'fax'. In the absence of even three root consonants, the template compromises one: *čitét* 'chat (on the internet)'. This also occurs when two consonants in the original word happen to be identical already, and cannot be further reduplicated: *tsitét* 'quote, cite' from German (and other languages) *zit-ieren*. Thus, Hebrew shows on the one hand considerable flexibility in adjusting both the replicated form and the demands of the template to accommodate a variety of verb-forms. On the other hand, however, it is consistent in assigning loan verbs to a rather marginal derivation template, one that is otherwise used for deliberate (planned) lexical creations, and which in its original meaning carries action-intensifying semantics.

This intensification aspect is found quite widely among the strategies for integrating loan verbs. Asia Minor Greek dialects integrate Turkish loan verbs by assigning to them one of several Greek inflection class endings, most commonly *-ízo*, which in Greek is used to derive verbs from nouns: *órkos* 'oath', *orkízo* 'I take an oath'. The original verb form is replicated in the Turkish 3SG past-tense: *aradízo* 'I search' from Turkish *ara-mak* 'to search', 3SG PAST-tense *aradı*; *anladǝzo* 'I understand' from *anlamak* > *anladı*; *örendízo* 'I learn' from *öğrenmek* > *öğrendi* (Dawkins 1916: 664–666). Moravcsik (1975)[5] points out similar devices in Hungarian, where a suffix used to derive denominal verbs from inherited nouns (*ful-el* 'to listen hard', from *ful* 'ear') is also employed to integrate loan verbs (*leiszt-ol* 'to accomplish', from German *leist-en*), and in Russian, where again the same suffix is used for native denominals (*nakaz-ova-t'* 'to command', from *nakaz* 'command') and for integrated loan verbs (*fix-ova-t'* 'to fix').

Verbalising suffixes are generally widespread. A verbalising prefix *ve-* is used in Biak, an Austronesian language of Papua, to integrate Indonesian loan verbs (van den Heuvel 2007: 332). Nahuatl borrows Spanish verbs by adding a verbalizing suffix *-oa* to the Spanish infinitive form: *cantar-oa-* 'to sing' (Jensen and Canger 2007: 406). Yaqui borrows the same suffix from Nahuatl and uses it in a similar way to integrate Spanish infinitives (Estrada Fernández and Guerrero 2007: 422–423). Aikhenvald (2002: 224) reports on the use of a verbalising suffix *-ta* in Tariana, an Arawak language of the Amazon, to integrate loan verbs from Tucano: *-besi-ta* 'to choose', from Tucano *besé*. In Shipibo-Konibo, a Panoan language of the Amazon basin,[6] Spanish verbs are taken over in the finite form of the 3SG present, to which a native suffix *-n* is added; thus *pierde-n-* 'to lose' from Spanish *pierde* 'loses'. This particular suffix has a transitivising meaning when combined with inherited roots: *raka-t-* 'to lie down' (intransitive), but *raka-n-* 'to lay' (transitive).

We find a similar usage of transitive/causative morphology in some dialects of Romani. In western varieties of Sinti (German Romani), the suffix *-ev-* is attached to loan verbs from German: *denkevel* 'to think' from German *denken*. The same suffix is used, as elsewhere in Romani, to derive transitives from intransitive verbs: *našel* 'to run away', *naševel* 'to drive someone away'. Other varieties of Romani retain other transitive/causative affixes along with Greek-derived tense/aspect and inflection class markers, of the kind described above: Crimean Romani has *pomniskerel* 'to remember', from Russian *pomnat'* 'remember', Gurbet Romani (in former Yugoslavia) has *pomožisarel* 'to help' from Slavic *pomož-/pomóći* 'to help'. The added segment *-is-* derives from the Greek aorist marker, while the affixes *-ar-* and *-ker-* are common Romani markers with transitive/causative meanings (the first goes back to Northwestern Indo-Aryan, the second is a more recent grammaticalisation of the verb *ker-* 'to do').

In some languages, added morphology supplements verbal meaning, not just grammatical status. In Indonesian, loan-verbs are normally integrated by means of an inherited prefix, as in *meng-akses* 'to access', *di-subisidi* 'to be subsidized' from Dutch *subsidie*, and *ber-dansa* 'to dance (Western dances)' from Portuguese (Tadmor 2007). Sakel (2007c: 569) reports that the Amazonian language Mosetén has only a small number of genuine verbs, or verbness markers. Verbs are generally formed as combinations of one of these markers and a non-finite element, and this is also the strategy that is applied in order to integrate Spanish loan verbs, drawing on one of two verbness markers. Spanish loan verbs are thus treated as non-finite (non-verbal) elements; their verbness is expressed by the modifier. In this fashion, Mosetén verbs can be derived from Spanish infinitives – *pasar-yi-* 'to happen', from Spanish *pasar* 'to happen' – but also from Spanish nouns: *suerte-yi-* 'to be fortunate', from Spanish *suerte* 'fortune'. A somewhat similar strategy can be found in the northern Australian language Jaminjung (Schultze-Berndt 2000: 142–144). Like many other Australian languages, it relies on a combination of two verbal elements, an uninflected preverb or 'co-verb', and a limited class of some three dozen inflecting verbs. Loan verbs from Kriol (an English-based creole) take the form of uninflected preverbs. Derivational markers such as the transitive marker *-im* are carried over from Kriol with the verb stem: *lukabta-im bun-ngangu* 'they looked after me'.

At the final end of the continuum we find languages that use actual lexical verbs in order to integrate loan verb stems. Japanese adds the verb *suru* 'to do': *sain suru* 'to sign', *esukēpu suru* 'to play truant' ('escape') (Loveday 1996: 118). Yiddish uses *zayn* 'to be' in conjunction with Hebrew masculine singular present-participles (in effect, the finite singular masculine present-tense form) to integrate Hebrew loans: *máskim zayn* 'to agree', from Hebrew *maskím* 'he agrees (etc.)'.

In a more or less coherent area stretching from the Caucasus and all the way to South Asia, languages tend to favour this 'light verb' strategy. The 'light' or 'adaptation' verb shows specialisation for valency: a distinction is made between transitive loans, which are normally integrated by adding the verb 'to do', and intransitive loans, to which the verb 'to be' or 'to become' is added. Adyghe (Höhlig 1997: 98–101) uses its verbs *sʲɪn* 'do' and *x̌°ɪn* 'become' to integrate Russian verbs. The Russian verb appears in the infinitive: *mešat' sesʲɪ* 'I disturb', *realizovat' x̌°ɪn* 'to fulfil oneself'. The strategy is well established, and is also used with older loans from Arabic and Turkish – *ḥisap sʲɪn* 'to calculate' (Arabic *ḥisāb* 'calculation') – though here the borrowed verb appears in a nominal form. Another Caucasian language with a similar system is Tsez, which uses its auxiliary verbs intransitive *-oq-* 'to become' and *-od-* 'to do' with a borrowed lexical element which may be a noun or an infinitive (Comrie 2004).

The replication of nominal forms rather than verbal systems is the traditional pattern in other languages of the area too: Kurdish has *temam kirin* 'to complete something' from Arabic *tamm* 'to complete' via Persian *temmām*, with Kurdish *kirin* 'to do', and *xilas bûn* 'to end' from Arabic *xallaṣ* 'end', with Kurdish *bûn* 'to become'. Persian shows *elām kardan* 'to anounce' and *elām šodan* 'to be announced', from Arabic *iʕlām* 'announcement', with Persian *kardan* 'to do' and *šodan* 'to become'. In some languages, the semantic distinction between the two light verbs does not quite convey syntactic transitivity, but rather the degree to which the subject has an agentive role, or is itself affected by the action (so-called 'unaccusativity'): Turkish has *kabul etmek* 'to accept' from Arabic *qubūl* 'acceptance', and *şahit olmak* 'to witness' from Arabic *šāhid* '(a) witness', the first (with *etmek* 'to do') indicating an agentive subject, the second (with *olmak* 'to become') an experiencer; Hindi has *taqsīm karnā* 'to divide' from Arabic/Persian *taqsīm* 'division' and Hindi *karnā* 'to do', and *hamrah honā* 'to accompany' from Persian *ham-rāh* 'road-companion' with Hindi *honā* 'to become', the latter similarly indicating that the subject is itself an undergoer/experiencer. Domari, an Indo-Aryan language that has been in intense contact with Kurdish (Iranian), Turkish (Turkic), and Arabic (Semitic) is in the process of grammaticalising its light verbs into affixes or augments. The verbs *-kar-* 'to do' and *-(h)o-* 'to be/to become' often appear in a contracted form when integrating Arabic verb loans: *štrī-k-ami* 'I buy' alongside *štrī-kar-ami*; *skunn-o-ndi* 'they reside' alongside *skunn-ho-ndi*. Here too, the semantic opposition signifies the subject as agent vs. experiencer. Thus we find transitive verbs such *fhimm-ho-mi* 'I understand', *ḥibb-ho-mi* 'I like', and *ʕallim-ho-mi* 'I learn' with the augment *-ho-* from the intransitive light verb 'to become', all of which express a subject that is an experiencer rather than an agent-initiator. As in the other languages that employ light verbs, in Domari too they are equally employed to derive verbs from indigenous nouns: *qayiš* 'food', *qayišk(ar)ami* 'I prepare food'.

Unlike the more established pattern in the area, Domari inserts Arabic verbal roots, rather than the Arabic nominal stem (so-called *masdar*). In the absence of an infinitive in Arabic, Domari selects a reduced form of the subjunctive, stripped of its person markers. The other languages in the area show a tendency toward similar developments, namely exploiting the established construction in order to integrate verbal forms. We saw this above for Adyghe in its integration of recent verbal loans from Russian. Kurdish–Turkish bilinguals frequently use structures like *anlamış kirin* 'to understand', based on the participle-like, 3SG past-tense evidential form of the Turkish verb in *-miş*. Turkish immigrants in Western Europe are frequently observed to use *yapmak* 'to make' instead of the older *etmek* 'to do' as a light verb, in conjunction with the infinitive forms of the donor language: *unterschreiben yapmak* 'to sign' from German *unterschreiben* (see Backus 1996 for numerous similar examples from Turkish in the Netherlands), and Hindi/Urdu makes use of English infinitives in constructions like *land karnā* 'to land'.

Rather than a group of segregated integration strategies of verbs, we find a continuum of devices. The theme of this continuum is not the structural effort that is made in order to accommodate verbs, but rather the degree to which the 'verbness' of foreign-origin verbs is recognised and accepted. Languages like Hebrew and Domari show that speakers apply considerable creativity and flexiblity when it comes to the structural adaptation and integration of loan verbs. While it is possible that some languages impose constraints on the isolation of verb roots,[7] there is no evidence to suggest that the length to which speakers of some languages go in order to integrate loan verbs is a product of any structural-typological constraints. As suggested already in Chapter 5, verbs accomplish, functionally speaking, two separate things. They are lexical signifiers that label events, activities, or states; and they also carry out the grammatical operation of anchoring the predication in the context of the utterance.

On the far side of the verb integration continuum, we find languages that treat borrowed verbs merely as lexical labels, but do not entrust them with anchoring the predication. The latter task is instead delegated to a separate, 'light' verb. This explains the emphasis on valency or agent/experiencer distinctions in the choice of light verb, for such distinctions serve a key role in defining the nature of the predication. At the other end of the continuum we find languages that recognise foreign verbs as both lexical labels (signifiers) and predicate-initiating devices. In between we find a variety of strategies. Many of the morphological devices are designed similarly to empower the lexical root to initiate a predication, either by emphasising its de-nominal character, or by assigning it valency, or by assigning it intensification qualities which similarly strengthen the activity side of the depiction and so move it closer, conceptually, to the role of a predication. A pre-requisite for the employment of loan verb adaptation markers is the availability in the recipient language of a morphological procedure to derive verbs from non-verbs. Whereas an isolating language like Vietnamese may rely to a considerable extent on the pragmatics of morpheme juxtaposition as a way of (indirectly) marking out word classes, flectional languages will often require an additional means of identifying derived verbs.

Some integration mechanisms serve as a token for the predication value, by highlighting an exclusive inflection class membership reserved for loan verbs. Arguably, the replication in Romani of Greek-derived aspecto-temporal and inflection class identification morphology activates associations with the original predicate-anchoring function carried by finite verb inflection, and so in this way it supports the conceptual association between the loan verb and a predicate. The same might be said for the choice of the prefix conjugation in Qafar Saho: it activates associations with the original Tigrinya conjugation. The question can then be asked, why speakers do not simply replicate loan verbs together with their original finite inflection?

There are several reasons for this. First, replicating the full verb inflection requires high bilingual proficiency, which is likely to counteract the spread of loans to monolingual parts of the speech community. Second, the import of loans along with their inflection would also create a compartmentalised system in which different inflection patterns, much more different from one another than distinct inherited inflection classes within a language, would coexist side by side. This

	Inherited: *phurjo(v)-* 'to grow old'		Turkish: *evlen-mek* 'to marry'	
Person	Present	Past	Present	Past
1sg	*phurjovav*	*phurilem*	*evleniim*	*evlendim*
2sg	*phurjo*	*phurilan*	*evlenisin*	*evlendin*
3sg	*phurjol*	*phurila*	*evlenii*	*evlendi*
1pl	*phurjova*	*phurilam*	*evleniis*	*evlendik*
2pl	*phurjon*	*phurilen*	*evlenisinis*	*evlendinis*
3pl	*phurjon*	*phurile*	*evleniler*	*evlendiler*

Figure 7.6 *Inherited and Turkish-derived verb conjugations in the Romani Kalburdžu dialect of Sindel, Northeastern Bulgaria.*

would counteract the natural tendency toward economy and consistency in the formal representation of functions.

Third, it can be argued that the choice of inflectional system in which to anchor the predication symbolises in effect the bilingual speaker's context-bound choice of 'language', even when the interaction is in the bilingual mode. In other words, while the selection of word-forms in an utterance may target the entire multilingual repertoire, the bilingual's compliance with a context-bound choice of language will manifest itself in the selection of a particular language as the carrier of the predication (just as the selection of a different language for the predication will signal non-compliance, or a marked choice). This gives us a somewhat more focused definition of the notion of 'matrix' language than Myers-Scotton's (1993b) idea of the consistency of system morpheme selection; it also allows us to explain why in some mixed languages, nominal inflection patterns differently as far as its source language is concerned from verb inflection, while the system of verb inflection itself is always consistent even in mixed languages, and not subject to any internal mixing by source (see Chapter 10). A convention by which the choice of finite verb inflection and so of predicate-anchoring strategy would be triggered by the choice of lexical item rather than by contextual constraints would constitute even for the proficient bilingual a partial breakdown of the principle of context-bound separation of 'languages'.

Despite these very powerful constraints, isolated cases of wholesale import of verb inflection along with loan verbs do occur. Perhaps the most stable case is that of a number of Romani dialects in the Balkans,[8] spoken mainly but not exclusively by Muslim populations,[9] who have been bilingual in Romani and Turkish for many centuries. In these dialects, Turkish verb inflection accompanies Turkish loan verbs. Figure 7.6 shows verb conjugations for an inherited (Indo-Aryan) verb, and a Turkish loan verb, in the Kalburdžu dialect of the village of Sindel, in northeastern Bulgaria. Note first of all that the morphological typology of verb inflection in Romani and Turkish is, however coincidentally, quite similar: Both languages employ a tense-aspect marker between the verb root and the subject concord marker, and in both languages the set of subject concord markers is fairly transparent and consistent. Moreover, there are even some – again, coincidental – similarities in the shape of forms, notably in the 1SG and 2SG of the past tense.

Nonetheless, the two systems are clearly distinct. What might motivate speakers to adopt Turkish verb inflection despite the constraints alluded to above? It appears that the key to the process is the acceptance of Romani–Turkish bilingualism as a constituting aspect of group identity. Both languages are spoken interchangeably in the home, as well as within the immediate community. When asked in the majority language, Bulgarian, to answer a question in *ciganski* (i.e. 'the Gypsy language'),[10] consultants often responded in Turkish, rather than in Romani. This full acceptance of bilingualism and the fact that there is, effectively, no domain separation and no contextual demarcation between Romani and Turkish in community-internal interaction, blurs the boundaries within the bilingual repertoire. It grants speakers a license to initiate the predication, at least in group-internal communication, randomly in either language. When choosing a particular lexical verb, speakers are thus at liberty to employ the finite verb inflection system that is most easily associated with that verb. Full bilingual proficiency throughout the community supports these choices, and helps to maintain a 'double' system, at least for a certain period. There are signs that in some Romani dialects of this 'type' Turkish verb inflection is infiltrating the inflection system of Romani verbs. In the Romani dialect of Ajia Varvara in Greece (Igla 1996), Turkish verbs retain Turkish inflection even several generations after emigration from Turkey and loss of competence in Turkish. However, the number of verbs conjugated in this way remains small. This is also the case in Crimean Romani, which had been influenced by another Turkic language, Tatar.

The incipient licensing of original verb inflection with loan verbs can be observed in Romani dialects of Greece, as well as in Russian Romani (cf. Matras 2002: 134; Eloeva and Rusakov 1990). Here too, it appears that alongside proficiency, acceptance of bilingualism as an aspect of group identity is an important pre-condition for the failure to integrate loan verbs. In the Romani dialect of Parakalamos in the district of Epirus in northwestern Greece (Matras 2004b), speakers tend to employ Greek morphology with spontaneous insertions of Greek lexical verbs, as with *jiriz-o* 'I return':

(6)   Epirus Romani:
           Ther-av   *kati*   buti   *ja* te   ker-av   akate   *prin*   te
           have-1SG   some   work   in order to   do-1SG   here   before   COMP

           jiriz-o   to kher
           return-1SG   to home
           'I have *some* work *to* do here *before* I *return* home.'

Many Greek-derived verbs that are used regularly, however, are adapted to Romani by means of loan verb adaptation markers – ironically, these markers are derived from Greek tense/aspect markers – and take inherited Romani inflection: *parakal-iz-ava* 'I thank' (Greek *parakal-o*), *aɣap-ez-ava* 'I love' (*aɣap-o*). This contrasts quite sharply with the Turkish-Romani varieties of Bulgaria, which do not distinguish between 'integrated' and 'non-integrated' Turkish loan verbs. In this respect, the phenomenon attested in Epirus (and in other Greek-Romani dialects, as well as in Russian Romani) is qualitatively different, although it sheds some light on the process of acceptance of bilingualism and loosening of the constraints on the differentiation of predication-language by context. Thus, an isolated sentence in Epirus Romani can take on the following shape (cf. Matras 2004b):

(7)   kon *bor-i*   te   *xtiz-i*   nje   kher   *xoris*   *karfja?*
        who can-3SG COMP build-3SG INDEF house without nails
        'Who can build a house without nails?'

(8)   na   *bor-o*   te   *diavaz-o*   soske   *prep-i*   te
        NEG can-1SG COMP study-1SG because must-3SG COMP

        vojt-iz-av   me   daj-a
        help-LOAN-1SG my.OBL mother-OBL
        'I cannot study because I have to help my mother'

In (7), both the modal verb *bori* 'can' and the complement verb *xtizi* 'build' are Greek, and both take Greek inflection. The preposition 'without' is a Greek loan, as is the word for 'nail'. The result is a sentence that contains more Greek material, including inflection, than Indic-derived or inherited Romani material. Nevertheless, it is the default choice in group-internal communication, and is not constructed in such a way as a result of any stylistic choice by the speaker, but simply due to the choice of lexemes, which in this case have no other, non-Greek-derived equivalent in the dialect. Note that in (8) we have altogether four verbs. The modal verbs *boro* 'I can' and *prepi* 'must' (impersonal) take Greek inflection, as does the lexical verb *diavazo* 'I study'; but the Greek-derived lexical verb *vojt-* 'to help' is integrated into inherited Romani inflection. In Epirus Romani, replication of donor-language verb inflection is regular and consistent with modal verbs, but only incipient in lexical verbs. This allows us to postulate the following hierarchy for the integration of verb inflection:

(9)   Integration hierarchy for verb inflection:
        modal/auxiliary verb > lexical verb

The borrowing of modals and auxiliaries is well-attested. Almost half of the sample languages considered in Matras (2007b) show matter replication of modal verbs, examples including Turkish *gerek* 'must' in Kurmanji, Arabic *lāzim* 'must' and *mumkin* 'can' in Domari, Arabic *lāzim* 'must' and *yumkin* 'can' in Western Neo-Aramaic, Arabic-derived *mungkin* 'can' in Indonesian, Spanish *tiene que* 'must' in the Pacific language Rapanui, Spanish-derived *nisisita* 'need', *debi* and *tieneki* 'must', and *puede* 'can' in the Pacific language Chamorro, *pudi* 'can' and *kiri* 'want' in Quechua, and *tyene ke* and *debe* 'must', *pwede* 'can', and *nesesita* 'need' in Otomi, Malay *harus* 'must' in Biak, and more. Arabic modals have diffused even more widely, including Turkish *lazim* and *mecbur* 'must', Swahili *sharti* 'must', *hitaji* 'need', and Urdu *lazmi* 'must' and (via Persian) *zarurat honā* 'need'. Evenki uses the Russian-derived impersonal modal *nada* 'necessary' (Grenoble 2000: 110–112). Romani dialects borrow word-forms such as Slavic and Romanian *musaj/musi-/muši-* and *triba/treba/trobu-* 'must', Slavic *mora* 'must' and *može* and *mog-* 'can', Turkish-derived *lazimi* and *medžburi* 'must', Swedish-derived *moste* 'must', German-derived *braux-* 'need', and Greek-derived *prep-* 'must' and *bor-* 'can' (see Matras 2002, Elšík and Matras 2006, Elšík and Matras 2008).

Modals are often borrowed as impersonal forms, which replicate a default third-person singular present-tense inflection of the donor language: Spanish *puede* 'can' and *tiene (que)* 'must' in various South American and Pacific languages are good examples, as are Slavic *može* 'can' and *mora* 'must' and Greek *prepi* 'must' in Romani dialects. The replication of finite inflection from the donor language thus begins in these impersonal forms. It may then spread to other tenses, as well as to person-inflected modals. The Greek Romani dialect of Kalamata (southern Greece) replicates the 3SG Greek tense and person inflection in both *prepi* 'must' (present tense) and *éprepe* 'had to' (past tense). Gurbet Romani in Serbia replicates alongside the Serbian 3SG form *mora* 'must' also the Serbian 1SG *moram* 'I must' and 2SG *moraš* 'you must'. Epirus Romani, as seen in (6)–(8), replicates Greek verb inflection with some Greek-derived lexical verbs, but adopts Greek-inflection wholesale with modal verbs: *boro* 'I can', *borusa* 'I could', and so on.

Further confirmation of the hierarchy introduced under (9) comes from Domari. We have seen that Domari applies a procedure of light verbs (currently undergoing grammaticalisation to verbalising affixes) to integrate Arabic lexical verbs. The borrowed Arabic modals *lāzim* 'must' and *mumkin* 'it is possible' are impersonal. Other modals and auxiliaries borrowed from Arabic, however, take full Arabic person and where applicable tense inflection. They include the aspectual auxiliary *kān* 'was', which indicates past-habitual (*kān džari* 'he used to go', *kānat džari* 'she used to go', etc.), the transition-modals *ṣār* 'to begin' and *baqi* 'to continue', as well as the nominal form *bidd-ī* 'I want', *bidd-ak* 'you.M want', etc., which is also replicated with its full Arabic inflection. It is noteworthy that the incorporation of Arabic inflection introduces a gender distinction into Domari in positions in which it is otherwise not indicated in the language (i.e. with present-tense verbs).

How can we explain the hierarchy depicted in (9), i.e. the greater likelihood of borrowed modals to attract replication of donor-language inflection than lexical verbs? Modality can be considered one of those grammatical operations that are vulnerable to malfunctions of the selection/inhibition mechanism. Though not as high on the scale as discourse operators or indefinites, modality represents the conditioning of the speaker's secure knowledge, therefore a potential reduction in the speaker's assertive authority and so a risk factor in the maintenance of stability in the relations between speaker and hearer in respect of their roles in the interaction. The same factor is also responsible for the hierarchy of borrowing within modality expressions, which was cited in the previous chapter: obligation > necessity > possibility > ability > desire. This hierarchy matches the one identified by Elšík and Matras (2006: 343, 2008) for the borrowing of modality markers in Romani dialects: necessity > ability > inability > volition. The greater the involvement of an external force in determining the modality of the proposition, the weaker the speaker's control over the truth and accuracy of that proposition.

7.4   Adjectives and lexical adverbs

Adjectives constitute a much smaller inventory than nouns and even verbs; indeed, in many languages adjectives are a very small class, and in some languages their mere existence as a separate word class is controversial. I am not aware of studies of the borrowing of adjectives into a language that lacks an adjective word-class in its indigenous inventory, but given that such languages are usually spoken nowadays in the vicinity of, and in a diglossic relationship with, languages that do have adjectives, the potential for such integration exists in principle.[11] Many of the figures cited above refer to the proportion of adjectives among the total number of loanwords, but not to the proportion of loans among the class of adjectives. For Selice Romani, Elšík (forthcoming) cites a figure of 42% (recent) loans among the total of adjectives represented on the 1430-wordlist. Of the 15 (English) adjectives on the 207 Swadesh list, Domari borrows 8 or 53% – slightly higher than the proportion of borrowings for the entire list. Maltese, by contrast, seems to have only two of the adjectives that appear on the list: the rather formal-institutional expression 'correct', Maltese *korrett*, and 'straight', Maltese *dritt*, both from Italian. The fact that these two are loans in Domari too, and one of them –'correct' – is also a loan in English, might indicate that some adjectives, like nouns, are semantically more prone to borrowing. Terms for 'big' and 'small' for instance appear to be more resistant to borrowing.

Colour terms are a useful measure, since we have an indication of which colour terms are more likely to appear in the world's languages and are therefore more 'basic'. If borrowing behaviour were to follow the hierarchy of the differentiation of colour terms, then one would expect it to run in the opposite direction to Berlin and Kay's (1969) hierarchy: black and white > red > yellow or green > blue. In other words, 'blue', the least likely (on this shortened version of the hierarchy) to be represented by an independent expression, would be the most likely to be borrowed. In Figure 7.7 Urdu, Domari, and Romani are all Indo-Aryan but have been in contact with different languages. Maltese is Semitic, Swahili is Bantu,

English	Swahili	Maltese	Lovari Romani	Domari	Urdu
red	-ekundu	aħmar	lolo	lala	laal
black	-eusi	iswed	kalo	kala	kala/siah
white	-eupe	abjad	parno	prana	safed
green	hijani	aħdar	zeleno	aḥdar	sabz
blue	bluu	blu	modro	azraq	asmān

Figure 7.7 *Inherited and borrowed colour terms in some languages.*

and English is Germanic. We can at least assume some similarities in the cultural relevance of colour terms in the respective societies, which have been in direct and indirect cultural contacts for millennia. As Figure 7.7 shows, the terms for 'black', 'white', and 'red' are indeed the most stable. Urdu borrows (from Persian) one of its two alternative expressions for black, *siah*, and its word for 'white', *safed*, putting 'red' at the top of the stability list. Indo-Aryan once had words both for 'green' and for 'blue'; indeed, the Indo-Aryan word for 'blue', *nīlam*, has even been borrowed into Dravidian languages (cf. Kapp 2004). The fact that Urdu, Domari, and Lovari Romani each borrow the terms (from Persian, Arabic, and west Slavic languages, respectively) does not point to a gap in the older system, but rather to the weaker stability of the term. In line with the prediction, 'blue' is the most unstable, being borrowed also into Maltese and Swahili (from English). The English word itself appears to have received semantic reinforcement from its French cognate *bleu*, as the original Germanic term *plaw/blaw* etc. meant 'grey' (cf. Biggam 1997).

Adjectives tend to be integrated syntactically into the position of the attribute in the recipient language. Hebrew positions adjectives of European origin after the noun: *yéled inteligénti* 'an intelligent boy'. Like nouns, adjectives tend to adopt the agreement morphology of the recipient language. German has relatively few borrowed adjectives, but treats them as native adjectives and they are assigned German agreement inflection: *ein cool-er Typ* 'a cool guy', *die cool-en Typen* 'the cool guys'.

But cases are frequently encountered where, in order to take on agreement inflection, adjectives must undergo derivational modifications, or where they are assigned to a specific inflectional class. Hebrew assigns all adjectives gender and number agreement markers, as it does with native adjectives. But loan adjectives are assigned to a particular inflection class, one that in Hebrew productively derives adjectives from nominals: *yardén* 'Jordan', *yardéni* (colloquial) or *yardení* (formal) 'Jordanian'; cf. *yéled inteligént-i* 'an intelligent boy', *yaldá inteligént-it* 'an intelligent girl'. Note that in formal Modern Hebrew, the inflectional ending carries stress with native adjectives – hence *yardení* 'Jordanian' – but not with loans.

Yiddish places adjectives in preposed position, and treats Hebrew loan adjectives in this way too. The inflectional integration of Hebrew adjectives into Yiddish, which also has gender and number agreement, depends on the phonological shape of the Hebrew form. Yiddish marks agreement on adjectives through vowel endings. When a Hebrew adjective ends in a consonant, a vowel ending is added directly to the default M.SG form of the Hebrew adjective: *šiker-e mentšn* 'drunken- PL people' (Hebrew *šikkōr* 'drunk. M.SG'). When the Hebrew adjective ends in a vowel (often as a result of the reduction of glottals or pharyngeals), an adjectival derivation suffix *-n-* is added: *mešige-n-e mentšn* 'crazy- PL people' (Hebrew *məšūgáʕ* 'crazy').

Romani generally applies a Greek-derived inflection ending *-o* to borrowed adjectives in the nominative singular (irrespective of gender), while other inflected forms are attached to the adjectival derivational ending *-on-*: *lung-o* 'long' (NOM.M.SG/NOM.F.SG), *lung-on-e* 'long' (NOM.PL/OBL.SG). Some dialects of Romani, however, have adopted adjectival endings from their contemporary contact languages. Burgenland Romani adopts German adjectival loans with a uniform ending *-i* – e.g. *brauni gra* '(a) brown horse'. The basis for the ending is a generalisation of the most frequent adjectival ending in the particular German dialect of the region.[12]

Languages that lack adjectival inflection altogether appear to avoid carrying over the original inflection of borrowed adjectives. Arabic for example has postposed adjectives that agree in gender and number with their head. This agreement pattern is sometimes preserved when entire Arabic-derived nouns phrases are used in older Persian and Ottoman Turkish texts. But in modern Persian and Kurdish, which do not show either gender or number agreement with adjectives (gender is lacking in Persian altogether), Arabic-derived adjectives simply follow the noun in the conventional Iranian attributive construction, appearing in the default (Arabic) M.SG form; e.g. Kurdish *çîrok-ên teqlîdî* (stories- ATTR.PL traditional) 'traditional stories' (the Arabic adjective with inanimate plural agreement would be *taqlīdi-yya*). Turkish, which lacks gender distinction and has no adjective inflection, similarly generalises the Arabic default forms, adapting them into its usual preposed position: *ciddi bir plan* 'a serious plan' (from Arabic *džidd-ī* 'serious- M.SG'). Urdu, which shows inflectional agreement of adjectives, generally prefers not to assign such agreement patterns to English-derived adjectives; consider the airport announcement *ye bilkul final elān hɛ* 'this is the absolute final call'. By contrast, English institutional titles may employ Latin inflectional endings in distinguishing between masculine *Professor Emeritus* and feminine *Professor Emerita*.

Maltese is an interesting intermediate case. Adjectives follow the noun, as they normally do in the principal contact language, Italian (and Sicilian). Like Italian, Maltese also has two genders. Some borrowed adjectives, namely those that end in a consonant, take the inherited (Semitic) inflection pattern, in which the M.SG is treated as default and has no identifiable vocalic ending, while the F.SG ends in -a: *f'kuntest modern* 'in a modern.M context', but *poeżija modern-a* 'modern-F poetry' (note that the original gender of the Italian loan nouns is preserved). Both the form and the position of the Maltese feminine singular adjective happen to agree with the form and position of the original Italian adjective. This leads to an analogy with the plural, where the Italian inflectional ending -i (Italian M.PL) is actually preserved: *toroq modern-i* 'modern roads'. A second type of Italian loan-adjective in Maltese ends invariably in -*ali*. We thus find *paġna prinċipali* 'main page', *paġna* being a feminine singular noun, but the same ending also appears in agreement with plural nouns: *soluzzjoni spiritwali għall-problemi ekonomiċi* 'spiritual solutions for economic problems'.

A grammatical operation that is related to adjectives and deserves our special attention in connection with borrowing is the derivation of non-positive (comparative and superlative) forms of adjectives. In most languages, this is done via morpho-syntactic means, through a specialised particle or affix, more rarely through suppletion (*bad – worse*). In contact situations in which the recipient language is the 'weaker' language – a minority, typically oral language, restricted to familiar domains – the grammatical markers and the procedure of non-positive adjective derivation are particularly prone to borrowing. Both Elšík and Matras (2006) and Matras (2007b) for the cross-linguistic sample establish the greater borrowability of superlative markers over comparative markers. This hierarchy can be explained in relation to the kind of activation of presuppositional information that is carried out by the two categories. The comparative procedure activates presupposed knowledge about an object of comparison. This already places the comparative on the side of those grammatical operations in which the speaker has to rely heavily on the listener, making it vulnerable to lapses in the control over the selection/inhibition mechanism. The superlative goes a step further. It sets the object of reference apart from the presupposed set of relevant objects, creating a mental demarcation or delimitation line. Superlative relations thus fall within the broad domain of contrast, exemption, and restriction, all of which are particularly contact-susceptible.

Romani dialects recruit comparative and superlative markers among the preposed, unbound or semi-bound markers of their various contact languages, such as Slavic *po*, Romanian *mai*, and Turkish *daha* for the comprative, Slavic *naj*, Hungarian *leg-*, Turkish *en* for the superlative. A bound comparative/superlative marker -*eder* had been borrowed into Proto-Romani from Iranian and continues to be used in many dialects. Sinti Romani for example uses it for the comparative – thus *sik* 'fast', *sikedər* 'faster' – and adopts the German superlative, including both its inflection ending and an accompanying preposition: *am sik-estə* 'fastest', (dialectal) German *am schnell-ste(n)*. The Spanish comparative and superlative marker *más* has entered several Central American languages, Nahuatl, Otomi, Yucatec Maya, Tzutujil, and others, as well as Autronesian languages like Tagalog, Hiligaynon, and Chamorro (Stolz and Stolz 2001). Speakers of

Kurmanji, Adyghe, and Aramaic in Turkey often use the Turkish particles *daha* (comparative) and *en* (superlative), which are also attested in Asia Minor Greek. Indonesian borrows a Javanese superlative particle *paling*. Yiddish has *grojs* 'big', *grejser* 'bigger', but *same grojs* 'biggest', using the Russian-derived marker *same*, which is also borrowed as a superlative marker into Kildin Saami.

Domari provides an interesting case. Its contact language, Arabic, employs a morpho-phonological template *áCCaC* to derive comparative/superlative forms from consonantal roots: *kbīr* 'big', *ákbar* 'bigger'; *zġīr* 'small', *ázġar* 'smaller'. This template cannot easily be isolated or integrated into the agglutinative-inflectional morphological structure of Domari, nor is it simple or even possible to break down Domari adjectives such as *tilla* 'big' or *kištota* 'small' into tri-consonantal roots for insertion into the Arabic-based derivation template. The solution adopted by Domari speakers is to borrow the full Arabic word-form for all comparative/superlative forms, resulting in complete borrowing-based suppletion of the inventory of adjectives: *tilla* 'big', *ákbar* 'bigger'; *kištota* 'small', *ázġar* 'smaller'. We thus see that the motivation to employ just one single structure across the repertoire for the operation 'comparative/superlative' overrides structural constraints as well as what are arguably lexico-structural inconveniences.

The word-class known as 'adverbs' is in many respects, certainly cross-linguistically, a 'non-category': while adverbs might have something in common in a given language as far as their position in a sentence is concerned, there is no general function in the sense of a language-processing operation that can be attributed to them. Consequently, we must differentiate between various functions when discussing the borrowability of so-called adverbs. Words like place deixis, indefinites, focus particles, and phasal adverbs, all of which often fall under the category 'adverb', will therefore be dealt with in the following chapter.

Lexical adverbs are derived in many languages from adjectives, and are often identical to adjectives: Turkish *çabuk* 'fast, swiftly'. Some languages rely on internal derivation strategies to derive adjectives from adverbs, and apply them to borrowed adjectives as well. Thus the Hebrew equivalent of 'intelligently' is *be-ófen inteligénti* lit. 'in an intelligent manner'. English too often employs its own adverb derivation procedure to French adjectives and nouns, rather than borrow French adverbs: *comfortable – comfortably, common – commonly, care – carefully*. Japanese can add a copula marker *ni*: *romanchikku ni* 'romantically' (Loveday 1996: 118). Maltese and Lovari Romani on the other hand tend to borrow full word-forms from the respective contact language, and as a result the typical adverbial endings become analysable to speakers: Maltese thus has *-ment* in Italian loans such as *verament* 'truly', *speċjalment* 'especially', while Lovari Romani has *-no/-nje* in Slavic loans like *specijalno, sistematičnje, objektivno* 'objectively'.

The class of lexical adverbs seems open to loans especially due to the fact that relative little use is made of it in everyday conversation, compared to more formal discourse. Languages often adopt adverbs in specialised contexts (*ipso facto, ex officio, de jure*), often as prepositional phrases. Prolific use of morphologically unaltered sentential adverbs from Arabic is found in Persian and Turkish, and Hebrew adverbs are used in Yiddish. Setting aside adverbs like 'swiftly', which mirror basic adjectives, and those that reflect professional/formal discourse, such as 'objectively', as well as those that belong to the closed sub-classes mentioned above – place deixis, phasal adverbs, etc. – we are left with a group of sentential adverbs whose function is to qualify the predication at the level of the interaction, and which therefore are closer in function to modalilty markers or even to discourse particles. I have elsewhere referred to them as part of a larger class of 'utterance modifiers' (Matras 1998a). Their principal function is to qualify the speaker's statement, and sticking to the explanatory model pursued from the beginning of this chapter, their vulnerability in bilingual contexts and their tendency toward fusion makes perfect sense. Consider Arabic-derived utterance modifiers or statement-qualifying adverbs of this kind in Turkish, such as *maale-sef* 'unfortunately', or *mesela* 'for example'; *belki* 'perhaps', which is shared throughout the area of the Caucasus (e.g. Adyghe), Anatolia (Turkish, Kurmanji, Neo-Aramaic), and beyond (Persian, Azeri); Adyghe borrowings from Turkish in Turkey such as *herhalde* 'apparently', *mesela* 'for example', *tabii* 'of course', *zaten* 'anyway', and corresponding Russian Adyghe borrowing from Russian such as *konečno* 'certainly', *objazatel'no* 'definitely', *polnost'ju* 'completely', *k sožalenju* 'unfortunately', *na primer* 'for example', *vsë ravno* 'equally', *prosto* 'simply', *značit* 'so-to-speak' (Höhlig 1997); Maltese borrowings from Romance *farsi* 'perhaps' and *ċertu* 'certainly'; all these may have a lexical core, in structural terms, but the label 'adverb' applied to them is misleading, since we are dealing with relatively grammaticalised items that operate at the interaction level, not at the level of straightforward naming or labelling, which is the property of content-lexical items. It is this particular trait that makes them easily borrowable.

8 Grammatical and phonological borrowing

8.1 Grammatical function words

8.1.1 Discourse markers and connectors

Studies published over the past two decades or so, beginning with the works by Brody (1987) and Salmons (1990), have established a widespread consensus that discourse markers occupy a position at the very top of the borrowability hierarchy. This holds true at least for the type of contact situations characterised by unidirectional bilingualism and diglossia, where the recipient language tends to be reserved for more personal, informal domains of interaction, and is often an oral and/or minority language. The unidirectionality of bilingualism and the fact that the bilingual mode will tend to dominate interaction in the recipient language both play an important role in situations where speakers license themselves to employ word-forms from the 'outside' language on a regular basis when interacting in the 'inside' language (cf. Matras 1998a, 2000c, 2007a).

Within the broader class of discourse markers and connectors, further borrowability hierarchies appear within functional and structural sub-classes. In Matras (1998a) I proposed the principle of 'pragmatic detachability'. This principle captures the tendency of a certain type of discourse marker to be detachable from the main sentential frame not just in a structural sense, as a result of their clause-peripheral position, but also from the bulk of the lexicon that speakers are more easily able to identify as appropriate in a particular context of interaction (see also Fuller 2001). Such markers – usually fillers, tags, interjections, and hesitation markers – are often not readily recognised or treated by speakers as genuine word-forms and are perceived instead as a kind of para-linguistic inventory of gesture-like devices that are exempted from context-bound selection and inhibition constraints. Even in situations in which speakers are aware of, and accept the status of such forms as language-specific, the pragmatic role of these devices as highly automatic conversational routines, and often also their structural composition – I am thinking here of 'verbal gestures' such as *uhuh* and the like –, make it difficult for speakers to maintain full control over their context-bound selection and inhibition, leading to selection errors.

High on the borrowing hierarchy is often the set of connectors. Once again, it is their function in discourse – to monitor and direct the hearer's participation in the interaction, and to process instances of a potential clash between hearer-sided expectation based on presupposition and the speaker's message – that makes connectors prone to selection errors, creates a free license for the insertion of foreign word-forms in the bilingual mode, and ultimately facilitates long-term borrowing. At the top of the subset hierarchy for connectors are those items around which speakers must 'work hardest' in order to sustain their authority in conversation: expressions of contrast and expressions of sequentiality. The first are 'vulnerable' due to the clash of expectations; this leads to the borrowability hierarchy based on contrast: but > or > and. The second require re-orientation toward a preceding proposition, establishment of new, shared ground as a point of departure, and a link to the subsequent proposition, and hence a rather complex and layered internal sequence of tasks all achieved through a single grammatical operation. Further items that stand out within the domain of connectors are those expressing justification, reason, and consequence.

Attestations of borrowings supporting these generalisations are numerous. Arabic-derived markers for contrast (*ama/amma/lākin/lakini* etc.) are found across a vast area from west Africa to the Caucasus and on to Southwest Asia, including in Hausa, Ful, Somali, Swahili, Lezgian, Turkish, Uzbek, Hindi, and Punjabi. Many of these languages also use the Arabic-derived disjunction marker *ya*, and some also an Arabic-derived addition marker *u/w* (cf. Matras 1998a, 2000c). Romani dialects always borrow 'but' from the contemporary or recent contact language (e.g. Slavic *no*, *po*, and *ali/ale*, Hungarian *de*, Turkish *ama*, Greek *ala*, German *aber*). Many Romani dialects also borrow 'or' and 'and'. These latter two are borrowed frequently, but are sometimes retained from an older contact language. Ajia Varvara Romani in Athens for instance has *ja* 'or' from its recent contact language, Turkish, but *ala* 'but' from its current contact language, Greek; Finnish Romani has *elle* 'or' from Swedish, but *mut* 'but' from Finnish; Manush Romani in France has German *un* 'and' and *otar* 'or', but French-derived *me* 'but', and so on (cf. again Matras 1998a and 2002, as well as Elšík and Matras 2006). Stolz and Stolz (1996, 1997) and Stolz (1996) document the high frequency in Central American and Pacific languages of Spanish-derived *pero* 'but', *o* 'or', *porque* 'because', *bueno* 'well', *ni* 'neither', and *sino* 'but, however', and Stolz (2007) identifies the Italian loans *allora* 'well, and then' *dopo*, *poi* 'and then', *dunque* 'thus, and so', as well as the connectors *però* and *ma* 'but', *o* 'or', and *e* 'and' in Molise Slavic, Italo-Albanian, Italo-Greek, and Maltese. Brody (1995) expands earlier work and documents discourse markers from Spanish in various indigenous languages of Central America.

Alves (2007: 351) lists more than a dozen connectors that were borrowed from Chinese into Vietnamese, among them *bèn* 'and then', *nhúng* 'but', *hoặc* 'or', *và* 'and', *tại* 'because', and *tuy nhiên* 'however'. Adyghe in Turkey borrows the Turkish conjunctions *ama* 'but', *ki* 'that', *çünkü* 'because', *ne . . . ne* 'neither . . . nor', and the discourse particles *yani*, *pek*, *tamam*, *işte*, *ki*, *ya*, and *hadi*, while Russian Adyghe borrows the Russian discourse particles *nu*, *vot*, *davaj* and the connectors *i* 'and' and *potomu čto* 'because' (Höhlig 1997). Tetun Dili, an Austronesian language of East Timor, uses alongside its native equivalents also the Portuguese conjunctions *purké* 'because', *para* 'in order to', *mezmu ké* 'although', *i* 'and', as well as the sequential and consequential markers *depoi* 'and then' and *entaun* 'and so' (Hajek 2006: 172). In Arnhem Land (Heath 1978: 136), the unrelated languages Nunggubuyu and Ritharngu share the form *yamba* 'because', while the unrelated Ngandi and Warndarang both have *aru* 'because'. Voorhoeve (1994: 661) describes the borrowing of conjunctions in the North Halmaheran languages of Indonesia. West Makkian for instance has the Malay loans *tapi* 'but', *jadi* 'therefore', *kalau* 'if', *sebap* 'because' (originally Arabic), and *terus* 'and then', while Sahu has *tapi* 'but', *ato* 'or', *kalo* 'if', *sebabu* 'because', and others. Evenki uses Russian-derived discourse markers *potom* and *posle* 'and then' (Grenoble 2000).

Of the sample languages covered in the volume by Matras and Sakel (2007; see evaluation in Matras 2007b), a significant number borrow all three coordinating connectors 'but', 'or', and 'and': Domari, Moseтén, Nahuatl, Kurmanji, Rapanui, Indonesian, Quechua, Otomi, Guarani, Kildin Saami, and Western Aramaic; languages that borrow only 'but' and 'or' are Tasawaq, Purepecha, Vietnamese, Rumungro, K'abeena, and Likpe. Macedonian Turkish borrows Macedonian *i* 'and' as well as *ili* 'or' and *a* 'or, whereas', but retains Turkish *ama* 'but', which is identical to Macedonian *ama* (cf. Matras 2004a). Jaminjung (Schultze-Berndt 2007) uses the borrowed Kriol *ani* 'but/only' alongside its native *bugu*, while only borrowed forms are used for addition and disjunction.

In some languages, borrowing of 'or' is attested without the borrowing of 'but'. Biak (van den Heuvel 2007) is reported to use the Indonesian disjunction marker *atau* 'or' and less frequently the addition marker *dan* 'and', but no contrastive marker is employed. Hup and Tariana both borrow Portuguese *ou* 'or' via Tukano (Epps 2007, Aikhenvald 2002), and Yaqui appears to borrow only Spanish *o* 'or' (Estrada and Guerrero 2007). This does not invalidate the overall observation that contrast is a semantic-pragmatic feature that facilitates borrowing, nor of course that clause-combining is an operational domain that is prone to contact-related change. Most likely, certain constraints of a structural and perhaps also a cultural nature (conventions on structuring discourse and expressing overt contrast) override, in some cases, what is otherwise an overwhelming tendency to borrow 'but' before 'or'.

Some of the most frequently borrowed subordinating conjunctions express concessive relations, causal relations, purpose, and conditionality (see examples above). These are once again the domains in which the relations between states of affairs depicted in the proposition are potentially controversial or beyond the speaker's domain of secure knowledge. This, of course, does not mean that other subordinators are not borrowed. Domari borrows its entire inventory of connectors, both coordinating and subordinating, from Arabic (Matras 2005a, 2007c). Chamorro too borrows a significant number of its subordinators.

Spanish-derived items include *antes ki* 'before', *asta ki* 'until', *desde ki* 'since', *despues ki* 'after', *fuera di* 'except', *konto ki* 'in spite of', *kosa ki* 'so that', *komo* 'if', *mientras ki* 'while', and a few more; conspicuously missing from the list of borrowings in Chamorro, however, are coordinating connectors (Toppin 1973: 148–151).

Another frequently borrowed connector is the relativiser or relative pronoun. Domari uses Arabic *illi*. The Romani dialects of Kaspičan and Sindel in northern Bulgaria have *ani* from the local Turkish dialect, while other Romani dialects in Bulgaria often combine the Romani inherited relativisers, which derive from interrogatives, with the Bulgarian relative particle *-to* (thus *kaj-to*, *kon-to*, etc.). Dialects of Romani in Russia and in Greece variably use borrowed relativisers – Russian *kotor-* and Greek *pu*, respectively – alongside inherited relativisers. Both Rapanui and Guarani employ the Spanish-derived relativiser *ke* (Fischer 2007, Rendón 2007b). Indonesian uses Sankrit-derived *bahwa* (Tadmor 2007), and Kildin Saami has replaced its original form by a Russian loan *kotor-* (Rießler 2007).

Factual complementisers appear to be more borrowing-prone than non-factual complementisers. Romani dialects, irrespective of location, generally distinguish the two types of complementiser, as do most languages of the Balkans. The original Romani factual complementiser *kaj* is often replaced, in the respective dialects, by Greek *oti*, by Bulgarian *či*, by Romanian-derived *ke*, by Italian *ke*, and by Hungarian-derived *hodž/hod/hoi*; the non-factual complementiser (inherited *te*) is virtually never replaced.[1] Other languages too tend to borrow just the factual complementiser. Khuzistani Arabic borrows Persian *ke* in factual clauses, and Likpe borrows an Ewe marker *bɔ́* (Ameka 2007). In such cases, the greater independence of the two events associated with factual complementation can be interpreted as a less secure connection between them, which in turn weakens the speaker's ability to vouch for the truth of the proposition. The result is a familiar rise in the tension surrounding the processing of the connector, and a higher likelihood of loss of control over the selection and inhibition mechanism.

Burridge (2006: 190) documents the use of English phrases such as *Ok, thank you* and, *Oh, I see* in Pennsylvania German conversation, and comments that the 'influence of English is particularly obvious in the minimal responses listeners use to indicate they are listening and to encourage the speaker to continue'. Along similar lines, Salmons (1990) had discussed the wholesale adoption of English discourse markers in Texas German as part of the overall convergence of communication patterns, including gestures. A further discourse-level borrowing phenomenon is the use of greetings. Here too, we find considerable volatility in bilingual contexts. German dialects have the forms *ade*, *tschü*, *tschu*, and *tschüß* deriving from French *adieu* 'goodbye'. The Arabic greeting *marḥaba* appears in Hausa *maraba* and Turkish *merhaba*, among many others. Colloquial Hebrew has *hi* and *bye* from English, *ahlan* from Arabic, and the combination *yallah bye!* 'bye, then!' from Arabic and English, which in turn is borrowed into Palestinian Arabic. Urdu has Arabic *shukriya* for 'thank you', as does Turkish (*teşekkür*), though middle-class, urban Turkish copies middle-class urban Persian in using French-derived *merci*. The reflexive-imperative *hadi* is common throughout the Balkans. To be sure, we are dealing in some of these cases with markers of social and religious identity, and with prestige-flagging devices. Nevertheless, the replication of matter around discourse-level, para-linguistic gestures also satisfies the need to simplify the management-apparatus of conversational interaction within the bilingual repertoire, and to establish uniform or at least compatible modes of reacting and intervening at the interaction-management level.

8.1.2   Phasal adverbs and focus particles

These categories are all related to the processing of presuppositions and relations between new information and presupposition background, or relevance (Sperber and Wilson 1986, Blakemore 2002). Phasal adverbs ('already', 'still', etc.) link events to expectations concerning their continuation and termination, focus particles ('even', 'too', 'only') evaluate entities and predications in relation to their membership in relevant presupposed sets and categorisations.

The borrowability of these elements is once again a product of their 'high-risk' impact in terms of the sustainability of a speaker–hearer relationship in the communicative interaction. As the speaker moves to prompt the hearer into activating presupposed knowledge, and further as the speaker puts forward propositions that challenge presupposed knowledge, resistance on the part of the hearer may be anticipated. It is in such instances that the speaker is susceptible to malfunctions of the selection and inhibition mechanism. Fusion of repertoire components with respect to the relevant grammatical operations is a way to pre-empt such malfunctions.

There is ample documentation of the borrowing of modal particles, phasal adverbs, and focus particles. Heath (1978: 100) describes how a number of bound affixes are shared by unrelated languages in the Arnhem Land region of northern Australia. They include *-ʔɲiriʔ* 'as well as, also', *-bugiʔ* 'only, still'. In Romani dialects, phasal adverbs and focus particles are always loans from European languages, but they are relatively stable compared to other borrowed function words such as connectors or discourse markers, indicating that they are high, but not highest on the scale for likelihood of borrowing. Thus some varieties of German Romani (Sinti) preserve Greek-derived *komi* 'still', but have German *schon* 'already' and *bloß* 'only', while Lovari Romani in Poland, Hungary, and Russia preserves Romanian-derived *inke* 'still', *aba* 'already', and *feri* 'only', and Burgenland Romani in Austria retains Hungarian-derived *meg* 'still', *imar* 'already', and *čak* 'only'. Adyghe in Turkey has Turkish *daha* 'still', and in Russia the Russian forms *uže* 'already' and *daže* 'even' (Höhlig 1997). Neo-Aramaic in southeastern Turkey borrowed *dîsa* 'again', *tene* 'only', and *hêj* 'still' from Kurmanji, and shares the forms *ħetta* 'even' and *faqat* 'just' with both Arabic and Kurmanji. Domari borrows all its relevant particles – *bass* 'only', *kamān* 'too', *ḥatta* 'even' – from Arabic. Turkish employs Persian-derived *henüz* 'still', *hem* 'too', and Arabo-Persian *hatta* 'even'. Maltese borrows Romance *diġa* 'already' and *anki* 'too'.

Both Matras (1998a) for a Romani sample and van der Auwera (1998) for a sample of European languages point out the greater susceptibility to borrowing of phasal adverbs indicating change (i.e. 'already') as opposed to continuation ('still'), in line with the explanation offered above on the degree of a 'risk' of a clash in expectations (change being less predictable and generally less easy to accept than continuation).

The adjective 'same' might be viewed as functionally related to focus particles, in its implicit reference to other members of a presupposed set. It too is frequently borrowed: Kurmanji employs Turkish *aynı*, Maltese has Italian *stess*, Romani often has Greek-derived *(v)orta* lit. 'straight, direct', or south Slavic *isto*.

8.1.3   Indefinites and interrogatives

Indefinites too belong to the explicit presupposition-processing apparatus. In using an indefinite the speaker is entrusting the hearer with the procedure of retrieval or imaginary substitution or supplementation of the relevant information within a specified ontological domain. Thus, with an expression like 'anywhere' the speaker is effectively laying down responsibility for specifying relevant information, while with an expression like 'somebody' the specific information is being withheld. All this adds up to the similar 'tension' or 'clash of expectation' effect already discussed above in connection with a number of other categories. Indefinites are therefore likely candidates for borrowing in situations of unidirectional bilingualism with weak normative support of the recipient language. Haspelmath (1997: 184–185) mentions a few examples of borrowing of indefinite markers, but admits to not knowing of any cases of borrowing of a complete indefinite pronoun. In the meantime, however, many additional cases have been documented, both of marker-borrowing and of borrowing of entire indefinite word-forms.

Otomi, for instance, borrows nearly the full set of Spanish indefinites: *kada kyen* 'everybody', *en kwalkyer parte* 'anywhere', *nunka* 'never', *syempre* 'always', and many more (Hekking and Bakker 2007), Mosetén borrows *nunca* and *siempre* (Sakel 2007c), and Guarani borrows the Spanish indefinites *alguno* 'somebody', *toda* 'everybody', and others. Tasawaq has Arabic-based *àlwáx-fò* 'sometime' and Tuareg-derived *fóóda* 'always' (Kossmann 2007). Turkish has borrowed Persian *her* 'every' and *hiç* 'no, any', as well as Arabic *şey* 'thing' in *bir şey* 'something', *hiç bir şey* 'nothing', as well as Arabo-Persian *bazi* 'some' and *bazen* 'sometimes'. Maltese employs Italian *kwalunkwe* 'any'.

Domari borrows the Arabic indefinite markers *kull* 'every', *ayy* 'any', and *wala* 'no(ne)', and combines them with the inherited Domari expression for person (*ekak*) and otherwise with Arabic expressions for thing, time, place, and so on. The word for 'always' is Arabic *dāʔiman*. All Romani dialects borrow indefinite markers, and many word-forms are also borrowed. Borrowed markers include

Slavic *(v)sako*, *ni-*, *bilo-*, Romanian-derived *vare-*, Turkish-derived *hič*, *her*, *bazi*, Hungarian *vala-*, and more. Borrowed indefinite word-forms are numerous and include Slavic *ništo* 'something, nothing, anything', Polish *zawsze* 'always', Romanian-derived *mereu* 'always', Hungarian-derived *šoha* 'ever, never' and *mindig* 'always', Greek-derived *čipota* 'nothing' and *kathenas* 'somebody', and many more (cf. Elšík and Matras 2006).

Contrasting with indefinites, interrogatives show much greater stability in contact situations. This is not a coincidence, but is inherently connected to their function: while interrogatives, arguably like indefinites, delegate a task of retrieving information to the hearer, the illocutionary force that accompanies interrogatives elicits this information directly and explicitly, to a level where it can be shared by the interlocutors rather than remain vague and unspecified, as is the case with indefinites. Thus even though they appear to highlight information gaps (from the speaker's perspective), interrogatives, once successfully employed, lead to explicit information being shared by the participants and thus to an expansion of the presuppositional domain. What we have called the 'risk-factor' of 'clash potential' is therefore not present here.

Nonetheless, interrogatives are not immune from borrowing, though attested cases are few in number. Those that stand out as more highly borrowable are the interrogatives for quantity ('how much') and time ('when'). Domari borrows both from Arabic – *qadēš?* 'how much/many?', and *waqtēš?* 'when?' – along with the determiner-interrogative *ayy?* 'which?'. Chamorro borrows Spanish *kuanto?* 'how much?'. Otomoi has Spanish-derived *ke?* 'what?', *ke tanto?* 'how much?', and *por ke?/ pa ke?* 'for what?' (Hekking and Bakker 2007). Hungarian Rumungro (or: Selice Romani; Elšík 2007) borrows two rather semantically specified interrogatives from Hungarian: *meddig* 'until when? for how long? until where?', and *merre* 'through where?'.

8.1.4   Expressions of temporal and local relations

Generic expressions of time, such as Spanish *ora* and Arabic *sāʕa* and *zaman*, serve as a basis for temporal expressions in many languages under the sphere of influence of these two idioms. Temporal deixis is occasionally borrowed, as in Adyghe *ozaman* 'then' (lit. 'that time', from Turkish, with Arabic *zaman* 'time'), Lovari Romani *atunčara* from Romanian *atunci* 'then', and Hungarian Romani *akkor* from Hungarian. Romani borrows its word for 'tomorrow' (*tajsa*, *taha*, *tehara* etc.) from Greek *taixia*, and Otomi has adopted a series of Spanish temporal expressions, including both *aora* 'now' and *ntonse* 'then' (Hekking and Bakker 2007). Vietnamese is reported to have borrowed its word for 'now', *hiện tại*, from Chinese (Alves 2007). Terms for days of the week are often borrowed into minority, oral languages from the formal language of education, media, and institutions, usually in colonial settings. We find Spanish borrowings in Quechua, Otomi Guarani, Biak, Purepecha, and Nahuatl, Kriol terms in Jaminjung, Arabic-derived terms in Indonesian, Portuguese terms in Hup, Russian in Kildin Saami, and so on (cf. Matras 2007b). Borrowing of expressions for times of day ('morning', 'noon', etc.) is usually linked to the borrowing of terms for days of the week, but is not as common as the latter. This reflects the greater relevance of weekly planning to institutional activity contexts.

The 'proximity/intimacy' constraint surfaces in connection with the borrowing of expressions of local relations too. More prone to borrowing are generally expressions of more peripheral and more complex local relations. These include relations that have complex reference points, such as 'between', 'along', 'through', and 'around', those that involve separation from a source, such as 'from', 'toward', 'against', and 'since', and especially those that convey contrast with a presupposed set, such as privative 'without' and 'except', and replacive 'instead of'.

Romani dialects tend to borrow prepositions like *pretiv/protiv* (Slavic) 'against', *is* (Slavic) and *fon* (German) 'from', *za* (Slavic) and *bis* (German) 'until', *de* (Romanian) 'since', *bez/brzo* (Slavic), *xoris* (Greek), *utan* (Swedish), and *oni* (German) 'without', *vmesto/namesto* (Slavic) 'instead', *osven*, *skluchenje*, *kromje* (Slavic), *in loc də* (Romanian) 'instead', and *ektos* (Greek) 'except for'. Thai and Khmer are reported to share their expressions for 'follow, along', 'by, with', 'from', and 'straight', and Indonesian borrows *sama* 'with' and *guna* 'for the purpose of' from Sanskrit (Tadmor 2004). Spanish *de* 'from', *por* 'for', and *para* 'for the purpose of' and *entre* 'between' are among the frequently attested borrowings in South- and Central American languages (see e.g. Stolz 1996), while Mosetén borrows Spanish *embesde* 'instead', *sin* 'without' *ashta* 'until', and *desde* 'from, since' (Sakel 2007a, Sakel and Matras 2008), and Chamorro has *desde* 'from', *asta* 'until', *sin* 'without', *pot* 'in order to', and *kontra* 'against', as well as, in fixed idiomatic expressions, *di* 'of' and *kon* 'with' (Topping 1973: 126–129). Maltese borrows *kontri* 'against' and *faċċata* 'opposite' from Italian.

Although more basic or core expressions of local relations are less likely to be borrowed, isolated cases can be found. While Persian and Urdu *bād* from Arabic *baʕd* 'after' could well have been borrowed first as a sequential marker 'and then, thereafter', Domari is exceptional in borrowing not just some of its core local relations expressions, but the great majority of them, from Arabic. Core prepositions borrowed from Arabic are *maʕ* 'with', *min* 'from', *baʕd* 'after', *ʕan* 'about', *ʕand* 'at', and *žamb* 'next to', in addition to *badāl* 'instead of', *bala* 'without', *bēn* 'between'. Some inherited (indo-Aryan) adverbial expressions of local relations, such as 'above', 'outside', and 'inside', are nevertheless retained. A possible explanation for this exceptionally high borrowing rate of prepositions is that Domari did not have prepositions when it first came into contact with Arabic. Most Indo-Aryan languages are postpositional; some, those in close contact and proximity to Iranian language, are circumpositional. One might have expected Domari to have undergone a similar development as Romani, where, apparently in contact with Greek and possibly other languages in Anatolia, postposed local expressions were recruited as material for the formation of new prepositions. It may be that the Domari speech community was simply too small, and language loyalty too weak, to trigger a creative process of this kind whereby a pattern would have been replicated using inherited linguistic matter.

8.1.5   Numerals

Given that quantifying objects is considered a very basic human cognitive ability,[2] it might seem surprising that many languages do, in fact, borrow numerals. It is even more striking that languages borrow numerals not primarily because these were absent prior to encounters with colonial trade; many languages that are known to have had inherited numerals have replaced them, or partly replaced them, or are in the process of replacing them, by numerals borrowed from a contact language. The borrowing of numerals is thus not 'gap-filling'; it is another one of those instances where participation in an activity context that is associated with a particular language leads to a generalisation of the relevant word-form from that language.

There are various isolated accounts of numeral borrowing. The North Halmaheran languages of the north Moluccas in Indonesia have borrowed the numeral 'nine' (*siwo, siworo, siwe*) from Austronesian, while one of the languages of the group, West Makian, also borrows the Austronesian numeral 'four', *fati* (Voorhoeve 1994: 661). But when comparing the borrowing behaviour of languages systematically it becomes clear that borrowing of numerals generally takes on a predictable path: first, it is triggered by a shift in favour of the donor language in contexts involving economic activity and possibly also institutional interaction, in a situation of unidirectional bilingualism. This leads to use of the borrowed numerals in interactions relating to those types of activity. The Betawi language of Indonesia borrows a complete set of numerals from Hokkien Chinese, but these are used only when referring to sums of money (Tadmor 2004). Chinese numerals are used in formal contexts in Vietnamese (Alves 2007). In Tagalog, speakers know and use numerals from Tagalog, Spanish, and English, and there is quite possibly a tendency to adapt the choice of numeral to the etymology of lexical item that the numeral accompanies, as far as it is known or assumed by the speaker. Romani speakers and Kurds generally use numerals from the majority language when citing dates, a task that is performed primarily in the context of official institutions.

In some situations, the sociolinguistic specialisation of loan-numerals for institutional use will lead to a generalisation of loans for the more abstract numerals, those that are beyond everyday counting abilities and are primarily in use in abstract, formal, and institution-bound calculations. Standard Indonesian borrows the numerals *laksa* 'ten thousand' and *juta* 'million' from Sanskrit, *milyar* 'billion' and *nol* 'zero' from Dutch (Tadmor 2004, 2007). Tasawaq borrows its lower numerals from Arabic, but its word for 'hundred' from Tuareg (Kossmann 2007); Romani in central Europe shows words for 'thousand' from Romanian (*miji*) and from Hungarian (*ezera*), Vietnamese uses a Chinese word for 'ten thousand' (Alves 2007), English borrows its terms for *zero*, *million*, and *billion* from Romance, Turkish has *sıfır* from Arabic for 'zero' and European *milyon* for 'million', and K'abeena has *zeeruta*, from Italian via Amharic, for 'zero' (Crass 2007).

More intense engagement in the relevant activity domains of the contact language will lead to borrowing of higher numerals (usually the tens, above twenty), followed gradually by lower numerals, with various cut-off points. The Pharas dialect of Asia Minor Greek borrows the Turkish terms for 'seventy', 'eighty', and 'ninety' (Dawkins 1916: 171).[3] Mosetén, Quichua, Nahuatl, and Biak borrow numerals above 'ten', while Hup borrows those above 'twenty'. The numeral 'ten' itself, along with 'five' and those below 'five', tend towards greater stability. Languages that borrow numerals in between the two include Swahili, which has *sita*, *saba*, *nane*, and *tisa* ('six–nine') from Arabic, and Romani, which has *efta*, *oxto*, *enja* ('seven–nine') from Greek. Swahili also has its higher numerals, from 'ten' to 'hundred', from Arabic (*ishrini* 'twenty', *thelathini* 'thirty', etc., to *mia* 'hundred'). Romani tends to retain an inherited word for 'twenty' and for 'hundred', but often has Greek words for the numerals in-between, though many dialects tend to replace these higher numerals through loans from their contemporary contact languages.

The borrowing exclusively of numerals above 'five' is attested for Tasawaq, Otomi, Guarani, Purepecha, Yaqui, and Kildin Saami (see Matras 2007b for details). Most Domari speakers in Jerusalem are equally unable to recall non-Arabic numerals above 'five', with the exception of 'ten' and 'hundred', although these are documented for speakers in the same community in the early 1900s (cf. Macalister 1914). Borrowing of numerals under 'five' is attested for Jaminjung, which has no native numerals above 'three' (Schultze-Berndt 2007), and for other Australian languages with similar, very basic and arguably non-numerical quantification systems. Chamorro has replaced its entire earlier system of numerals, which was still attested in the early twentieh century, with Spanish loans (Topping 1973: 166–167). Thai uses Chinese numerals above two, and Khmer uses Thai numerals (of Chinese origin).

It appears, then, that while higher and more abstract numerals are vulnerable to borrowing due to their association with formal contexts of use, and numerals in general may become borrowing-prone through intensification of economic activity in the (potentially) donor language, the proximity constraint protects 'salient' numerals, primarily those below 'ten' or 'five', but sometimes also 'ten' and even 'hundred'. With the latter two exceptions, and the exception of 'zero' whose affinity is toward the formal-abstract numerals, most attested cases add up to support an implicational hierarchy of numeral borrowing: higher > lower numerals (see Chapter 6; cf. Elšík and Matras 2006, Matras 2007b).

Interestingly, while higher cardinal numerals are more borrowing-prone, the opposite is true for ordinals. Persian borrows only Arabic-derived *evvel* 'first', and Romani dialects tend to borrow 'first' from their contemporary contact language, but derive all other ordinals through a regular derivation affix (*-to*, itself borrowed from Greek). Indonesian borrows its word *pertama* 'first' from Sanskrit (Tadmor 2004). English is a seeming exception, having borrowed *second* but not *first* from Romance, though it confirms the general tendency to use borrowings in order to mark out the exclusivity of lower ordinals, which tend to be prioritised; here, borrowing is a supplementary strategy to internal suppletion.

8.1.6   Place deixis, demonstratives, and personal pronouns

Deictic and anaphoric elements are among the categories for which relatively few instances of borrowing are attested. Chamorro is a rare exception in borrowing the demonstrative *este* from Spanish, which is added to a three-term demonstrative paradigm (Topping 1973: 112–113). Tadmor (2004) reports that Thai and Khmer share their forms *ni/nih* 'this' and *nú:n/nuh* 'that'. Voorhoeve (1994: 661) suggests that deictic *ne* 'this' in North Halmaheran languages of Indonesia 'could be' a borrowed form from Austronesian. (In Volga-German, the Russian demonstrative *eto* is borrowed, not in its function as a demonstrative, however, but rather in its function as a filler; see Anders 1993 and discussion in Matras 1998a.) Rumungro (Selice) Romani borrows the Hungarian deictic prefixes *am-* and *ugyan-*, which are combined with Romani deictic stems (Elšík 2007). Spanish *la* is used as an anaphor in Guarani (Rendón 2007b), and the Arabic resumptive pronoun *iyyā-* is sometimes used in Domari in relative clauses. Domari also employs the Arabic reflexive expression *ḥāl-* '-self' and the reciprocal *baʕd*.

Place deictics are at least as rare among confirmed borrowings. Some Romani dialects of the Balkans have *orde* 'there', the origin of which is possibly Turkish or Azeri *orda/ordä*, as well as *inća* 'here', possibly from Persian *īndžā*, though both etymologies require further investigation. The Sinti dialect of Romani as spoken in the historical German-language enclave around Temeshoar in Romania borrows German-derived *doti* 'there'.

The borrowing of personal pronouns has received some attention in the literature, mainly owing to the fact that pronouns are usually considered reliable indicators of genetic relatedness of languages and are assumed to be stable and reistant to borrowing (see for example discussion of pronoun borrowability in connection with the classification of some North American languages: Nichols and Peterson 1996, 1998, Campbell 1997). Wallace (1983) had proposed that this view of pronouns is biased to some extent through the model of pronominal forms in Indo-European, and pointed out some essential differences between the functionality of the primarily deictic and anaphoric devices which we call 'pronouns' in Indo-European languages, and the more elaborate role that pronouns have, for example in languages of southeast Asia, in labelling social relations among interlocutors. Wallace's conclusion is that the stability of pronouns tells us more about the function of pronouns in a particular language and the culture to which they belong, than about the borrowability-in-principle of pronominal forms.

Siewierska (2004: 274–277) mentions just over a dozen cases of borrowed pronominal forms that are attested or suggested in the literature. Almost all of them fall into one of two categories: They either involve the expansion of a system to include the semantic specification 'inclusive/exclusive', or else they belong to the Southeast Asian type of participant referentiality. Thomason and Everett (2001) make an emphatic case for the borrowability of pronouns, citing on the whole similar examples, to which they add three additional example types. The first is the specific case of the Amazonian language Pirahã. It is argued that Pirahã borrowed its entire set of pronouns from Tupi-Guarani, and the form resemblance between the two paradigms appears to support this case. The intriguing aspect about Pirahã is the fact that there is no evidence for early bilingualism, though recent investigations seem to contradict the impression that the Pirahã have always been monolingual (Sakel 2007b). It also appears that pronouns are not normally used in Pirahã conversation, suggesting that borrowing may have served a distinct referential purpose; the paucity of descriptive material makes the case difficult to judge. The second type of evidence cited in support of the claim are person endings on verbs; I would argue that these have a separate function, one that is related to the conveying of finiteness and the anchoring of predications, discussed earlier in this chapter.

The third type mentioned by Thomason and Everett are mixed languages such as Chavacano and Mednyj Aleut. The implicit assumption is that general processes of borrowing can be compared with the specific processes that lead to the emergence of mixed languages. This view is, however, controversial. The view among many researchers is that mixed languages result from deliberate, conscious creations (see Chapter 10), and this view has been expressed on occasion by Thomason herself (cf. Thomason 1999).[4] Surely, if mixed languages are the product of social circumstances and communicative needs that are quite distinct from ordinary situations of language contact, then the structural outcomes that they manifest cannot be taken as a measure with which to evaluate ordinary situations of contact. Mixed languages often show pronouns that pattern with the lexifier language, rather than with the grammar language, to use an oversimplified characterisation of the typical structural 'split'. The process is similar to the disguising of pronouns along with content-lexemes in other in-group forms of speech, such as cryptolects (cf. Smith 1998).[5] It is therefore motivated by different factors than the conventional borrowing of grammatical or even of lexical word-forms.

This brings us back to the frequently cited examples from Southeast Asian languages. In Southeast Asian societies, speakers are accustomed to making fine-tuned social judgments when referring to themselves and to the hearer (see e.g. Iwasaki and Horie 2000 for a recent discussion of Thai). The system of terms of address is, as a result, complex and adaptable. It includes not just inherited deictic forms, but also nominal forms such as 'self', 'friend', 'follower', 'supporter', 'servant', or 'slave', as well as body-parts such as 'hair of the head' or 'underneath foot'. As social constellations change, for instance as a result of urbanisation or inter-ethnic contacts, the complex system of referring to speaker and hearer incorporates new forms. As a result, some languages and language varieties show several layers of borrowings which serve so-called 'pronominal' functions. Wallace (1983) mentions Sanskrit nominal terms of reference as well as Chinese, Javanese, Dutch, Arabic, and English pronouns in Jakarta Malay, English and Amoy Chinese pronouns in urban colloquial Thai, and French pronouns in the Vietnamese speech of the westernised upper classes in Vietnam. A particularly noteworthy case is that of the Amoy Chinese pronouns *goá* 'I' and *lú* 'you', which were used as in-group markers among Jakarta's Chinese when speaking Malay, and were eventually adopted by the Malay population through contact with Chinese merchants and overseers. Wallace's (1983: 587) conclusion is that in these cultures, 'the social values of human grouping and ranking attached to pronouns promote their transfer, loss, and gain'.

Tadmor (2004) similarly cites borrowings of pronouns in various Southeast Asian languages. Standard Indonesian borrows its 1SG pronoun *saya* from Sanskrit, Betawi borrows its 1SG and 2SG forms, *gué* and *lu*, respectively, from Hokkien Chinese, and its honorific 1SG and 2SG forms, *ané* and *énté*, from Arabic, Urban peninsular Malay borrows 1SG *ai* and 2SG *yu* from English, Javanese borrows its 1SG honorific form *kulò* from Sanskrit and its 1PL honorific *kitò* from Malay, and Thai borrows 1SG *ay*, 2nd person *yu*, 3SG.M *hi*, 1PL *wi*, and 3PL *de* from English. Ongoing shifts in a participant-reference system are described by Ho-Dac (2002: 111ff.), who shows how Vietnamese–English bilinguals in Australia use the English pronouns *me* and *you* while conversing in Vietnamese in order to avoid the complex system of possible solidarity or hostility marking that can be associated with the corresponding Vietnamese form (see also Thai 2007).

We must therefore be cautious not to draw general conclusions about 'pronouns' on the basis of systems such as those employed in Southeast Asian languages. These systems rely on lexical expressions, which differ inherently from the function of deixis as they encode much more specific labelling information than is contained in person deixis. Participant expressions of this type are perhaps more closely related, functionally speaking, to terms in English (and other European languages) used for formal address, such as *Majesty*, *Your Honour*, *Eminence*, *Sir*, *Madame*, *Master* – all terms that are often borrowed in European languages (note the Romance origin of all these English terms). Their borrowability stems from the need to label and re-label new types of social roles and social relations. In this sense, their language-contact behaviour is akin to that of content-lexemes.

A more 'grammatical', language-processing oriented motivation for the borrowing of pronouns is the need to match the system of categorisation of the two languages, or to maintain just a single categorisation system across the linguistic repertoire. Such levelling usually affects the type of categorisation represented by pronouns, such as animacy, gender, and inclusive/exclusive, and the procedure employed is often to recreate the model patterns drawing on inherited linguistic matter (or through loss of inherited material, in the case of a reduction in categorical distinctions, e.g. the loss of gender). In a few rare cases, levelling is achieved by borrowing word-forms. Thus, van der Voort (2000: 158) suggests that some pronominal forms in Kwaza, an isolated Brazilian language, in particular the first-person inclusive *txa'na*, could be a loan from Tupí-Guaraní languages, and Voorhoeve (1994: 661) identifies the 1PL exclusive pronouns *ngomi, imi* of North Halmaheran languages as Austronesian loans. Carlin (2006: 320) reports on the borrowing of an exclusive 1PL pronoun *amna* from Carib (from Waiwai, usage pattern from Trio) into Mawayana, an Arawak language of Suriname.

This leaves us with the question whether there are any 'straightforward' cases of pronominal borrowing. Several reported cases are controversial, or difficult to verify. The borrowing of Spanish *este* in Chamorro seems to have prompted speculation as to whether the 1SG pronoun *zo* might also be a Spanish borrowing (*yo*), but clear evidence is lacking. Foley (1986: 210) had pointed out similarities between some of the pronominal forms of two Papuan languages, Iatmul and Kambot, which are said to be at best very distantly related. Iatmul is said to have been the powerful and prestigious group, and if borrowing did occur, it is likely that it was from Iatmul into Kambot. Intriguingly, none of the forms are functional equivalents in the two languages: The first- and second-person forms cited by Foley change persons; the third-person form changes number. The case was recently challenged by Aikhenvald (2007a) on the grounds that the word-forms as reported by other sources do not actually bear a strong resemblance to one another, and that there is no attestation for any earlier trade contacts between the Iatmul and Kambot peoples. According to Campbell (1997: 340, citing Kenneth Hall in personal communication), Miskitu borrowed its independent 1SG and 2SG personal pronouns from Northern Sumu; the historical analysis however is not accessible.

As we've seen for other grammatical categories, Romani provides an excellent sample of structural borrowing due to intense contacts, unidirectional bilingualism, the prevalence of the bilingual mode in conversation, lax normative control over language use, and a variety of languages with which the dialects of Romani are and have been in contact. Figure 8.1 shows several attested cases of borrowing of pronominal forms into dialects of Romani from their respective contact languages.

Early Romani (see Matras 2002, Elšík and Matras 2006) is assumed to have had the pronominal forms *ov* 'he', *on* 'they', which are continued in most dialects of southeastern and central Europe, while in other areas prothetic consonants *j*- and *v*- are added. The remarkable development attested in the top three dialects – Hungarian, Slovene, and Thracian Romani – is the copying of plural affixes from the contact languages into the inherited plural pronominal form. This is made possible as a result of three conditions.

First, the accidental similarity in forms between the Romani pronouns and those of all three contact languages: in each case we have a monosyllabic form, beginning in or consisting of a back vowel. Second, the fact that the contact

	3sg	3pl	Model	3sg	3pl
General/Early Romani	*(v-, j-) ov*	*(v-, j-) on*			
Hungarian Romani	*ov*	*on-k*	Hungarian	*ő*	*ő-k*
Slovene Romani	*ov*	*on-i*	Slovene	*on*	*on-i*
Thracian Romani	*ov*	*on-nar*	Turkish	*o[n-]*	*on-lar*
Molise Romani	*jov*	*lor*	Italian	*il*	*loro*

Figure 8.1 *Borrowed pronominal forms in some Romani dialects.*

language shows an exclusively agglutinating formation of the plural pronoun, consisting of the singular pronoun with the addition of a plural suffix. (In Turkish, the underlying form in *o[n]-* becomes apparent when non-nominative case endings are added; thus *onu* 'him.ACC', *ondan* 'from him', etc.) And third, the fact that this plural suffix is identical to the general, nominal plural suffix used in the language. This makes the plural affix easily transparent and analysable.

It is thus the plural affix, not the actual pronominal form of the respective contact language, that is borrowed into Romani. What we see is a fusion not of forms, but of the procedures that are used to derive the plural from the singular forms. Note that the respective plural suffixes are only diffused into the Romani pronominal forms, and not carried forward into any inherited nominal forms, though borrowed nouns from the respective languages may retain their original plural endings when used in the plural.

The exception is the borrowing of a word-form in Molise Romani. It is the only genuine case in Figure 8.1 of the borrowing of a pronominal word-form. Intriguingly it is once again the 3PL that is affected by contact. This can lead us to infer that it is not just the model in the contact languages – the transparent marking of plurality on the pronoun, and the way it matches the marking of plurality on nouns – that attracts the change, but that there is also an internal motivation to renew the 3PL pronoun. This is in fact confirmed by the frequent internal renewal of the 3PL and its substitution, for instance, through Romani demonstratives. Partial borrowing or even borrowing of the full word-form provides another option for this renewal process to go forward.

Thomason and Everett (2001) are thus correct in emphatically insisting that pronouns *can* be borrowed. The more interesting question, however, seems to be why there are so few straightforward examples of pronoun borrowing. The answer seems to lie in the absence, by and large, of a motivation to borrow pronominal forms. For all the categories surveyed so far in this chapter, we have been able to identify either a discourse-functional, language-processing related motivation for borrowing, sometimes triggered by the association of the donor language with specific domains of activity, and always triggered by the need to balance and control the repertoire in bilingual situations. None of the specific motivations named above appears to apply to pronouns.

They do not provide labels for unique referents in the sense discussed above, i.e. specific terms for institutions, products, or procedures; they are not associated particularly with certain activity domains, as for instance higher numerals may be; they do not involve any manipulation of the presupposition domain or management of the interaction roles, and do not have the 'clash' potential at the interaction level between speaker intentions and hearer expectations; in fact, they signal harmony between speaker and hearer in relation to the deictic field of reference. Indeed, when either of these functions *is* filled by pronouns, as in the case of the complex labelling system of social roles in many Southeast Asian languages, then pronouns appear to be as borrowable as other categories of the lexicon. Thus, pronouns may be borrowable in principle. But in practice, in deictic and anaphoric function they show very low borrowability due to the absence of any of the functional features that tend to motivate borrowing. One lesson to be drawn is that the postulation of a category of 'pronouns' is questionable, and perhaps even quite meaningless in this context. One is better off distinguishing lexical labels or content-words from deixis and anaphora.

8.1.7   Negators, possessors, and existentials

These categories constitute a kind of 'rest class' of elements that have pragmatic-semantic saliency among the grammatical categories, that is, they express some essential and salient semantic relations that are likely to have some kind of structural manifestation in every language. Not many examples of direct borrowing of word-forms can be found for these categories.

According to Epps (2007), the verb *ni-* 'to be' in Hup appears to have been borrowed directly from Tukano, which also has a verb (and copula) *ni*. The Hup and Tukano copulas function in similar ways, although it is more obligatory in Tukano, while in Hup it appears only in the presence of certain tense-aspect-modality markers.

Some varieties of Sinti Romani have borrowed the dialectal German negator *nit*, which follows the finite verb, as it does in German: *me džinau nit* 'I don't know'. Other Sinti varieties use the German-derived emphatic particle *gar*, roughly 'indeed', as a negation particle: *me džinau gar* 'I don't know'. This functionalisation is internal to Sinti, and appears to have derived via the German expression *gar nicht* 'not at all'. The only known word-form borrowing in Romani with the meaning of possession is the Polish verb *ma-*, borrowed into Polish Romani (*majinav* 'I have').

In Domari, the Arabic copula is adopted as a periphrastic expression of the habitual aspect, which is one of its original functions in Arabic. However, while in Arabic this is the only expression of the existential verb – *(huwwe) kān marīḍ* 'he was ill.M.SG' – in Domari it co-exists with the inherited enclitic copula and simply reinforces the past tense: *pandži kān mišt-ēya* 'he *was* ill-COP.PAST'. Domari also borrows the Arabic negator *mišš* in non-lexical predications – *pandži mišš mišt-ēk* 'he *not* ill-COP.M.SG' = 'he is not ill'. The Arabic negator *mā...-š* accompanies all Arabic-derived inflected verbs (modals and auxiliaries) in Domari: *pandži mā kānš mišt-ēya* 'he was not ill'.

Other cases of direct borrowing of word-forms in these domains come from Spanish influence on a variety of languages. The Spanish copula *está* is used in Otomi (in the form *ta*) and in Rapanui, which also has Spanish *tengo* 'to have' is employed in Rapanui (Fischer 2007). In Chamorro, *está* is used in a way that is somewhat similar to the use of the Arabic copula in Domari, namely to express past-tense existential predications (Topping 1973: 89). The Spanish negator *no* is reported to be replacing the negative circumfix *mana...chu* in Quechua, as well as the negative prefix *nd-* in Guarani (Rendón 2007b). Spanish *sin* 'without' is occasionally used as an expression of negation in Chamorro (Topping 1973) and in Mosetén (Sakel 2007c).

8.2   Morphological borrowing

8.2.1   Derivational morphology

As discussed in Chapter 6, bound morphology has been observed to be relatively resistant to borrowing compared with both lexical items and grammatical function words. In defining morphological borrowing, we must distinguish the mere acceptance of morphology along with borrowed lexical items, from the diffusion of morphology beyond the borrowed lexicon itself; and further, between 'backwards diffusion', that is, replication of borrowed morphs in connection with pre-existing, inherited lexicon, and 'forward diffusion', that is, the productive use of borrowed morphs with newly acquired vocabulary. A good example is the Turkish agentive derivational suffix *-ci/-çi*, which has been borrowed into Iraqi Arabic as one of a number of Turkish derivational suffixes (Masliyah 1996). It entered into the language with Turkish loans, such as *aġšamçi* 'a (watch)man who does the evening shift', from Turkish *akşam* 'evening', or *çayxançi* 'tea-shop proprietor', from Turkish *çay* 'tea', and Persian-derived *xan* (*hane*), 'house'. Based on such loans, the suffix is replicated and applied to existing Arabic words, as in *kēfçi* 'party-goer' (from *kēf* 'fun'), *ʕaraqçi* 'one who likes Araq (a spirit)', even reinforcing existing agentives, as in *bawwābçi* 'doorman', from *bawwāb* 'doorman'. It then continues to diffuse 'forwards' and is applied to new loanwords, as in *gōlçi* 'goalkeeper', from English 'goal'. At the very least, backwards diffusion is a pre-requisite for recognising a 'morphological' loan, as opposed to a mere portion of a lexical loan.

Perhaps the most common morphological borrowing is found in the domain of nominal derivation. Nominal derivation is generally an area in which languages tend to show diversity and proliferation of functional devices. This is in line with the tremendous range of referential meanings that are covered by nouns, and the need for subtle semantic categorisations within the class of nouns. Quite prominent on the list of attested borrowing of nominal derivation markers are markers of agentivity. Kedang (eastern Indonesia) for instance has borrowed the Indonesian agentive suffix *-wala* (which on its own can mean 'Sir, master, lord'), which in turn is an Indo-Aryan borrowing into Indonesian. The suffix is productive in Kedang: thus *during* 'to sell', *durungwala* 'seller'; *lile* 'to look', *lilewala* 'onlooker' (Samely 1991: 67). Tetun Dili borrows the agentive suffix *-dor* from Portuguese: *hemu* 'to drink', *hemudor* 'one who drinks habitually' (Hajek 2006). Agentive suffixes borrowed from Spanish include Quechua *-dor* and Tagalog *-ero*.

Colloquial Modern Hebrew has adopted a series of agentive suffixes from European languages, mainly via Yiddish; among them are *-ist* (*bitsu'íst* 'doer', from *bitsúa* 'implementation'), *-er* (*mafyonér* 'mafiosi', from *máfya* 'mafia'; *protektsyonér* 'one who enjoys patronage, well-connected person', from *protéktsya* 'patronage, protection'), and *-nik* (*kibútsnik* 'member of a Kibbutz'). Various diminutives are also borrowed from Yiddish, including Germanic-derived *-le* (*xamúdale*, *xamúdile* 'cutie (F/M)', from *xamud/á* 'cute'), and Slavic-derived *-čik* (*baxúrčik* 'a [nice, adorable] young man', from *baxúr* 'young man'). Many of these suffixes are loans that have been borrowed into Yiddish from Slavic languages.

Romani dialects borrow a series of agentive and diminutive affixes from various contact languages. Common in particular are diminutive/diminutive feminine *-ic-* *-ica/-icka-* and agentive *-ari*, which are shared by several languages in the Balkans; thus Sinti Romani has *Sint-íca* 'a Sinti woman', and *rechtsprech-ari* 'a community elder, judge' (from German *Rechtssprecher* 'arbiter'). The Turkish agentive suffix *-ci*, which is rather common in the Balkans, is also used in Sepetçi Romani: *xoxamdžis* 'lier', from the Romani verbal root *xoxav-* 'to tell a lie', and Greek M.SG nominative inflection *-is*.

Borrowing of other nominal derivation is perhaps less common, possibly due to the cross-linguistic diversity but also lower saliency of other, more specialised forms of nominal derivation. Thus Romani borrows a Persian suffix *-in* denoting fruit trees in words like *ambrolin* 'pear tree', alongside *ambrol* 'pear', both Persian loans, and extends it to further items, such as *akhorin* 'hazelnut tree', from *akhor* 'hazelnut'. Although applied to very few words, the suffix appears still to be productive in some dialects. Vlax (Transylvanian) Romani applies it to a Romanian loan in *prunin* 'plum tree'. Maltese borrows a productive singulative suffix *-ata* from Italian (Borg and Azzopardi-Alexander 1997: 280): *xemxata* 'sunstroke', from *xemx* 'sun'.

Occasional borrowing of word-class changing derivation is attested. English *-able* and *-(e)ous*, both of Romance origin, derive adjectives within both the Romance and Germanic lexical components: *feasible* alongside *loveable*, *edible*; *courteous* alongside *righteous*. English *-ment* of Romance origin derives nouns from verbs, as in both *argument*, and Germanic-based *bereavement*. In some Romani dialects, the suffix *-imos* from Greek derives abstract nouns from Romani verbs and adjectives: Vlax Romani *sastimos* 'health' from *sasto* healthy, *marimos* 'struggle' from *mar-* 'to fight'. Another suffix of Greek origin in Romani, *-to*, derives ordinal numerals from cardinal numerals: *dujto* 'second', from *duj* 'two'.

Borrowing of verb-deriving morphology appears to be quite rare. A rather isolated example is Lovari Romani *-áz-* from Hungarian, found in a limited number of inherited words, such as *bučáz(in)-* 'to work', from *buči* 'work'. The borrowing of derivational morphology in the verbal domain is normally limited to semantic modifiers, such as English *re-* (as in Romance-derived *retire*, but also Germanic *relive*) or *dis-* (*disengage*, but rarely found with Germanic roots, such as *disbelieve*). Romani dialects in contact with Slavic languages primarily in Poland, Russia, and Slovakia, and to some extent also Romani dialects in contact with Latvian, Lithuanian, and Greek, borrow aktionsart-derivational prefixes (often referred to as 'aspect'): In Russian Romani we find, based on *dava* 'I give', *dodava* 'I add', *obdava* 'I embrace', *otdava* 'I confiscate', *piridava* 'I hand over', *podava* 'I obtain', *rozdava* 'I hand out', *vydava* 'I give away'. In Latvian Romani we find, based on *dža-* 'to go', *iedža-* 'to go in' and *piedža-* 'to approach', and in some Greek Romani dialects we find *dikh-* 'to see', and *ksanadikh-* 'to see again'. It appears that Greek aspectual prefixes of this kind have diffused widely into Aromanian (Vlachi) dialects in northern Greece.

Although it is a pre-requisite and a trigger for morphological borrowing, lexical borrowing on its own does not seem to constitute a very powerful motivation to replicate derivational procedures. Considering the amount of Romance vocabulary in English and the transparency of the derivational morphology that is contained in it, the diffusion of productive Romance derivational morphology into inherited (Germanic) lexemes in English must be described as rather modest. The same pertains to other languages that have borrowed a massive amount of lexical content words, such as Maltese, Tagalog, and Chamorro. An important pre-condition for the diffusion of morphology is its structural transparency (see discussion in Chapter 6, and cf. Field 2002). This explains the low borrowability of Arabic morphology, which is highly fusional, into Turkish and Persian, which have both borrowed a massive amount of vocabulary from Arabic, while on the other hand Iraqi Arabic, having been in contact with Turkish during the Ottoman rule and later through occasional contact between Arabs and Turkmen in northern Iraq, but never under massive pressure from Turkish or in a situation of widespread bilingualism, borrows a number of Turkish derivational affixes.

Apart from structural constraints on the transparency of morphemes and the existence of a large pool of model lexical items from which to extract them, it appears that a certain attitudinal profile is necessary in order to turn an available resource into a productive resource. A major component of this profile is full and widespread bilingualism, which may explain the differences between the extent to which Slavic-derived verb aktionsart markers spread in Romani dialects; speakers wish to be able to make the same category distinction when describing events in one interaction context as they do in another, and generalising the relevant morphological inventory for the entire linguistic repertoire, i.e. the wholesale borrowing of the set of 'aspect' or aktionsart prefixes, allows them to do this. By contrast, Romance-derived verbal modifiers such as *re-* and *dis-* were diffused in English primarily via a bilingual elite and its literature.

This also explains the wide diffusion of European (Yiddish-mediated) derivational morphology within colloquial Hebrew, but its rather modest appearance in formal, written styles of Modern Hebrew. The first generation of speakers of Modern Hebrew, in the early 1900s, licensed themselves to full access to certain salient word-derivational resources of their repertoire, irrespective of interaction context; i.e. when speaking Hebrew they continued to make use of the very same procedures as in their native languages (recall that borrowing into early Modern Hebrew constitutes borrowing into a second language that was in the process of being nativised).

8.2.2   Inflectional morphology

A major difference between inflectional and derivational morphology in language contact situations is that derivational morphology almost always accompanies borrowed lexicon; in other words, when borrowing a word like *government* in order to represent its semantic concept, we are also borrowing its entire derivational composition from the source language. We become, as speakers, semi-conscious of the fact that we have replicated not just a word, but also a morphological procedure, once we borrow another word that utilises the same procedure, such as *arrangement*. As discussed in the previous section, this paves the way to the extension of the procedure to pre-existing, inherited roots, to compose words such as *settlement*. Inflectional morphology does not operate in this way. Inflectional morphology is applied at the sentence level, not at the word level, and so within the framework of the utterance of the recipient language; it does not, by default, accompany individual words, since it is not an inseparable component of the meaning of those words, and hence not directly relevant to the goal for which the word is being borrowed in the first place (namely specificity of reference). This is the major difference between derivational and inflectional morphology, and the main reason why the borrowing of inflectional morphology is rare compared to that of derivational morphology.

The one exception is inflectional morphology that accompanies the single word, notably the expression of plurality.[6] Even without widespread bilingualism, English tends to adopt, at least in some styles, Latin plurals for nouns like *phenomenon* PL *phenomena, fungus* PL *fungi*, even though these are in decline and gradually assimilating to the wider body of nouns (thus *forum* PL *forums*; cf. German *Paradigma* 'paradigm', PL *Paradigmata* alongside *Paradigmen*). The long-term replication of plural forms is consistent with the occasional retention of plural inflection by bilinguals during codeswitching, as seen in Chapter 5. Persian adopts Arabic nouns along with their Arabic purals: *entexāb* 'election', PL *entexāb-āt*. Yiddish retains the Hebrew plural marker *-im* in Hebrew loans such as *xavéjrim* 'friends', and uses it productively with some European loans, such as *doktójrim* 'doctors', from *dóktor*. Vlax Romani adopts the Romanian-derived plural suffix *-uri/-ura*, which diffuses backwards to replace plural markers of earlier European loans, as in *foruri* 'towns', from Greek *foros*, and forward to new loans from subsequent contact languages, as in *šefturi* 'business opportunities', from German *Geschäft*, though it does not combine with pre-European vocabulary. Epirus Romani, by contrast, adopts the Greek plural ending *-imata* which is applied consistenly to all indigenous masculine nouns ending in a consonant: *vast* 'hand', PL *vastimata*; *kher* 'house', PL *kherimata*. Other Greek-derived inflectional endings are generally productive in Romani, having been borrowed into Early Romani and are extended to subsequent loan vocabulary: Kaspichan Romani (northern Bulgaria) has Turkish-derived *džam-is* 'mosque', PL *džam-ides*. Latvian Romani has *doktor-is* 'doctor', PL *doktor-ja*.

A wealth of inflectional morphology is also borrowed into the verb system of Romani and its various dialects. Early Romani had borrowed the Greek tense-aspect inflectional markers *-Vn-*, *-Vz-*, etc. (present) and *-is-* (past) along with Greek-derived verbs, and subsequently generalised them to verbs from other contact languages. Thus we find in the Balkan dialects of Romani forms like *analadi-s-ker-djom* 'I understood', where the form *anladi* is the Turkish inflected past-tense 3SG form *anal-dı* 'understood', the *-(i)s-* is the Greek aorist marker, *-ker-* is the causative/transitive marker that integrates the loan verb, and *-djom* the past-tense 1SG inflection. In this respect, we may argue that the borrowed Greek markers have assumed a role within Romani morphology that is partly inflectional (since tense specification continues to be part of it, at least in some dialects) and partly derivational (as they mark out particular verbs as loans). Greek also contributed the 3SG present-tense person concord marker *-i*, which in many Romani dialects is limited to loan verbs, as in Arli Romani of Kosovo *pomožin-i* 'he/she helps', but in Slovene Romani is generalised to all verbs, replacing the inherited Romani 3SG present-tense concord marker. Slovene Romani also borrows the Slovene/Croatian person concord endings for the 2PL – *kerdž-ate* 'you.PL did', and the 1PL – *mothav-amo* 'we say'.

Some Romani dialects – Crimean Romani, and Romani dialects of northern Bulgaria, for example – borrow parts of their person concord set from Turkish (for details, see Elšík and Matras 2006: 136) This process is evidently triggered by two factors: first, the tendency to retain Turkish verb inflection with Turkish-dervied verb stems; and second, analogies based on chance similarities between the inherited Romani and Turkish conjugations. The similarities and the resulting new forms or 'semi-borrowings' are summarised in Figure 8.2. Essentially,

	Romani (inherited)		Turkish			Romani new form
Person	Present	Past	Present	Past	Nominal	Past
1SG		-om/-em/-im	-Vm	-Vm	-Vm	
1SG		-an	-sVn	-Vn	-Vn	
1PL	-as	-am	-Vz		-VmVz	-am-Vs
2PL	-en	-en	-sVnVz	-VnVz	-VnVz	-en-Vs

Figure 8.2 *Borrowing of Turkish person concord markers into Romani.*

there is an analogy between the Romani 1st and 2nd person forms in *-m* and *-n*, respectively, and the corresponding Turkish forms in *-m* and *-n*. This is no doubt supported by the presence of similar nominal possession suffixes in Turkish, which facilitates the adption of the Turkish form *-Vz* as a generic plurality marker, leading to the emergence of past-tense 1PL *-amus* etc. and past-tense 2PL *-enus* (and phonological variants). This is in a sense reminiscent of the development described above for the 3PL pronominal form in some Romani dialects: the agglutinative marking of plurality through a borrowed morpheme, based on analogies with an external model and inspired by coincidental similarities between the indigenous form and the model.

A somewhat similar development is found in Asia Minor Greece (Dawkins 1916: 59ff.), where the Silli dialect adds *-iniz* to the concord endings of the 1PL and 2PL. Dawkins emphasises the appearance of this new form specifically with Greek medio-passives, which usually have intransitive and inchoative meaning, and which in Greek resemble the existential verb. Thus, Dawkins cites *kimúmistiniz* (other dialects: *kimúmisti*) 'we slept', as well as *xastarimístiniz* 'we were ill' (from Turkish *hasta* 'ill'), and *kimástiniz* (other dialects: *kimásti*) 'you.PL' slept, alongside *xastarístiniz* 'you.PL are ill'. Gardani (in press: 73) points out that Turkish *-iniz* is a possessive marker, and proposes that it was borrowed as a general marker of pluralilty without regard to person. Although this explanation of the functionality of *-iniz* seems plausible, as Figure 8.2 shows Turkish *-VnVz* has a certain consistency in marking not just the 2PL of lexical verbs, and possession, but also the copula; this seems to have been the source of its adoption specifically into the Greek morpho-semantic domain of inchoatives/medio-passives.

There thus appear to be two pathways for the adoption of finite verb morphology. The first is through the adoption of loan verbs and the retention of their original inflection – in all likelihood first with modals and auxiliaries, where applicable, and then with lexical loan verbs. From there, the affixes are diffused backwards to inherited verbs. This seems to have happened with the Greek 3SG ending *-i* in Romani and with the borrowed person markers in Slovene Romani.

Affix	Function	Source	Recipient
-ḏu	ergative-instrumental	Ritharngu	Ngandi
-miri	instrumental	Ritharngu	Nunggubuyu > Warndarang
-gu	genitive-dative-purposive	Ritharngu	Ngandi
-wala	ablative	Nunggubuyu	Warndarang

Figure 8.3 *Diffusion of inflectional morphology among Arnhem Land languages (based on Heath 1978).*

The second possibility is an analogy, based on perceived structural similarities, between the inherited markers and those of the contact languages; this appears to have been the development in Balkan Romani dialects and in Asia Minor Greek in contact with Turkish.

Evidence of cross-linguistic diffusion of productive nominal inflection is extremely rare. One of the few documented cases is Heath's (1978) investigation of contact between several languages in the Arnhem Land region of northern Australia. As a result of a pattern of contacts among the neighbouring languages, Ritharngu (belonging to the Yuulngu family, an isolated sub-branch of the Pama-Nyungan phylum) is the source of borrowings into Ngandi and Nunggubuyu (both part of the same sub-branch of the so-called 'prefixing' languages); Nung-gubuyu is the source of borrowing into Warndarang (which belongs to a separate sub-branch of the 'prefixing' group); and Ngandi is also the source of some borrowings into Nunggubuyu. The morphemes that are borrowed between the languages cover a variety of derivational and adverbial (modal) functions; they also include a series of nominal inflection markers (see Figure 8.3).

These data contrast rather sharply with the evidence collected from other scenes of intense contact and grammatical diffusion, where the borrowing of actual morphological forms especially in the domain of nominal inflection is generally absent. It is certainly possible to view Heath's findings as a clear statement that borrowing in this domain is not excluded, and as an indication that further cases may yet be identified. It is also necessary, however, to admit that in the three decades or so since Heath's findings were published very few if any parallel cases have become known that show diffusion of nominal inflection markers, despite an upsurge of descriptive work on previously lesser-known languages. To be sure, the analysis of borrowing in regions such as Arnhem Land has to proceed hand in hand with general linguistic reconstruction and the identification of genetic relations among languages, without which it is impossible to rule out that common forms result from shared inheritance. Despite advances in this area, some basic issues in historical reconstruction in this and other regions remain unsolved, and so we lack clarity about the mode and often the direction of diffusion of individual morphs. Interestingly, Heath (1978: 105) concludes that in Arnhem Land, case, number, and noun-class affixes are diffusible, along with affixes marking derivation, negation, and functions like the inchoative and thematiser. On the other hand, independent pronouns, demonstrative stems and adverbs, as well as verbal and pronominal affixes, are not diffusible. This contrasts partly with other proposed generalisations on borrowing, if not with respect to the individual functional categories then at least with respect to their status as bound and unbound morphemes (cf. e.g. Field 2002). It also contrasts with analyses proposed for other regions in Australia, where diffusion of pronouns, for instance, has been proposed, but remains highly controversial.[7]

From the communicative perspective of the bilingual speaker, the inconvenience of re-structuring paradigms and isolating abstract markers when it comes to templates like nominal case, which operate on the purely formal-sentential level of syntactic relations, appears to outweigh the possible advantage of being able to categorise nouns in the same way with respect to their sentential role, irrespective of interaction context (i.e. choice of 'language').[8] We will see in Chapter 9 that such syncretisation of role categorisation can often be achieved at a 'lower' cost, by re-organising inherited linguistic matter. Nonetheless, we must conclude that while we are able to explain the rarity of borrowing of case markers and other items of inflectional morphology, there appear to be situations in which speakers display an aptitude to prioritise matter replication even in these domains.

8.2.3   Articles and classifiers

Our final category in this survey of matter replication is grammatical morphemes that are not bound, but semi-bound. Their function is to categorise nouns. Both appear to be of limited distribution in the languages of the world; in fact, their distribution even as categories, irrespective of actual matter-form, is to a considerable extent areal. We shall revisit this aspect of articles and classifiers in Chapter 9. At the moment we are concerned with matter replication of the articles and classifiers. Attestations are rather rare. One of the most outstanding cases of matter diffusion in this domain of structure is the borrowing of Chinese noun-classifiers into Vietnamese, Korean, and Japanese, where they may accompany attributes such as demonstratives or numerals. Alves (2007) presents an inventory or the relevant forms in Vietnamese (Figure 8.4).

Other cases include the borrowing of postposed classifiers in the eastern Indo-Aryan languages Oriya (*-ṭa, -ṭī*), Bengali (*-ṭā, -ṭī, -khānā*), and Assamese (*-to, -zɒ n, -khɒ n*, etc.), probably from Tibeto-Burman (cf. Masica 1991: 250).

Borrowing of matter-forms of definite and indefinite articles is rare. Articles may sometimes accompany borrowed words, re-analysed as part of the word – as in the case of Spannish *azucár* from Arabic *ʔas-súkkar* '(the) sugar', or Chamorro *lamasa* from Spanish *la mesa* '(the) table' – but such forms are not productive as articles, and indeed are combined with the definite articles of the recipient language to convey definiteness. Chamorro does use Spanish-derived articles – indefinite *un* and definite *la* and *las* – in some cases, namely in the case

Vietnamese	Chinese	Category
bàn	壁 (bì)	a unit for flat surfaces (table, hand, foot)
bản	本 (běn)	a unit for scripts, reports, compositions
căn (SV gian)	間 (jiān)	a unit for houses
chiếc (SV chích)	隻 (zhī)	(1) a unit for vehicles cars, boats, planes, (2) a pair of chopsticks
cuốn (SV quyển)	卷 (juǎn)	unit for books
đạo	道 (dào)	unit for laws, orders, decrees
đỉnh	頂 (dǐng)	unit for mountains
đoạn	段 (duàn)	unit for sections, paragraphs, passages
đôi	對 (duì)	couple of shoes, chopsticks, husband/wife
môn	門 (mén)	unit for a subject/field of study
phát	發 (fā)	unit for a shot of a firearm, an injection
tòa (SV tọa)	座 (zuò)	unit for buildings
vị	位 (wèi)	unit for people of high status
viên	員 (yuán)	unit for officials
viên	丸 (wán)	unit for small, round things (pills, tablets, bullets, etc.)

Figure 8.4 *Borrowed Chinese classifiers into Vietnamese (from Alves 2007: 347).*

of *un* as a numeral, or else in fixed expressions such as *un dia* 'once upon a time', or *oran alas dos* 'two o'clock' (Topping 1973: 136–137). A rare case of definite article borrowing are the Jewish Aramaic dialects of Iraq, which have borrowed the (Southern) Kurdish definite article -*ek* (or -*ăk*; cf. Khan 2004: 295).[9] Epirus Romani shows an indefinite article *njek*, which appears to be a blend of inherited Romani *(j)ek* and Albanian *një*. Aikhenvald (2007b) reports on the borrowing of the Tok Pisin indefinite article and quantifier *wanpela* 'a/one' into Manambu, a Ndu language of the Sepik area of Papua New Guinea, though limited to the function of introducing new participants into discourse.

The absence of widespread matter-borrowing in the domain of articles contrasts sharply with the replication of nominal plural endings, and questions, at least at first glance, the relevance, in the discussion context of long-term borrowing, of the category of 'early system morpheme' (Myers-Scotton and Jake 2000). One way to interpret the conflict between the behaviour of nouns during codeswitching, when they are often accompanied by articles, and the fact that articles are not borrowed as productive devices, is to assume that codeswitchers, as fluent bilinguals, have access to the grammatical apparatus to which articles belong, but that the dissemination of borrowed nouns throughout a monolingual population filters out such grammatical adjuncts. This is not an entirely satisfactory account, since it fails to explain the absence, by and large, of article borrowing even in situations where bilingualism is widespread.

The answer appears to lie in the degree of transparency and consideration of the referential individuality of nouns, as offered by the various nominal categorisation devices. Derivational procedures that mark agentivity or diminutiveness are highly transparent, para-lexical devices that effectively act like compounding devices. They therefore occupy the top position on the matter-borrowabilty continuum for nominal modifiers (1). Noun classifiers are based on a semantic categorisation of nouns and are therefore rather transparent devices. This explains their high degree of acceptance along with loan nouns, and their possible subsequent backwards diffusion into the inherited inventory of nouns. Plurality is based on the momentary categorisation of a noun in terms of quantity and is therefore volatile, but still transparent. It occupies the next position on the scale. The definite and indefinite article indicate a noun's pragmatic status in discourse, which is both volatile and less obvious than e.g. plurality. With case-markers, categorisation is based on the semantic-syntatic role in a phrase, with little consideration of the noun's individuality, permanent semantics, or presupposition status:

(1)   Likelihood of borrowing of nominal modifiers
         derivation marker > classifier > plural marker > definiteness marker > case
         marker

Naturally, there may be interaction among the devices, with case markers appearing only with definite or only with animate nouns. Gender too is a form of categorisation, though in practice it is usually embedded into the marking of definiteness, or case, or both. The purpose of the hierarchy in (1) is not to offer a comprehensive theory of nominal categorisation, but to point out the essential distinctive features of certain devices that are relevant to their likelihood to be candidates for borrowing. Note that in flectional languages, the lower positions on the hierarchy tend to be highly differentiated and multi-layered, making replication in a different system difficult. We would therefore predict that if a case marker is found to have been borrowed, then it is likely that it was borrowed from a system in which it had no parallel function such as marking out gender or number.

8.3   Constraints on matter replication

The present chapter cannot serve as an encyclopaedic survey of cases of cross-lingusitic matter replication; that is still an outstanding endeavour. The purpose of the modest survey undertaken here was to introduce the factors that promote and possibly also impede borrowing around particular functional categories. This agenda is based on the assumption that it is the functionality of categories, and not merely their structural representation, that motivates bilingual speakers to generalise a form in the repertoire and adopt it for use irrespective of the choice-language of the interaction context, thereby making it part of another 'language', available and accessible to other speakers and possibly to other generations of speakers, whether bilingual or monolingual.

Evidence for the functionality-trigger was derived from the fact that even within a single category, different members of the category or 'paradigm values' may differ in their susceptibility to contact, without differing significantly in other relevant features such as structural complexity or position in the sentence. The assumption that function drives borrowability is further anchored in the acceptance that words are not just slots in a sentence, but are meaningful devices on which speakers rely to convey information and attitudes, as well as to establish and maintain social relations with others. In this perspective, we view borrowing not merely as a plain modification of an abstract 'system', but as an activity in which speakers engage, and which is goal-oriented.

Several different goals of borrowing were described, which can be reduced essentially to two principal motivations: to modify patterns of social interaction, and to modify patterns of language processing during communicative interaction. Speakers are more likely to be aware, to some extent at least, of processes belonging to the first domain than of those belonging to the second. The first has much to do with the referential resources of language and its suitability and adaptability to negotiate various kinds of social activities. The second has more to do with the degree to which speakers are able to exercise control over the mental organisation of their linguistic repertoire; in this domain, those phenomena that catch our attention as diachronic modifications in the repertoire of structures that we define as a particular 'language' are often the ultimate result of lapses on the part of speakers in exercising such control.

In any instance, and regardless of trigger or motivation, a change in the structure of language represents the acceptance of an innovation by the speech community or sectors within it. This brings us to consider one of the first and foremost constraints on borrowing, namely the setting and directionality of bilingualism and speakers' attitude toward language change. An almost trivial point is that matter replication will be restricted if contact remains superficial and if bilingualism remains marginal. Nevertheless, as mentioned above, even superficial communicative interaction in new constellations and with members of new population groups may bring about some borrowing. Marginal and superficial bilingualism, however, will almost never impose a burden on speakers' mental processing of their linguistic repertoire; we are therefore unlikely to witness any of the changes that result from repertoire-management problems in such situations. This means, in effect, that superficial language contact is unlikely to lead to any borrowing in the domain of grammar and grammatical operations.

Sector-specific or 'filtered' bilingualism such as elite bilingualim is also likely to limit the extent of borrowing in the domain of grammar, for similar reasons: the need to actively manage a bilingual repertoire remains the property of few. Nevertheless, in such situations the replication of grammatical forms by a small elite may trigger a process of internal language change through which the sector of bilinguals act as agents of change within their larger, mainly monolingual society. Prestige then acts as a secondary factor, one that supports the spread of an innovation throughout the speech community. The successful spread of an innovation can be constrained by institutionalised intervention. Institutions are generally slower to adopt change than individuals and informal social groupings. Some institutions, such as those that promote and engage in literacy and literary activities, are even entrusted with safeguarding and so propagating a particular form of language. Their intervention may slow down any processes of innovation diffusion that may be underway. Thus we find that languages that have a tradition of native literacy and are used as languages of formal interaction in institutions are less likely to show grammatical borrowing. Once again, what this means at ground level is that, in an attempt to answer to the expectations of institutions, bilingual speakers will be more reluctant to give in to lapses of control over their linguistic repertoire and will remain more conscious of the need to maintain the contextual separation of repertoire subsets.

A social inhibition against the lifting of 'demarcation boundaries' with the linguistic repertoire may also exist as a result of community traditions that are not, or are less, institutionalised. Especially in smaller, tight-knit communities, language loyalty may be an important manifestation of social identity. Taboos against language mixing have been reported for various areas of the world, including Amazonia (Aikhenvald 2002, Epps 2001 and 2007), Northwest Melanesia (Ross 1996, 2001), and Northwestern California (O'Neil 2006). Quite often, though, such taboos target only clearly recognisable tokens from another language, i.e. phonological word-forms. They may therefore block the replication of linguistic matter, but not that of linguistic patterns, which I discuss in the next chapter.

One outcome of the above survey that might surprise some readers is the fact that there seem to be rather few constraints of a purely structural nature on the borrowability of linguistic matter. I have shown how speakers will often find a way to overcome typological incongruencies that hinder the smooth integration of loans, by bypassing the structural difficulties. Thus, a postpositioning language may adopt a preposition from a contact language and use it in a position following the noun, as in the case of Hindi/Urdu *bād* 'after' or Turkish *rağmen* 'despite' and *kadar* 'up to' (the latter two derived from preposed Arabic attributive adverbs). Languages adopt various kinds of strategies in order to overcome the difficulties of isolating lexical verb roots and inserting them into the recipient language's finite-inflectional component paradigms, as seen in the cases of languages that borrow verbs as nominals or infinitives (as in Turkish and Adyghe), or in the case of Hebrew, where an abstract consonantal root is identified and extracted to be inserted into an inflectional template. And Domari speakers allow themselves the inconvenience of complete suppletion in their inventory of adjectives in order to be able to utilise the Arabic marking of comparison, which cannot otherwise be morphologically isolated. Such examples must prompt us to treat with caution proposed constraints on 'system incompatibility' and predictions that borrowing is only possible if the borrowed morpheme can be accommodated into the morphological structure of the recipient language (cf. Field 2002: 40–42).

A difficulty that always accompanies the discussion of borrowability is the impossibility to disprove that something may not occur. While we can accept concrete cases as evidence for borrowing, the absence of a described case does not necessarily imply that certain borrowing patterns are impossible. This, coupled with the enormous diversity of examples of matter replication, suggests that little that is productive can emerge out of a discussion on the existence or absence of absolute constraints on borrowing. The emphasis in this and the previous chapter has therefore been on speakers' motivation to engage in borrowing; the process was defined as the lifting of context-bound constraints on the selection of a form in communicative interaction, and consequent generalisation of this form within the individual's bilingual repertoire, at its initiation stage, and the subsequent spread of this very process through a relevant sector of the speech community, whether bilingual or monolingual. Since borrowing is inititated by individuals, their motivation to borrow is a key towards understanding the process.

The frequent borrowing in a particular domain of language function deserves an explanation just as much as the rarity of borrowing in a certain domain. Any explanation must address the issue of the motivation to borrow with respect to the functionality of the particular category. The actual outcome of change in a particular language-contact situation will invariably involve the scales considered above, which depict in effect the interest that speakers have, whether consciously or not, in allowing their language to change around a particular function. The surrounding, facilitating factors, such as language attitudes and the nature of bilingualism, will define the extent to which borrowing is allowed to proceed.

8.4 Mechanisms of contact-induced change in phonology

8.4.1 General considerations

Phonology has a somewhat ambiguous position in between the two types of structural replication – that of *matter* and that of *pattern* (see Chapters 6 and 9). Phones and phonemes can be produced and perceived, and that gives us the impression that they constitute concrete shapes, or linguistic matter. On the other hand, sounds are independent of the meaning of the words and morphs in which they appear. Unlike our examples of matter and pattern, the production and replication of phonological forms is subject to physiological constraints, most notably the difficulty to master new sound forms in adulthood. It is therefore more difficult to exercise control over the sound-producing apparatus than over the selection of word-forms (matter), or of features such as a particular rule of word-order variants (pattern). This makes the domain of sound production even more vulnerable to 'interference' phenomena than other areas of structure. If the selection and inhibition mechanism is further constrained by physiological factors, then speakers will be less successful in discriminating distinct sets of sounds to accompany distinct, context-bound sets of word-forms and other structures.

Phonological replication – or 'interference', 'transfer' or borrowing' – may affect any level of sound structure: the articulation of individual phones or phonemes within words, length and gemination, stress and tone, prosody and intonation. Borrowings in phonology have often been considered as strategies to fill so-called 'structural gaps' in the recipient system (cf. Winford 2003: 55–56). The notion of 'gap' is vague, however, given that languages are generally considered in descriptive linguistics to constitute autonomous, self-contained, and functional systems. I will therefore avoid the idea of 'gaps' and continue to focus on speakers' motivation to produce effective utterances in order to perform communicative tasks.

Taken from this perspective, contact-induced change in phonology is the result of speakers' inability or reluctance to maintain complete and consistent separation among the phonological systems of two languages. There are several kinds of processes that lead to the lifting of strict phonological demarcation. The integration of word-forms into the recipient system can lead to changes to these word-forms themselves, without affecting the recipient system. This occurs most frequently when a foreign word is introduced into the recipient language by just a small group of bilinguals or even semi-bilinguals, and spreads across the speech community to monolinguals, who are not familiar with the original sounds of the donor language. In such situations there is strong loyalty toward the recipient language and generally only superficial acquaintance with the donor language. The integration of the French-derived word *current* has no consequences for the phonological system of English. Integration into English results in a change to the phonology of the word itself: ['kʰʌrənt] shows shift of stress to initial position, aspiration of the initial consonant, lowering of the first vowel and reduction of the vowel in the second syllable to a centralised one, and a change to the quality of the trill /r/. In Jordanian Arabic, the English-derived word 'puncture' is rendered as *banšer* ['banʃær], showing voicing of English /p/ to /b/, lowering of the vowel in the first syllable from /ʌ/ to /a/, reduction of the palatalised cluster /kt'/ or /ktʃ/ to a post-alveolar sibilant /ʃ/, de-centralisation of the pre-final vowel /ɐ/ to /æ/, and the presence of a trilled /r/ in the coda. Once again, there is no modification of the recipient phonological system to accommodate the new word. Instead, the word itself undergoes modification.

In a second kind of process, sounds that appear in borrowed word-forms but are normally absent from the system of the recipient language may be replicated along with the word-form itself, leading to an enrichment of the sound inventory of the recipient language. Phonological enrichment of this kind may be quite subtle. German integrates the English word forms *Baby* and *Computer*, and with them sound sequences that are not normally present in German in such positions, namely [eɪ] in the first word, and [ju] in the second, but both sounds are in principle available for production as combinations of German sounds. German *Dschungel* 'jungle' on the other hand contains a phoneme /dʒ/, which is alien to the German system, and in fact is often pronounced [tʃ] by many German speakers. Kurdish integrates many Arabic words and with them often the sounds that they contain, such as the pharyngeal fricatives /ħ/ and /ʕ/, as in *haywan* 'animal', pronounced [ħaj'wɑːn], or *se'et* 'hour', pronounced [sæ'ʕæt].

This kind of process typically occurs in situations where bilingualism is fairly widespread. Bilingual members of the speech community, who are aware of the original, donor-language pronunciation, make an effort to authenticate the borrowed word by replicating its original phonology. Since the donor language enjoys some form of prestige, often due to associations with commerce, technology, knowledge, or other kinds of innovation or power, the replication of original donor-language pronunciation is imitated by many monolinguals (i.e. non-speakers of the donor language) as well, leading to the spread, within the recipient language, of the new phonemes in the relevant loanwords. This testifies to speakers' respect toward the donor language and to their flexibility in the use of their own native language (the recipient language). It indicates that speakers are content to award the phonologically 'authentic' replication of lexical loans higher priority than to the preservation of the coherent phonological structures of their native language.

We can speak of system convergence when speakers are uncomfortable maintaining a separation of phonological sub-components within their repertoire and seek to draw instead on just a single inventory of sounds (including rules on the distribution of sounds) when communicating, irrespective of interaction context and so of choice of language. In a community of second-language learners, this may be due to a reluctance or inability to acquire full command of the phonological system of the target language. As a result, words in the target language are produced with the phonology of the native language. The substrate effect may lead to a group-particular 'accent' (e.g. in the case of an ethnolect), or in the event of language shift to the emergence of a new native variety of the target language with its own distinctive phonology. The collective substrate effect is no different in principle from what we call 'accent' or 'interference' at the level of the individual speaker. In South Asian English the phoneme /t/ (in English an aspirated dento-apical stop) is usually pronounced as an unaspirated retroflex [ʈ]. Members of the Greek-speaking minority in Turkey[10] tend to converge the Turkish back vowel [ɯ] and front vowel [i] (grapheme representation <ı> and <i>, respectively) into just a front vowel [i], as well as to avoid velarised /l/, thus rendering the Turkish word *balık* [ba'lɯk] 'fish' as [ba'lik].

Finally, in a situation of established and prolonged bilingualism, speakers of one language, often a minority language, may adjust the inventory of sounds and the rules that govern their distribution to match those of another, often a dominant contact language, seeking here too the advantages of not having to maintain a context-oriented separation of sound inventories within their bilingual linguistic repertoire. In Polish and Russian varieties of Romani, aspiration, which is absent from the sound inventories of the contact languages, converges with the velar fricative [x], which is the nearest point of articulation and is also the sound used by speakers of Polish and Russian to render the glottal fricative [h] in foreign words. This results in the pronunciation of the Romani aspirated set of consonants /ph, th, kh/ as [px, tx, kx], as in *pxen mange!* 'tell me!' In Domari, the phoneme /p/ as in /pandži/ 'he, she' is currently undergoing voicing under the pressure of the Arabic system, which lacks a voiceless labial stop but possesses a voiced one, /b/. The outcome is either an in-between pronunciation, showing a lenis [p̥], or else alternation between [p] and [b] in the relevant position.

Figure 8.5 provides an overview of the four types of contact-induced phonological change, with typical speaker profiles and language attitudes for each. Type A is distinct, in that it involves no change to the phonological system but only a change to individual words, while Types B–D all involve some degree of modification to the system as used by speakers on a regular basis. Nonetheless, there are resemblances among the types in individual aspects. Types A and B are similar in revolving around individual borrowed words. Types A and C are similar in that both involve the transfer of native language features onto foreign material. Types B and D are similar in that both involve the adoption of foreign sound patterns and their integration into the native language. Types C and D share, as mentioned above, the fact that speakers try and avoid having to select sounds from two distinct inventory sets, and to this end generalise just one set of sounds to be used in both 'languages', that is, in all interaction contexts.

There are points of overlap between the various types, and so they should not be understood as covering contact situations on a wholesale basis. The borrowing of word-forms along with their sounds may trigger or accelerate processes of convergence, with new phonemes diffusing 'backwards' to substitute inherited phonemes in selected words. In some varieties of Kurdish in southeastern Turkey and northern Iraq, the Arabic-derived pharyngeal phoneme /ħ/ is not just retained in Arabic loans such as [ħaj'wɑ:n] 'animal', but it also substitutes the inherited glottal fricative /h/ in selected inherited words: [ħæʃt] 'eight', originally [hæʃt]. The retention of donor-language phones and phonemes in borrowed words may also be selective. Kurdish imports the Arabic pharyngeal in [ħaj'wɑ:n] 'animal', but substitutes the quality of the original Arabic long vowel – cf. Arabic [ħaj'wa:n] – by the quality of the nearest native-Kurdish long vowel [ɑ:]. And so in a single contact situation – Kurdish–Arabic bilingualism – we can identify several different types of process: replication of original phonemes in loanwords, convergence of phoneme systems (through the adjustment of phonemes in inherited words to match those of the contact language), and substitution of phonemes in loanwords through inherited sounds.

Type	Process	Description	Speakers/ Bilingualism	Language attitudes
A	Phonological adaptation of word-forms	Replicated word-forms are adjusted to match the sound patterns of the recipient language	Semi-bilinguals or monolinguals	Strong loyalty towards, and stability of the recipient language; superficial contact
B	Borrowing of phonological features along with word-forms	Borrowed and inserted word-forms maintain (fully or partly) the original sound patterns of the donor language ('authentication')	Fairly widespread bilingualism	Flexibility in the use of the recipient language, prestigious bilingualism
C	Convergence of systems during second-language acquisition	Word-forms of the target language are systematically adjusted to match the sound patterns of the native language	Emerging bilingualism; stable minority bilingualism; emergence of ethnolect or language shift	Strong group identity coupled with a need (pressure) to acquire the target language
D	Convergence of systems in stable, intensive bilingualism	Sound patterns of the native language are adjusted to match those of the second language	Intensive and widespread bilingualism	Second language is 'prestige' language

Figure 8.5 *Types of processes leading to contact-induced phonological change.*

How can we explain convergence and borrowing in phonology? From the point of view of handling the multilingual repertoire, there is a functional motivation favouring consistency in the types and points of articulation as well as the distribution rules of allophonic variation and suprasegmentals, regardless of the speech situation in which language users find themselves. This motivation exerts pressure toward convergence of the two phonological 'systems' in the speaker's repertoire. At the same time, social norms, awareness of identity, and loyalty toward the group associated with the home language may counteract levelling within the phonological repertoire by demanding conformity to the established pronunciation norms. The process of phonological borrowing is therefore usually

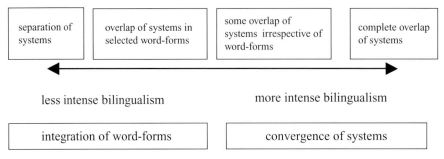

Figure 8.6 *Connections between intensity of bilingualism, type of accommodation process, and overlap between phonological systems.*

an outcome of compromises between these two pressures. Compromise is shaped by the nature and intensity of contact, especially by the degree and directionality of bilingualism and the degree to which phonology is a factor in flagging group loyalty. Contact-induced phonological change can therefore be represented as a continuum (Figure 8.6).

8.4.2   The phonological integration of word-forms

The processes of phonological change arising from the integration of loans into a recipient system are essentially part of what Weinreich (1953) described as processes of phonological 'interference'. They involve a re-definition of places and modes of articulation and so of phones and phonemes in a word in such a way that matches the phonological system of the recipient language: Speakers perceive similarities between a sound X in one language, and a sound Y in another. These similarities usually derive from shared features in the position of articulation of the two sounds, sometimes also in the mode of articulation. On this basis, one sound is allowed to represent the other. The process has two possible directions. In Types A and C (Figure 8.5), speakers re-interpret the sounds in a loanword or target language by matching them to sound patterns of the recipient or native language. This procedure of *approximation* enables the production of foreign word-forms within a familiar phonological framework. In Type D, phonological convergence, speakers modify individual sounds within the existing framework based on an external model. As we shall see in the next section, this may involve direct replication of foreign sounds, as in Type B, but it may also involve *approximation*, as in Types A and C.

Application of a rule on allophonic phone distribution to a loanword can result in the loss of a feature in one of that word's phonemes. Turkish shows final de-voicing of stops, and applies this to the loanword *arap* 'Arab', from Arabic *ʕárab*. The same example also shows how integration can lead to the omission of phonemes that are not part of the phoneme inventory of the recipient language: the voiced pharyngeal fricative /ʕ/ is lost. A sub-type of phoneme omission is the simplification of phoneme clusters, a frequent occurrence due to the greater probability that pairs of languages will not share complex clusters: Hebrew *páncer* 'puncture' shows reduction of the English cluster [ktʃ] through omission of the velar stop and retention merely of an affricate, while Jordanian Arabic *banšer* shows further reduction of the affricate to just its fricative component.

The omission of certain features during phoneme replication can be disruptive to the system as a whole and it may result in a reduction of minimal pairs. Khasanova (2000) describes how speakers of Manchu-Tungusic and Paleo-Siberian languages of the Lower Amur basin in Russia's far east fail to distinguish groups of Russian palatal consonants, and thus merge Russian *vet'er* 'wind' and *večer* 'evening' (both *večer*), and simplify Russian initial clusters (*vmesto* 'together' > *mesto*). This occurs both when speaking Russian, and when integrating Russian word-forms into their own languages.

Probably one of the most common forms of phonological integration is phoneme substitution through phonemes of the recipient language that share some of the features with the original sound, allowing an approximation of the foreign sound through native material. Turkish *hanım* [haˈnɯm] 'lady' shows several substitutions compared to its Kurdish and Persian origin word *xānim* [xɑːˈnɪm]: the initial velar fricative is replaced by a glottal, and the qualities of both vowels change. A similar development occurs in Japanese *terebijon* 'television': three of the consonants are replaced with approximations, each sharing at least one salient feature with the original phoneme that it replaces (usually place of articulation rather than mode), in an attempt to replicate the word-form using native phonology. Phoneme substitution is common, since phonemes, by definition, are combinations of articulatory features. Any pair of languages is more likely to share *some* features of a given phoneme than the *precise combination* of features in the form of a complete phoneme. It follows that individual features can be matched across languages more easily than complete phonemes. A 'milder' form of integration is phone substitution, where the phonemes are preserved but their phonetic qualities are adapted to the recipient language: Hebrew *ramzór* 'traffic light', pronounced [ʀamˈzoʀ], is borrowed into Palestinian Arabic as [ramˈzoːr]; note the different pronunciation of /r/ and the lengthening, in Arabic, of the vowel in stressed position.

Loanwords may accommodate to syllable and stress structure. In Turkish *gurup* 'group', and *istasyon* 'station', from European languages (French/English), an initial cluster CC, which violates Turkish syllable structure rules, is avoided, albeit in different ways. In the first example it is re-interpreted as CVC, anticipating the original nucleus /u/. In the second case, it is rendered as VCC, drawing on an epenthetic vowel. Accommodation of loanwords to Japanese syllable structure involves a general re-interpretation of (C)C-codas as CV, thus affecting both simple consonants and final clusters: *kyatto-fūdo* 'cat-food', *baransu* 'balance'. In Domari, despite a general tendency to converge with Arabic, Arabic-derived words are assimilated into the inherited stress system. Thus the name *áḥmad* 'Ahmed' shows shift of stress in the accusative case: *aḥmad-ás*.

Above I discussed 'authentication' as a motivation for the retention of foreign sounds in loanwords. Replication of the original sounds presupposes of course that speakers are able to identify and produce those sounds, and so it requires a fair degree of bilingualism at least on the part of the sector of innovators within the speech community. Monolinguals may acquire the new phonemes too in an attempt to imitate the innovators. Thus, the Arabic-derived pharyngeal consonants are used in Arabic-derived loanwords in Kurdish dialects of southeastern Turkey and northern Iraq irrespective of individuals' proficiency in Arabic. In the cross-linguistic sample discussed in Matras (2007b), almost all languages incorporate loanwords along with at least some of their original phonemes, which are new to the recipient system. Examples are Macedonian Turkish /ts/ with Macedonian loans, the Vietnamese sounds /ʃ/, /f/. /v/, and /z/ with Chinese loans, the Domari pharyngeals /ħ/ and /ʕ/ used in Arabic loans, and Imbabura Quichua /b/, /d/, /g/, /ʋ/, /ʒ/, and the vowels /e/ and /o/ in Spanish loans. The Turkish–Greek bilingual population of Asia Minor Greek retained /ʃ/ in Turkish loan words: *düšündüzo* 'I think, consider' (Dawkins 1916: 67–68). According to Hajek (2006: 168–169), Tetun Dili (an Austronesian language of East Timor) borrowed half of its entire consonant inventory of twenty-two from Portuguese, some with reinforcement from Malay. In terms of occurrence frequency, contact-related change is more likely to affect consonants than vowels (Matras 2007b). The reason behind this hierarchy is the fact that consonant inventories are generally larger and so the potential for lack of correspondence between consonant systems in contact is higher, resulting in greater pressure to adjust the consonant system.

Some modifications to the recipient system entail changes merely to the distribution of internal phonemes. In French-derived loanwords, German tends to substitute a nasal vowel in final position by the nasal-velar /ŋ/, which is part of its inherited inventory of sounds: *Restaurant* /ʀɛstoːˈʀaŋ/. The nasal-velar, which is otherwise a rather marginal phoneme in German, thereby gains in frequency and environments in which it appears.

Preservation of some of the original, donor-language phonological features of loanwords can lead to the exemption of loanwords from general phonological rules that apply to the inherited component of the language. German final stress, as in *Restauránt*, is limited almost entirely to loanwords. In Romani, by contrast, the stress in inherited words falls on the inflectional segment, as in *rakl-ó* 'boy-M.NOM', *rakl-í* 'girl-F.NOM', while loanwords are permitted to retain their root-stress, as in Greek-derived *fór-o* 'town-M.NOM', and the general European loan *prezidént-o* 'president-M.NOM'. A similar rule applies in Modern Hebrew, where loan nouns are permitted to retain root-level stress: cf. inherited *yéled* 'boy', PL *yelad-ím*, but *studént* PL *studént-im*. In Turkish, loanwords are often exempted from vowel harmony, which is normally applied in inherited words even within the lexical component: *haliç* 'bay, Golden Horn', from Arabic *xalīğ* 'gulf, bay'.

Individual phoneme borrowing in loanwords can have an effect on the system as a whole beyond just the enrichment of the phoneme inventory. In Modern Hebrew the borrowing of word-forms with initial /f/ and /v/, such as *faks* 'fax' and *veterinár* 'veterinary', de-stabilises the inherited system of complementary distribution of stops and fricatives /p:f, b:v, k:x/, where fricatives only occur in positions that follow inherited (Ancient Hebrew) long vowels. It is not the only de-stabilising factor, however, but joins other changes such as the merger of /ħ/ and /x/ and the appearance, as a result, of /x/ in initial position, and the merger of historical /w/ with /v/, with similar consequences. Nonetheless, the changes trigger random variation, which leads to uncertainty especially among younger speakers as to the identity of the consonant in paradigms that contain morpho-phonemic stop/fricative alternation. We thus find non-standard *šopéxet* 'she spills' (standard *šoféxet*) alongside non-standard *nitfás* 'he was caught' (standard *nitpás*) (cf. Matras and Schiff 2005). In Kurdish, the borrowing of the Arabic pharyngeals /ħ/ and /ʕ/ interferes with the system of closely positioned glottals /h/ and /ʔ/ by adding what is perceived as another set of 'gutturals'. This leads to frequent substitution, both of a pharyngeal through a glottal in loans, as in Kurdish /sæˈhæt/ 'hour' from Arabic /ˈsaːʕa/, but also of glottals in inherited words through pharyngeals: Kurdish /hæʃt/ often becomes /ħæʃt/.

8.4.3   Convergence of phonological systems

Speakers of Jerusalem Domari (Matras 1999a) are all fluent in Arabic. In fact, Arabic is the dominant language not just outside the home (except for limited communication with other Dom of the same generation in the tiny community), but for cross-generational communication in the home. It is not surprising therefore that Domari has adopted many of the Arabic sound patterns. Firstly, since all Dom are bilingual, all Arabic phonemes are retained in Arabic loanwords. And since loanwords constitute the greater part of the overall vocabulary and even a significant portion of basic vocabulary, Arabic-derived phonemes are extremely frequent in Domari speech. Some features of Arabic phonology are integrated into the inherited Indic (pre-Arabic) component of the language. The most salient of those is the pharyngealisation of stops. In Arabic, this is a regular phonological opposition within the system of stops. In Domari, some words are consistent in showing stop-pharyngealisation, e.g. [tˤaːtˤ] 'heat'. Others show variation, e.g. [kɪʃtˤoːˈtˤa] 'small', also [kɪʃtoːˈta]. Complete convergence is found in the phonetic realisation of phonemes, which matches that of the corresponding Arabic phonemes entirely, e.g. in the allophonic distribution of [ɑ] (in the environment of pharyngealised consonants, among others) and [a] (in other environments).

While all Arabic phonemes are preserved in Arabic loans, there are only two phonemes in the inherited inventory of Domari that do not also exist in Arabic. The first is the affricate /tʃ/. This phoneme is currently undergoing change as a result of indirect Arabic influence. In Palestinian Arabic, the voiced affricate /dʒ/ has become interchangeable with its de-affricated counterpart /ʒ/: Arabic [dʒamb, ʒamb] 'next to'. Domari takes over the very same development, and the two sounds become interchangeable here too: Domari [dʒandi, ʒandi] 'they go'. Arabic has no voiceless counterpart, but in Domari the weakening of affrication spreads to voiceless /tʃ/, giving [tʃoːˈni, ʃoːˈni] 'girl'. The other Domari sound that is not shared with Arabic is /p/, which, under pressure of Arabic, is in the process of merging with /b/. A factor that slows down the process is the presence of several word pairs that rely on the contrast, as in *payyom* 'my husband', *bayom* 'my wife'.

By definition, convergence increases the similarities between the phonological inventories of the two languages. The introduction of pharyngealised consonants into Domari from Arabic increases the complexity of the Domari system. But convergence may also lead to the elimination of some of the phonemes of one of the languages. In most of the Anatolian Greek dialects, inherited /θ, ð/, which are absent in the contact language Turkish, are avoided and replaced by /t, χ/ or by /d, r/ respectively (alternation being dependent on dialect, as well as on the position of the sound): *peðí > perí* 'child', *iða > ira* 'I saw' (Dawkins 1916: 74–79). Some varieties of Purepecha lose the opposition between retroflex /ʈ/ and flap /r/, as well as between central /ɨ/ and front /i/, resulting in a system that matches that of Spanish (Chamoreau 2007: 466 467). In Macedonian Turkish, /h/ in most positions, especially initially, undergoes weakening and frequent omission as a result of contact with Macedonian and Albanian, which lack such a phoneme. Speakers of so-called Oriental varieties of Modern Hebrew, whose ancestors were native speakers of Arabic, Persian, Aramaic, Kurdish, and Judeo-Spanish, lack the inherited Hebrew diphthong /ey/, which is missing from these substrate languages, and replace it with the monophthong /e/: *becá* 'egg' (standard *beycá*), *ex* 'how' (standard *eyx*). Convergence may also take the form of segmental substitution especially when it is the outcome of collective language learning. The following substitutions are characteristic of the English of Pennsylvania German speakers: dark /ɫ/ > clear /l/, /dʒ/ > /tʃ/, /ʌ/ > /ʊ, ɔ/, /ɪ/ > /ɛ, ə/ in unstressed positions, loss of voice in word final obstruents (Burridge 2006: 192–193).

The replication of allophonic variation is a common pathway for convergence. In Khuzistani Arabic, the uvular stop /q/ acquires a velar fricative allophone /ɣ/, based on the variation among the two sounds in the contact language Persian. Phonological rules may also undergo convergence. Polish Romani shows final de-voicing of consonants, like the contact language Polish: *kamaf* 'I want' (cf. other Romani dialects *kamav*). Some Anatolian Greek dialects partly adopted the Turkish pattern of vowel harmony in inflectional segments, applying it selectively to the Greek-derived inflectional morpheme *-Vzo* in combination with Turkish-derived verb roots: *istedízo* 'I wish', *anladózo* 'I understand', *düşündüzo* 'I think, consider', *oturdúzo* 'I sit down' (Dawkins 1916: 67–68). Romani dialects in contact with Slavic languages tend to adopt the rules of consonant palatalisation in the environment of a palatal vowel, especially /i/.

8.4.4 Contact-susceptibility within phonology

While in Chapter 6 we were able to suggest scales of contact-susceptibility for grammatical categories, there does not seem to be a particular reason why certain phonemes should be universally more borrowable than others. Although articulatory and auditory factors may play a role in determining the ease of production or perception of certain phonemes, there is no obvious hierarchical difference between the meaningful processing of one phoneme and that of another. We do seem to find a hierarchical relationship between layers of meaningful sound sub-systems, however: prosody seems to be more prone to cross-linguistic replication in contact situations than segmental phonology, with stress figuring in-between the two. The position of tone – which shows a high tendency toward areal clustering – may be considered somewhat problematic since it correlates strongly with the morphological typology of languages and so with internal diachronic developments. But tone too appears to be related to prosody (intonation and stress) in its contact-susceptibility.

As discussed in Chapter 6, our method for determining the contact-susceptibility of categories or structural 'layers' relies on sampling. For phonology in particular, different types of samples may show different outcomes. Comparing the phonological contact-behaviour of Romani dialects (cf. Matras 2002: 205), we find that prosody is at the top of the hierarchy of adopted features; the geographical location (by country or region) of Romani dialects is often identifiable even to those who lack any knowledge of Romani, by associating their prosody with that of their contact languages. Stress appears next on the scale. The conservative stress pattern in Romani is on the final inflectional segment of the word (with the exception of three additional sets of 'external' suffixes). Romani dialects in Western Europe (Britain, Germany, Italy, Scandinavia, Finland) have adopted a strong tendency toward word-initial stress, while those in a zone in central Europe (Hungary, Slovenia, Croatia, Slovakia) show a moderate tendency toward penultimate stress, in both cases replicating the patterns of the contact languages.

A secondary development accompanying the shift of stress in Romani is the acquisition of vowel length. In the central European zone, long vowels tend to correlate with stressed syllables and are not necessarily phonemic, while in Western Europe vowel length is a stable feature of the system. Vowels and changes to vowel quality are also more readily adopted into the inherited lexicon than consonants. Some Balkan dialects of Romani show reduction of the nucleus to /ə/, as in *khər* 'house' from *kher*, and Baltic dialects show raising and centralisation of /-a/ to /-ɨ/ as in *sɨr* 'how' from *sar*; dialects in contact with Turkish often show rounding of vowels, as in *kerdüm* 'I did' from *kerdjom*. The integration of consonants into the inherited lexical component follows in final position. Replication of consonants is otherwise common, of course, in loanwords. Among the inherited consonants that are most susceptible to change are semi-vowels and liquids: initial /j/ changes to /dž/ in some dialects in contact with Hungarian,

/l/ is velarised to /ł/ and subsequently to /w/ in dialects on contact with Polish, and /r/ usually acquired the point and mode of articulation of its counterpart in the contact language, thus German Romani [ʀ]. Also susceptible to convergence are highly marked consonants, when they are absent from the inventory of the contact language. Thus German Romani loses aspiration in /čh/, reducing it to [tʃ], while Greek Romani substitutes the post-alveolar articulation by a dental one: [tsa'vo] for *čhavo* 'boy' [tʃʰa'vo]. The results of the Romani sample can be summarised in the hierarchy in (2), which captures changes to the inherited phonological system in the dialects:

(2)   prosody > stress > vowel length > vowel quality > semi-vowels and
        liquids > complex consonants > other consonants

In the cross-linguistic sample (Matras and Sakel eds. 2007), the contact development that is reported on most frequently is the borrowing of consonants (see Matras 2007b: 36–40). This follows from the fact that new phonemes are more frequently introduced within loanwords. Since the inventory of consonants in any given phonological system is usually larger than the inventory of vowels, two languages in contact are more likely to differ in their consonant systems than in their vowel systems. Loanwords are therefore more likely to introduce more new consonants than new vowels. This finding does not, therefore, contradict the results of the Romani sample. Moreover, the volatility of prosody is confirmed by the cross-linguistic sample too. Several pairs of languages are reported to share prosodic features with their current contact languages: Domari, Nahuatl, Rapanui, Rumungro, and Indonesian, and to some extent at least also Kurdish, some varieties of Yiddish, Hup, and Kildin Saami. This is more than can be said about any other area of phonology, where we find borrowings and convergent tendencies, but no tendency toward wholesale convergence (with the exception of Jaminjung and Kriol, which largely share their phonological systems; Schultze-Berndt 2007).

Evidence of the borrowability of prosody is confirmed in other studies, too. Burridge (2006: 192) reports that the most obvious influence of Pennsylvannia German on the English of Canadian Mennonites occurs at the prosodic level, with a characteristic intonation that is transferred into English. Matisoff (2001: 320–323) points out the high diffusability of tones and other prosodic features in Southeast Asia. Non-tonal languages such as Vietnamese, Tai, and Hming-Men have borrowed tones along with lexical items from Chinese, but tones are also borrowed from a more prestigious language in languages that already have tones, as in the case of Tai and Chinese borrowings into Mien. Finally, tonal languages assign tones to borrowings from toneless languages. The argument in favour of a contact-induced development is strengthened by the fact that it is difficult to reconstruct shared tones for the respective proto-languages. Matisoff attributes the diffusibility of prosodic features partly to what he calls the 'perceptual salience' of the rise and fall of the human voice. He points out that intonation is the first linguistic feature that babies seem to acquire from the language surrounding them.

The high susceptibility of prosody to contact might be a result of two inter-connected factors. The first is the peripheral role that prosody has in conveying meaning and the fact that it is prototypically a form of expression of emotive modes, operating at the level of the speech act and the utterance, rather than the word level. This allows speakers to mentally disconnect prosody more easily from the matter or shape of words associated with a particular language, making it prone to change and modification in contact situations. The second factor may be the proven neurophysiological separation between prosody and other aspects of speech production (cf. Schirmer *et al.* 2001, Friederici 2001; see also McMahon 2005), making prosody more difficult to control. Both factors may contribute to the fact that foreign 'accents' are most persistent in the area of prosody.

9   Converging structures: pattern replication

9.1   Defining pattern replication

9.1.1   Distinguishing matter and pattern replication

Models of bilingual speech production have tended to focus on the modes and conditions for selection of lemmas or word-forms from the lexicon (cf. Green 1998, Clyne 2003, Paradis 2004, Ijalba, Obler, and Chengappa 2004, Costa 2004, Kroll and Dussias 2004). Less attention is given to other aspects of language organisation, which we shall refer to as patterns or constructions (for the latter see Goldberg 1995, Croft 2001). We must assume that constructions also have a mental representation of some kind, that they are equally part of a 'task schema' that is assembled in order to pursue a communicative goal, and so that they are equally subject to the control of a selection and inhibition mechanism.

In Chapter 2 we noted the child's effort to comply with the selection of context-appropriate word-forms while at the same time allowing himself some flexibility in recruiting patterns from within his entire linguistic repertoire. While word-forms were in such instances subjected to tight selection and inhibition control, patterns and constructions appeared to be selected with the aim of maximising communicative efficiency. This suggests two possible paths, which are not incompatible with one another: the first is to select the construction which, due to its use on a routine basis, is most easily associated with the targeted task-schema; in other words, it is the construction that 'comes to mind' first. The second is to select the construction that appears most appropriate since it is highly specialised for the needs of the particular task-schema. Recall Ben's attempt to re-structure, during Hebrew discourse, a specialised form of address (based on the German politeness form) that had been used in a particular position in the role-play (Chapter 2, Example 17).

The liberty to freely scan the entire repertoire for an appropriate, task-effective construction, while at the same time limiting the selection of word-forms to those that are context-appropriate, suggests that the control and inhibition mechanism can treat word-forms and patterns/construction in a differentiated manner. In the concluding remarks to Chapter 8 we mentioned societies that have strict norms on the avoidance of word-form replication. Such societies are not at all confined to remote and isolated, tight-knit communities such as those described by Aikhen-vald (2002) and Epps (2007) for the Amazon, by Ross (1996, 2001) for Melanesia, or by O'Neil (2007) for northern California. Many modern nation-states maintain institutions such as the French, the Turkish, or the Hebrew language academies, which are entrusted with counteracting the infiltration of foreign word-forms, sometimes by banning their use in the public domain, and usually by promoting nativised alternatives (see Zuckermann 2003 for a discussion of Hebrew nativi-sation strategies of lexical items). It appears that word-forms are more easily identified with the set of interaction contexts in which they are normally used. They are more easily controlled and selected, and their selection is used to flag the social cohesion of a group and adherence of the individual speaker to that group.

When discussing pattern replication we are talking about the differentiated selection of word-forms and constructions. Under construction I understand a mental procedure that involves a meaningful combination of items at various possible levels: the association of a word-form with its semantic meaning, the mode of combining word-forms and the retrieval of new meanings from such combinations, and the ordering of word-forms. Each of these is volatile: thus in the expression *hurry up*, the meaning of *up* is altered as a result of the combination. In some languages, the presence or absence of a definite article accompanying the word is significant to the meaning of that word. In others, the presence or absence of a copula form in present-tense existential predications can be meaningful. In many languages, the alternation between subject-verb and verb-subject order conveys a semantic opposition (see Matras and Sasse 1995). All of these examples show constructions that could be replicated from one interaction context into another, and are thus, in principle, 'borrowable'.

Silva-Corvalán (1994: 133, 168ff.) regards the transfer of features from one language into another as a strategy that bilinguals use in order to cope with the need to communicate in two different linguistic systems. She follows Weinreich (1953) in attributing language maintenance coupled with a step-by-step progres-sion of change, to speakers' sense of 'language loyalty', i.e. to a state of mind that attributes a high value to the language. In this context, we might view the replication of patterns as a kind of compromise strategy that allows speakers to continue and flag language loyalty through a more or less rigid choice of word-forms and at the same time to reduce the load on the selection and inhibition mechanism by allowing patterns to converge, thus maximising the efficiency of speech production in a bilingual situation.

To be sure, constraints on the distribution of matter and pattern replication are not just social; structural factors may play a role too. As we shall see, the replication of patterns depends on the ability to match a new pattern to available word-forms. Speakers of Sinti Romani for instance replicate the German lexicalised aktionsart pattern as found in constructions such as *ich mache auf* 'I open', literally 'I make up'. They do so by identifying pivotal features of the pattern and by matching them with corresponding inherited word-forms in Sinti.

The result is the Sinti verb *kerau pre* 'I open', based on a composition of *kerau* 'I make' with the local relations expression *pre* 'up, above'. A similar replication of the German *ich mache zu* 'I shut', literally 'I make to', is impeded, however, by the absence of an isolated word-form with a dative-allative meaning (Sinti uses synthetic suffixes to indicate dative-allative case). As a result, German *zu* is borrowed directly, and we get *kerau zu* (or rather: *cu*), 'I shut'.[1] There is thus an interplay and mutual conditioning of matter and pattern replication.

There also appear to be general preferences in applying matter or pattern replication to particular categories. As we shall see later on in the present chapter, some domains of structure that are rarely affected by matter replication, such as definite and indefinite articles, or tense-aspect and case inflection, show many cases of pattern replication. Naturally, syntagmatic formations are open exclusively to pattern replication.

The distinction between matter and pattern replication is well established in the literature on language contact (cf. Matras and Sakel 2007a, Sakel and Matras 2008): Haugen (1950) speaks of the 'importation' of form versus 'calque', a term which has become widespread to denote pattern replication especially at the level of single-word semantics, but also at the phrase and clause level. Gołąb (1956, 1959) separates 'substance' from 'form', while Johanson (2002) speaks of 'global copies' and 'selective copies'. Weinreich (1953) too describes two distinct modes of interference. The first involves borrowing from a 'source' language to a 'recipient' language and is compatible with our notion of matter replication. The second is described by Weinreich as a change in the function of morphemes which takes place in a 'replica language', inspired by a 'model language'. The latter were referred to by Weinreich as 'cases of convergent development' (see also Rozencvejg 1976). The term 'convergence' has since been used almost synonymously with 'calque' and 'pattern transfer' (see Heath 1984: 367). Geographical zones in which pattern transfers are widespread among a group of languages have been referred to since Weinreich (1958) as 'convergence areas', an alternative to the more rigid-sounding notion of a 'linguistic league' (*jazykovoj soyuz* or *Sprachbund*) advocated by Trubetzkoy (1928), and later simply as 'linguistic areas' (see Campbell 2006).

Silva-Corvalán (1994: 4–5) defines 'convergence' as the general acquisition of structural similarities between languages. Focusing on a case of language attrition (the use of Spanish by second- and third-generation immigrants in Los Angeles), where a growing number of native speakers are abandoning the language in a growing number of interaction domains, she notes an internal tendency toward simplification, overgeneralisation, and category reduction. This tendency is accelerated by bilingualism, but does not necessarily involve direct replication of the structures of a source language.[2] Myers-Scotton (2006: 271) attributes a more definite role to bilingualism in stating that 'convergence... has all the surface-level forms from one language, but with part of the abstract lexical structure that underlies the surface-level patterns coming from another language' (cf. also Bolonyai 1998).

Pattern-sharing among languages is recognised as a common and characteristic feature of second-language acquisition. Substrate influence is often acknowledged in the formation of pidgins and creoles, and is sometimes even seen as the principal factor that is responsible for their grammatical structures (see Lefebvre 1993, 1998). Thomason (2000: 323; 2001) takes for granted that the present-day similarities among languages of the Ethiopian Highlands or South Asia go back to large-scale, unidirectional bilingualism and what is referred to as 'shift-induced interference', that is, a population of speakers abandoning their ancestral language and shifting to a new, superstrate language into which they transfer features of the old language (e.g. Dravidian speakers shifting to Indo-Aryan languages in South Asia).

Shift-induced interference is not, however, the only source of pattern replication. Numerous authors point to the sharing of patterns among languages that have co-existed in situations of prolonged bilingualism, either uni-directional or reciprocal. Ross (1996, 2001) describes situations of almost wholesale pattern replication (i.e. comprising all relevant domains of grammar) in Melanesia, referring to the phenomenon as 'metatypy'. As defined by Ross in the particular case-studies, metatypy is the product of orientation toward a prestigious outsider language by fluent native speakers, in a situation that is constrained by attitudes that disfavour the replication of concrete, easily identifiable word-forms from an outside language. Aikhenvald (2002: 13) attributes the replication of patterns to multilingual diffusion in linguistic areas, while predicting that one-to-one language contact will involve the levelling of structures (and if accompanied by diglossia, also a considerable influx of loanwords). Numerous examples of the import of patterns from a prestigious language are attested in smaller or 'insider'-languages, in situations of diglossic, unidirectional bilingualism such as Yiddish, Macedonian Turkish, Romani, Aramaic, and Khuzistani Arabic, none of which have attracted any significant population of second-language learners.

Thus, it does not seem possible to map pattern replication exclusively to any specific type of multilingualism or language contact situation. What conditions pattern replication appears to be situated at a much more specific, micro-level of discourse strategies, which are governed by constraints relating to structure, communication goal, and language attitudes. For some structures, such as the organisation of information at the clause level through word order and phrase order, pattern replication is the only option through which to syncretise the mental planning operations behind the production of utterances. For other structures, like the syncretisation of case-representation or tense-aspect arrangements, there is a clear preference for pattern over matter replication, irrespective of type of contact. Apart from structure, language loyalty may block matter replication and favour the exclusive transfer of patterns as a means of simplifying control over the bilingual linguistic repertoire. On the other hand limited opportunity or motivation to immerse fully in a second language may result in consistent replication of patterns from the native language while using correct word-forms of the target language.

9.1.2   Convergence and grammaticalisation

Pattern replication is characterised as a change to an inherited structure of the 'replica' language, inspired by a structure of the 'model' language. This normally involves a change in the meaning and possibly also in distribution. This recognition prompted the search for an appropriate theoretical framework with which to describe the process – one that would combine aspects of the study of contact with the analytical tools that are available to describe 'language-internal' change in meaning and distribution of structural material. Givón (1982) was one of the first to apply the notion of *grammaticalisation* to the processes of functionalisation of lexical material to mark grammatical relations in Creole languages. Combining the grammaticalisation notion with the recognition of substrate influence, Keesing (1991) argued that the expansion of complex grammar in Melanesian Pidgin through internal processes of grammaticalisation is accelerated by mapping grammatical meanings of the substrate language onto word-forms of the superstrate or lexifier language. With reference to Southeast Asia, Bisang (1996, 1998) similarly interprets language contact as one of the key determiners of specific grammaticalisation pathways and so of the emergence of new constructions. Contact is thus regarded as a trigger for grammaticalisation processes (cf. Hopper and Traugott 1993: 63–93).

The question arises what motivates speakers to replicate patterns, and how this motivation leads to the specific pathway of contact-induced gramamticalisation processes. In a situation of intense bilingualism coupled with a loyalty toward language maintenance, it seems advantageous for bilingual speakers to be able to syncretise the mental planning operations applied while interacting in each of the languages. In order to do this, they exploit the meanings and functions of inherited structures and enhance them to carry out organisation procedures that are replicated from the model language. The adoption of Balkan syntactic features in Romani and Balkan varieties of Turkish proceeds in such a way, with interrogatives and correlatives taking on the functions of subordinators (Matras 1994: 67, 241–243, Matras 1996b, 1998b, 2004a).

Haase (1991) notes that bilingual speakers are motivated to avail themselves of the expressive means of both languages, and thus wish to have equal constructions at their disposal in each language; but they can only do so if they are able to identify parallel items in the two languages as translation equivalents. This means that the grammaticalisation process begins by matching lexemes to one another and adapting the range of meanings expressed by the lexemes of the replica language to those expressed by the parallel lexemes in the model. The basis for the matching procedure is the polysemy of the word in the model (cf. Nau 1995), which represents both a concrete and a more abstract meaning. A good example is the German word *auf*, which has the concrete lexical meaning 'up, on', but in combination with the verb *machen* 'to make' takes on a non-compositional modification function that cannot be directly derived from its concrete semantics (compare with English *give up*). Speakers will inevitably direct their attention to the more concrete meaning when searching for a match in the replica (as in Sinti *pre* 'up, on, above'). The match will then lead to the emergence of a more abstract meaning. This proceeds along a hierarchical scale that resembles the unidirectionality path of language-internal grammaticalisation from more concrete, lexical meanings to the more abstract, grammatical functions (cf. Nau 1995: 175–176, Haase 1991: 169).

Heine and Kuteva (2003, 2005) list several typical grammaticalisation tracks that can be triggered by contact: the expansion of a construction from minor to major use patterns including an increase in frequency, an extension of its distributional context, extension across categories, and the emergence of new categories (Heine and Kuteva 2005: 44–75). The general unidirectionality of grammaticalisation is manifested in these types of change through the rise of novel meanings, semantic bleaching or blurring of existing meanings as concrete lexemes take on more abstract grammatical functions, loss of morpho-syntactic properties that are associated primarily with the content-lexeme (as in the case of nouns that are grammaticalised into location expressions, or interrogatives that are used as subordinators), and possibly also through an erosion or reduction of phonetic substance.

Contact-induced gramamticalisation is triggered according to Heine and Kuteva (2005) by the need to replicate a function that exists in the model language. Speakers of the replica language map that function onto an existing lexeme in the replica, resulting in its functional extension along a path of grammaticalisation. Alongside canonical contact-induced grammaticalisation, Heine and Kuteva identify two further sub-types: the first is referred to as 'replica grammaticalisation' and covers those instances where the original grammaticalisation path behind the structure in the model is conceptually accessible to speakers, and is replicated in the replica language (2003: 539, 2005: 92). A possible candidate is the grammaticalisation of the Macedonian Turkish relativiser (Matras 1998b, 2004a) *ne* based on the original interrogative meaning 'what', which follows the same path as the model relativiser *što* (both 'what' and a relativiser) in Macedonian.

The second type is referred to as 'polysemy copying' (Heine and Kuteva 2005: 100–103). This entails a shift in meaning inspired by a model language, but without a change in the grammatical status of the item in question. Polysemy-copying therefore does not involve strict grammaticalisation, and tends to be found primarily in the extension of lexical meanings or what Haugen (1953) had called 'loan translations'. A possible candidate would be Modern Hebrew *kélev kar* based on (northern) German *kalter Hund* 'a layered cake based on biscuits and chocolate fudge', literally 'cold dog', or equally the Québec-French translation of English *hotdog* as *chien chaud*.

The boundaries among sub-types should not be seen as rigid, however, but rather as a continuum of different options. The principal gain in viewing pattern replication from the perspective of gramamticalisation theory is the realisation that contact-induced change is not arbitrary, but tends to follow certain predictable pathways. These pathways are a product of conceptualisation and categorisation strategies that guide speakers into making certain choices and creatively exploiting their existing inventory of linguistic structures to enable new procedures of language processing and event representation.

9.1.3   Pattern replication and creative pivot-matching

At least two issues arise in conjunction with pattern replication that are not directly addressed within the grammaticalisation model. The first concerns exceptions to the unidirectionality hypothesis. The hypothesis itself is not unique to contact-induced grammaticalisation, but carried-over from general grammaticalisation theory.[3] While it makes sense that speakers will seek to exploit the potential of more concrete meaning in order to express abstract functions, a model must also account for the rare exceptions. German and Italian, for instance, share the use of anaphoric expressions to represent deictic meaning (*Sie* in German, *Lei* in Italian). Some contact situations may lead to the loss of categories, as in the loss of the definite article in Baltic-Northeastern Romani, or the loss of gender in some dialects of Yiddish.

A further issue with the grammaticalisaiton model is its focus on gradual development. There is no doubt that some contact-induced changes in the distribution and meaning of internal structures only emerge gradually. Silva-Corvalán (1994: 134ff., 166–167) describes contact-induced changes in syntax and morpho-syntax as a gradual process of step-by-step modification of contexts of use of a construction, beginning at the discourse-pragmatic level. The syntactic permeability of grammar is thus first evident in nonce syntactic borrowing, i.e. the occasional use of a construction with a new meaning or in a new environment. There is also no doubt that the propagation of innovations throughout a speech community is a gradual development. Nonetheless, the occurrence of what Silva-Corvalán describes as 'nonce syntactic borrowing' itself demands an explanation and accommodation within a model of pattern replication. The examples of creative use of morpho-syntax by second-language learners (Chapter 4) and of Ben's creative transfer of patterns (Chapter 2) show that speakers are able to come up with new constructions, not just new meanings and usage contexts, spontaneously. Whether or not such constructions will lead to change is a separate issue, and one that has to do with the social parameters of the bilingual community and not with the actual shape or meaning of the constructions themselves. It is equally difficult to see how a construction such as the Macedonian Turkish postposed, finite relative clauses *adam ne gel-di* 'the man who [what] came' could have evolved only gradually as an alternative to the Turkish gerundial construction *gel-en adam* literally 'the coming man'. The point is that speakers' creativity itself must be accounted for in the model, not just society's acceptance of it.

Following from an earlier model presented in Matras (1998d), Matras and Sakel (2007a) propose a scheme according to which pattern replication is firstly selected after the elimination, due to various factors, of matter replication, and is then translated into a procedure by which pivotal features of the model construction are identified and replicated in the replica language. This may or may not entail the grammaticalisation of elements in the replica language, and the process may be either gradual or abrupt. The model is thus able to accommodate a variety of cases which on the grammaticalisation model would have to be treated as exceptions. The scheme presented in the following is a further elaboration on the 'pivot-matching' model discussed in earlier work.

Both the grammaticalisation and the pivot-matching model agree that speakers map abstract functions from one language onto word-forms of another. But how does this actual mapping proceed? The speaker aims at pursuing a particular communicative goal, embedded into a particular communicative context. This is transposed into a concrete linguistic task for which an appropriate task-schema (see Green 1998) needs to be assembled from within the linguistic repertoire. Scanning through the entire repertoire, the speaker identifies a construction that would serve this particular task most effectively (Figure 9.1). This might be a routine task-schema that has recently been implemented and so its effectiveness lies in the speaker's ability to select it rapidly. Or it might be a construction that captures the more subtle, perhaps inter-personal aspects that are associated with the task, and it is therefore preferred over one that is more general and therefore perhaps less effective. In any event, a search is underway for the optimal retrieval procedure of a suitable construction. Now, the special feature of our model is that we assume at this stage that the speaker has the entire repertoire at their disposal and does not 'block' or 'de-activate' any particular language 'system'.

However, the speaker is of course conscious of the need to meet certain expectations of the interlocutor. This too is part of the effectiveness of the task-schema: a linguistic structure will not be effective if it is not understood by the interlocutor, or if it is understood but rejected by the interlocutor as contextually inappropriate, or if it is understood by the bilingual interlocutor and accepted but interpreted as a marked, stylistic choice (which might then be interpreted as irony, anger, rejection of cooperation, and so on; cf. Myers-Scotton 1993b, 2002a, Li Wei 2005). All this makes the choice of context-appropriate word-forms essential to the success of the linguistic task-schema.

Let us assume, however, that the optimal construction that was identified does not have an established structural representation that is appropriate for the present context, i.e. it is mentally available to the speaker but is not part of the routine of verbalisation in the present interaction context (or context type). The speaker then tries to optimise communicative efficiency by combining the selected construction with context-appropriate word-forms (as portrayed in the grey-shaded area in Figure 9.1). In order to do this, the speaker re-assembles the construction by isolating its pivotal features. There can be any number of such features. For example the English construction *I am cold* might be

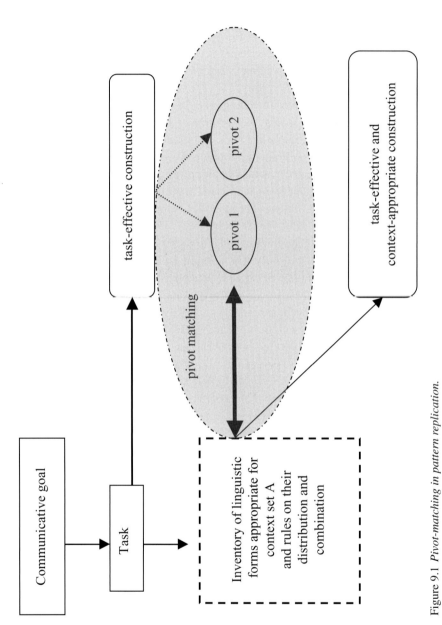

Figure 9.1 *Pivot-matching in pattern replication.*

interpreted as having a simplex pivot consisting merely of an existential construction that carries a specific semantic content.

The construction pivot is then matched to the inventory of context-appropriate forms. This inventory includes not just word-forms, but also their formation and combination rules. When Ben makes use of the English construction in German- and Hebrew-speaking contexts (Chapter 2, Example 15), for example, he accommodates by choosing appropriate word-forms and morpho-syntactic combination rules. The outcome in German is *ich bin kalt*, which very closely matches the original template, but in German differs in meaning (indicating a physical attribute rather than an experienced feeling). Mapped onto Hebrew, different formation rules apply to the existential construction: it consists in the present tense of a subject followed immediately by the non-verbal predicate which agrees with the head in gender and number. The outcome is thus *ani kar*. As a result of the application of pivot-matching, pattern replication does not necessarily lead to isomorphism, but rather to a one-to-one match between constructions or even just construction types. This kind of process is spontaneous, not gradual. The speaker is being creative in selecting and putting together building blocks that will ensure maximum communicative effectiveness in carrying out the task and accomplishing the communicative goal.

This creativity has the potential of increasing and enriching the inventory of forms and structures that speakers have at their disposal in a given set of interaction contexts. But there is also the risk of misjudging the acceptability of new constructions. Second-language learners and less experienced, less mature, or less proficient bilinguals may sometimes make selections based on the misguided expectation that they will be successful. They may or may not convey the intended meaning; and they may also trigger ridicule and alienation. Interlocutors' reactions are therefore crucial to the chances of a new construction to be genuinely effective, to be accepted, to be used by the speaker again, and to be replicated by others and so eventually lead to language change.

9.2   The distribution of pattern replication

From our discussion in the previous section it is clear that pattern replication is in general a much more volatile and opportunistic strategy than matter replication. While the latter is driven primarily by a need to participate in and communicate about a range of social activities and to reduce the processing load around certain types of operations, pattern replication derives from an individual speaker's scan for an optimal construction through which to communicate local meanings. The initiation and successful propagation of new, replicated constructions therefore seems to take on a much more erratic course. As a result, it appears rather difficult to postulate general hierarchies of convergence.

Nonetheless, some authors have suggested the following progression of convergence (cf. Stolz and Stolz 1996, Ross 2001):

(1)   discourse > clause > phrase > word

By contrast, Romaine's (1995: 64) hierarchy appears to suggest almost the exact
opposite:

(2)   lexical items > morphology (derivational > inflectional) > syntax

Silva-Corvalán (1994) approaches the issue of convergence from the perspective of simplification in a situation of ongoing language attrition (reduction of
communicative functions), and finds that simplification begins at the level of
morphology, continues to the level of the lexicon, and then finally reaches the
level of syntax. This is different from both (1) and (2) and appears to show that
simplification due to language attrition does not take on the same structural progression as convergence in situations of language maintenance. Heine (2005a)
for example emphasises how the syntax of a language can be deeply affected by
contact.

   If our assumption is true that pattern replication is often a result of speakers'
experiments and their chances of successful propagation, then we would indeed
expect an erratic rather than orderly pattern of diffusion of convergent structures.
Nonetheless, the overall message that can be derived from the observed hierarchies of matter replication (Chapter 6) suggests that bilingual speakers face
particularly strong pressures in coping with distinct procedures of organising and
managing the discourse and the arrangement of propositions in discourse. On
this basis, we might expect the pressure to converge the inventory of constructions in the repertoire to begin with those that organise complex propositions. We
would expect the structure of complement clauses, adverbial clauses, and relative
clauses and embeddings as well as the structure of coordination to be targeted
first in the process of convergence, to by followed by convergence at the phrase
and word level. This would mean that any two languages that share a pattern
of organisation of nominal case marking, for example, or aspectual or person
marking on the verb, as a result of contact, might also be expected to share their
patterns of complementation, relative clause formation, and so on.

   Such a hierarchy can, it appears, be postulated for most linguistic areas (see
below); it is extremely rare to find an area that is characterised by a particular pattern of word-level morphology, but does not share patterns of clause-combining.
Some hierarchies may also appear within sub-domains of structure. There is some
evidence to support the generalisaton that word order change begins at the level
of the nominal phrase, where it firstly targets more loosely combined elements
in the possessive construction, then proceeds to other attributes (which behave
more generically as attributes, such as lexical adjectives and determiners); it will
only then proceed to the verb phrase, where existential predications are the most
prone to convergence, followed by the lexical predication (see Matras 2007b).

The documented history or at least the inferable history (on the basis of writ-ten documentation of closely related languages) of several languages in contact supports this scenario: Balkan Turkish (also the European Turkic languages Gagauz and Karaim) have adjusted their clause-combining strategies to those of the surrounding European languages but have generally retained their agglutina-tive morphology. Verb-final word order and postpositions are retained in Balkan Turkish, but the possessive construction is being re-structured and the copula in existential constructions appears in non-final position. In Romani, the change to verb-medial order (from a reconstructed Indo-Aryan verb-final pattern) as a result of contact with Byzantine Greek comes along with the re-organisation of all subordinate clause types, the shift from postpositions to prepositions, and the introduction of pre-posed definite articles, though the genitive-possessive con-struction remains distinct (GEN-head) due to the specific morphological agree-ment marking.[4] Aramaic from the regions of southeastern Turkey and northern Iraq has complementation and other clause-combining strategies that are almost identical to those of Kurmanji, a similar arrangement of constituents in possessive constructions, and a (relatively young) analytical copula, but has preserved its verb-medial word order.

9.2.1   Lexical semantics

Pattern replication in the area of lexical semantics (lexical 'calquing', or 'loan translation') appears to proceed independently of pattern replication at the grammatical level, partly as a result of speech communities' conscious and organised efforts to nativise lexicon. The creation of neologisms based on loan-translations or similarly sounding words is central to many language planning strategies, and institutions such as language academies and language committees are often entrusted with the task of creating such lexemes.

Early twentieth-century German introduced terms like *Fernsehen*, a literal calque on 'television' (lit. 'remote-vision'), which is still in use, and *Fern-sprecher* 'telephone' (lit. 'remote-speaker'), which has fallen out of use and has been replaced by *Telefon*. Turkish loan-translates 'computer' as *bilgi-sayar*, lit. 'information-counter', while the word for 'school' draws on the inherited root for 'to read', *oku-*, adding a pseudo-derivational ending *-l* to form *okul* 'school', resembling both French *école* and English *school* in its sound and shape. Hebrew neologisms that exploit both inherited word-forms and sound-similarities include *mexonít* 'car' (cf. Russian and Yiddish *mašína*, German *Machine*, etc., and the Hebrew root *k/x.w.n*), *ge/ge'é* 'gay' (Hebrew *g.ʔ* 'proud'), and *tso'aní* 'Gypsy' (Russian *cigan*, Yiddish *tsigejner*; Biblical Hebrew *ts.ʕ.n* 'drift, roam', but also *tsoʕan* 'Egypt', coupled with the tradition of ʕ-g alternation, cf. Hebrew *ʕaza* 'Gaza', etc.) (cf. Zuckermann 2003, who refers to such cases as 'Phono-Semantic Matches').[5]

In terms of our model of pivot-matching, both phonological similarities and polysemy might trigger an association between the model and the target item in the replica language. A frequent case of lexical pattern replication in Ben's vocabulary is the use of Hebrew *yodéa* 'knows', occasionally also of German *wissen* 'to know', with respect to acquaintance with persons, as in *atá yodéa otó?* 'do you know him?', Hebrew *atá makír otó?*, based on the scope of usage of English *know*. 'Semantic scope' captures the difference between the English and Hebrew verbs more appropriately than the reference to 'polysemy' with respect to English *know*, and it is this scope of meanings that is replicated, drawing on the lexeme *know* as a pivot and on its default, less specialised and more frequent translation equivalent as a pivot-match.

Consider an example from a young English–German bilingual with English as a dominant language:

(3)   a. Bilingual child's German:
Er ist grösser denn   mir.
he is bigger PART me.DAT
'He is bigger than me'

b. German:
Er ist grösser als   ich.
he is bigger than I.NOM
'He is bigger than me'

Here we are dealing essentially with a combined morpho-phonological pivot. The selection of dative *mir* 'to-me' in German is triggered by the English model containing an oblique form of the 1SG in *m-*. The relevance of phonology becomes even clearer in the selection of German *denn* as a match for English *than*. The German form serves as a modal particle, and in some varieties also a temporal particle (*denn* 'then', in competition with Standard German *dann*), but it does not introduce the object of comparison.[6] Its selection to match the English pivot is in part due to its function as an uninflected, potentially multi-purpose particle, and due to its sound similarity to English *than*.[7]

Silva-Corvalán (1994: 171) reports on the extension of word-meanings in words that resemble English words in their surface forms, as in Spanish *parientes* 'relatives' acquiring the meaning 'parents', and *papel* 'paper' acquiring the meaning '(news)paper'. Further types of lexical extensions include what Silva-Corvalán (1994: 184) refers to as 'relexification', which is in fact the insertion of Spanish word-forms into English syntactic blueprints: *eso es por qué nosotros fuimos p'allá* 'that is why we went there', Spanish *por eso (es qué) nosotros fuimos p'allá*. Situated at the intersection of lexicon and grammar are changes in the combinations governed by lexemes (Silva-Corvalán 1994: 175–177): *sabía como hablar español* 'he knew how to speak Spanish', Spanish *sabía hablar español*.

Ross (2001: 145) discusses convergence in the collocational domain among Takia (Austronesian) and Waskia (Papuan) in Melanesia. In both languages, the expression 'the palm of my hand' has the literal meaning of 'my hand's liver':

(4)   a. Takia:
           bani-g   ate-n
           hand-1SG   liver-3SG

        b. Waskia:
           a-gitiŋ   gomaŋ
           1SG-hand   3SG.liver

The expression 'I am waiting' literally means 'I am putting my eye':

(5)   a. Takia:
           mala-g   ŋi-ga
           eye-1SG   1SG-put

        b. Waskia:
           motam   bete-so
           1SG-eye   put-1SG

Note that the expressions are not isomorphic; there is no one-to-one correspondence between the morphemes of the equivalent lexemes. Rather, each is created within the rules of its own self-contained system, but they share a general design. It is for this reason that it is justified to speak of *patterns* that share a *pivot* – in this case the specific combination of the two lexical entities 'eye' and 'put'.

Collocations attract pattern replication because they do not literally mean what the combination of words render. Instead, the combination has a metonymic and sometimes even a metaphorical function. Collocations are thus hard to translate and their metonymical or metaphorical effects are often unique and difficult to copy through existing word-forms without resorting to creative pattern replication. In the Lower Volta Basin (Ameka 2006: 137–139), several different languages, including Ewe, Likpe, Akan, Nawuri, and Ga, lexicalise concepts in similar ways. The verb 'to believe' is formed by combining the lexical roots for 'to receive' and either 'to eat' or 'to hear', while 'to expect' is a combination of 'see/look' and 'way'.

Lexical items that are perceived as matches may undergo similar grammaticalisation processes in contact situations. Heine and Miyashita (2008) show how contact has supported the diffusion across neighbouring (related and unrelated) European languages of a grammaticalisation pattern of the verb 'threaten' as an expression of epistemic modality (indicating an imminent, undesired event). Enfield (2003) devotes a book-length study to the emergence of shared meanings and functions based on a lexeme with the general basic meaning ACQUIRE in various languages of Southeast Asia, including Lao, Khmer, Vietnamese, Hdmong, and Kmhmu Cwang, and others, belonging to several different language families (Mon-Khmer, Tai-Kadai, Sinnitic, Tibeto-Burman). Enfield argues that, in addition to similar language-internal grammaticalisation paths, diffusion or copying from one language to another at various historical stages in the development of the lexeme has promoted a shared cluster of functions that tend to be occupied by the respective ACQUIRE lexeme of each language (Lao *daj*, Khmer *baan*,

Hmong *tau*, Vietnamese *đu'ọ'c*, and so on), and which include 'come to have', 'succeed', 'can', 'know and have ability for'.

Pattern replication may also affect the level of individual grammatical function words. Numeral systems are a good example: Kurmanji replicates Turkish in replacing single-lexeme numerals for numerals above ten with combination lexemes ('ten-and-one'). Vigesimal systems are shared by Basque and French, while Indonesian adopts a Javanese tag-lexeme indicating 'teens' and re-organises its earlier system of numeral juxtaposition above ten accordingly (Tadmor 2007). The distribution of inclusive and exclusive pronouns often follows areal patterns; the Tok Pisin forms *yumi* 'we (inclusive)' and *mipela* 'we (exclusive)' are a favourite example of substrate-based calquing in this domain. In South Asia, the distinction between inclusive and exclusive pronouns, of non-Indo-Aryan origin, has spread to Indo-Aryan languages such as Marathi, Gujarati, and Rajasthani (Masica 2001). Imbabura Quechua is reported to have developed a polite form of the second-person pronoun *kikin* on the basis of Spanish *Usted*, and in some heavily Hispanicized varieties of Guarani the inherited distinction between inclusive and exclusive is dissolved (Rendón 2007a, 2007b).

9.2.2   Clause-level typology

As predicted above, numerous examples can be found of pattern replication at the level of clause combining. Kurmanji and Neo-Aramaic of Zakho (northern Iraq), for instance, share their pattern of modal and factual complementation. In both languages the main clause appears first, followed immediately by the complement verb in the subjunctive, which is then followed by the indirect object:

(6)   a. Kurmanji:
            ez di-xwaz-im   her-im   mal-ê
            I PROG-want-1SG go.SUBJ-1SG home-OBL

         b. Neo-Aramaic (Zakho):
            ana g-ib-ən   āz-in   l-bēsa
            I   PROG-want-1SG   go.SUBJ-1SG to-home
            'I want to go home'

Note once again the absence of absolute isomorphism: the formation of the indirect object differs, with Kurmanji using an oblique case while Aramaic relies on a preposition. But the overall layout, the positioning of constituents, and the use of cross-referencing devices – person-agreement markers, dependent mood (subjunctive), overt pronouns – is similar.

Convergence of modal complementation structures is one of the well-known features of the Balkan languages, often referred to as 'infinitive-reduction' or 'infinitive loss' (cf. Joseph 1983). Two lesser-known languages of the Balkans – the dialect of Turkish spoken in the Balkans, and Romani – also undergo similar changes and adapt to the prevailing pattern of finite marking of the modal complement clause (cf. Matras 1998b):

(7)   a. Macedonian Turkish:
          (o) istiyor   git-sin
          3SG want.3SG go-3SG.SUBJ

       b. Macedonian:
          toj   sak-a   da   id-e
          3SG want-3SG COMP go-3SG

       c. Romani (Balkans):
          ov   mang-el-a   te   dža-l
          3SG.M want-3SG-IND COMP go-3SG.SUBJ

       d. Greek:
          (aftós) thel-i   na   pa-i
          3SG   want-3SG COMP go-3SG
          'He wants to go'

The relevant developments in each of the two languages, Turkish and Romani, will have occurred at different places, in different times, and in all likelihood in contact with different languages. Note that here too isomorphism is only partial. Turkish arrived in the region with the Ottoman conquests from the late fourteenth century onwards, with continued settlement throughout the Ottoman period, much of it directly from Anatolia (cf. Friedman 2003, Tufan 2008). Different patterns of contact-induced grammaticalisation in the individual Turkish dialects of the Balkans indicate that convergence was to some extent at least a product of orientation toward the local contact languages, no doubt reinforced by contacts among the Turkish-speaking populations within the regions, and by migrations. The model for Macedonian Turkish is thus likely to have been Macedonian, as well as Albanian.

Although finite subordination based on a Persian model was common in written Ottoman Turkish,[8] Turkish generally relies on nominal infinitives in canonical modal complements. In Macedonian Turkish the infinitive construction disappears almost entirely, and in its place an existing finite option is generalised (see discussion in Matras 1998b, 2004a). Note that while the other languages rely on a non-factual complementiser to introduce the modal complement (Macedonian *da*, Greek *na*, Romani *te*; other Balkan languages have comparable forms), Turkish makes use of its rich inflectional potential and assigns the historical optative mood in 3SG *-sin* to the subjunctive position. The embedded verb is thus indicated in a sufficiently different way from a factual indicative complement, and a semantically specialised complementiser becomes redundant. Thus, the pivotal functions of the construction – finite subordination, non-factual (non-indicative) marking of the complement verb – are replicated in an idiosyncratic way, exploiting inherited resources.

Romani arrived in the Byzantine Empire (Anatolia and westwards) in all likelihood around the tenth or eleventh century, and was in contact with Greek for several centuries before a dispersion of populations began, within the Balkans and beyond, in the late fourteenth century. While we have no historical documentation on pre-European Romani, it can be assumed that earlier forms of the language had, like other New Indo-Aryan languages, infinitives and other converbal clause-linking constructions. These are lost in Romani and instead finite complementation prevails. Romani grammaticalises an inherited correlative pronoun *ta* which assumes the function of a non-factual complementiser *te* (see Matras 1994).

Macedonian Turkish also undergoes a rather spectacular re-organisation of its relative and adverbial clause structure, losing Turkish nominal-participial and gerundial constructions of the type *gönder-diğ-i mektüp* 'the letter that he sent' ('send-PART-3SG letter') and replacing them with finite subordinated clauses, introduced by newly grammaticalised subordinators such as the relativiser *ne* (derived from the interrogative 'what') (see Matras 1998b, 2004a):

(8)   üç   yüz   mark para   al-ır-dı   bir mektup ne   gönder-ir-di
        three hundred mark money take-AOR-PAST one letter   REL send-AOR-PAST
        'He used to take three hundred marks for each letter that he sent'

A change in the opposite direction is documented by Dawkins (1916: 201) for the Anatolian Greek dialect of Silli. Modern Greek has a post-nominal, finite relative clause that is introduced by a general, uninflected relativiser: *to peðí pu íða* 'the boy that/whom I saw'. Turkish by contrast has, as we saw above, preposed participial-gerundial constructions that are inflected to mark the subject of the relative clause: *gör-düğ-üm çocuk* 'the boy that I saw' (lit. 'see-PART-1SG boy'). Note the absence of a definite article in Turkish. Silli Greek replicates the Turkish construction type by selecting pivotal functions: the entire relative clause is preposed, in attributive position, to the head. The head is determined by the relative clause itself, and so a definite article is absent. These are the two features that are shared with the Turkish construction. Note that Silli Greek retains the finite verb ('I saw'), and so there is no replication of patterns at the level of verb morphology. Note also that the Silli Greek relative clause continues to be introduced by a relativiser (albeit one that differs from Standard Modern Greek).

(9)   Silli Greek (Dawkins 1916: 201):
        kyat íra   perí
        which I-saw boy
        'The boy that I saw'

Convergence of clause combining strategies may thus take different structural directions. Heath (1978: 128–129) reports on convergence in the use of suffixes to indicate adverbial and relative clauses in the languages of Arnhem Land in northern Australia. In Ritharngu (Yuulungu family, Pama-Nyungan phylum) the suffix -*ŋu*, originally an adjectival suffix, is added to the verb in a finite clause which would otherwise be an ordinary main clause, to indicate adverbial clauses ('having gone, I returned') or relative clauses ('I who had gone, returned'): *wa:ni-na-ŋu* 'having gone'. In neighbouring Ngandi ('Proto-prefixing' phylum) there is similar use of the subordinating affix *-ga-*: *ṇi-ga-ṛiḍ-i* 'the one who went; having gone' (cf. *ṇi-ṛiḍ-i* 'he went').

Changes in word-order structure are usually assumed to be gradual, emerging via loss of pragmatic specialisation of secondary word order variants. Macedonian Turkish retains its SOV order, contrasting with the surrounding languages in the Balkans, but it does show convergence in the position of the copula in existential predications. While in Turkish the copula is enclitic, Macedonian Turkish places the non-verbal predicate after the copula (Matras and Tufan 2007, Tufan 2007):

(10)   Hised-ıl-mes   ki   vardır   sonbaar
        feel-PASS-NEG.AOR COMP exist.COP.3SG autumn
        'It does not feel like [= that there is] autumn'

(11)   Siz i-dı-nız   ev-de
        you COP-PAST-2PL house-LOC
        'You were at home'

The arrangement of existential predication may show even more radical changes than just the positioning of the copula. Neo-Aramaic in east Anatolia and northern Iraq has developed an enclitic present-tense copula, modelled on the enclitic copula of Kurdish, while earlier forms of the language (much like other present-day Semitic languages such as Arabic and Hebrew) did not have a present-tense existential verb. By contrast, Northeastern dialects of Romani in contact with Russian tend to lose the present-tense copula under the influence of the Russian non-verbal predication.

Changes in verbal predications seem to require either a very prolonged period of contact or very intense impact of the contact language and relative isolation of the replica language. German Romani (Sinti) has maintained most of the canonical word-order rules of Romani despite massive influence from German; at the level of word order it nevertheless replicates the German rule on verb–subject inversion when the first constituent position of the sentence is occupied by a third entity:

(12)   a. Sinti Romani:
           koj   his   mri   bibi
           DEIC was my.F aunt
        b. German:
           da   war meine Tante
           DEIC was my.F   aunt
           'My aunt was there'

Among the dialects of Romani, only the very isolated Zargari variety spoken in Iran shows a shift to verb-final word order, under the impact of both its close contact languages Azeri and Persian:

(13)   Zargari Romani (Baghbidi 2003: 139):
         mu   phrāl   madrasa dža-l-a
         my.M brother school   go-3SG-IND
         'My brother goes to school'

A similar development, in the very same region, affects the Neo-Aramaic dialect of Saqqez in Iranian Azerbaijan:

(14)   Saqqez Neo-Aramaic:
         tara-kē   plix-li
         door-DEF open.PAST-1SG
         'I opened the door'

9.2.3   Phrase-level typology

In Chapter 8 I mentioned the scarcity of examples of matter replication of definite articles, but their high susceptibility to pattern replication. Stolz (2006) discusses the geographical patterning of types of definite and indefinite articles in European languages in quite detail. Europe can be said to have four principal zones as far as the distribution of the definite article is concerned: Western Scandinavia has postposed articles, Western Europe in general has preposed articles, the Balkans have postposed articles, and central-eastern Europe (from Croatia to Finland) has no definite articles. An isolated zone comprises Greek, which has preposed articles. The geographical patterns are particularly interesting since the appearance of definite articles in many European languages is fairly recent, emerging over the past millennium or so. Some developments are even more recent. Romani developed a preposed definite article (M.SG *o* < *ov*, based on a demonstrative *ov*) through contact with Greek sometime after the tenth century AD, and Sorbian, a Slavic language, developed a preposed definite article *ton/ta/to* (also based on demonstrative pronouns) through contact with German over the past few centuries (Lötzsch 1996).

The Balkan area is particularly striking because of the similar development of postposed articles in languages that are not directly related: Romanian (Romance) *munte-le* 'the mountain', Macedonian and Bulgarian (Slavic) *voda-ta* 'the water', Albanian (Inro-European isolate) *mik-u* 'the friend'. A further indication of the volatility of definite articles in contact situations is the loss of overt marking of definiteness. Definite articles are lost in the Northeastern dialects of Romani, in contact with Polish and Russian (Matras 1999b). Khuzistani Arabic shows selective retreat of definiteness marking in some constructions, in contact with Persian, which has no overt marking of definiteness. The article disappears from the head noun of a postposed relative clause that is introduced by a definite relativiser. Note that indefinite heads in Arabic take attributive relative clauses that are not introduced by relativisers, but follow the head directly (*mara šift-ū-ha* 'a woman that I saw'). The presence of *lli* in (15) thus makes the definite article (*l-mara* 'the woman') redundant:

(15)   Kh. Arabic (Matras and Shabibi 2007):
          mara   lli   šift-ū-ha   xābar-at
          woman REL saw-2PL.M-3SG.F called-3SG.F
          'The woman that you saw called'

Evidence for the contact-susceptibility of determiners is widespread from other areas of the world; Bella Coola, a Salish language of the northwest Pacific coast of North America, has developed deictic affixes that are similar to those of the neighbouring Wakashan languages (they are enclitic in Wakashan, but both proclitic and enclitic in Bella Coola), while the related Salish languages express deictics as preposed, unbound particles (Beck 2000: 42–45).

Phrase-level replication of patterns can involve the order of constituents and their modifiers. One of the more frequently affected functions is word order in the possessive construction. Grenoble (2000: 108) reports on change in the possessive construction in Evenki, under Russian influence:

(16)   a. Older Evenki:
          ətirkə:n orortin
          old.man deer.PL.POSS.3PL

      b. Russian:
          olen-i   starika
          deer-PL old.man.GEN

      c. Russian influenced Evenki:
          orortin   ətirkə:n
          deer.PL.POSS.3PL old.man
          'The deer of the old man'

Macedonian Turkish from the town of Gostivar (Tufan 2008, Matras and Tufan 2007, 219–220) similarly reverses the order of the possessor and object of possession, under influence from the neighbouring languages, Macedonian and Albanian:

(17)   a. Macedonian Turkish:
          ruba-lar-i   damad-ın
          clothes-PL-3SG.POSS groom-GEN

      b. Macedonian:
          ališta-ta   na zet-ot
          clothes-DEF to groom-DEF

      c. Albanian:
          teshat e   dhandrit
          clothes ATT groom

      d. Turkish:
          damad-ın   eşya-lar-ı
          groom-GEN clothes-PL-3SG.POSS
          'The groom's clothes'

Note that the languages continue to employ very different morphological procedures to mark out the possessive construction. Macedonian Turkish retains
its suffix-marked genitive-possessive construction, with inflectional endings on
both the head (the object of possession) and the attribute (the possessor). The
only extent to which it converges with the other languages is in the order of elements, which is interpreted as the pivot feature of the neighbouring construction.
Naturally, reversing the order of elements is a much simpler adjustment to the
construction than any morphological changes. It is of course the rich inflectional
morphology of Turkish that allows the change in word order to take place in the
first place without affecting the meaning of the possessive relationship.

Note however the similarities and differences between the Macedonian and
Albanian constructions. Macedonian employs a preposition with a rather general
semantic meaning of direction, positioned in between two definite nouns. Here,
there is no flexibility of word order. The Albanian construction looks remarkably
similar, in that here too a grammatical function word is inserted between the object
of possession and the possessor. This function word is a postposed attributive
article which agrees with both the head and the attribute. It is thus morphologically
very different from the Macedonian morphemes, yet the pivotal setup of the two
constructions – the Macedonian and the Albanian – is remarkably similar, not
just in word order, but in the expression, in between the two constituents, of both
definiteness and a possessive-attributive relation.

Two further examples show that changes in the possessive construction may
affect morphological marking as well. In Domari, a 'canonical' construction,
recorded a century ago by Macalister (1914) and still present, though rare, in
contemporary speech, agrees in its word-order characteristics with the possessive
construction of other New Indo-Aryan languages. Nowadays, most speakers of
this moribund language (cf. Matras 1999a) use a construction that is calqued on
Palestinian Arabic. Its pivotal features are the word order possessed-possessor
(replacing the older possessor-possessed), the explicit marking of agreement with
the possessor through a person suffix on the possessed, and the oblique marking
of the possessor:

(18)   a. 'Canonical' Domari:
           bɔy-im   kuri
           father-1SG.OBL house

        b. Palestinian Arabic:
           bēt-o   la-ʔabū-y
           house-3SG.M   to-father-1SG

        c. New Domari construction:
           kury-os   bɔy-im-ki
           house-3SG.NOM father-1SG.OBL-ABL
           'my father's house'

Khuzistani Arabic undergoes a reanalysis of the morphology of its attributive
constructions – involving both nouns as attributes (possessive construction) and

adjectives (see Shabibi 2006, Matras and Shabibi 2007). In Arabic, adjectival attributes follow the head noun, and agree with the head noun in gender, number, as well as in definiteness (19a). Nominal attributes, by contrast, are conjoined by means of the attributive *Iḍāfa*-construction, whereby only the dependent (genitive) noun is overtly marked for definiteness (19.b):

(19)   Standard Arabic (and other dialects):
          a. l-walad l-kabīr
             DEF-boy DEF-big.M
             'The big boy'

          b. walad l-mudīr
             boy DEF-director
             'The director's son'

In Persian, both types of attributes are treated in the same way: the attribute (whether adjectival or nominal) follows the head, and an attributive particle (called the *Ezafe* marker) mediates between the two:

(20)   Persian:
          a. pesar-e bozorg
             boy-ATTR big
             'The big boy'

          b. pesar-e modīr
             boy-ATTR director
             'The director's son'

   The pattern in Khuzistani Arabic matches the Persian arrangement (note that, as in other dialects of Arabic, the definite article *l-* assimilates to dental consonants, resulting in gemination of that consonant):

(21)   Khuzisiani Arabic:
          a. walad č-čibīr
             boy DEF-big.M
             'The big boy'

          b. walad l-modīr
             boy DEF-director
             'The director's son'

   Given the similarities in word order between the Arabic and Persian constructions, it was easy for bilingual speakers to identify the Persian (definite) attributive marker *-(y)e* as the pivotal feature of the Persian construction. This was matched with the grammatical marker that conjoined the corresponding words in the Arabic construction, leading to a re-interpretation of the function of the Arabic definite article in this construction. (Note that Persian does not have a definite article.) As agreement in definiteness is dropped in adjectival attributions (21a), we may speak of an extension of the nominal attribution or possessive construction in Khuzistani Arabic to adjectival attributions as well, following the Persian model of uniting the two functions.[9]

The conflation of two constructions is an interesting challenge to the unidirectionality hypothesis in grammaticalisation theory, which normally assumes that extension (of meaning or of distribution context) will lead to the emergence of new categories and more differentiation will emerge. Silva-Corvalán (1994: 182–183) describes how pragmatically neutral word order in the source language is reproduced with word-forms of the replica language by allowing a highly marked construction to lose its special effect: Thus *tengo dos más meses* 'I have two more months' replaces the default order *tengo dos meses más*, and the prepositioning of adjectives in *la más importante persona* 'the most important person' replaces the unmarked Spanish order *la persona más importante*.

Ongoing convergence can be observed in Domari in connection with the position of attributive adjectives. Like other Indo-Aryan languages, Domari inherits preposed attributive adjectives that agree in gender and number with the head: *till-a zara* [big-M boy] 'the big boy'. Arabic, by contrast, has postposed adjectives (see 19a):[10] *l-walad l-kbīr*. Domari also possesses a non-verbal existential construction, in which adjectives may take the role of predicate. The adjective then follows the head, and an enclitic copula is attached to it: *zara till-ēk* [boy big-PRED.M] 'the boy is big'. This construction is being generalised as the default attributive construction, due to its similarities in the order of constituents with the corresponding attributive construction in Arabic:

(22)   a. Domari:
          er-a   zara till-ēk
          came-M boy big-PRED.M
          'the big boy arrived' (lit. 'the boy, being big, arrived')

        b. Arabic:
          iža   l-walad   l-kbīr
          came.M DEF-boy DEF-big.M
          'the big boy arrived'

Considerable syncretisation of this kind is seen at the phrase level among the unrelated Melanesian languages Takia (Austronesian) and Waskia (Papuan). Note the identical position of morphemes, and the presence of near-complete isomorphism (Ross 1996: 191):

(23)   a. Takia:
          tamol tubun uraru en
          man   big   two   this

        b. Waskia:
          kadi bi-biga itelala pamu
          man   PL-big   two   this
          'these two big men'

(24)   a. Takia:
             ŋai tamol an   ida
             I   man   DET with.him

         b. Waskia:
             ane kadi mu   ili
             I   man DET with.him
             'the man and I'

So far we have seen changes in the order of constituents, the presence of overt marking of categories such as definiteness and the function assigned to morphemes. The place of adpositions is usually believed to be an integral part of a language's overall typology and slower to change than other patterns of word order (such as subject and verb position) to which greater flexibility is attributed. But changes do occur. It is quite reasonable to assume that, being an Indo-Aryan language originally formed in central India, Romani had postpositions before coming into contact with Byzantine Greek (or perhaps already with Persian–Indic frontier languages) (see Matras 2002). Present-day Romani dialects are almost exclusively prepositional; agglutinative case endings are referred to by a minority of writers as 'postpositions', but this is done primarily in order to foster an image of Romani as a very different, non-European language. The consensus view of Romani is clearly that of a prepositional language (cf. Friedman 1991). Nevertheless, a number of dialects have developed postpositions out of elements that are elsewhere in Romani used as prepositions (and which, prior to Early Romani in the Byzantine Empire, had been, in all likelihood, used as postposed location adverbs). The change is attested in Romani dialects in contact with postpositioning languages – Finnish and Turkish, respectively:

(25)   a. Finnish Romani:
             panah minutt-esko   pālal
             five   minute-GEN.SG after
             'after five minutes'

         b. Romani of Sliven, northern Bulgaria:
             i   štar   zis-en-dar palal
             DEF four day-OBL.PL-ABL after
             'after four days'

Macedonian Turkish is also beginning to show the adoption of prepositions, replicating the Macedonian pattern, in what is otherwise a strictly postpositional language (cf. Matras and Tufan 2007):

(26)   a. Macedonian Turkish:
             güzel   neka Meryem
             beautiful like Meryem

    b. Macedonian:
       ubava   kolku Merjem
       beautiful like   Meryem

    c. Turkish:
       Meryem kadar   güzel
       Meryem as.much beautiful
       'As beautiful as Meryem'

While phrase level structures are usually thought of as determined to a large extent by typological 'type', we see that changes at the phrase level can and do occur as a result of contact, in the order of constituents and the mapping of functions to morpho-syntactic structures, leading at times to what might be considered typological 'hybrids'.

9.2.4   Morphology and morphological paradigms

    Generalisations on borrowability mention paradigmaticity as one of the constraints on borrowing, influencing in particular the scarcity of borrowing within inflectional morphological paradigms (e.g. Field 2002, van Hout and Muysken 1994). It is not made clear in most discussions whether such predictions should apply only to the replication of linguistic matter, or also to patterns. While it is difficult to evaluate the prominence of morphological pattern replication quantitatively or in terms of frequency in comparison with other domains, such as clause- or phrase-level syntax, there is a wealth of examples of convergence in paradigms, from the paradigmatic arrangement of unbound functions words to that of inflectional morphology.

Tense and aspect systems show a continuum and often even combinations of semi-bound and bound morphological material. Bao (2005) discusses the re-arrangement of the aspectual system in Singapore English, where the particle *already* is used to match the completive aspect expressed by the Chinese particle *le*, English *ever* calques the experiential expressed in Chinese by *guo*, the verb *got/finish* matches the Chinese emphatic expressed by *yŏu/wán*, and English *never* conveys the negative expressed in Chinese by *bù*. Bao analyses the emergence of this system as a case for relexification based on a Chinese substratum. The target language is thus a kind of fossilised interlanguage variety spoken by second-language learners. Note, however, that the learner population has not abandoned their first language Chinese, and so we are not dealing with *shift*-induced interference. The procedure is essentially no different from other cases of 'pivot-matching': a construction is selected from the repertoire and replicated by re-constructing pivotal features around a new set of word-forms.

One of the well-known features shared by the Balkan languages is the use of an analytic future particle, derived from the verb 'to want', which is followed by an inflected verb: Greek *tha pao* 'I shall go', Romanian *voi cînta* 'I shall sing', Bulgarian *šte vidja* 'I shall see', (Balkan) Romani *ka dikhav* 'I shall see'. Burridge

(2006: 183) mentions the emergence of a future tense in Pennsylvania German that employs the auxiliary *geht* 'to go' (*es geht ihm happene* 'it's gonna happen to him'). Grammaticalisation of 'go' for the future is common even without contact (cf. Modern Hebrew *ani holéx lixtóv lo* 'I am going to write to him', Palestinian Arabic *ana rāḥ amšī ʔal-balad* 'I'm going to walk to town', in independent developments), but is largely absent from German dialects, and so in the case of Pennsylvania German, English will have had a role at least in accelerating an internal grammaticalisation process, if not triggering it. Khuzistani Arabic develops a remote past (pluperfect), calquing the use in Persian of an auxiliary 'was' (Matras and Shabibi 2007):

(27) a. Khuzistani Arabic:
      mən rəħ-ət lə-l-bīet, huwwa mā-rāyəħ   čān
      when went-1SG to-DEF-home he NEG-going.SG.M was.3SG.M

   b. Persian:
      vaɣti raft-am xūne, ūn na-rafte būd
      when went-1SG home he NEG-gone was.3SG.M
      'When I went home he had not gone away'

The Amazonian languages Tucano (Tucanoan family) and Tariana (Arawak family) provide an example of convergence that infiltrates the inflectional system. Both share the same tense and evidentiality distinctions in which past-tense verbs are marked for four different sources of information: direct (visual), non-visual, inferred, and reported. In all cases a unique suffix on the verb indicates the type of evidential (Aikhenvald 2002: 118). Another example of convergence of inflection morphemes is the aspectual and mood system of languages in East Anatolia (cf. Chyet 1995, Matras 2000c). The languages involved include Persian and Kurmanji (Kurdish) (Iranian branch of Indo-European), various dialects of Neo-Aramaic (Semitic), Western Armenian (Indo-European isolate), as well as Levantine Arabic (Figure 9.2). All share the basic morphological layout of the finite, present-tense verb: A progressive-indicative aspectual prefix appears in the first position, followed by the root, which is followed by person suffixes (Arabic, a more recent arrival in the region, maintains person affixes in prefixed position, marking gender and number through suffixes; the progressive prefix *b-* is often attributed to an Aramaic substrate). The subjunctive is marked either by the absence of the progressive-indicative prefix, or by a specialised subjunctive prefix, with Kurmanji alternating between the two options.

Convergence proceeds even further among Aramaic and Kurdish. Khan (2004: 445) notes the reduction, with no obvious language-internal motivation, of a root consonant in the Neo-Aramaic verb 'to come', so that its form can resemble the corresponding form in Kurdish. Khan appears unaware of the possible Kurdish affix *t-* (normally *d-* but de-voiced with this particular verb) which represents the progressive-indicative. Added to the paradigm, the resemblance between the two languages is striking not just in the morphological layout but also in the form of person affixes and in the form of the verbal root itself (Figure 9.3).

	'I see' present indicative			'I see' present subjunctive		
	ASPECT	ROOT	PERSON	ASPECT	ROOT	PERSON
NE Aramaic	k-	-xāz-	-in/yan	ø	-xāz-	-in/yan
Turoyo Aramaic	ko-	-ḥoz-	-eno/ono	ø	-ḥoz-	-eno/ono
Kurmanji	di-	-bîn-	-im	ø/bi-	-bîn-	-im
Persian	mī-	-bīn-	-æm	(ø)/be-	-bīn-	-æm
W Armenian	gə–	-desn-	-em	ø	-desn-	-em
Arabic	b- -a-	-šūf-	[zero]	ø -a-	-šūf	-[zero]

Figure 9.2 *Layout of the present-tense finite verb in languages of East Anatolia.*

	Aramaic		Kurdish	
person	indicative	subjunctive	indicative	subjunctive
3SG.(M)	k-e	he	(t-)ê	b-ê
3PL	k-en	hen	(t-)ên	b-ên

Figure 9.3 *Aramaic and Kurdish forms for 'to come'.*

Matter and pattern replication are not always mutually exclusive, and we find convergence in domains in which concrete morphemes are sometimes borrowed. Ameka (2006, 2007) reports on Likpe, where the 3PL pronoun form *mɔ́* is attached as a suffix to certain kin terms to mark plurality (*ant-mɔ́* 'father-PL'), copying the formal identity between the 3PL pronoun *wó* and the nominal plural marker in Ewe. Jendraschek (2006: 148) points out the similarities between the marking of plurality on 'pronouns' (i.e. indefinites and interrogatives) in Spanish – *uno/unos* 'one/some', *quién/quiénes* 'who/-PL', *cuál/cuáles* 'which/-PL' – and Basque *bat/batzuk, nor/nortzuk, zein/zeintzuk*.

Morphological alignment is considered one of the stable features of languages that is normally shared only by genetically related languages (cf. Nichols 1992). An example of contact-induced shift in alignment patterns are the agreement systems of Kurmanji and various dialects of Neo-Aramaic. In Kurmanji, ergative alignment emerged as a result of the generalisation of the past participle (to compensate for the loss of the Old Iranian past-tense inflection). Subsequently, a distinction arose between the agreement patterns and mode of marking the subject/agent in transitive and intransitive verbs. Transitive verbs show zero-agreement or agreement with the direct object, and their agent appears in the oblique case. Intransitive verbs agree with their subject, and this agreement is indicated by a set of subject-agreement markers that arose through a synthetisation of the copula with the past participle. Subjects of intransitive verbs appear in the nominative case. In Aramaic, a similar generalisation of the passive-participle took place in past tenses, as a result of which the older person inflection was lost. The agent of transitive verbs became marked as a prepositional object, using the dative/benefactive/allative preposition *l-*. This preposition was later integrated into the past-tense verb or participle, forming in effect a new set of transitive agreement markers. As in Kurmanji, intransitive verbs acquired a new set of past-tense subject concord markers, which arose from the old copula forms, and which now function as intransitive agreement markers.

(28)   a. Kurmanji:

> ez   rabû-m   û   min   derî vekir
> 1SG.NOM stood.up-1SG and 1SG.OBL door opened.

      b. Saqqez Neo-Aramaic:

> qīm-na,   tara-kē plix-li
> stood.up-1SG.ITR door-the opened-1SG.TR
> 'I stood up and opened the door'

The Vaupés region provides another, yet more complex example of similar systems of cross-referencing affixes (Aikhenvald 2001: 9). Note that glosses[11] are almost identical, but there are no shared morphemes:

(29)   a. Tucano:

> dɨporó-pɨ-re   ni'ki   masɨ
> long.ago-LOC-TOP.NON.A/S one.CL:HUMAN person
>
> a'to-ré   etâ-wɨ̃
> arrive-3SGNF.REM.P.VIS here-TOP.NON.A/S

      b. Tariana:

> payape-se-nuku   paita   nawiki
> long.ago-LOC-TOP.NON.A/S one.CL:HUMAN person
>
> di-uka-na   aĩ-nuku
> 3SGNF-arrive-REM.P.VIS here-TOP.NON.A/S
> 'A longtime ago a man arrived here'

Given the difficulty – on which there is wide agreement (cf. Field 2002, Moravcsik 1978, van Hout and Muysken 1994) – of recognising the semantic function of highly flectional morphemes in another language and the consequent difficulties in replicating such morphemes, how do tightly convergent inflectional systems as seen in the previous examples arise? Mithun (2004) discusses the Wakashan, Chimakuan, and Salishan language families of the Pacific Northwest, which are not related but have developed very similar hierarchical systems of pronominal affixes. These are highly complex and highly unusual systems, in which person interacts with agentivity in competition over the position, suffixed to the verb, in which they are likely to appear. Mithun attributes the similarities to a shared process involving the grammaticalisation of independent pronominal

	SL Portuguese	SL Malay	SL Tamil
Nominal case:			
NOM	ø	ø	ø
ACC	-pə < *para* 'for'	-na < *nya* 'that'	-a(y)/-e
GEN	-su(wə) < *sua* 'his/her'	-pe(i) < *punya* 'of'	-ṛa, -ooṭe
LOC	-(u)ntu < *junto* 'together'	-ka < *deka* 'near'	-(i)la(y)/-(i)ṭṭa(y)
Verbal category:			
POTENTIAL	lo- < *logo* 'soon'	a(n)ti- < *nanti* 'soon'	-pp-an
CONDITIONAL	kan(da)- < *quando* 'when'	-kalu < *kalu* 'if'	-al

Figure 9.4 *Some case markers and verbal categories in Sri Lankan Portuguese and Sri Lankan Malay, and their etymologies (based on Bakker 2006).*

forms to person affixes that became specialised for certain functions and occupied the same positions in the phrase. These person affixes later on underwent synthetisation in each of the systems, in independent internal developments.

Mithun's (2004) proposal might also explain the facts of the shared layout of aspect, mood, and person markers in East Anatolian languages (Figure 9.2). In fact, the more recent emergence of a progressive-indicative prefix *b-* in Levantine Arabic, based on the preposition *b-* 'in' as well as the historical analysis of the origin of the progressive affixes in the other languages (cf. Kurdish *di* 'in' > *d-* progressive prefix, Aramaic *ke* 'as' > *k/g-* progressive prefix, etc.) nicely confirm this. A further example of convergence where Mithun's scenario is applicable is the emergence of suffixed case markers from prepositions and prefixed verbal categories from (largely) unbound auxiliaries in Sri Lankan Portuguese and Sri Lankan Malay, both of which arose as creoles and were subsequently in contact with the highly inflectional language Tamil. Bakker (2006) compiles a variety of sources on the basis of which he presents the case for convergence; selected features are repeated in Figure 9.4.

A further pathway for morphological convergence is through re-analysis and levelling of functions within the paradigm of the replica language. Fertek Greek from the Cappadocia region in central Anatolia adopts the Turkish agglutinative arrangement of case markers, drawing on its own inherited system of morphemes (Dawkins 1916: 113–114). While Greek has a declension-sensitive inflectional system, where a single morpheme may integrate several meanings/functions (e.g. GEN.SG.F), Fertek Greek moves toward an agglutinating type in reducing the meanings of each morpheme: Thus *-yu* (originally M.SG.GEN) marks exclusively

	Greek	Fertek Greek	Turkish
'wife'	yinék-a	nék-a	kadın
'wives'	yinék-es	nék-es	kadın-lar
'of the wife'	yinék-as	nék-a-yu	kadın-ın
'of the wives'	yinék-on	nék-es-yu	kadın-lar-ın

Figure 9.5 *Genitive case marking in Fertek Greek (based on Dawkins 1916).*

the genitive, independently of gender and number, like Turkish -ın in the model. It can be combined with other markers of singularity or plurality into a layered case structure, as in the Turkish model (Figure 9.5).

Yet another development type leading to morphological convergence is the re-distribution of affixes among different semantic functions, to match the form–function mapping of the model language. Tenser (2008) describes how the distribution of semantic functions among the case-marking system of Northeastern Romani dialects – especially Russian, Lithuanian, and Latvian Romani – mirrors that of Russian, the principal contact language during a prolonged period:

(30)   a. Latvian Romani:
        jow dykh-el man
        he see-3SG 1SG.OBL

    b. Russian:
        on vid-it menya
        he see-3SG 1SG.ACC/GEN
        'He sees me'

    c. Latvian Romani:
        man na sys khere
        1SG.OBL NEG was.3SG home

    d. Russian:
        menya ne bылo doma
        1SG.ACC/GEN NEG was.3SG.NEUTR home
        'I was not at home'

(31)   a. Russian Romani:
        leste sys raklori i rakloro
        3SG.M.LOC was.3SG/PL girl and boy

    b. Russian:
        u nevo bылi doč' i sын
        to 3SG.ACC/GEN was.3PL daughter and son
        'He had a daughter and a son'

Romani LOC (*Russian* GEN)	
Possessor:	'he has a sister'
External possessor:	'my nose hurts'
Location:	'next to me'

Romani ABL (*Russian* prep + GEN)	
Source:	'from me'
Partitive:	'two of them'
Privative:	'except for her'
Object of comparison:	'taller than you'

Romani INSTR (*Russian* INSTR)	
Comitative:	'with me
Instrumental:	'with a knife'
Promotion to state:	'I became a chef'
Time of day:	'tomorrow'

Romani OBL (*Russian* ACC/GEN)	
Direct object:	'he sees me'
Negative existence:	'I wasn't there'

Figure 9.6 *Replication of Russian semantic map of case-representation in Baltic-North Russian dialects of Romani (after Tenser 2008).*

c. Lithuanian Romani:
   mande   dukh-al   nakh
   1SG.LOC hurt-3SG nose

d. Russian:
   u menya bol-it   nos
   to   1SG.ACC/GEN hurt-3SG nose
   'My nose hurts'

Note how in (30), Romani employs the unmodified oblique (not followed by any specific semantic case marker) case to match the Russian accusative/genitive; this is the marking of both the direct object and the subject of negative existence. In (31), Romani uses its locative case to match the functions of the Russian preposition *u*+genitive/accusative to mark the possessor and external possessor. Both patterns differ from the canonical Romani marking of all subjects in the nominative and of possessors in the oblique. The wholesale re-mapping of the case system in this way suggests that the entire Russian 'semantic map' of case representation has been replicated in Romani (Figure 9.6).

The nominal inflection domain may also undergo category convergence. The distribution of noun classifiers shows strong tendencies toward areal clustering, which must be interpreted as a tendency toward convergence in these domains. Epps (2007) discusses the incipient system of nominal classifiers in Hup, which classify inanimates by shape and animates by gender, which is being adopted from Tucano. Although gender shows less obvious macro-areal distribution, changes to gender systems can be observed in several contact situations. Developments affecting gender marking that occur in the cross-linguistic sample (Matras 2007b) include a shift in unmarked gender from feminine to masculine in Mosetén, the loss of neuter gender in Northeastern Yiddish (in contact with Lithuanian and Latvian), as well as some marginal phenomena such as the loss of gender in pronouns (in Selice Romani in contact with Hungarian) as well as in Zakho Aramaic (in contact with Kurdish, which lacks gender differentiation in the 3SG.NOM). Silva-Corvalán (1994: 4) reports on the loss of adjective gender marking in some varieties of Los Angeles Spanish.

Word-derivation is a further area of morphology where pattern replication is observed. Jendraschek (2006: 158) discusses how Basque calques a word-derivation procedure on Romance (and possibly English), employing the prefix *berr-* with an original meaning of 'new' as well as 'twice' to express iteration: *ikusi* 'see' and *berrikusi* 'revise', *aztertu* 'examine' and *berraztertu* 're-examine', etc. Both Tucano and Tariana show a morphological passive derivation and can use passive morphology on intransitive verbs to indicate impersonal meaning. In addition, Tariana also developed a periphrastic causative construction as a result of contact with East Tucanoan (Aikhenvald 2002: 114-116). Recent contact-induced grammaticalisation leads to the emergence of causative, passive, and reflexive markers in Hup (Epps 2007), and to a reflexive in Likpe (Ameka 2007).

Romani dialects in contact with languages that possess a productive morphological causative, such as Turkish and Hungarian, have developed a fully grammatical use of the inherited transitive/causative suffix *-av-*, which can be added to almost any verb: *ker-* 'to do', *ker-av-* 'to make somebody do'. In other Romani dialects this suffix is on the whole lexicalised and so limited to a contained number of verbs such as *dara-* 'to fear', *darav-* 'to frighten'. Romani dialects also tend to re-shape their passive constructions based on the contact language. Early Romani had a productive morphological passive, based on the gramamticalised verb *-jov-* 'to become', affixed to the verb root, closely mirroring the passive derivation of Greek. This construction continues in most dialects, in some way or other. However, dialects in contact with Slavic languages as well as Romanian have begun to generalise a mediopassive construction involving the active verb followed by a reflexive pronoun, which is expanding at the expense of the old synthetic passive. In German and British Romani, the synthetic passive has been abandoned altogether and passive constructions are periphrastic, drawing on the independent verbs 'to be/to become'.

9.3   Linguistic areas

9.3.1   Methodological issues

The Balkans had attracted the attention of historical and descriptive linguists quite early on as a region in which a cluster of structural-typological features is shared among languages that are not directly genetically related. In what was the first attempt to enumerate and describe these features, Sandfeld (1930) proposed that at least some were a result of the cultural impact of Byzantine Greek. It is clear though that some features, such as the postposed definite article or the analytical comparative particle, which are common to other languages of the region but does not appear in Greek, could not have arisen as a result of Greek influence. A substrate hypothesis had attracted support until fairly recently (cf. Solta 1980), reasoning that forerunners of the present-day Balkan languages had been acquired by a local population who spoke so-called Daco-Illyrian and Thracian dialects – the structural features of which remain entirely obscure and open to speculation.

Alongside attempts to reconstruct the historical developments in the Balkans, linguists also took an interest in the theoretical value of the region's languages and the similarities among them. The Balkans provided confirmation that language change can proceed not just in a way that follows the traditional tree-model, with branches and sub-branches diverging from one another, but also in a way that corresponds to the wave model, which had originally been conceived to capture the spread of innovations among closely related and mutually comprehensible varieties of a single language. The impression that structural innovations can 'jump the language boundary' inspired a re-evaluation of language classification models. Trubetzkoy's (1928) term 'linguistic league' – still popular today in its German version *Sprachbund* – can be seen as an attempt to allow for the possibility of a group of languages that are closely related structurally but not genetically, a concept that had not been previously entertained by the comparative method in linguistics.

Aware of the gradational nature of relatedness based on acquired (rather than inherited) features, Weinreich (1958) warned against the metaphor of closed membership in a 'league' and proposed instead to view the Balkans as a *convergence area*. The term 'area' highlights the geographical proximity that is a historical pre-requisite for contact (at least in pre-globalisation society), while 'convergence' flags the reality of a situation like the Balkans, where a cluster of typical features is distributed in a variety of patterns across a group of languages. Weinreich had, several years earlier, provided the theoretical framework for transfer and interference that explained the mode in which structural features can be diffused across language boundaries (Weinreich 1953). But by highlighting the gradational aspect of linguistic areas Weinreich introduced a dilemma into the discussion that remains unresolved to this very day: if areas are defined as a gradient of contiguous languages that share features as a result of contact, where is the cut-off point between 'conventional' cases of one-to-one contact, and genuine 'areas'? Surely not every situation of contact in which convergence takes place can be regarded as a 'convergence area'?

Work on other regions where contact-based structural similarities were found, such as that by Emeneau (1956) on South Asia and by Greenberg (1959) on Africa, contributed to a consolidation of the notion of convergence areas – referred to in these two studies and thereafter as 'linguistic areas' – and created a small but growing pool of case-studies from which scholars began to extract commonalities in order to arrive at a general definition. Factors mentioned as part of such proposed definitions include the number of structural features that are shared by the languages of the region (and are known to have been acquired through contact rather than through genetic affiliation or chance similarity), the number of unrelated languages or even of language families that are represented in the area, evidence of a history of trade and cultural contacts, and more (see Campbell 2006 for an overview of proposed definitions).

Discussions of linguistic areas have tended to focus on shared patterns, rather than the replication of linguistic matter. Superficially this can be taken to suggest that convergence is the mutual adaptation of languages to one another, rather than the replication of structures from a dominant language. In actual fact, the dominance of one language over others is not excluded from the definition of linguistic areas. Thomason for example (2001) views shift-induced interference as one of two types of contact that may result in the emergence of a linguistic area. The reality is that there is no avoiding the gradational nature of linguistic areas, in every respect: firstly, some areas involve replication of matter as well as patterns, as in the case of the diffusion of connectors, phasal adverbs, indefinites, and a huge amount of vocabulary items among the languages of Anatolia and the Caucasus, or the diffusion of vocabulary, derivational affixes, and interjections across languages of the Balkans. Second, in many one-to-one contact situations we find replication of pattern as well as matter. This has been demonstrated both for the speech of immigrants in the environment of a dominant majority language (Silva Corvalán 1994, Savić 1995, Clyne 2003, and more), and for regional or minority languages such as Basque (Haase 1991), Asia Minor Greek (Dawkins 1916), Hup (Epps 2007), or Domari (Matras 1999a).

One of the solutions to the problem of gradational participation in an area is to identify relations between core and periphery. Work by Masica (1976) on the South Asian area, and by Joseph (1983) on the specific case of the Balkan infinitive, concludes that with respect to individual features (and, in South Asia, with respect to a group of features) diffusion centres can be defined in which a feature is more consistent, or in which more features tend to cluster. Individual languages or groups of languages within the area can be identified as centres, and their locations will constitute the geographical core of the area. Joseph identified residual uses of non-finite forms in Romanian, Albanian, and Greek, and the most consistent reduction of the infinitive in Macedonian. In this way, areas can be described following the same method as traditional dialectology, namely by plotting isoglosses for selected features.

In a seminal paper that breaks with much of the older ways of defining areas by counting the number of features and languages, Masica (2001) argues for an isogloss-based approach that would take into consideration both the wider distribution of a feature, and smaller regions with a high density of shared structural traits. Masica illustrates that features are not properties of areas, but that areas are rather an outcome of a conspicuous intersection of features/isoglosses: the infinitive-reduction isogloss covers a coherent area that is in fact much greater than the Balkans, and SOV word order is found across an area that includes, but is much larger than, South Asia. Minimally, then, a linguistic area can be defined by a single feature that is areally patterned and crosses linguistic-genetic bound-aries (Masica 2001: 212). Rationally, any conspicuous density of cross-genetic isoglosses is a likely candidate for more careful investigation of the histori-cal circumstances that supported the diffusion of innovations across language boundaries.

While areas appear to be products of language contact, the actual reconstruction of contact is problematic in regions where many questions about the linguistic history and even the linguistic-genetic makeup of the region remain unclear. There is therefore a risk inflating the notion of 'linguistic area' by simply attributing similarities on a wholesale basis to contact developments. A good example is Australia. Whereas Dixon (2001, 2002) argues that similarities between many languages and language sub-groups of Australia are a result of diffusion rather than genetic inheritance, most Australianists tend to agree on the existence of a large phylum, called Pama-Nyungan, which covers most of the Australian languages with the exception of those situated in the extreme north of the continent (cf. O'Grady and Hale 2004, Evans 2005, Bowern 2006).

At the other end, the investigation of areas as contact zones has given way to a new direction – 'areal typology' or 'areal linguistics' (cf. Muysken 2000b). This involves pre-selecting a geographical region that is known to have been the scene of cross-cultural contacts and trade during a significant period in its history, and then taking an inventory of the linguistic features of this area. Areal typology has focused on regions such as the Mediterranean (Ramat and Stolz 2002, Ramat and Roma 2007), the Circum-Baltic region (Dahl and Koptjevskaja-Tamm 2001), and Europe as a whole (van der Auwera 1998 and other works of the EUROTYP[12] project; Heine and Kuteva 2006). This approach also gave rise to the World Atlas of Language Structures (Haspelmath, Dryer, Gil, and Comrie 2005) which maps the occurrence of selected structural features in various regions of the world. Not all of these investigations have yielded clear results of areal patterns; the Mediterranean, for example, may have been the scene of trade and cultural contacts but it is not the meeting point of an outstanding number of structural isoglosses. At the very least, areal typology has contributed to a sharpening of our view of linguistic areas: while similarities among languages are not always a result of contact, cross-cultural contact will not always lead to intense processes of linguistic convergence.

9.3.2   Profiles of linguistic areas

Despite a growing number of descriptions devoted to individual con-tact zones, many of them involving more than just two or even three languages, the comparative investigation of linguistic areas is still in its infancy. This is partly to do with issues of definitions and the nomenclature-related difficulty of assem-bling a sample of representative 'areas'. It is also an outcome of greatly varying standards of descriptions and gaps in exemplification, which make it difficult to assess data from a wide range of areas in an in-depth and comprehensive manner. The present section is merely a brief supplement to two recent overviews of linguistic areas (Thomason 2001: 99–126, Heine and Kuteva 2005: 172–218), and to two recent collections that contain a selection of relevant case studies (Aikhenvald and Dixon 2001, Matras, McMahon, and Vincent 2006).

Europe is an example of a rather loose linguistic area, where most bundles of relevant isoglosses separate the continent into sub-areas – often a western and an eastern zone, sometimes northwest and southeast (see especially Stolz 2006). Some of the typical features of Europe as a linguistic area include the presence of a transitive verb 'to have', a word order pattern in which S precedes O, the 'have'-perfect, use of a relative pronoun strategy in relative clauses, and the presence of a participle passive (cf. Heine and Kuteva 2006). Within Europe, the **Circum-Baltic** area has received attention recently in areal typology (Stolz 1991, Dahl and Koptjevskaja-Tamm 2001, Koptjevskaja-Tamm 2006). It encompasses the Scandinavian languages, Finnish and Estonian, Karelian, Veps, Lithuanian and Latvian, Saami, Polish, Russian, Belarussian, Yiddish, Karaim, Baltic Romani, and other smaller languages. Typical features include polytonicity and initial stress, case alternation marking total vs. partial objects, nominative object in various constructions, oblique marking of non-canonical subjects, and evidential mood.

The **Balkans** area has attracted much attention, though there are not many comprehensive overviews of features that include exemplification from all languages. The most widely cited languages that represent the area are Romanian, Bulgarian, Macedonian, Albanian, and Greek, as well as Aromanian or Vlach. At least three more languages belong to the area, namely Romani (Indo-Aryan),[13] the Balkan dialects of (Ottoman) Turkish, and Gagauz (another Turkic language). Features include the use of finite subordination in modal complement clauses, a distinction between the subordinators used to introduce factual and non-factual complements, merger of the historical dative and genitive and a general reduction of case marking, postposed definite articles, an analytic comparative particle, similar patterns of word order variation, pronominal object reduplication, a vowel system consisting of /a, e, i, o, u, ə/, and a tendency toward palatalisation of dentals and velars around front vowels. There is also word-form diffusion of modal particles and interjections as well as of cultural terminology (e.g. food), and diffusion of a number of nominal derivation affixes (agentive, diminutive, feminine) (cf. Hinrichs 1999, Sandfeld 1930).

Africa (especially west and central Africa) might be considered a further macro-area, which is more reasonably sub-divided; but some general shared features include the presence in phonology of tones, vowel harmony, and a contrast between oral and nasal vowels, and in morphosyntax the presence of noun classes and serial verbs (see Dimmendaal 2001). The **Ethiopian Highlands**, the home of languages of the Semitic, Cushitic, and Omotic groups, among others, show glottalised consonants, pharyngeal fricatives, SOV word order, preposed subordinations, postposed auxiliaries, and the use of converbs for coordination (Bisang 2006, Ferguson 1970, Greenberg 1959).

Mesoamerica constitutes a more 'classic' case of a linguistic area in which a large number of features spread across many genetic families in a contained geographical zone. The families involved include Mayan, Otomanguean, Mixtecan, Uto-Aztecan, and more. Features incude final devoicing of sonorants, voicing of obstruents after nasals, vowel harmony, implosives, and retroflex fricatives in phonology; and in morphosyntax the presence of nominal possession of the type 'his-dog the man', the use of relational nouns (person-inflected location expressions), a vigesimal numeral system, non-verb-final word order, numeral classifiers, noun incorporation, and several widespread semantic calques (see Campbell, Kaufman, and Smith-Stark 1986).

The **Pacific Northwest** of North America (Thomason 2000: 319, 2001, Mithun 2004) features the language families Salishan, Wakashan, Chimakuan, and others. Languages of the region typically have verb-initial word order, sentence-initial negation, a weak lexical noun/verb distinction, numeral classifiers, a system of lexical suffixes, possessive pronominal affixes and a hierarchical system of pronominal agreement suffixes, minimal case systems, many suffixes but few prefixes, and a series of shared features in phonology, including labialised dorsal consonants, a velar/uvular distinction in dorsals, /ts/ affricates, and a common sound change from velars to alveo-palatals.

The **South Asian** area includes languages belonging to the Indo-Aryan, Dravidian, and Munda language families (Masica 1976, Emeneau 1956). Its features are retroflex consonants, SOV word order, postpositions, dative subject constructions, causative morphology, use of converbs for clause combining, absence of a definite article, a case-marking system that is sensitive to animacy, suffixing morphology, use of echo-words, widespread use of quantifiers, and more.

Southeast Asia includes several language families, among them Mon-Khmer, Tai-Kadai, Hmong-Mien, Sinnitic, and Tibeto-Burman. Shared features include the absence of case marking and gender and the absence of cross referencing or fusional affixing, the presence of numeral class constructions, verb serialisation, parallel lexicalisations, sentence-final particles, topic-prominence, sentential nominalisations, and the presence in most languages of lexical tone (cf. Enfield 2003: 51, Matisoff 2001, Bisang 1996).

Anatolia has not yet been discussed or studied intensively as a linguistic area, but many of its features can be traced back to historical developments of the past millennium and longer thanks to extensive written documentation on at least some of the languages. Present-day and recent languages of the area include Turkish (partly), Azeri, Kurmanji, Zazaki, Aramaic, Laz, Asia Minor Greek, Arabic, as well as Persian and Domari. Shared features include the use of finite subjunctives in modal complements, a verb template {aspect/mood-root-person-tense}, an enclitic copula, a postposed particle 'too', uvular /q/, the opposition /ɑ/:/æ/, as well as widespread pharyngeals in Arabic loans, shared focus and modal particles, the use of light verbs (mainly 'to do' and 'to become') for derivation and loans, echo expressions, similar 'either . . . or' constructions, and a *ki*-subordinator (Haig 2001, Matras 2000c, Chyet 1995).

Siberia as a linguistic area includes languages from the Tungusic, Eskimo-Aleut, Samoyedic, Mongolic, Turkic, Nivkh, Yukaghiric, Ob-Ugric, and other families. They tend to show a contrast /m, n, ŋ, ñ/, morphological marking of desiderative and reciprocal, subordination with a case-marked nominalised verb, a prolative case ('along'), and a distinction between dative/allative and instrumental/comitative (Anderson 2005).

Arnhem Land in northeastern Australia (Heath 1978) shows diffusion of a number of grammatical morphemes across unrelated language sub-groups, including case, noun class, number, and derivation affixes, and the presence of reduplication, enclitic pronouns, similar pronominal systems, and similar clause combining strategies (subordinating affix).

The list seems to be open, and researchers have identified convergence phenomena extending to several unrelated languages in numerous other regions, including East Timor (Hajek 2006), the Lower Volta Basin (Ameka 2006), Western Nilotic (Storch 2006), the Burgenland district in southeastern Austria (Houtzagers 2000), the Cape (Güldemann 2006), the Mediterranean (Ramat and Stolz 2002, Ramat and Roma 2007a), the Sepik River Basin in New Guinea (Foley 1986, Aikhenvald 2007a), the Vaupés region in the Amazon basin (Aikhenvald 2001, 2002, 2003, Epps 2006, 2007), the languages of Sri Lanka (Bakker 2006), and more.

9.3.3   An outlook on language convergence

Part of Thomason's (2001) definition of a linguistic area is its emergence scenario – either as a setting of prolonged multilingualism, or else as a case of substrate influence and collective language shift. Aikhenvald (2002) similarly distinguishes between linguistic areas as the outcome of multilingual constellations, and so-called 'one-to-one' contacts, arguing that the first will involve primarily the diffusion of pattern, while the second will show diffusion of word-forms. As noted above, while it is certainly the case that some cases of prolonged and stable multilingualism, such as the Vaupés region or the Melanesian cases discussed by Ross (1996, 2001), show primarily pattern replication, there are other areas of stable multilingualism, such as Anatolia, where word-form diffusion accompanies pattern diffusion, and there are also cases of one-to-one contact that are characterised by both matter and pattern replication.

Indeed, the boundary between multilingual developments and one-to-one contacts remains fuzzy even within individual linguistic areas. Romani for example is assumed to have acquired many of its Balkan features in contact with Byzantine Greece, which explains its use of a preposed definite article and the absence of a central vowel (at least from the inventory inherited by present-day dialects; some dialects have acquired a central vowel through later contacts). Heath (1978) describes the patterns of multilingualism in a region within Arnhem Land in some detail. Multilingualism is said to have been common in traditional society, and was considered an 'aspect of social relationships' (Heath 1978: 15). Yet not all languages were in contact with all other languages: the Ritharngu (Yuulngu family) had contacts especially with Ngandi but also with Nunggubuyu (both part of the same sub-branch of the 'prefixing' languages); Ngandi and Nunggubuyu were in contact with one another; and Nunggubuyu was also in close contact with Warndarang (of a separate sub-branch of the 'prefixing' group). Bakker (2006) too describes how in Sri Lanka, speakers of a Portuguese-based Creole and speakers of a Malay-based Creole were both in contact with speakers of Tamil, but not with one another. Based on the Tamil model, Sri Lanka Portuguese and Sri Lanka Malay show remarkable similarities (see above), despite the absence of direct contacts between them. Moreover, due to many centuries of contact between Tamil and Sinhalese, Sri Lanka Portuguese and Sri Lanka Malay resemble Sinhalese as well, despite the absence of direct contact.

It might therefore be argued that it is not possible to define linguistic areas at all: it is unclear how many features and how many languages they involve, it is unclear whether or not they must show a history of cultural contact or even evidence of linguistic contacts, it is controversial whether they are limited to certain types of contact or multilingualism, or to certain types of borrowing (matter or pattern). Indeed, Campbell (2006) proposes that linguistic areas are not a self-contained phenomenon but cases that can be adequately described using common concepts in contact linguistics. There is in other words no need to define linguistic areas as a distinct phenomenon. Bisang (2006) is somewhat more reserved, but similarly points out the difficulties of defining a restrictive area in which a density of shared features can be found across all languages, and proposes instead to replace the notion of an area by that of multiple 'zones of contact-induced structural convergence' (2006: 88).

This leaves us with two issues of interest. The first is the precise mechanism that enables the diffusion of features across languages and language-genetic boundaries. The second is one of epistemological interest, namely how to explain the reality which many linguists have hitherto been referring to as a 'linguistic area'? The answer to the first question was provided in the analysis of pivot-matching and pattern replication: bilingual speakers (including language learners) might syncretise planning operations across their repertoire of linguistic structures, while respecting the context-bound selection of appropriate word-forms. The result is an innovative construction in the chosen language of interaction, which becomes the 'replica-language'. In order for these innovations to be propagated, there needs to be a situation of tolerance or an approach of non-intervention with language use on the part of the immediate social environment. Such tolerance is nevertheless coupled with sufficient social pressure to ensure the maintenance of the replica language as a symbol of social identity (or in the case of learners, to embrace the new language).

Linguistic areas stand out due to two conditions: First, the repetition of the process of construction-borrowing for not just one or two constructions, but for a conspicuous number of structural features in a variety of structural domains. Second, and here lies the difference between one-to-one convergence and linguistic areas, the very same or a similar scenario needs to be repeated several

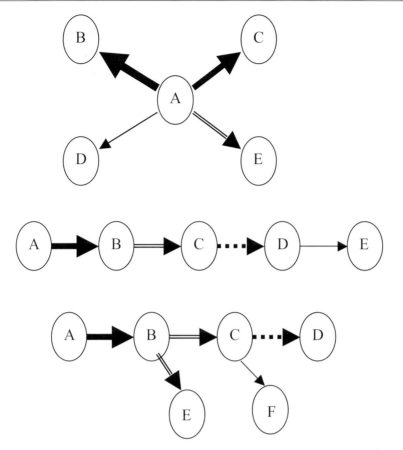

Figure 9.7 *Types of diffusion of structural patterns across languages; the various arrow shapes indicate unequal selection and diffusion of features across language pairs.*

times among pairs of contiguous languages. This can happen in several different ways: the model language might be in contact with several different languages, or there might be a kind of chain reaction, with each language serving as a model for a further contiguous language; or a combination of the two, as depicted in Figure 9.7.

The conditions for the emergence of linguistic areas are summarised in (32):

(32)   Conditions for the emergence of linguistic areas:
    a. Bilingual speakers are fairly uninhibited to generalise patterns across their linguistic repertoire, but are relatively conscious and respectful of contextually appropriate selection of word-forms.

    b. There is lax parental and societal control over the spread of innovations in the form of patterns, allowing the propagation of replicated patterns and so leading to language change, while at the same time loyalty to the replica language, ensuring language maintenance.

    c. Repetition of a. and b. across pairs of contiguous languages, resulting in
      a fairly dense, easily recognisable cluster of isoglosses representing
      shared structural patterns (and possibly also phonological forms).

The result of this scenario is a cluster of isoglosses that encompass a particular geographical region. There must be a sufficient density of shared isoglosses for linguists to give the region their attention as a linguistic area. Linguistic areas are therefore not real-life entities. Rather, they are constructions by linguists, who choose to grant their attention to situations in which, as a result of socio-historical coincidences, a series of conditions are met, and to label this kind of situation in a particular way.

10   Contact languages

10.1   The birth of a language

Linguists are rarely able to observe or document the 'birth' of a
language, or even to pinpoint its precise time of emergence. Languages are
transmitted from one generation to another and even phases in the history of a
single language, let alone the breaking away of varieties to form new idioms, are a
result of a gradual accumulation of changes over many generations. The exception
are languages that emerge as a result of language contact. Such languages have
been referred to as 'contact languages' (see Thomason 1997c and 1997e, Sebba
1997, Bruyn 1996). By this definition we exclude from the notion of 'contact
languages' cases of heavy borrowing that are a result of prolonged contact over
many generations and so of gradual accumulation of change, and concentrate on
those where the rise of a new idiom is relatively abrupt – often within just one or
two generations (cf. Bakker 1996, 2000a, Bakker and Muysken 1995).

A defining feature of contact languages is their function as a new medium of
communication, the need for which arises in a situation of cross-language interaction among population groups in a variety of settings, ranging from minimal
social contact and just occasional encounters for the purpose of trade, on to regular interethnic communication in a common socio-economic framework, and on
to intense social contacts among groups speaking different languages within the
same community and even within the same household.

Not all contact situations give rise to new languages, and not all languages used
in contact situations are also contact languages. The term *lingua franca* refers
to languages that are used for interethnic communication, i.e. in interactions in
which the participants have diverse background languages. But a lingua franca
may or may not be a contact language. Thus, English is used as lingua franca
in numerous international business transactions, and Russian is used as lingua
franca in encounters among members of various nations in Central Asia and the
Caucasus, but neither language emerged as a result of a situation of contact. On
the other hand, Nigerian Pidgin English and English-based Kriol of northern
Australia are both the product of cross-language interactions, and are widely
used among members of diverse ethnic and linguistic backgrounds as a means of
communication.

Although one occasionally comes across suggestions that a language's role as lingua franca will inevitably influence its structure – allowing for instance greater variability in style, or large-scale vocabulary import – there is no agreed parameter on the basis of which to assess such claims, and the term 'lingua franca' remains strictly confined to the sociolinguistic role of the language concerned, with no direct implications as to its structural composition. The case differs somewhat for *koiné*. This term relates to a variety of a language that serves as a means of communication among speakers of related varieties or dialects; in effect, a koiné is a lingua franca used among speakers of related dialects. There is however a general understanding that the role of a koiné entails a certain amount of structural levelling and cross-dialectal accommodation, processes that occur much more easily when the speech varieties involved are related and to some extent at least mutually comprehensible.

Another type of speech variety employed in contact situations is *foreigner talk* (see Chapter 4). Although here we might say that the emergence of the variety is abrupt, catering to the specific contact situation, and that it has far-reaching structural implications (especially the simplification of the target language), foreigner talk does not typically undergo any long-term conventionalisation and remains a largely improvised register, which we might best define as an ad hoc selective employment of structures from a speaker's linguistic repertoire. Those instances in which foreigner talk does undergo, or contribute toward conventionalisation and the emergence of a new speech variety inevitably involve the participation of the population of 'foreigners' or second-language learners itself; any conventionalisation of foreigner talk is thus part of the process of *pidginisation* (see below).

Finally, language contact situations may lead to the emergence of a collective interlanguage with a population of bilinguals learning and sometimes shifting to a second language. It is extremely difficult in such situations to determine either the pace of change, or the point at which the 'new', contact-shaped form of the language is sufficiently distinct from the 'old' form to merit classification as a separate language. Zuckermann (2003), following in the footsteps of Wexler (1990), suggests provocatively that the revitalised form of Hebrew spoken in Israel today is sufficiently different from earlier forms of Hebrew to be considered a separate, only partly related language, but this view is not generally accepted (see Comrie 1991), even though the evidence for Judeo-Arabic, Aramaic, and Ladino substrate influences in Israeli Hebrew goes far beyond both Wexler's and Zuckermann's narrow focus on the Yiddish and European substrate (see Matras and Schiff 2005). Bakker (2006: 153) discusses the convergence of Sri Lankan Portuguese and Sri Lankan Malay to Tamil (see also Chapter 9), which has led to a radical shift in the typological structure of the languages, but is unable to argue conclusively for a rapid change within one or two generations (although some evidence seems to support such an interpretation); in any event, the point of departure in these cases is a creole, already a contact language in its own right, and this fact appears to be highly relevant in assessing speakers' flexibility to re-structure their speech based on the model of the contact language.

The key feature defining a contact language is thus the absence of direct continuity from a single, identifiable predecessor variety – what Thomason and Kaufman (1988) refer to as 'broken transmission'. The term has effectively a double meaning. At the practical sociolinguistic level, it suggests that the language acquired and adopted by a young population is not the language transmitted to it by the parent generation.[1] At the more abstract level of language classification, it suggests that the language of the younger population is not based on any single transmitted, ancestral variety, but on a combination of sources. As a result, the conventional criteria of the comparative method cannot be applied in order to determine the new language's genetic affiliation or linguistic 'parentage'.

Two types of contact language matching this characterisation have so far been identified in the literature: the first are pidgin and creole languages, the second are mixed languages (also referred to by a variety of other names, such as 'bilingual mixtures', 'bilingual mixed languages', and 'split languages'). The principal challenge facing the study of contact languages is to relate their particular structural profile to the circumstances of their emergence and the purpose for which they are created and used. However, despite the young age of many contact languages, the precise circumstances of their emergence and a detailed picture of the linguistic input involved in the process are missing. For this reason especially, conclusions drawn from observations on contemporary situations of linguistic creativity in language contact situations form a vital part of the analysis: language play among bilinguals (cf. Golovko 2003), simplification and creativity strategies among language learners (e.g. Clyne 1968, Goglia 2006), and foreigner talk provide important clues alongside all other language contact phenomena such as those discussed in the previous chapters – codeswitching, fusion, and matter and pattern replication.

10.2   Pidgins and creoles

10.2.1   Definitions and key features

Pidgin is a cover-term for languages that arise from situations of semi-communication among a population of potential interlocutors who have no single language in common. In this respect, pidgins might be seen as a kind of makeshift lingua franca: they are created by speakers who draw on items within their various linguistic repertoires in order to enable inter-ethnic communication in a limited set of interaction contexts, usually for a restricted set of activities. For this reason, pidgins do not have native speakers. Typical situations in which pidgins arise are trade contacts and work organisation. Under conditions of more-or-less equal partnerships, pidgins might be based on an equal share of each group's linguistic input, thus creating a makeshift linguistic repertoire to which all participants contribute. This appears to have been the case in Russenorsk, a marine trade pidgin used during the nineteenth century in encounters between Norwegian and Russian sailors in the Arctic sea, which had vocabulary items of both Norwegian and Russian origin (Jahr 1996).

Labour pidgins, by contrast, are typically unbalanced, reflecting the power relations between the caste of employers, who often belong to a single ethnic-linguistic group, and that of labourers, who belong to another group and in many situations come from a variety of different ethnic and linguistic backgrounds. Colonial trade pidgins tend to be unbalanced as well, having their base in the colonial language – e.g. Arabic, Portuguese, English, or French; this reflects the dominance of the colonial power in the import of manufactured goods and often ideas on religion and social order. An unbalanced pidgin is one that emerges in a situation where the referential component of the makeshift lingua franca (that is, the content lexicon) is created largely through unidirectional accommodation to the linguistic repertoire of the dominant group. This repertoire thus acts as the primary *lexifier* of the pidgin. The great majority of documented pidgins emerged in the context of European colonial expansion and therefore have a European colonial language as their lexifier. Debates surround the processes that give rise to non-referential, grammatical operations in pidgins (see Section 10.2.2 below).

It is usually assumed that pidgins begin their 'life-cycle' as an informal, makeshift medium, sometimes referred to as 'jargon' (cf. Hall 1962, 1966, Mühlhäusler 1986, Muysken and Smith 1995). We might envisage this stage as the experimental employment of referential structures by a speaker and their adjustment subject to feedback from the interlocutor on their comprehensibility, in other words, subject to their role in successfully achieving communicative goals. Typically, at least in the emergence process of unbalanced pidgins, refer-ential structures are gradually selected in interactions of speakers of the lexifier language, leading to the stabilisation of a functionally limited, *shared reper-toire* of referential structures – or 'stabilised pidgin'. This repertoire gradually becomes independent of interactions with speakers of the lexifier. In interactions among non-speakers of the lexifier language it undergoes expansion of both the referential inventory of items (e.g. through processes such as makeshift lexical composition, or reduplication) and of the operational or grammatical domain of structure. It is this expansion that turns pidgins into 'languages in their own right'. The process of stabilisation and expansion is gradient, and different pidgins may show different extents of developments.

A consistent shift on the part of a population to a pidgin may give rise to a *creole*, the native language of the subsequent generation for whom the pidgin served as the principal input language in infancy. The majority of documented creoles emerged in the context of the European enslavement of African populations, either in plantations in the Americas and the Indian Ocean, or in forts or outposts and other ventures of European colonisation in Asia and the Pacific. In many of these regions, creoles are now used alongside the colonial language that had served as their lexifier in complementary sociolinguistic roles. The creole (or in some cases pidgin) is normally the *basilect* or language of the home and informal activities. The colonial language usually serves as the *acrolect* – it is the standard, written variety that is used in the public domain in formal interactions as well as in writing. In-between these two ends of the continuum we find various forms of the creole that are influenced by the standard, lexifier language and which are referred to collectively as *mesolect*. They often serve various purposes of semi-formal communication, such as informal interaction in an institutional setting, or the discussion of institutional, technical or academic topics in an informal setting; and they often predominate in urban settings (see Hackert 2004). While the mesolect is distinguishable as a system from both the basilect and the standard, it is open to considerable variation (cf. Patrick 1999). The term *post-creole continuum* is used to characterise this flexibility in the relationship between creole and standard (cf. Sebba 1997: 210–212, De Camp 1971). Examples are the co-existence of French-based Haitian Creole and standard French in Haiti, and of English-based Jamaican Creole and English in Jamaica.

English-based pidgins and creoles are often divided into Atlantic and Pacific (see Holm 2000: 91–101). This is not just a geographical division, but a classification that is at least in part historically motivated as well as structure-based. The group of Atlantic creoles includes those of the Carribean, such as Jamaican and Bahaman Creole English, Gullah of the coast of South Carolina and Georgia, and a long list of English-based creoles spoken along the eastern mainland coast of Central America (e.g. in Belize, Nicaragua, and Panama). English-based pidgins and creoles of West Africa, such as Sierra Leone Krio, Liberian and Nigerian Pidgin English, also belong to the Atlantic creoles. Similarities in both lexicon and grammar appear to point to a shared origin of the Atlantic creoles in West African English-based trade pidgins, which were carried into the western Atlantic area with the displacement of West African slaves to Atlantic plantations (see Hancock 1986, McWhorter 2000). Some of their grammatical features, such as verb serialisation, appear to be attributable to the typological features shared by the West African substrate languages. Similarities among Atlantic pidgins were reinforced by the two-way traffic between colonial outposts in West Africa and the Caribbean plantations from the seventeenth century onwards (cf. Holm 2000: 92). The English-based Pacific pidgins and creoles include Hawaiian Creole, Tok Pisin in Papua New Guinea, Solomon Islands Pijin, Bislama in Vanuatu, and the pidgins and creoles of northern Australia. Some of these show substrate features that are common in Austronesian languages, such as a distinction between inclusive and exclusive pronouns, the use of a transitivising suffix on verbs, and the use of a classifier-like suffix with various modifiers (cf. Keesing 1988).

French-based creoles are found in West Africa, the Caribbean (e.g. Haitian Creole, Antillean Creole of Guadeloupe, Martinique, Dominica, Trinidad, and Guyana), the Indian Ocean (Mauritius and Réunion), and New

Caledonia in the Pacific. Portuguese-based pidgins are found in West Africa (Cape Verde, Guinea, São Tomé), India, Sri Lanka, and Macao, and Dutch-based creoles include Berbice Dutch Creole in Guyana and the now extinct Negerhollands of the Virgin Islands. The absence of Spanish-based plantation creoles is regarded by McWhorter (2000) as evidence that creoles did not emerge in the plantations themselves, but grew out of trade pidgins based on Portuguese, Dutch, French, and English that had their origin in West Africa. Palenquero is a Spanish-based Creole that developed among run-away slaves in northern Colombia. Papiamentu, spoken on the Netherlands Antilles islands of Curaçao, Aruba, and Bonaire, is often considered a Spanish-based creole, but appears to have had its origin in a Portuguese-based West African pidgin spoken by slaves who were brought to the islands and later shifted towards Spanish (Kouwenberg and Muysken 1995, Holm 2000: 76–80).

Several other creoles are the result of mixtures and shifts. Zamboangueño or Chabacano, spoken by a population of mixed European–Asian origin on the Philippines island of Mindanao, is a mixture of Hiligaynon (Austronesian) and a creolised form of Spanish, the latter based on a re-lexified Portuguese pidgin (Frake 1971, Forman 1972). Lipksi (1992) suggests that it was formed at the Spanish garrison in Zamboanga by repatriated slaves from across the Philippines, while others relate it more directly to Manila Bay Creole Spanish. Sranan and Saramaccan, both English-based creoles spoken in Suriname, have been heavily influenced by Dutch and Portuguese, respectively (Adamson and Smith 1995, Bakker, Smith, and Veenstra 1995, Migge 2003). Ndyuka, a descendent of Sranan, is spoken by descendents of run-away slaves in Suriname, and has contributed to the emergence of the mixed Ndyuka–Trio trade pidgin along with Trio, an indigenous Carib language (Huttar and Velantie 1997).

Pidgins and creoles based on other languages include Juba Arabic of southern Sudan and Arabic-based Nubi of Uganda and Kenya (Owens 1997, Wellens 2005); Sango, a creole that developed out of a pidgin based on the Ubangian (Niger-Congo) language Ngbandi and is now widely spoken and even has official status in the Central African Republic (Pasch 1997); Fanakalo, a Zulu-based (Bantu) pidgin of southern Africa; Kitúba, a creole spoken in western Zaire and the Republic of Congo, based on Kikongo (Bantu) (Mufwene 1997); Nagapidgin, a restructured variety of Assamese; Bazaar Malay, Baba Malay, and numerous other simplified varieties of Malay spoken throughout the Indonesian Archipelago and New Guinea; Hiri Motu, an interethnic lingua franca based on Motu, an Autronesian language of Papua New Guinea (Dutton 1997); Lingua Geral, a lingua franca based on Tupi used in the Amazon basin; Chinook Jargon, an interethnic pidgin of the Pacific Northwest (Thomason 1983); the now extinct Pidgin Delaware based on the Eastern Algonquian language Unami in the regions of the Hudson River, Long Island, and northern New Jersey (Goddard 1997) and Greenlandic-based Eskimo trade pidgin (van der Voort 1995). Basque-based pidgins were employed in the North Atlantic in the sixteenth century (Bakker 1987,

1989), and Rabaul Creole German or *Unserdeutsch* was spoken until recently on New Britain Island in Papua New Guinea (Mühlhäusler 1977, 2001). This brief survey is by no means exhaustive.

While pidgins and creoles display a great variety of grammatical structures, certain structural properties can be said to be characteristic if not constitutive of the creole 'type'.[2] The most obvious of those is the reliance primarily on content lexemes of the lexifier language, ignoring or reducing grammatical morphemes that are semantically less transparent. In this regard, pidgin and creole formation resembles the hierarchy of morpheme borrowing and, more importantly, the hierarchy of morpheme acquisition in second-language learning (see Chapters 6 and 4). McWhorter (2005, 1998) regards as prototypical features of creoles the reduction and often complete disappearance of any inflectional morphology, as well as the absence of non-compositional derivational morphology, i.e. of morphology such as that represented by the English word *understand*. To these McWhorter adds the absence of phonological tone as a meaningful device to distinguish between morphemes. Discussions of general properties of pidgins and creoles are presented by Bickerton (1981), Bakker (1995), Holm (2000: 106ff.), and Winford (2003: 275–286, 319–329), which serve as a partial basis for the following remarks.

In phonology, most creoles have at least a five vowel system consisting of /a e i o u/, while Atlantic creoles tend to have /ɛ/ and /ɔ/ as well, and so a seven-vowel system resembling that of many West African languages. Creole vowel systems usually lack length opposition and rounded vowels. English vowels such as /æ, æi, ɑi, ʌ, ɔ, ɔʊ/ are often substituted: Tok Pisin *kot* 'coat', *dok* 'dog', *trai* 'try', *sapos* 'suppose'. The adherence to a West African syllable pattern CVCV results in forms such as Saramaccan *teki* 'take', *seri* 'sell', *fisi* 'fish'. Creoles tend to reduce consonant clusters, resulting in forms such as *tan* 'stand' in English-based Caribbean creoles, *yesidee* 'yesterday' in Jamaican Creole, or *amaun* 'amount' in Tok Pisin. English dental fricatives /ð, θ/ generally merge with the stops /d, t/ and affricates are usually reduced. Some Atlantic creoles retain West African co-articulated stops such as /kp/ and /gb/ and pre-nasalised stops like /nd/ and /mb/ in words of African origin; in some cases, these stops spread to European words from the main lexifier language, e.g. Haitian Creole *ntirɛlmā* 'naturally' (French *naturellement*). Palatalisations are common in positions preceding palatal vowels, though in many creoles post-alveolar articulations are substituted by dentals: Saramaccan *fisi* 'fish', Tok Pisin *was* 'watch'.

The creole lexicon is composed of items from the lexifier language, retentions from substrate languages, and internal creations. Creoles often display calques on substrate language elements: the structure 'rain/water' + PROG + 'fall', as in Jamaican Creole English *ren a faal* 'it's raining', is shared by a number of creoles, such as Haitian Creole French and Papiamentu Creole Spanish, as well as by West African languages such as Yoruba, Twi, and Kongo (Holm 2000: 121). Another substrate feature is reduplication for semantic emphasis and as a way of marking intensification, reiteration, or superlative.

The most characteristic features of creoles are probably found in morphosyntax. Creoles tend to have SVO word order, with little or no inflectional morphology and only minimal derivational morphology (the latter is usually limited to word-class changing derivation and nominal agentives). The prototypical verb system of creoles shows a tense opposition between an unmarked and an anterior form, an aspectual opposition between unmarked and non-punctual (progressive or habitual), and a modality opposition between unmarked and irrealis (cf. Givón 1982). Some creoles also have a completive aspect. In the pidgin stage, tense is normally indicated by the use of temporal particles. A characteristic feature of the creolisation process is the emergence of grammaticalised tense, modality and aspect particles, usually based on verbs of motion: cf. Saramacccan anterior *bi* from 'been', irrealis *o* from 'go', and habitual *ta* from 'stand/stay'. The particles can be combined; their linear arrangement tends to follow the same pattern in all creoles, namely tense first, followed by modality, followed by aspect – hence 'TMA': Saramaccan *mi bi-o-ta-njan fisi* 'I would have been eating fish' (cf. Bakker, Post, and van der Voort 1995: 250–252).

The use of serial verbs is widespread in creoles. Their meanings are usually directional, degree marking, aspectual, and argument introducing: Sranan *mi teki fisi seri* lit. [I take fish sell] 'I sold the fish' (Muysken and Veenstra 1995: 291, 306). Negation is usually marked by the placement of a negation particle before the verb. Many creoles have separate copula forms for adjectival predications, nominal predications, and predications expressing location. The verb 'say' is often used in serialisation to introduce a complement. Nouns lack either gender or plural inflection, but some creoles use determiners or quantifiers as pluralising markers: cf. Tok Pisin *bik-pela bisnisman* 'big businessman', *sam-pela sikman* 'some patients' (Verhaar 1995: 164, 414). Case and gender oppositions are also missing from the system of pronouns, though some Pacific creoles distinguish inclusive and exclusive pronominal forms, based on substrate influence from Austronesian and other languages: Tok Pisin *yumi* 'we (inclusive)', *mipela* 'we (exclusive)'. Definite articles are generally not taken over from the lexifier language, but appear as the outcome of internal grammaticalisation processes. Prepositions are likewise grammaticalised, sometimes from verbs or adjectives. Frequently, a general locative preposition is modified by adverbial expressions, or used in an abstract sense which is then specialised in conjunction with the verb: Melanesian Pidgin *ol meri long kantri* 'women in the country', *toktok long hevi bilong helt* 'talk about the difficulties of health', *moa long 40 meri* 'more than 40 women' (Sebba 1997: 52). Possession is usually expressed through juxtaposition, sometimes accompanied by a preposition: Melanesian Pidgin *hevi bilong helt* 'the difficulties of health'; Ngukurr-Bamyli (northern Australia) Creole *dog blanga dadi* 'a dog of Father's' (Sandefur 1979: 106). While conjunctions vary, the pronominal form for 'he' is often used in the meaning of 'and', and the preposition 'with' often functions as 'and' expressing accompaniment.

10.2.2   Emergence scenarios

The fact that we are able to make such detailed generalisations about the structures of dozens of languages that evolved in different places, at different times, by and large among different population groups, presents linguistic theory with the challenge of how to account for the link between similar sociolinguistic circumstances of communication and a particular structural profile of a language to which these circumstances give birth. The first factor that comes to mind is the simplification process involved in unguided, spontaneous second-language acquisition. As we saw in Chapter 4, unguided language acquisition tends to focus on the imitation and replication of lexical items with clear referential meaning, while leaving operational (grammatical) functions to makeshift constructions or often to constructions that are guided by the speaker's native language. The speech of Turkish labour immigrants in Germany ('Gastarbeiter') in the 1970s–1980s for instance (Chapter 4, Examples 5–6) shows absence of verb morphology, of plural marking, of nominal case, and of adjective agreement, generalisation of a single negator, and the use of adverbs to indicate verbal tense. It also shows the absence of a copula and definite articles and OV word order, which are all features of Turkish.

Foreign workers' German or *Gastarbeiterdeutsch* is not the only simplified, makeshift variety that has similarities with early-stage pidgins. A simplified form of Arabic is being used by household and construction workers from the Philippines, India, and Indonesia in the Gulf states (United Arab Emirates, Kuwait, and Oman).[3] Its features include the absence of plural marking, an analytical expression of possessiveness (with *ta-li* 'of-me'), absence of morphological agreement between nouns and modifiers, absence of definite and indefinite articles, generalisation of a single negation pattern, generalisation of the 3SG.M.PRES form of the verb for all persons and tenses leading in effect to the loss of verb morphology, use of the particle *awwal* 'first, once' accompanying the verb to express past tense, and loss of distinctive phonemes through substitution of both /x/ and /q/ by /k/, and of the pharyngeals /ħ/ and /ʕ/ by the glottals /h/ and /ʔ/, respectively. While the lexicon is entirely Arabic, Spanish-derived *chico* is used for 'child', apparently introduced by Philippinos.

Such features are often evaluated as a reduction of the structures of the target language due to limited access to target-language input. This assumes that the goal of learners is invariably to adopt the form of the target language that is spoken by native speakers. We must remember, however, that the process of unguided learning, especially for the purpose of restricted communication in a limited range of social activities, is not necessarily oriented towards the model of the target language, but towards efficiency of communication in those specific interaction contexts in which interethnic communication is necessary (see Goglia 2006). Processes such as the generalisation of word-forms or paradigm reduction, along with occasional insertional switching and the creative introduction of improvised constructions, can be viewed in this light as innovative strategies that facilitate communication, rather than mere target-language simplification. At any rate, learners' predictable interlanguage strategies and their fossilisation or stabilisation appear to have played a major role in the formation of pidgins.

Some scholars have gone a step further and attributed similarities among pidgins to an actual historical pool of shared structures. The idea of a *monogenesis* of pidgins takes on a variety of different shapes. The most speculative hypothesis, which is quite impossible to either prove or disprove, views all pidgins and creoles as deriving from a medieval Romance-based pidgin spoken around the Mediterranean coastal regions, termed *Lingua Franca* (hence the technical term *lingua franca*), which was introduced into West Africa by European traders. This created the basis for a Portuguese-based pidgin which was subsequently relexified in numerous new contexts as a result of the dominance of various European colonial languages, and carried among trade outposts and on to overseas plantations. A watered-down version of the same hypothesis traces colonial pidgins back to a West African Portuguese Pidgin without relating it to a medieval predecessor. This version relies largely on the fact that the Portuguese were the first European colonial trade power to make contacts in West Africa; that Portuguese-based creoles were the first to be widely dispersed throughout the Caribbean, the Indian Ocean, China, and the Philippines; that many Portuguese outposts and settlements were overrun and lost to other European powers, their non-European populations consequently shifting to accommodate to a new lexifier language; and finally on the wide diffusion of a small number of Portuguese words such as *savi* 'know' and *pikinini* 'child' in a large number of pidgins and creoles (cf. Stewart 1962, cited in Goodman 1987: 362–363; Whinnom 1965).

Alternative explanations for the similarities shared by pidgin and creole languages have been offered from two distinct theoretical directions. On the formalist side, generative approaches regard creolisation as a kind of structural scrambling process that triggers the re-modelling of surface-level structures in accordance with a supposedly pre-defined Universal Grammar. In this respect, creole genesis is likened to processes of first-, rather than second-language acquisition. This view is associated most closely with the works of Bickerton (1981, 1984) on the so-called 'Bioprogram' or 'Phylogenesis' hypothesis, which proposes that in the absence of clearly organised, full linguistic input from a pidgin-speaking parent generation, children draw on their innate linguistic abilities to transform the input they receive into a full-fledged language. Creoles thus owe their similarities to the universal shape of innate grammar.

On the functionalist side, grammaticalisation theory regards pidginisation as both motivated and shaped by the pragmatic need for basic communication, which leads to the selection of only the most salient referential structures (cf. Givón 1979, 1982). Numeral modifiers, quantifiers, and in most cases pronouns[4] tend to draw directly on forms and accompanying meanings of the lexifier language, while more abstract and highly grammaticalised elements of the lexifier language tend to be lost in the process of language acquisition and simplification. Creolisation, in turn, is driven by the need for expanded communication means, especially by the need to fill gaps in the representation of abstract functions. The lexical material from the lexifier language provides the source for the necessary grammaticalisation processes through which new operational structures evolve (cf. Keesing 1991, Bruyn 1996, Plag 2002). For example, typical sources of reflexive forms in creoles are lexifier-language pronominal forms, nouns expressing body-parts (such as 'body', 'head', 'skin'), and intensifiers such as 'same' and 'self' (Heine 2005b). The role of motion and state verbs such as 'go', 'be', 'stay', in the formation of tense, modality, and aspect particle was already mentioned above (cf. Givón 1982, Sankoff 1990).

A position that has become known as the 'substratist' approach to creoles attributes many developments in grammar and other areas of structure to the influence of the native languages during the process of pidginisation that preceded creole formation – West African languages for the Atlantic creoles (Boretzky 1983), and Oceanic-Austronesian languages for the Pacific creoles (Keesing 1988). Among the Oceanic substrate features mentioned by Keesing is the presence in Pacific creoles of a transitivising suffix, mirroring the transitivity marker of indigenous languages: compare Solomons Pidgin *(luk)luk* 'look', *luk-im* 'see', *sut* 'shoot', *sut-im* 'shoot (something)', with Kwaio (Southeastern Solomonic Austronesian language of Malaita) *(aga)aga* 'look', *aga-si-* 'see', *fana* 'shoot', *fana-si-* 'shoot (something)' (Keesing 1988: 120). Specific research has also been devoted to a number of Caribbean creoles. For the creoles of Suriname, socio-historical research has identified as potential substrate languages the Gbe languages of western Nigeria, Benin, Togo, and eastern Ghana, varieties of Kikongo spoken in Zaire and northern Angola, and Akan/Twi and Gã of Ghana, and these languages were also identified as significant contributors to the lexicons of Suriname creoles (Migge and Smith 2007: 5). Berbice Dutch Creole derives at least a quarter of its basic vocabulary from Eastern Ijo, a Nigerian language. Unusually for a creole, it contains inflectional morphology, which is also derived from Eastern Ijo: a plural marker *-apu*, and a past-tense marker *-tε*. The enclitic locative marker *-anga* is also of Eastern Ijo origin (Kouwenberg 1994).

Lefebvre (1998, 2004) selects Fongbe, a Niger–Congo language of the Gbe cluster, as representative of the putative substrate languages of Haitian Creole, and argues on the basis of structural comparisons between the two languages that Haitian Creole, and thus creoles in general, are the result of a process of 'relexification' of the substrate language. This model assumes that learners with limited access to the target language rely on an acquisition strategy that involves mere substitution of lexical items from their native language by corresponding items of the target language (French, in the case of Haitian Creole), with no actual acquisition of the target language grammar (cf. also Winford 2006). Some of the lexical placeholders are subsequently reanalysed, while at a later stage contact among contiguous creoles and especially between the creole and its lexifier contributes yet further to shifts in meaning and structural change, rendering the final shape of creoles with its contemporary manifestation. The distinction between pidginisation and creolisation is thus removed in favour of a three-stage account of creole genesis, beginning with relexification, followed by reanalysis and dialect levelling.

Other authors have taken a less wholesale approach to substrate influence. Kouwenberg and LaCharité (2004) compare reduplication patterns in English-based creoles of both Jamaica and Suriname with corresponding structures in the Niger–Congo languages Gbe and Igbo, and find evidence of substrate transfer in a number of very specific constructions. McWhorter (1997: 21–39) emphasises the relevance of homogeneity across a variety of potential West African substrate languages such as Akan, Ewe, Fon, Gã, Yoruba, Igbo, and others in the organisation of serial verb constructions – cf. for instance Fon *kòkú sɔ́ jiví mà kwíkwí* [Koku take knife cut banana] 'Koku cut the banana with a knife' – to the continuity of similar constructions in Saramaccan: *a tei goni suti di pingo* [he take gun shoot the pig] 'he shot the pig with a gun'; cf. also Arends, Kouwenberg and Smith (1995: 107–108). Holm (2000: 210) mentions the use of the verb 'surpass' or 'exceed' to indicate comparison with adjectives, based on a West African model: cf. Ewe *so lolo wu tedzi* [horse big exceed donkey] 'the horse is bigger than the donkey', Krio Creole English *olu big pas in padi* 'Olu is bigger than his friend', Haitian Creole French *Boukinèt bèl pase Marí* 'Boukinèt is more beautiful than Mari'.

Migge and Winford (2007) argue for a differentiated approach to substrate influence. They hypothesise that a number of factors condition and constrain substrate transfer, including the presence of similar categories across a variety of substrate languages involved in the process (varieties of Gbe, in the case of Surinamese), and the availability of lexifier morphemes to represent these functional categories. They conclude that substrate influence was definitely involved in the formation of the TMA system of Surinamese creoles, but that it was not the only contributor, and that processes of internal change played a role as well.

A so-called 'superstratist' view attributed to Chaudenson (1992) and Mufwene (1996) regards pidgins and creoles as varieties of the lexifier or superstrate language, much like any other variety, though shaped by the particular circumstances of contact, migration, or displacement of a 'founder generation'. Mufwene (1996, 1997a, 2001) effectively seeks to 'de-construct' prevailing notions on pidgins and creoles, rejecting the idea that they constitute a particular language type. Mufwene's alternative is to approach each and every idiom individually and investigate its own particular language history. Pidgins and creoles are names given in a somewhat arbitrary manner, according to this view, to a series of speech varieties that emerged during a certain period, as a result of contact between Europeans and non-Europeans, and are sometimes extended to further languages on the basis of partial similarities with the first group. In fact, these various idioms all constitute part of a larger continuum ranging from makeshift varieties or 'jargons', through to indigenised varieties of the standard colonial languages, foreigner and immigrant varieties, non-standard koinés, and other languages affected in some way or another by contact. Mufwene also contradicts the view that pidgins and creoles arose abruptly, and attributes their formation and development to similar processes as are exhibited in other, gradual situations of language change.

Arends (1993) proposes a similar interpretation, which he refers to as a 'gradualist' hypothesis (see also Arends and Bruyn 1995; cf. Thomason 2001: 183–188). Based on interpretations of historical sources documenting early forms of creoles and the social circumstances under which they were employed by speakers, Arends (1993: 373) suggests that creolisation is not unigenerational, but a long and gradual process extending over a number of generations. The criticism is directed in particular against Bickerton's (1981) universalist Bioprogram idea, which views the materialisation of creoles as a catastrophic event in which all parts are put into place at once by (first) language learners. Arends (1993: 376) suggests instead that the process is continuous, that it is carried out by adult speakers rather than by children, that it is a process of second rather than first language acquisition, and that it is differential (i.e. leading to a variety of outcomes in different cases) rather than uniform.

Leaving aside Bickerton's Bioprogram, many of the other approaches to creole genesis are not entirely irreconcilable with one another. McWhorter's (2005, 1997) model of creole genesis offers an interesting synthesis of views. McWhorter (2000) rejects suggestions that creoles emerged on plantations independently of pidgins, and considers them instead to be direct descendents of West African trade pidgins used as lingua francas and indeed even as markers of a collective African identity by the displaced population of slaves on plantations. McWhorter's explanatory model assumes that during the genesis stage of pidgins, speakers are not interested in acquiring full command of the (lexifier) target language, but rather in having an effective means of communication that can serve the rather limited needs of a small set of interaction contexts and activities. The development of creoles from here onwards constitutes a cline. Some varieties, such as Berbice Dutch Creole, enjoyed a stronger homogeneous linguistic background during their emergence stage and consequently show greater or more consistent substrate influence. Others, like Réunionais, which was used for a long period in a situation of somewhat looser social distance between population strata, acquired greater superstrate influence during its genesis.[5] Creoles may also differ in the extent of contact influence from the lexifier language after genesis. In all creoles, speakers make use of those simplified structures inherited from the pidgin stage and expand them through processes of internal grammaticalisation (cf. McWhorter 2005: 72–101).

According to McWhorter (1998, 2005), it is due to their young age and their origin in simplified varieties employed in a limited set of interaction contexts – pidgins – that creoles constitute a particular language type with the following characteristics: absence of inflectional morphology, absence of non-compositional derivational morphology, and absence of distinctive, meaningful tone. All three are structures that require a prolonged diachronic development: intense grammaticalisation and synthetisation in the case of the former two, significant erosion of meaningful syllables in the case of the latter. McWhorter's ideas on the emergence of creoles are well in line with the notion developed in the previous chapters that speakers have their full linguistic repertoire at their disposal at all times, and that speakers make choices within this complex linguistic repertoire that are guided by the goals of communication and contextual appropriateness. In the context of limited interaction in an interethnic setting, speakers will make use of those components of a lingua franca that are both accessible and necessary to sustain communication; they will also avail themselves of constructions and even word-forms from their native language(s), to the extent that these can be understood and appear acceptable to a significant proportion of potential interlocutors; and they will engage in the creative composition of makeshift constructions to express relations for which an adequate, established structure is missing.

10.3   Mixed languages

10.3.1   Definitions and explanatory accounts

While there is no uniform view of what precisely constitutes a mixed language, it is generally understood that mixed languages show mixtures that are distinct, either qualitatively or quantitatively, from other cases of contact-induced change. As a sub-group of contact languages, mixed languages are considered to be mixed to the extent that their genetic affiliation cannot be ascribed to just one particular lineage (cf. Thomason and Kaufman 1988), while the absence of simplification processes as part of their genesis makes them distinct from pidgins and creoles.

In Chapter 2 (Example 38) we witnessed Ben's playful and deliberate mixing of languages amounting in effect to making non-conventional combinations of elements from the complex linguistic repertoire in order to create special effects in discourse. The example – with omission of accompanying turns – is repeated here as (1):

(1)   (Hebrew-defined context; italicised insertions from German):
       Where do I get a *Lappen*   so I can *wisch* my *Gesicht*?
       'Where do I get a *wash cloth* so I can *wipe* my *face*?'

The example derives from a rather late phase in the child's surveyed history of linguistic socialisation, indicating not just a relatively high level of proficiency in the languages, but also a relatively high degree of confidence, enabling him to take communicative risks and to try and manipulate language for special effects. It also illustrates that in the course of such language manipulation the complex linguistic repertoire can be scrambled and demarcation lines within it re-defined.

In the cited example, this re-definition does not occur at random. Grammatical operations within the utterance, including clause structure and inflections, are taken from one language, while the lexicon is taken from another.

The choice of both languages in the mixed utterance – English grammar, German vocabulary – defies the convention of selecting Hebrew as the language of interaction with the father. The example thus shows a double contrast, sending a message of double inconsistency: inconsistency in the choice of language for the interaction with the father, and inconsistency in the selection of grammar and vocabulary components within the utterance itself. It is the disruption of harmony at these two levels that lends the utterance its humorous effect. Two important observations can be made on the basis of (1): first, in pursuit of special conversational effects fluent bilingual speakers, even young bilinguals, are able to control their repertoire in such a way as to purposefully defy conventions on both situational selection of forms and the structural composition of utterances. Second, a natural way to compartmentalise the selection of structures within an utterance is to separate the grammatical blueprint of the utterance from its key content words.

Heine (1969, cited in Mous 2003a: 4), writing with reference to the Ma'a language of Tanzania (also called 'Inner Mbugu'), was one of the first to point out the existence of mixed languages in which different sub-systems – grammar and lexicon – derive from different languages. This view remained controversial until quite recently. Greenberg (1999) denied that a 'truly mixed language' (i.e. one that derived its vocabulary and grammar from two different sources) could arise by a natural process, and interpreted the case of Ma'a as gradual borrowing of Bantu grammar into a Cushitic language. Thomason and Kaufman (1988) and Thomason (1997a) argue in favour of the existence of mixed languages that cannot be genetically attributed to either of their sources, but agree essentially that the process that led to the emergence of Ma'a is one of gradual replacement of a Cushitic grammar by Bantu grammatical inflections. The specific arguments put forth by Thomason (1997a) in support of this scenario – the retention of some Cushitic grammar, and supposed evidence of different periods of Bantu influence – are both contentious (see Mous 2003a: 75ff.).

The more likely scenario appears to be that Ma'a arose as a mixed language when speakers of a Cushitic language shifted to a Bantu language, but retained command of significant portions of the original Cushitic vocabulary (see below). In terms of its historical progression, this scenario appears to be the reverse of the process of 'relexification', which Muysken (1981, 1997) describes for Media Lengua, a variety of Quechua in which speakers consciously substitute native vocabulary items on a wholesale basis with vocabulary from Spanish. The notion that such processes can occur gradually, as proposed by Thomason and Kaufman (1988), is refuted by Bakker and Mous (1994; see also Bakker and Muysken 1995) on the grounds that there is no evidence of a continuum between cases of heavy lexical borrowing, where no more than 40% of the vocabulary is replaced, and mixed languages like Ma'a or Media Lengua, which recruit 90% of their vocabulary from a language that is different from the source language of their grammar (see also Stolz 2003).

Bakker (1996, 1997a; see also Bakker and Mous 1994, Bakker and Muysken 1995) therefore proposes that the processes that are responsible for the formation of mixed languages are distinct from those that lead to heavy borrowing. Mixed languages are defined by Bakker and Mous (1994) as languages that have distinct source languages for their lexicon and grammar, or show a 'lexicon-grammar split'. This split is regarded by Bakker as the result of a process of conscious creation coined 'language intertwining'. The process is considered to be abrupt in most cases, leading to the emergence of a new language within one generation. It is tightly embedded into the social process of ethnic identity formation, and the resulting mixed code is seen as an overt manifestation of a new, mixed identity (cf. also Croft 2003). Language intertwining therefore occurs in small communities that are undergoing a process of identity crystalisation, either as a result of migration or acculturation or due to wide-scale intermarriage and the emergence of mixed households. The split between lexicon and grammar is regarded by Bakker as natural: lexical substitution is conscious, while the employment of grammar is intuitive, with function words falling in between the two. This makes mixed languages to some extent predictable.

The role of bilingualism in general and codeswitching in particular has received much attention in discussions of mixed languages. Myers-Scotton (1992, 1998, 2003) emphasises formal-structural similarities between the lexicon–grammar split in mixed languages, and insertional codeswitching in which, according to the Matrix Language Frame model (see Chapter 5), the only permissible items from the Embedded Language are content-morphemes. Myers-Scotton proposes a process of '(Arrested) Matrix Language Turnover', by which a speaker population shifts from one Matrix Language to another, incorporating the old ML as a new Embedded Language. From the conversation-analytical perspective, Auer (1999) hypothesises that mixed languages or 'fused lects' can emerge when codeswitching becomes regular and predictable, and loses its discourse-level meaningfulness.

Bakker and Muysken (1995) and Backus (2003) contend that insertional codeswitching virtually never manifests the consistency, regularity, and predictability seen in the split of lexicon and grammar in mixed languages. However, McConvell and Meakins (2005) seem to provide evidence in support of a gradual conventionalisation of codeswitching patterns in the context of ongoing language shift: recordings made during the 1970s–1980s among bilingual speakers of the northern Australian language Gurindji and Kriol (an English-base creole) show codeswitching patterns that are characterised by the use of Kriol syntax and verb morphology and Gurindji case-inflection on nominal elements. This recurring pattern of language mixing, in conjunction with the decline in proficiency in Gurindji, provided the principal linguistic input for the younger generation of speakers. It has subsequently been conventionalised in Gurindji Kriol, a mixed language in which the use of elements of different source languages is overwhelmingly stable and no longer subject to choice based on social or discourse-level considerations.

This and other investigations of mixed languages – Vakhtin (1998) on Copper Island Aleut, Mous (2003) on Ma'a, O'Shannessy (2005) on Light Walpiri, Matras *et al.* (2007) on Angloromani – emphasise the role of language death and language shift in the formation of many, though by no means all, mixed languages. Adding a functional dimension to Myers-Scotton's (1992) idea of a 'turnover' of languages, I have proposed (Matras 2000a) that a 'functional turnover' in the status of the old community language – from an everyday means of communication to a primarily emblematic medium – may lead to 'selective replication' of structural material. This will target primarily the lexicon, but possibly also some grammar, which suffices for the new, emblematic functions that are now assigned to the old lect. A process of 'lexical re-orientation' was postulated to account for the deliberate recruitment of content lexemes from an external source. This leads to the creation of a mixed language in situations in which there is otherwise continuity of the community language, i.e. language maintenance rather than shift, e.g. in Media Lengua (cf. Muysken's 1981 'relexification').[6] There is growing consensus that the creation of mixed languages is not only a conscious act by speakers, but a deliberate one. Thomason (1997d, 1999) identifies deliberate choices made by speakers as one of several mechanisms that can lead to language change, and Golovko (2003) provides empirical evidence of adult bilinguals' language play where speech is manipulated to reflect a hybrid cultural identity, thus constituting an 'identity act' (cf. Croft 2003). The 'deliberate creation' hypothesis is a key to understanding the different functions that mixed languages have, and the range of structural profiles that they exhibit.

10.3.2   Structural profiles and the functionality cline

Mixed languages can be arranged on a functional cline. At its extreme end we find those mixed languages that have developed into everyday family and community languages. At its opposite end we find lects whose use is limited to a number of rather narrow and specialised communicative functions. Smith (1995) has observed that some mixed languages exist in a 'symbiotic' relation to one of their source languages, that is, the mixed idiom is a variety of a non-mixed language spoken by a larger, neighbouring community, with which it shares most aspects of morphosyntax and phonology. Users of the mixed language also have command of the non-mixed form of the language, which may even be their default everyday speech variety.

Jenisch (also: Yenish, Yeniche) is one of these 'symbiotic' mixed languages and representative of what might be described as 'cyptolects' or secret, in-group vocabularies that rely on foreign lexicon to disguise meaning. Jenisch varieties are used by populations in southwest Germany, Switzerland, and Austria, who call themselves *Jenische*. They appear to have been formed around the seventeenth century as a network of travelling families engaged in various itinerant service occupations. Jenische largely became sedentary from the eighteenth century onwards, but maintained their itinerant occupational profiles and cross-regional social networks. They also absorbed other Travellers and members of minority communities such as Gypsies and Jews who, for some reason or other, had left their own communities. Jenisch is a limited lexicon, usually comprising several hundred lexical items in the vocabulary of any individual user. The words are inserted into dialectal German conversation, usually in order to exclude outsiders or to flag group solidarity and group membership. The composition of the Jenisch vocabulary is not uniform, but characteristic of specific local communities and often subject to considerable individual variation. Typically, Jenisch varieties consist of a lexical core that goes back to the historical *Rotwelsch* or German-based secret jargon. These are often figurative and metaphorical formations such as *Zündling* 'lighter' for 'fire', or words of obscure origin that take on a German-like structure, such as *Blamm* 'beer'. The core is supplemented by words of Hebrew origin adopted from the secret language of Jewish traders, as well as many words of Romani origin. In the Jenisch of Unterdeufstetten (cf. Matras 1998e), a village in southwest Germany on the Württemberg–Bavarian border, some 30% of the vocabulary derives from Romani, and another 10–15% is Hebrew (non-German elements are italicised):

(2)   *schäfft* a *lawe Tschai, nasch* mit'r   ins   *Tschiben*
        is   a bad girl   go   with.her to.DEF bed
        '[She]'s a bad girl, go to bed with her'

(3)   *nasch* zum   *Ruach* und *mang* mir   *Maro*
        go   to.DEF farmer and ask   me.DAT bread
        'Go to the farmer and get me some bread'

In (2), the words *schäfft* 'is' and *law-* 'bad' derive from Hebrew (*šev-* 'to sit', *lav* 'not'), and entered Jenisch via the Jewish in-group cryptolect, apparently through occasional contact with Jewish traders or the absorption of Jews into the community. The words *Tschai* 'girl', *nasch* 'go', and *Tschiben* 'bed' are all of Romani origin, as are *mang* 'ask, beg' and *Maro* 'bread' in (3), while *Ruach* comes from the Rotwelsch component. Jenisch is thus a perfect example for lexical re-orientation: it recruits lexical content-vocabulary from a variety of sources and employs it occasionally, and entirely at the speaker's discretion, in order to disguise meaning or flag in-group solidarity.

Another symbiotic mixed language of southwest Germany and neighbouring areas is Lekoudesch, also known by related names such as Lechoudesch and Lottegorisch (Matras 1988, 1991, 1996a, Klepsch 1996, Meisinger 1902), or in the Netherlands as Louter Lekoris and Losche Nekôdesch (Moormann 1920, 1922). The name is a euphemistic extension of the term for the language of the Hebrew scriptures – *Loschn ha-koudesch* 'the holy tongue'. Lekoudesch was used by Jewish cattle-traders at markets as a secret language, but it also contributed to the consolidation of group-identity among the men involved in the trade. It recruits its special vocabulary primarily from Ashkenazic Hebrew, the unspoken language of northern European Jewish communities used in prayer, religious education, and formal community transactions. Hebrew lexicon was inserted into the rural Judeo-German ethnolect, which was closely related to the southwestern German dialects.

Rural Jewish communities practically ceased to exist in Germany after World War II, but knowledge of Lekoudesch was retained for a further generation among non-Jewish farmers who in their youth had been hired by Jews to help drive cattle to the markets, a task which usually involved a several-day journey on foot. The following examples were recorded in 1984–1985 from a group of such users in the village of Rexingen, near the Black Forest region of southwest Germany (see Matras 1991). The host language is the local Swabian dialect of German; Hebrew insertions are italicised:

(4)   Der *schäfft* de ganze *Jomm* im   *Uschpiss*, un duat immer
       he sits   the whole day in.DEF pub   and does always

       harme schasskenna und *meloucht lou.*
       much drinking   and works   not
       'He *sits* all *day* in the *pub*, and *drinks a lot*, and *doesn't work*.'

(5)   Die *Goja*   isch *haggel doff*, dia kennt-m'r *lekächa.*
       the woman ist   all   good her can-one   take
       'The *woman* is *very pretty*, one could *sleep* with her.'

(6)   *Lou dibra,* d'r *Guj* schäfft!
       not talk   the man is
       'Don't talk, there's man there! [=a stranger is listening]'

Note that Lekoudesch shares its copula *schäff-* (Hebrew *šev-* 'to sit') with Jenisch. Other Hebrew-derived items in Examples (4)–(6) are the nouns *Jomm* 'day' (Hebrew *yōm*), *Uschpiss* 'pub' (Hebrew from Aramaic *ušpīz*, Greek/Latin *hospitio*), *Goj/a, goya* '(non-Jewish) man/woman, stranger' (*gōy/a*), adjectives and adverbs *haggel* 'all, entirely' (*hakkōl*), *doff* 'good' (*tōv*), and *harme* 'much' (*harbe*), the negation particle *lou* (*lō*), the verbs *dibr-a,* 'to talk' (*dibber*), *lekäch-a* 'to take' (*lakax*), *schass-kenn-a,* 'to drink' (*šaθa*), and the derived verb *melouch-t* 'works' (from the Hebrew noun *məlaxa* 'work').

In addition to content-words with referential meaning, both Jenisch and Lekoudesch recruit cryptolalic or 'disguised', foreign word-forms for a limited number of grammatical categories, namely non-verbal predications (copula) and negation. These categories might be described as 'pragmatically salient' in respect of the overall propositional meaning conveyed by the utterance: whether something is present or absent is essential to the message, and is therefore in need of potential means of encryption (cf. Matras 1998a, 2003). Note that Examples (4)–(5) show an opposition between the locational-existential predication, for which the Hebrew-derived copula is used, and the adjectival predication, which employs the German copula. Other grammatical word-forms, such as pronouns, prepositions, articles, auxiliaries, and along with them all inflectional morphology is dialectal German. This employment of foreign-lexicon grammatical material does not seem related to the accessibility of such material. Depending on their degree of religious education, Jewish men will have had active reading knowledge and possibly even writing knowledge of Hebrew and so will have been able to produce a much greater range of word-forms and categories, including grammatical categories, than what appears in Lekoudesch. From the similarities in the type of lexical categories it appears that the recruitment of external vocabulary is tailored not to availability, but to expressive needs.

The purpose of both Jenisch and Lekoudesch is to be able to convey meaning in a *group-internal perspective, at the level of individual utterances*, whether for the purpose of humour and in-group solidarity (see discussion in Matras 1996a), or for the purpose of actually excluding bystanders. Note that the sample sentences documented above, which have been provided by users in recollection of their actual use of the code, tend to contain taboos, derogatory comments about others, warnings, and 'conspiracy' instructions. In this respect, the 'languageness' (Thomason 1997c) of codes like Lekoudesch might in fact be questioned: both structurally and functionally they are clearly distinct from the everyday notion of 'language' as a potentially all-purpose means of communication, and are limited instead to a very specific domain of speech acts, utilising a lexical reservoir of limited scope (though this reservoir can potentially be extended).[7]

Mixed codes like Jenisch and Lekoudesch also figure at the extreme end of the cline with respect to the degree of bilingualism that is involved in their emergence. In Jenisch, language contact only plays a peripheral role. The core of the Jenisch lexicon goes back to a monolingual cryptolect that recruits its material through language-internal creative derivation processes. Jenisch relies in addition on material that is imported from speech varieties that are regarded as having similar cryptolectal functions (irrespective of the fact that both Hebrew and Romani also have additional, non-cryptolectal functions in their respective communities). The mixed character of Jenisch vocabulary is therefore in the first instance a reflection of the need to enrich the special lexical reservoir through new items that have not yet been compromised and through fashionable lexical items. This enrichment process relies on contacts with other itinerant or marginalised populations. In the case of Lekoudesch, bilingualism is largely passive, involving an unspoken language. Yet again, the recruitment of Hebrew items as a lexical reservoir is purely opportunistic in the sense that it makes use of available lexical material for cryptolectal purposes. A similar case of a cryptolect that relies on an unspoken language is the speech of the Abdal or Äynu of Anatolia, central Asia and Chinese Turkestan (Xinjiang), which consists of the insertion of special vocabulary of Persian origin into Turkish, Azeri, or Uyghur (Ladstätter and Tietze 1994).

Angloromani occupies a nearby position on the continuum (see Matras *et al.* 2007). Like other so-called 'Para-Romani' varieties (cf. Bakker and van der Voort 1991, Boretzky and Igla 1994, Bakker 1998, Matras 1998c, Matras 2002), it is an in-group lexical reservoir of Romani-derived word-forms – primarily lexical content-words. Speakers of Angloromani usually have knowledge of several hundred Romani-derived words. Unlike Jenisch and Lekoudesch, Angloromani also includes some grammatical function words such as personal pronouns and demonstratives, expressions of local relations and location deixis, some expressions for time, numerals, a few indefinites such as 'nothing' and 'something', negators, as well as some productive word-derivation strategies that are inherited from inflectional Romani (*mas* 'meat', *masengro* 'butcher'; *del* 'to give', *delliben* 'gift').

Like other Para-Romani varieties, Angloromani is the product of language shift and the abandonment of (inflected) Romani as an everyday language of the family and community. This suggests that its formation involved some degree of bilingualism, albeit in the context of language obsolescence. Romani was spoken in Britain by a small minority beginning with the arrival of the first Roma in the British Isles in the fifteenth century and until the second half of the nineteenth century, after which it underwent a rather rapid decline.[8] The use of Romani words in English utterances is documented already in the seventeenth century, suggesting that Para-Romani or Angloromani may have been used as a mixed in-group register even before the decline of inflected Romani (see Bakker 2002). Nevertheless, sources from the late nineteenth and early twentieth century point to a gradual rise of indiscriminate mixture of inflected Romani and Romani insertions into an English sentence frame, followed by a consistent use of English sentences into which Romani words are inserted. The latter is the pattern that prevails today among the Romani Gypsies of England and Wales, though even this use of Romani is largely limited to the occasional insertion of Romani words into individual English utterances (examples from Matras *et al.* 2007; Romani-derived words are italicised):[9]

(7)   *Kekka pen dovva, rakli's trash!*
        'Don't say that, [the] girl's scared!'

(8)   *Maw* be *rokker*ing in front of the *mush* and *rakli!*
        'Don't be talking in front of the man and [the] girl!'

(9)   *Ol* the *obben* coz when the *rakli*s *jel*s I'm gonna *mor* yas.
        'Eat the food coz when the girls go I'm gonna kill you(PL)!'

(10)   She's a *chikli rakli* – look at the *chik* everywhere!
        'She's a dirty woman – look at the dirt everywhere!'

(11)   *lesti*'s *savv*ing at *mandi*
        'he's laughing at me'

A key factor in the retention of a Romani-derived lexicon is no doubt the maintenance of a tight-knit community structure with its own set of values, a very specific socio-economic profile based on an itinerant service economy, and semi-nomadism and marginalisation leading to minimal social contacts with the majority society. This resembles key features of the rural Jewish communities of southwest Germany and the Jenische. Like Lekoudesch and Jenisch, Angloromani is best characterised as an *emotive mode* (Matras *et al.* 2007). Its basic function is to ground the utterance in a very particular domain of intimate knowledge and attitudes that is shared only by members of the community. Secrecy and warnings, as in Examples (7)–(8), are concrete manifestations of this function, as are intimate expressions of care and responsibility (9), evaluations (10), and sharing of distress and other emotions (11).

Ma'a or Inner Mbugu, spoken in the Usambara mountains in Tanzania, provides evidence that selective replication under similar circumstances may also lead to the emergence of a language with a broader range of functions. It is also a symbiotic mixed language, based on what the speakers call 'normal' Mgubu, a Bantu language that is similar to Pare or Chasu, which is spoken north of the Usambara region. Speakers refer to themselves in Mbugu as *vaMbugu* and in the in-group form of their language as *vaMa'á*, hence the term *Ma'a* for the in-group variety or 'Inner Mbugu'. When discussing the differences between the varieties, speakers use the language labels *kiMbugu* and *kiMa'á* (Mous 2003a: 1). The surrounding language is the Bantu language Shambaa. Speakers generally know Mbugu, Shambaa, Swahili, and Pare. Mous (2003a: 8) defines Inner Mbugu as a parallel lexicon, but one that has a lexical range that is as complete as that of Normal Mbugu and is used by some speakers for all topics of conversation.

Mous (2003a: 17–50) reviews a series of historical scenarios and concludes with a rather complex proposal for the origin of the group, involving several migrations, splits, language shift, and intermarriage with other groups. The principal elements of the proposal and the various alternative scenarios that underlie them are these: The Mbugu people's economy and social identity revolves around cattle raising, and this makes them distinct from neighbouring populations. The Mbugu once had knowledge of an Old Kenyan East Cushitic language, which appears to have been abandoned in favour of Bantu Pare (Chasu). They also had contacts with Iraqw/Gorwaa, and possibly assimilated speakers of this language into their own group, and with the Maasai, for whom they provided services. The need for a parallel lexicon arose as a means of flagging a separate identity as an economically specialised, possibly ethnically mixed population of former migrants. The various languages that played a role in the history of the group, namely the old East Cushitic language (which remains unidentified), South Cushitic Iraqw/Gorwaa, and Nilotic Maasai, were exploited as sources for the parallel lexicon, alongside a number of internal (Pare-based) strategies of lexical manipulation (see also Mous 2003b: 213). These include truncation of suffixes, addition of final *é*, and substitution of a consonant with /ʔ/ or /ɧ/ (Mous 2003b: 215–216).

Ma'a or Inner Mbugu is thus largely a parallel lexicon which substitutes the lexicon of Normal Mbugu in conversations that are marked as 'group-internal'. Apart from content words, the parallel lexicon has its own structures for the possessive construction, possessive affixes, demonstratives, quantifiers, agreement patterns of some modifiers, some expressions of time (e.g. 'today', 'yesterday'), expressions of local relations, conjunctions, personal pronouns, numerals, and greetings. Content words have by and large the same meaning and grammatical properties (e.g. nominal class affiliation) as the words they replace:

(12)   Normal and Inner Mbugu narrative excerpts (Mous 2003a: 9) (numerals refer to Bantu nominal class affixes):
   a. NM hé-na   m-zima   é-tang-we   kimwéri m-fumwa w-a
      IM hé-ló   mw-agirú é-sé-we   kimwéri dilaó   w-a
         16-have 1-elder   1-call-PAST.PERF Kimweri king   1-CONV

      NM i-i i-sanga l-á   lusótó
      IM yá i-dí   l-á   lusótó
         this 5-land 5-CONV Lushoto

   b. NM hé-na   i-zuva i-mwe áa-tanga   va-mbugu na   va-shamba
      IM hé-lo   i-'azé i-wé áa-sé   va-Ma'a na   va-sitá
         16-have 5-day 5-one 1.PAST-call   2-Mbugu with 2-Shambaa

      NM na   va-asu   vá-vata vá-zé-m-hl-la   ma-diyo-ake
      IM na   va-áriye vá-so   vá-zé-m-hand-ía ma-gerú   ku'u
         with 2-Pare 2SUBJ-go 2SUBJ-it-1-apl 6-bananas   his

   c. NM íji va-mbugu v-á-he-fika   ila'i
      IM íji va-Ma'a v-á-he-hé   twái
         now 2-Mbugu 2-PAST-16-arrive there

   d. NM kwá kubá   te-vé-kund-ye   vá-ronga   io   ndima
      IM kwá kubá   te-vé-dúmú-ye   vá-bó'i   ka   nyamálo
         with reason NEG-2-want-PERF 2.SUBJ-make DEM.2 work

   a. 'There was an elder called Kimweri, king of this land Lesutho.
   b. On a certain day he called the Mbugu, Shambaa, and Pare people to go and plant his banana trees.
   c. Well, the Mbugu arrived there.
   d. Because they didn't want to do this work...'

Like Angloromani, Ma'a or Inner Mbugu appears to have arisen from a situation of language obsolescence, with speakers retaining a selection of structures and employing them within the overall framework of the new language as an in-group code. While the functions of Angloromani are limited and resemble those of cryptolects, Ma'a, although symbiotic, is used at the level of entire stretches of discourse and not just at the utterance level.

Media Lengua is another mixed language that is apparently used at the discourse level, though documentation of its actual use is limited. Unlike our previous cases, Media Lengua arose in a situation of acculturation, when Quechua-speaking men from a number of villages in Equador were employed in the construction of railways in the early twentieth century, spending prolonged periods away from home in a Spanish-speaking environment (Muysken 1981, 1997). The mixed idiom that they created was imported back to their villages and became a token of the families' and community's social identity. The principal feature of Media Lengua is the substitution of Quechua content lexemes by

Spanish word-forms, hence Muysken's (1981) characterisation of the process as
're-lexification'. While all inflectional morphology as well as word order and
most clause-combining strategies are Quechua, the Spanish lexicon also includes
grammatical vocabulary such as (singular) pronouns (to which Quechua plural
markers are added to form the plural pronouns, based on the Quechua model),
demonstratives, indefinites pronouns, negators, adverbs, and numerals:

(13)   Media Lengua (Muysken 1997: 377):
         a. *Media Lengua*-ga   *así* Ingichu-munda *Castellanu*-da *abla*-na
            Media Lengua-TOP thus Quechua-from Spanish-ACC talk-NOM

            kiri-xu-sha   *no abla*-naku-ndu-mi   *así*, chaupi-ga *Castellanu*
            want-PROG-SUBJ not talk-PL-SUBJ-AFF thus half-TOP Spanish

            laya *i*   chaupi-ga Ingichu   laya *abla*-ri-na   ga-n.
            like and half-TOP Quechua like talk-REFL-NOM be-3pl.

         b. *Isi*-ga   *asi nustru barrio*-ga   *asi   kostumbri*-n   *abla*-na.
            this-TOP thus our   community-TOP thus accustomed-3pl talk-NOM

         a. '*Media Lengua* is *thus* if you *want* to *talk Spanish* from Quechua but you
            can't, then you *talk* half like *Spanish and* half like *Quechua*.
         b. In *our community* we are *accustomed* to *talking this* way.'

Media Lengua is therefore also a symbiotic mixed language: speakers are fluent
in Quechua as well as in Spanish, and mixing takes place by conscious and deliberate choice, albeit not in a random but in a conventionalised manner. Muysken
(1981, 1997) notes that the presence of Spanish discourse markers constitutes
an exception to the relexification principle, as they do not directly substitute
equivalent Quechua word-forms. This is not surprising, if we recall the general
susceptibility of discourse markers to borrowing, in particular from a dominant
language in situations of unidirectional bilingualism. However, it does show that
the processes involved in the formation of mixed languages are often multilayered
and can therefore not be accounted for by just a single mechanism or principle
(cf. Matras 2000a). In the case of Media Lengua, lexical re-orientation (or: lexical substitution, relexification) combines with the more ordinary, commonplace
process of grammatical borrowing from a dominant language.

   Copper Island Aleut (also: Mednyj Aleut) emerged in the Commander Islands
off the coast of Kamchatka in the Russian north Pacific. Aleut settlers were
brought to the island by the Russian American Company from the early 1800s
onwards, with larger groups of settlers arriving in the second half of the nineteenth century. The population eventually consisted of Russians, Aleuts, as
well as so-called 'Creoles' of mixed Aleut-Russian parentage (cf. Golovko and
Vakhtin 1990; Golovko 1994, 1996). A key role is sometimes attributed to this
mixed community in forming the mixed Aleut-Russian variety (cf. Bakker 1996,
1997a and elsewhere). Golovko (2003) attributes the mixture to the conventionalisation of conscious language mixing by a more diverse population of
bilinguals.

While Thomason (1997) views Copper Island Aleut as a case of borrowing of Russian elements into Aleut, Vakhtin (1998: 321) emphasises that the type of mixture attested in Copper Island Aleut cannot be explained as the outcome of a borrowing process, either of Russian elements into Aleut, or of Aleut elements into Russian. He proposes instead that the mixed variety arose in a situation of 'cross-generational sociolinguistic tension'. According to Vakhtin's scenario, a young, bilingual generation of Aleut and mixed origin, whose dominant language was Russian, made a conscious effort to maintain the language of their parent and grandparent generation by replicating Aleut structures, albeit selectively. Access to Aleut may have been reinforced by renewed contact to other population groups who were at the time still Aleut speakers. Thus, Vakhtin suggests that Copper Island Aleut was a kind of 'invention' of the younger generation who wished to restore the 'language of the elders'.

A key assumption in this scenario is that the 'inventor' generation spoke Russian as its native language, and used Russian grammar as the primary base for the new language (cf. Vakhtin 1998: 326). This contrasts with Thomason's (1997b: 462) assertion that the overall structure of Copper Island Aleut 'shows clearly that the language is basically Aleut, with Russian features incorporated into the Aleut base'. Thomason appears to base her impression primarily on a quantitative measure of vocabulary items, coupled with an itemised count of grammatical categories. However, it is the actual identity of the individual grammatical categories, not their mere quantity, that is the key to reconciling the structural facts of Copper Island Aleut with the socio-historical data. Consider the following examples, from Golovko (1996: 65–71); Russian-derived elements are italicised:

(14)   ula-ng
         hous-1SG
         'my house'

(15)   aniqju-χ saĝan-*it*
         baby-SG sleep-3SG.PRES
         'the baby *is* sleep*ing*'

(16)   *oni* taanga-χ   su-la-*jut*
         they alcohol-SG take-MULT-3PL.PRES
         '*they are* buy*ing* alcohol'

(17)   *ona* hiχ ta-*it*   *čto*   *ona ego* liaχ ta-*it*
         she say.3SG. PRES COMP she him love.3sg.PRES
         '*She* say*s that she* love*s him*'

While isolated nominal entities may appear exclusively Aleut, as in (14), verb inflection and categories that immediately accompany verb inflection such as subject and object pronouns and word order are consistently Russian (15–17). As a result, sentences such as (16–17) strongly resemble the various cases of lexical substitution discussed above. The major difference is the retention of

Aleut nominal inflection (including possessive inflection) which accompanies Aleut nouns. Along with Aleut nouns, grammatical nominals from Aleut also appear, namely demonstratives and indefinite pronouns, as well as numerals and some adverbs. Combinations of morphemes within the Aleut noun phrase retain Aleut word order (cf. Example (14)).

The crucial historical development in the Copper Island community was the shift to Russian as the language of the predication, triggering with it the use of Russian clause-organisation grammar. Naturally, this will have been accompanied by the adoption of Russian vocabulary, though the latter is not really relevant to the process that gave rise specifically to the mixed language of Copper Island, for speakers are all fluent in Russian anyway. Our focus in seeking to understand the mixed variety must be on the attempt to replicate Aleut structures once Russian became dominant. The deliberate attempt to keep Aleut alive succeeded in targeting Aleut vocabulary, for the obvious reasons that make vocabulary items more easily accessible and retrievable. It also succeeded in maintaining nominal inflection as a feature accompanying individual nouns and apparently even more complex nominal constructions. But it failed to keep Aleut as the language of the predication and so as the language in which the proposition is anchored and hence the primary language of the utterance (see Chapters 5 and 6).

Copper Island Aleut is thus essentially similar, within the typology of mixed languages, to the processes observed in Angloromani and Ma'a: it is the product of language obsolescence and ongoing language shift, partly suspended in the process in order to be able to use Aleut-derived structures selectively for emblematic purposes of identity-flagging at the level of full conversation. The fact that nominal inflection accompanies Aleut nouns illustrates that speakers do not necessarily process 'grammar' on a wholesale basis, but that functional distinctions are as much part of the 'inner' or 'intuitive' part of language processing as is the discrimination of lexical content morphemes from other morphemes. The notion of lexicon–grammar split does not fully capture the complexity of the process. When Bakker (2003: 124) writes that 'It [Copper Island Aleut] is not intertwined since there is no clear lexicon-grammar dichotomy as in the intertwined prototype', then the problem appears to be not the language, but the prototype (cf. Matras 2003).

In fact, Copper Island Aleut is not entirely unparalleled in its structural composition. In the community of Lajamanu in the Northern Territory of Australia, a mixed variety is spoken by young adults in their twenties, and is currently being transmitted to young children as their native language (O'Shannessy 2005). Referred to as 'Light Walpiri', it is a mixture of Walpiri (Paya-Nyungan), Aboriginal English or Kriol, and English. It draws most verbs and its verbal morphology from Kriol, its nouns from Walpiri and English, and its nominal inflection from Walpiri, while creating its own innovative system of auxiliaries that is diagnostic of the variety. In the following examples from O'Shannessy (2005: 49–50), Walpiri elements are italicised:

(18)   fence-*rla*   yu-rra   shat-im-ap *ngula-j*
        fence-LOC   2sg-NFUT   shut-tr-UP   ANAPH-FOC
        'Lock *that one* up *inside* the fence'

(19)   Japayi i-m   trip-im *watiya-ng*
           3SG-NFUT   trip-TR   tree-ERG
        '*The tree* made Japayi trip'

O'Shannessy (2005) distinguishes between Walpiri and Kriol/English codeswitching and Light Walpiri, citing the following features: Light Walpiri lacks the Walpiri preverb-verb construction and Walpiri auxiliaries; instead, Walpiri-derived verbs use the Kriol transitive marker -*m* and are accompanied by an innovative auxiliary system, based on Kriol-derived forms. Light Walpiri also shows re-distribution of the Walpiri-derived ergative and locative case suffixes, assigning equivalent affixes with different shapes not, as in Walpiri, on the basis of the syllable structure of the word, but based on its source language. All this shows that Light Walpiri constitutes what Bakker (2003) refers to as an 'autonomous system' – a mixed language system that is independent of the systems and rules of its respective source languages.[10]

Another mixed language of the Northern Territory of Australia is Gurindji Kriol, a mixture of Gurindji and English-based Kriol (McConvell and Meakins 2005). The language is the product of contacts between the Gurindji people, who worked on cattle stations, and the white pastoralists who ran the stations. Its emergence parallels the decline of the traditional Gurindji language, which is now highly endangered. Gurindji Kriol was formed during the 1960s–1970s and is now being passed on to the next generation independently of its two source languages.

Structurally, Gurindji supplies case-marking as well as nominal derivational morphology, possessive pronouns, and emphatic pronouns and demonstratives, while Kriol supplies verb morphology and basic lexical verbs, conjunctions, and numerals. The lexicon, including grammatical function words, is mixed, though some general patterns can be identified (McConvell and Meakins 2005: 11). Gurindji-derived are verbs describing bodily functions, states, motion and impact, and nouns describing plants, body-parts, in-law and grandparent kin, while Kriol-derived are expressions for close kin, colours, temporals, and directionals. Other domains, such as nouns describing people, food and animals, quantifiers, adjectives, and interjections, show a mixture of both source languages.

Moreover, for some nouns, expressions are available from both source languages, indicating that Gurindji Kriol has not yet entirely completed its process of stabilisation; two forms, one from each source language, exist for one third of the words on the Swadesh list (McConvell and Meakins 2005: 15). Nonetheless, McConvell and Meakins (2005: 12) report that Gurindji Kriol is the main language of communication in the home, the community shop, the council office, and a variety of other domains. Traditional Gurindji is used only by elderly people and mostly in the home and in some religious ceremonies, while Kriol is used exclusively in interaction outside the community. Thus, Gurindji Kriol has become the everyday community language:

(20)   Gurindji Kriol (from McConvell and Meakins 2005: 11); Gurindji-derived items are italicised:

a. *nyawa-ma* wan *karu* bin   plei-bat   pak-*ta*   *nyanuny*
   this-top   one child PAST play-CONT park-LOC 3SG.DAT

   warlaku-ywaung-ma
   dog-HAVING-TOP

b. tu-bala   bin plei-bat.
   two-NUM past play-CONT

c. I   bin   tok-in   la   im:
   3SG PAST talk-PROG PREP 3SG

d. 'kamon *warlaku partaj ngayiny*   leg-*ta*.'
   come.on dog   go.up 1SG.DAT leg.LOC

e. *Ngalo*   plei-bat   *nyaway-ngka*
   1SG. INC play-CONT this-LOC

a. '*This* one *kid* was playing *at* the park *with his dog.*
b. *The two of them* were playing.
c. And the kid said to him:
d. "Come on *dog, jump up on my* leg.
e. *You and I* can play *here.*"'

Citing McConvell (2002), McConvell and Meakins (2005: 14) explain the retention of Gurindji nominal inflection in Gurindji Kriol as the result of an asymmetrical pace in the turnover of grammar from one language to another in the context of ongoing language shift, coupled with the discontinuation of the process mid-way. This asymmetrical pace targets verb grammar first in dependent-marking noun-coding languages, resulting in cases like Copper Island Aleut and Gurindji Kriol. In head-marking verb-coding languages, nominal grammar is targeted first, resulting in the retention of verbal grammar from Cree in Michif.

Michif is the only documented mixed language that is spoken by a population that has at least partly lost contact with either of its source languages. Spoken in the Canadian provinces Saskatchewan and Manitoba and in adjoining regions in the United States (North Dakota) it evolved as a result of the settlement of French-Canadian fur traders and their liaisons with indigenous Cree-speaking women, which gave rise to a community of mixed households – the Métis – in the early nineteenth century (cf. Bakker 1997a and 1994, Bakker and Papen 1997). The language is still spoken today, albeit by few speakers scattered in different communities, and has thus survived as an autonomous, native language for nearly two centuries.

Michif retains Cree verbs and verb inflection, some nouns and their possessive inflection, personal pronouns, demonstratives, and indefinites, some negators and most adverbs. Word order in the verb phrase is based on Cree, as are some subordinating structures and conjunctions. French elements in Michif include most nouns and their modifiers such as definite and indefinite articles, numerals, prepositions, adjectives, and possessive pronouns, nominal agreement inflection, as well as adverbs and some conjunctions:

(21)   Michif narrative extract (from Bakker 1997a: 5–6) (French items are italicised):

a. *un vieux* ana ayi *un vieux* opahikêt ê-nôhcihcikêt, you see,
   an old   this uh an old   trapper   trapped

b. êkwa ayi *un matin*   êkwaniskât ahkosiw, but kêyapit ana
   and uh one morning woke-up   be.sick   still   this-one

   wî-nitawi-wâpahtam *ses pièges*.
   want-go-see   his traps

a. '*An old* this uh *an old* trapper was trapping, you see,

b. and uh *one morning* he woke up sick, but he still wanted to go and see to *his traps*.'

(22)   Michif fairy-tale extract (Matras and Bakker 2003: 3):

a. kayâs   *une fille La Cendrieuse* kî-isinihkâ-sô-w.
   long.time.ago a   girl the Cinderella PAST-name-REFL-3

b. avec o-mâmâ-wa   kî-wîki-w *puis trois ses soeur(s)*
   with poss-mother-obv PAST-live-3 and three her sisters

c. *La Cendrieuse* mâka   *tout* kî-piskeyiht-am *tout*
   the Cinderella however all PAST-clean-it   all

d. *La maison, le   plancher* kî-kisîpêkin-am
   the house   the floor   past-wash.by.hand-it

a. 'A long time ago there was *a girl* called *Cinderella*.

b. She lived *with* her mother *and her three sisters*.

c. *Cinderella*, however, cleaned *everything*.

d. She washed *the house, the floor*.'

Bakker (1997a) explains the overall mixture in Michif as a tendency toward the 'classic' intertwining procedure, which combines the lexicon of one language with the grammar of another. In this particular case, the procedure is constrained by the specific typological profile of the two participating languages. In Cree, verb stems cannot be isolated as lexical entries and so they cannot be substituted by French verb-roots. In French, modifiers such as definite and indefinite articles are proclitic to the noun and are therefore likewise inseparable from the stem. But as we have seen, Michif is not the only mixed language that defies the lexicon–grammar split. Indeed, 'grammar' must be defined only in the narrowest sense of 'productive inflectional morphology' to allow us to identify even a single language in which the split among the source language for grammar and lexicon is entirely consistent.

The question arises, therefore, whether it is at all possible to define a structural prototype for mixed languages, or whether the only feature that defines them as a unique sub-type of contact language is the history of their emergence coupled

with an unusual – by comparison with cases of gradual borrowing – combination
of sub-components. McWhorter (2005: 247–259) suggests that mixed languages
('intertwined languages') are no different in principle from creoles. With reference to cases like Angloromani and Ma'a, he points out that proficiency in the
lexifier language is not a requirement for the emergence of mixed languages.[11] It
follows that mixed languages cannot be regarded a priori as 'bilingual mixtures',
as Thomason (1997c, 2001) refers to them. McWhorter interprets the inclusion
of inflectional morphology in mixed languages – an apparent contradiction to
his own 'creole prototype' definition – as part of the creole cline, and so no
different in principle from the inclusion of individual morphemes from Eastern Ijo in Berbice Dutch Creole or the presence of Hiligaynon morphology in
Zamboangueño. He concludes that mixed languages are simply creoles that have
arisen in situations in which there was only a single substrate, and so speakers
were able to transfer greater morphological complexity from the substrate when
learning the target, lexifier language.

McWhorter's proposal dismisses the fact that the creators of mixed languages
have very different motivations for mixing or even shifting to another language
than the creators of the pidgins that gave rise to creoles: The first are typically
in a process of acculturation and identity-shift, the second are in search for
a basic medium of interethnic communication in the absence of a common
language. It does not therefore seem in any way constructive to regard Romani,
for example, being the lexifier language of Angloromani, as functionally parallel
to Portuguese as the lexifier of the Angolar creole or to English as the lexifier of
Sierra Leone Krio. The functions of 'lexifier' in the two situation types are quite
distinct. Nonetheless, McWhorter's attempt to apply the notions of 'substrate'
and 'lexifier' to the emergence of mixed languages, implying a hierarchical rather
than an equivalence relationship between the contributor languages, deserves
some consideration. It is, for one, well in line with the proposal made in Matras
(2000a, 2003) concerning the distinct roles of the source languages involved in
the process.

The key to understanding the structural profiles of mixed languages is not, as
in the formation of creoles, the need to find an adequate medium for communication, but the interplay of language retention and language shift and the search for
a compromise variety – with whichever range of functions – that can constitute a
bridge between the two. In the centre of the process is a compromise between the
anchoring of the predication, carried out on the basis of structures derived from
one of the languages, and the bulk of referential or at least the more stable (nominal) referential resources of the language, namely content lexicon or vocabulary.
It is noteworthy that none of the mixed languages documented so far shows a mixture within the inventory of finite verb inflection, i.e. among the means that anchor
the predication (cf. Matras 2003). These are always consistent, and also tend to
pattern with the word-order rules of the verb phrase and the complex clause.

The mixed language prototype is thus not a lexicon–grammar split, but a split
between finite verb inflection or the 'predication-anchoring language', and the

bulk of referential lexical vocabulary, or 'content-reference language'. This kind of split can be explained in terms of the language processing mechanism and especially the mechanism of selection and inhibition of wholesale components within the repertoire: the anchoring of the predication is the more intuitive, less conscious mental act. It therefore reflects the overall social and communicative orientation of the speaker. In symbiotic mixed languages, the language of the predication is always the 'outer' language that is used for a greater number of functions, usually as the default or 'unmarked' choice. Moreover, in cases where the overall sociolinguistic development in the history of the community follows the direction of language shift, the predication derives from the new, dominant, and powerful 'outside' language. Ma'a, Angloromani, Copper Island Aleut, Light Walpiri, and Gurindji Creole all represent cases where the language of the predication has shifted and the mixture is an attempt to partially maintain an old community language.

By contrast, the referential means of the language are those that are more easy to target in a conscious effort. Lexicon is more easily disguised, distorted, or manipulated in cryptolects and symbiotic mixed languages, it is more easily extracted from scripture or through superficial contacts with other groups, it is more easily preserved in situations of language loss, and it is more easily inserted consciously in an emblematic fashion. All of this derives directly from the very same inherent functional properties that make content-lexicon more easily borrowable than finite verb inflection (see Chapters 6–7).

The two Australian cases provide rare insights into the ongoing process of mixed language creation by a young generation that is acquiring the mixed languages as a native tongue. Both cases confirm that there is a type of mixed language that arises through speakers' partial resistance to language shift in small communities, resulting in the selective replication from elements of the 'old' language. Interestingly, in many cases speakers even apply the term used for the old language to the new, mixed variety: Copper Island Aleut speakers call their language 'Aleut', Angloromani users call their mixed variety 'Romani' or 'Romanes', and Gurindji Kriol speakers call their language 'Gurindji'.

This 'preservation' type is distinct from the 'acculturation' type, where elements of an outsider language are adopted selectively, often in a situation in which the 'old' language is still preserved, by and large, and is not at all endangered. Media Lengua shows such accommodation to an 'outer' language in its lexicon, but the predication of the 'old' language is retained, in line with the retention of Quechua as the all-purpose community language. Michif, too, represents a case of maintenance of the predication language, which derives from the language of the indigenous population that was not, during the period of emergence of Michif, endangered or undergoing shift or obsolescence.

Mixed languages differ from creoles primarily through the fact that they do not evolve from the need for an improvised means of *external* communication, a pidgin, based on a simplification of a target lexifier. Rather, they are a means for *internal* communication, based not on structural simplification but on *selective* replication from a target lexifier, a process that often includes inflectional mor-phology from the lexifier as well as other abstract grammatical operators. The key to the unique mixture, which defines the mixed language prototype, is the con-scious and deliberate differentiation between the source of predicate-anchoring operations (finite verb inflection) and the source of much and sometimes most of the referential lexicon.

10.4   The position of contact languages

Contact languages show structural profiles that are distinctively dif-ferent from those that arise through gradual processes of contact-induced change. Yet the individual mechanisms that give rise to these structural profiles can be observed in the communicative behaviour of bilinguals already from a very young age: insertion and replication of content-lexical elements from another language, creation of new constructions through pivot-matching and pattern replication, and manipulation of repertoire components for discourse-strategic effects. Some of these are shared by semi-bilinguals or second-language learn-ers, who equally make use of makeshift pattern replications, of isolated content-morphemes (stripped of inflection), and of mere selective replication of gram-matical operators in order to sustain communication in new sets of interaction contexts.

Nonetheless, the particular density with which these strategies are employed in the birth of new languages, and the conditions that lead to the long-term stabilisa-tion of the new structures that emerge as a result, are non-trivial. They are part of a recurring type (and sub-types) of sociolinguistic constellation that favours the concentrated employment of these particular strategies. Such constellations invite speakers to make creative use of their linguistic repertoire as a whole, encourag-ing both opportunistic, task-driven, and emblematic, effect-driven lifting of the mental demarcation among sub-components of the repertoire, and prompting a re-definition and re-drawing of boundaries.

Contact languages are non-trivial, since it takes a particular punctuated event to 'scramble' the linguistic repertoire in such an intense way. The enormous scale on which such events are attested just from the past few centuries might prompt us to speculate about the extent to which conditions had arisen in earlier phases of human history that were favourable to the emergence of contact languages – from mass enslavement and population displacement to the coming together of different groups to form a new, small, and tight-knit community, and on to nomadism and migrations of service-providing clans or tribes. All things being equal, each and every such event of the past might have given rise to one or several contact languages. The potential implications of this realisation to historical linguistic theory are enormous (cf. Bakker 2000b, Matras 2000c): it is possible that numerous languages around the world originated in pidgins or mixed languages. This imposes severe limitations on the traditional comparative method in historical linguistics, which is not equipped to deal with contact as a force that triggers the emergence of new languages, and it invites skepticism in respect of the chances of applying the method successfully to the majority of the world's languages, for which we have no written record and no proof for the absence of past events that may have led to a scrambling of repertoires and the rapid emergence of new combinations of sets and subsets of grammar and vocabulary.

A final point to reiterate is the recognition that new languages can emerge from speakers' strategic use of their repertoire with only partial inhibition on the context-appropriate selection of both matter and pattern, or in deliberate and overt defiance of such inhibition constraints. This realisation must encourage us to approach contact languages not merely from a purely descriptive viewpoint of drawing inventories of their structural profiles, but from the point of view of the discourse-strategic value that the mixture has for its speakers. In creole studies, the evaluation of structural components of creoles as reflecting strategic compromises in speakers' old and new repertoires is by now well established. Recent work on mixed languages has emphasised both the acculturation aspect of the mixture, and in relevant cases the act of resistance of language loss and the attempt to award the 'old' language a kind of afterlife.

11   Outlook

How can the study of language contact contribute to our general understanding of language use, language change, and the structure and perhaps even the ancient evolution of the language faculty itself? In this final chapter, I briefly take up three issues: the availability of the linguistic repertoire, the relation between individual innovation and language change, and the layered structure of grammar.

11.1   The multilingual speaker's repertoire

The first issue concerns the speaker's command of 'linguistic systems'. The traditional position in descriptive and formal linguistics is to view contact through the metaphor of two 'systems' that somehow come into direct contact with one another. We have seen evidence that, although multilingual speakers become experienced in separating communication routines and so in effect in demarcating sub-components of their overall linguistic repertoire, that repertoire remains active at all times. Repertoire components cannot, it seems, be shut down wholesale for the duration of a communicative interaction. Instead, the bilingual speaker must suppress or inhibit the activation of each and every lexeme, phonetic realisation or semantic construction that at a given moment may be functional but not appropriate to the ongoing interaction context.

We have plenty of evidence that the entire, multilingual repertoire continues its presence, so to speak in 'alert mode', in all interactions. Consider first the time that it takes an infant to acquire the rules on appropriate context-bound selection (and inhibition) of word-forms, and later of constructions. This acquisition process entails a development that is social and behavioural, and has been proven to correlate directly with the behavioural input that the infant receives in conversation. Next, there is evidence from pathological language conditions, whether as a result of injuries or other impairment (aphasia or agrammatism), or a temporary strain on the speech production mechanism. Both may result in a weakening of the ability to select 'correct', i.e. context-appropriate structures, and to rule out those that are associated with another 'language' and other contexts. This weakening may be prolonged, as in language impairment, or instantaneous, as represented by so-called bilingual speech production errors, slips of the tongue or 'wrong' or 'inappropriate' language choices.

We have seen that language learners will often draw on elements of their linguistic repertoire as a whole in order to make communication most effective. They will incorporate into their attempts to communicate in the target language not just phonetic and phonological realisations that were acquired with and are anchored along with their 'first' or earlier language(s), but also constructions (i.e. meaningful relations among elements) and in some cases even specific word-forms. These are regarded from a formal perspective as 'errors', 'interference', or 'negative transfers', but in effect they enable communication by allowing users to exploit a greater potential of their linguistic repertoire in order to sustain communicative interaction. Accordingly, where second-language learners act as agents of language change, for example in situations of language shift or pidginisation and creolisation, the outcome – the emergence of a new speech variety, be it through a gradual or abrupt process – will display features belonging to the original repertoire in its entirety, including in all likelihood aspects of phonology, morpho-syntactic constructions, and possibly even word-forms of the original or 'substrate' language(s).

Finally, we have also witnessed that multilingual speakers are able to use their repertoire creatively. Rather than simply block or shut off complete linguistic 'systems', in conversations with other multilingual individuals they will exploit subtle nuances in meaning differences, evoke context-specific associations by selecting words that are associated with those contexts, authenticate the replication of those words by copying their original phonology, and even draw on the contrast of languages to structure the internal cohesion of the discourse and to navigate sequences in the interaction. This ability is tightly linked to the degree of linguistic maturity and the ability to take conversational risks for the sake of creating special conversational effects. But we saw that even the young bilingual child is capable of employing the contrast of languages strategically in this way. Even demonstrative word-plays are part of the active bilingual's manipulative usages of the repertoire as a whole. Such discourse strategies that demonstrably defy demarcation boundaries among repertoire subsets may in some circumstances undergo sedimentation and lead to the formation of mixed languages.

The effects of language contact in conversation and speech production strongly suggest that 'language systems' are social constructions, not natural entities that have an independent existence in speakers' minds. Speakers are, of course, by and large conscious, as long as they are in full control of their speech production mechanism, of the context-appropriateness of individual word-forms and other structures, and moreover of entire sets and clusters of structures. But this context-appropriateness is, as we saw, the product of gradual socialisation and it is subject to lapses and errors as well as to conscious intervention and scrambling by speakers themselves.

11.2   Multilingual speakers as agents of language change

In traditional formal-descriptive approaches to contact linguistics, a distinction is commonly made between 'individual' and 'societal' bilingualism. Individual bilingualism is regarded mostly as a psychological and developmental issue, and has been excluded, by and large, from most discussions of contact-induced change or the typology of language convergence. Structural change that is induced by contact has been attributed instead to social processes, such as the imposition of a new language on an entire population, or the sudden need to create a makeshift language for the purpose of interethnic communication. While it is obvious that isolated individuals are not in a position to introduce changes that will shape a language's diachrony, it is also crystal clear that no societal process can lead to language change unless it prompts individuals to innovate their own speech. Language change is thus always the product of innovations that are introduced by individual speakers in the course of discourse interaction, and which find favourable conditions of propagation throughout a sector within the speech community, and on to the speech community as a whole.

This realisation has led us to search for and identify the mechanisms of contact-induced change not in macro-level societal processes, but in concrete, local discourse strategies that individual speakers pursue in conversation. To be sure, some of these strategies appear in response to societal processes, e.g. the need to learn another language. Certainly, the chances of successful propagation of new strategies is dependent on social circumstances; thus a deliberately mixed utterance is only likely to become the norm in a tight-knit community that is undergoing some kind of re-packaging of its community and ethnic identity. Nonetheless, the origin of a *structural* change is the employment of an innovative structure as a means of expression at the utterance level.

As depicted in Figure 11.1, typical creative strategies in bilingual settings can be arranged on a continuum, from those that are applied by the speaker in a non-voluntary and non-conscious manner with no intention to evoke any special effects in discourse, and on to those that are deliberate manipulations of the default rules on the well-formedness of the utterance, employed for special attention, key, and mode. For the first side of the continuum, the term 'strategy' might not be entirely appropriate, since there is no reflection involved on the part of the speaker. Nevertheless, innovations falling on this side of the cline are not random, either. They include the selection malfunctions discussed in Chapters 2 and 4, and the reaction to them in the form of a relaxation of the control mechanism around the relevant structures, as discussed in Chapter 5. Thus, these are innovations that are functional to the organisation of the utterance and the discourse, despite the fact that they are not planned or deliberate. Next on the continuum we find the process of pattern replication through pivot-matching (also called 'calquing' or 'convergence'). Resorting to such strategies is often not a matter of choice, or at least not a choice that has stylistic goals. Nevertheless,

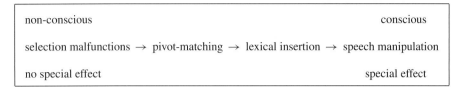

non-conscious			conscious
selection malfunctions $\rightarrow$ pivot-matching $\rightarrow$ lexical insertion $\rightarrow$ speech manipulation			
no special effect			special effect

Figure 11.1 *The continuum of contact-induced creativity and innovation.*

speakers are often aware of the replicative nature of pivot-matching. In fact, some pivot-matching procedures, in particular in the lexical domain, are the property of the literary language and may even be backed by language planning institutions (as in the creation of neologisms). Not depicted on Figure 11.1 is the position of prosody, which tends to be replicated in a non-conscious manner.

The insertion of word-forms fills an entire scope of functions, from the more spontaneous selection of a word due to its context-particular associations and on to the replication of a word for special stylistic effects. Again, Figure 11.1 does not explicitly depict phonology, but we can treat phones and phonemes as accompanying the integration of word-forms and the replication of original sounds from the donor language as an effort to authenticate the replication of word-forms. Finally, deliberate or conscious mixing in manipulated utterances occupies the extreme position on the continuum for special conversational effects.

Change resulting from the generalisation of any of these strategies naturally involves the neutralisation of special circumstances under which the innovation occurs, and its generalisation to potentially all modes of interaction. One-off speech production errors or malfunctions become tolerated and stabilised, new constructions and word-form insertions become routine, and the special effect of deliberate language mixing is reduced somewhat to a regular emotive or assertive mode, and in the rare cases of Michif, Gurindji Kriol, Light Walpiri, and perhaps a few other languages, to the default mode of interaction.

By and large, the strategies depicted in Figure 11.1 (with accompanying features in phonology) cover the principal types of structural change that can be triggered by contact: the adoption of grammatical markers as a result of category-specific 'fusion' of the representation of certain grammatical operations in the repertoire; the generalisation throughout the repertoire of constructions and form–meaning mapping; the adoption of content-lexemes; and the intertwining of subcomponents by category. Other outcomes of language contact, such as simplification or indeed enrichment of morphology, for instance, are mere by-products of these principal strategies, arising from either the adoption or non-adoption of certain grammatical markers or the generalisation of certain patterns.

It is important to note once again that all these strategies are available already to the young bilingual at a stage of relative maturity and confidence in conversational interaction, and are employed wherever possible in the immediate interaction environment. They do not require large-scale societal processes to be set in motion. We must thus carefully distinguish between the triggers of language change and the emergence of structural innovations, and the processes that may or may not lead to the propagation of those innovations. As far as propagation is concerned, I have taken issue in various places in the preceding chapters with the expectation that the type of change will necessarily reflect either the direction of language orientation – that is, language maintenance on the one hand, language shift on the other – or the type of linguistic co-existence – diglossia and language specialisation on the one hand, so-called language equilibrium on the other. In fact, we find situations of language shift in which both patterns and word-forms are replicated from the substrate language, we find cases of pidginisation and creolisation that involve replication of substrate-language word-forms and even some grammatical morphemes in addition to patterns, we find diglossic situations where pattern replication is extensive in addition to the adoption of grammatical operators and word-forms, and of course a whole range of structural admixtures in the very colourful pool of mixed languages.

The crucial factors in the propagation of innovations in contact situations appear to be, rather, the directionality of bilingualism, and the extent of control and pressure that is exerted on speakers to conform to more established speech norms. Language shift may in principle take place with hardly a trace of substrate influence when there are tight regulatory target norms to adhere to, and motivation and an opportunity to acquire those norms. Consequently, ethnolectal features in the speech of immigrant communities in larger urban centres tend to be limited perhaps to prosody and some phonetic patterns, to a small number of constructions, and to a small inventory of culture-specific word-forms. This is rather marginal by comparison to pidgins and creoles, where a learner population has little motivation and perhaps little opportunity to acquire the target language and seeks instead a makeshift mode of communication. In the case of smaller languages in a diglossic situation, the unidirectionality of bilingualism will license the use of structures from the majority language because speakers of the smaller language are more likely to employ a bilingual mode as a default choice in many types of interaction. But the presence of normative and institutional support, such as literacy in the minority language, will slow down the pace and the extent of change even here. The so-called cases of linguistic equilibrium are in effect cases in which group loyalty is strong enough to discourage overt word-forms or linguistic matter that is perceived as context inappropriate, but at the same time there is lax normative control with respect to speakers' innovative use of new constructions or patterns.

11.3   Contact and the layered architecture of the language faculty

The final point to consider is the recognition that different components of grammar and structure react differently to the pressures exerted by the need to manage a multilingual (i.e. a context-differentiated) repertoire. This alerts us to a layered structure of the grammatical apparatus of language and in effect assigns to language contact the role of an external force that shakes the bottle and allows the different ingredients of its content to become, to some degree at least, visible.

A basic division exists between overt shapes of morphs, which are more easily associated with particular sets of interaction contexts and so more easily identified as belonging to a particular 'language', and patterns of form–meaning mapping, which are potentially more opaque in their affiliation. A further basic division is that between content-lexemes or 'labelling'-vocabulary, and grammatical morphemes. Though there is no doubt a continuum between the two, the more semantically transparent morphs are more readily isolated and replicated, especially when their meaning evokes unique contextual associations. Semantically independent morphs – content words, and among those nouns, and among those unique referents or names for institutions etc. – are more likely to be borrowed, are easier for the very young bilingual child to assign to different languages and keep as synonyms, easier to acquire and to employ in a situation of non-guided second-language learning, and easier to manipulate and 'camouflage' in deliberate language mixing. There appears therefore to be stronger analytical control over the production and processing of content lexemes, or generally of morphs with a semantically transparent content.

A further distinct layer that becomes transparent in its high vulnerability to contact phenomena is the grammatical apparatus that is entrusted with managing the interaction and qualifying the relations between propositions and the shared, presupposition-based expectations of the speaker and the interlocutor. These range from semi-lexical verbal gestures in the roles of tags and fillers, on to discourse markers and connectors, to focus particles and modality markers, and on to an assortment of operators that process clashes with expectations (indefinites, comparisons with a set, exceptions, etc.). Here too, we are not dealing with a clearly definable class in absolute terms, but with a cline. The more involved an operator is in regulating the interactional participation of speaker and listener, the more likely it is to be affected by malfunctions of the selection and inhibition mechanism, and the more likely it is (in relevant constellations) to be compromised in favour of the corresponding form from the dominant language, thus eliminating the need to apply the selection and inhibition mechanism altogether around the particular function. This in effect leads to fusion or the wholesale borrowing of a class of operators. Items that are involved in processing expectations and especially anticipated clashes of expectations fall under this category since they take on a more intensive role in regulating the interaction-oriented relations between speaker and hearer.

The question arises, why this particular class of operators is so vulnerable, and what makes it more difficult to control? It appears that, on a cline, the operations involved here are more gesture-like and automated, and less reflected or analytic. It is interesting to note the connection with prosody, which is similarly contact-vulnerable, and is also separate from the more analytical neurofunctional processing domain that controls segmental phonology (see Schirmer *et al.* 2001, Friederici 2001; cf. also McMahon 2005). The study of language contact cannot, on its own, supply all the answers. But it is tempting to regard discourse-regulating operations as a separate, perhaps more archaic layer in the evolution of the language faculty. It is perhaps a layer that has its earliest roots in the kind of intuitive prosodic expression that we can find in animal communication, while its later development is shaped by the uniquely human acquisition of the ability to regard the interlocutor as an intentional agent (see Tomasello 1999), and to reach out and try and influence the interlocutor's course of action – an ability which may well have been the trigger for the subsequent evolution of human language.

Speakers' reduced ability to control and differentiate the selection of appropriate (correct-language) word-forms around such functions is apparent already in the way that expressions of modality and particles lag behind in the emergence of bilingual synonyms in the bilingual infant, and is further exemplified by the extreme volatility of this class of elements in the discourse of bilinguals, as illustrated in Chapters 4 and 5. These facts match up nicely with the consistent pattern in implicational hierarchies of grammatical borrowing, which show an overwhelming tendency for the relevant class of operators to be affected first and most extensively by contact-induced language change in the domain of grammatical lexicon and grammatical morphology.

A further domain of differentiated functionality that is worth pointing out is that of deixis and anaphora. Though no absolute constraints apply, it is striking that under normal circumstances of language contact and contact-induced change, not much happens to the actual word-forms involved in these functions. They are not conspicuous as targets of bilingual speech production errors, they do not seem to provide extensive difficulties for learners, nor are they frequently borrowed. In some sense, deixis and anaphora are at the opposite end compared to discourse operators and the like; while the latter are gesture-like and automated and are accompanied by the apprehension of a clash between speaker and listener, the former rely on firm and stable harmony between speaker and listener at least in respect of the indexical orientation coordinates within which the expressions operate. It is no coincidence that those seeming exceptions – personal pronouns that are borrowed in normal situations of contact – are not strictly speaking or inherently deictic or anaphoric in nature, but have a strong lexical-terminological component (see Chapter 8).

Finally, a unique position is occupied by the grammatical elements that initiate the predication. The predication is the core of the utterance, probably the most outstanding basic structural feature of the human language faculty. When we speak of accommodating language choice to contextual parameters, we mean accommodating the initiation of the predication to the context, for it is the predication that carries and manifests that choice. This accounts for the difficulties in switching around predicates, the structural inconvenience of adopting lexical vocabulary in the domain of verbs and predicates, and the consistency with which even mixed languages select only one set of structures for the initiation of the predication. Once again, the study of language contact cannot possibly on its own resolve the question of the position of predication-initiating grammar within the overall language faculty. But if discourse markers, prosody, and the like are the more instinct-based, less analytic layers of grammar, content-morphs with high semantic transparency are the more analytic, and deixis and anaphora are further abstractions that rely on the establishment of a firm and stable shared attention and orientation field, then it seems that the predication is the expression of the contextualisation of messages in an activity setting that is guided by behavioural rules and conventions.

Notes

1   Introduction

1 And other works in the Functional-Pragmatics tradition; cf. Rehbein (1977), Ehlich (2007), and contributions contained in Bührig and Matras (1999).

2   An emerging multilingual repertoire

1 For the most part, no formalised schedule of observations or recording was followed. During the early period of lexical acquisition, and up to the age of 1:11, active vocabulary use at home was logged systematically. Occasional observations covered interaction with the child-minder outside the home. From 1:11 onwards, notes were taken occasionally and some interactions were recorded. Observations during the later period covered mainly interactions with the father or situations in which the father was present.

2 Also referred to as 'language-neutral' or 'family' words; cf. Lanvers (2001).

3 This figure is based on an accumulated inventory of active vocabulary items taken up to and during a particular week at the age of 1:9. The child is, at this age, acquiring new items on a daily basis.

4 Of the tokens that can be assigned to more than one language, 12 can be regarded as either German or Hebrew, 12 as German or English, 2 as Hebrew or English, and 14 as German, Hebrew, or English.

5 Cf. German *Willst du gucken* 'do you want to have a look?', Hebrew *atá rocé larédet?* 'do you want to descend?'

6 Terms for foods (Figure 2.1) happen to show a high proportion of words that are identical or nearly identical in two or more languages, and so their actual position with respect to the adoption of bilingual synonyms is difficult to evaluate.

7 For a discussion of metalinguistic awareness see Lanza (1997: 64-69).

8 See Matras (1998a) for a discussion of *fusion* in this sense. Cf. Meisel (1990), who characterises the lack of grammatical separation between languages in Bilingual First Language Acquisition as *fusion*.

9 From Hebrew *yašén* '(he) sleeps'.

10 At the age of eight, Ben reads intensely in English, and has a fluent reading knowledge of German as well as exposure to more formal styles of German through various media. Hebrew, by contrast, continues to be used primarily in oral conversation with the father and occasionally with friends and relations. Ben is familiar with the Hebrew alphabet, but does not have actual (practised) reading knowledge of Hebrew, and his familiarity with formal Hebrew vocabulary and morpho-syntax remains limited.

11 Note that in German, the verbal particle is separated from the main lexical stem and follows when the verb form is finite, as in *ich nehme auf* 'I record', but is adjoined to the stem and precedes it in non-finite constructions, as in *ich habe aufgenommen* 'I have recorded'. The Hebrew finite verb 'took' appears to be treated here by analogy to the finite verb in German, even though colloquial German would normally favour the perfect (non-finite, participial) form of the verb in the past tense.

12 Here again we have, arguably, a case of de-grammaticalisation, from a more abstract preposition which operates on an individual noun, to a more concrete adverbial expression which modifies the entire predication.

13 For codeswitching as a 'skilled manipulation' of languages see Poplack (1980: 581).

14 Two exceptions are recorded: At the age of 3:10, during a visit to Israel, Ben refers in Hebrew to 'harvesting' as *lidróš* – an integration of German *dreschen*. At the age of 5:6, he refers to 'shallow water' (in a pond) as *máyim šlulím*, evidently a contamination of Hebrew *redudím* 'shallow' and the English word, but apparently also triggered through association with Hebrew *šlulít* 'pond'. Both instances go unnoticed by the child, and are obviously errors in the choice of subset items.

4   Acquiring and maintaining a bilingual repertoire

1 See Hoffmann (1991: 50–52) for a table overview of studies published up to 1990.

2 For more subtle differences between age groups and the effect of the social environment on children and adolescent learners see Dimroth (2007).

3 This does not mean, of course, that syntax and information structure are free from transfer and interference. Clahsen and Felsen (2006), for example, argue that speakers are more likely to achieve native-like command of word-level structures than of complex syntactic structures, and Carroll and Lambert (2003) demonstrate learner difficulties and transfer at the level of discourse organisation.

4 Broadcast on 'Dispatches', Channnel 4, 9 June 1997.

5 In earlier discussions of bilingual aphasia, two opposing views were represented, which Paradis (1990) had termed 'the extended system' hypothesis and the 'dual system' hypothesis. Subscribers of the first advocated a model of processing according to which there is just one storage system that accommodates elements from both languages, and that therefore access to both language systems follows the same pathway. Supporters of the second underline the existence of separate neural networks underlying the activation of each language, and support a differentiated representation of the languages, albeit without disputing that they are both stored in the same language area.

6 More evidence that non-equivalent impairment involves functional tasks rather than storage area comes from the fact that some patients can speak a language spontaneously but are unable to translate into it, or vice versa (cf. Green 1998).

7 This involves a preposed, stress-carrying particle *ken* 'yes': *kén haya!* 'Yés (there) was!'

8 Newsnight, BBC 2, 7 June 2004.

9 Note that the second class could also contain the first one, which similarly serves monitoring-and-directing operations. In the specific case of Examples (8)–(9), however, we know that there is no cognitive malfunction, but a gap in pragmatic proficiency.

Similarly, in (10) we can trace the speaker's inability to suppress the German tags to incomplete pragmatic proficiency.

5   Crossing the boundaries: codeswitching in conversation

1 *familja* 'family' in segment (e) is an ambiguous case. It appears integrated, as seen by the assignment of the Romani inflection ending *-a*, but it is not entirely clear whether it belongs to the layer of words taken over from German, or whether it may have entered the language in earlier stages, as a result of contact with other languages. Moreover, in this particular excerpt it is introduced by the hearer in segment (d), and so would not be able to count as a case of spontaneous integration by the speaker even if it turned out not to be an established loan in common use in the community.

2 In these and the following examples, acute accent indicates the stress position and is not part of either German or Romani orthography.

3 Heveen Ali Kurdi, personal communication.

4 Broersma and De Bot (2006) find empirical and experimental evidence in support of Clyne's triggering hypothesis, but they also note the challenges that it poses to models of bilingual speech production: the trigger is assumed to operate at the surface level, while code selection is assumed by most models to take place at the lemma level.

5 Romaine (1989: 159) by contrast admits that a pragmatic approach to codeswitching is strictly interpretative and is unable to offer predictive rules.

6 For the term in connection with codeswitching see Maschler (1994).

7 Major household retailer.

8 Auer's (1999) example of a 'fused lect' is, however, the Sinti-Romani dialect spoken in Germany, as described by Holzinger (1993). Arguably, this dialect merely shows extensive lexical and grammatical borrowing from German. Auer's suggestion that codeswitching may undergo a kind of sedimentation and lead to language change has been cited quite frequently, but the particular structural characteristics of a 'fused lect' remain largely undefined.

9 But see Ho-Dac (2002: 111ff.) for a discussion of the insertion of English *you* into Vietnamese discourse as a strategy of avoiding the complex social system of distance and solidarity expressed by native Vietnamese terms of address.

10 For a discussion of the strategy of 'compound verbs' in English–Panjabi codeswitching see Romaine (1995: 131–141, 154ff.).

11 Examples provided by Dörte Hansen-Jaax, 1992 (recorded in 1990).

6   The replication of linguistic 'matter'

1 German has upper-case spelling of the initial letter in nouns: *Computer, Internet*.

2 It is possible that some languages show structural differences between the expression of the various values belonging to the category of 'coordinating connectors' – for instance, expressing one meaning through a free standing, clause initial particle, but others through bound, postposed suffixes. Such structural factors may be relevant to the borrowability of an item in a given language contact situation. However, across a sample of many different languages, such structural factors are unlikely to replicate themselves. Moreover, there is no evidence within the sample of a link between structural representation and a behaviour that is aberrant from the general

hierarchy. Finally, in languages that do represent all three values in a structurally compatible way, their semantic-pragmatic functions are the only relevant distinctive features. Thus, we are left with the cline of 'contrast' as the relevant dimension that conditions the relative borrowability of an item.

3 Based on the RMS (Romani Morpho-Syntax) Database: www.romani.humanities. manchester.ac.uk

4 The sample covers the following languages (names of respective chapter authors and/or data contributors in brackets): Tasawaq (M. Kossmann), K'abeena (J. Crass), Likpe (F. Ameka), Katanga Swahili (V. de Rooij), Khuzistani Arabic (M. Shabibi), Domari (Y. Matras), Kurmanji (G. Haig), NE and Western Neo-Aramaic (G. Khan, W. Arnold), Macedonian Turkish (Ş. Tufan), Kildin Sami (M. Rießler), Yiddish (G. Reershemius), Rumungro (V. Elšík), Manange (K. Hildebrandt), Indonesian (U. Tadmor), Biak (W. van den Heuvel), Vietnamese (M. Alves), Jaminjung (E. Schultze-Berndt), Rapanui (S. Fischer), Nahuatl (A. Jensen), Yaqui (Z. Estrada and L. Guerrero), Otomi (E. Hekking and D. Bakker), Purepecha (C. Chamoreau), Quechua and Guarani (J. Rendón), Hup (P. Epps), Mosetén (J. Sakel), as well as Wichi (A. Vidal), Maltese and Chamorro (T. Stolz).

5 Thomason and Kaufman (1988: 51) for instance state that marked features are less likely to be borrowed than unmarked features.

7 Lexical borrowing

1 The Loanword Typology project led by the Linguistics Department at the Max-Planck-Institute for Evolutionary Anthropology in Leipzig is such a project, whose findings, however, were not yet available at the time of writing (www.eva.mpg. de/lingua/files/lwt.html).

2 Swadesh's list includes not just words like 'fire', 'smoke', 'water', and 'wind', but also 'river', 'road', 'sand', 'snow', and 'mountain', which are arguably not at all universally familiar concepts.

3 It appears that the two lists used are similar, but not identical. Borg and Azzopardi-Alexander (1997) cite some Semitic words, such as *niexef* 'dry', for which Stolz (2003) was only able to find a Romance equivalent (*xott*). Stolz also counts *qarn* 'horn' as an Italian loan, but it is clearly Semitic, albeit one of a small number of ancient words shared by Semitic and Indo-European (see Levin 1995).

4 The comparison with Jewish Neo-Aramaic of Sulemaniyya (Iraq) is interesting: Khan (2004: 443) gives the proportion of (mainly Kurdish, some Arabic) loans in the overall lexical inventory by category as 67% for nouns, 48% for adjectives, 53% for particles, and 15% for verbs.

5 See also ALT Discussion List posting, 3 January 2003.

6 P. Valenzuela, ALT Discussion List posting 1 January 2003.

7 With reference to Michif, a Cree-French mixed language, Bakker (1997a) argues that there is no mixture or substitution involving lexical verbs since the structure of the Algonkian verb does not allow isolation of a lexical verb root.

8 I.e. a geographically dispersed cluster of dialects spoken in Bulgaria, Macedonia, southeastern Romania, and western Turkey; note that the dialects are not all related in terms of their dialect classification within Romani, and that in turn related dialects may differ in their treatment of Turkish loan-verbs. For more information see

the online Romani Morpho-Syntax (RMS) Database of the Manchester Romani Project.

9 It is not uncommon for Romani populations in the Balkans to shift from one religion to another, and so religion is not always a stable ethnographic indicator of group-identity.

10 As part of fieldwork carried out by the Manchester Romani Project.

11 Bakker (1997a) discussed the use of French adjectives in the mixed language Michif, whose other 'parent' language, Cree, has only a very limited class of independent adjectives. Being a mixed language, however, Michif is not a good example for the borrowing of adjectives into a language where the adjective class is missing or limited.

12 Such generalisation is also common in learner varieties of German, where adjectives often end in a default -e, imitating a common pattern in non-standard German.

8   Grammatical and phonological borrowing

1 An indirect exception is Slovene Romani, where it appears that the two forms first merged in *te/ti*, as they did in Welsh Romani and in some German Romani dialects, and this general form was later replaced by Slovene/Croatian *da*.

2 But see Gordon's (2004) claims about the Amazonian Pirahã tribe.

3 Lekoudesch, the secret language of Jewish cattle-traders in Germany and the Netherlands (Matras 1991), employs the Hebrew letters as numerals, as was common in the Hebrew tradition, with the exception of 'seventy', 'eighty', and 'ninety', for which the Hebrew numerals are used. This is quite widespread in different varieties of the 'language' (or rather vocabulary), and could indicate that different sources these numerals and the others.

4 But contrast the discussion of speaker's conscious choices in Thomason (1999) with the position expressed in Thomason (1995) that mixed languages are the product of ordinary processes of contact-induced change.

5 There are numerous examples. Dixon (1980: 60, 67) mentions Luritja, a Western Desert language of Australia, which has special pronominal forms that are reserved for avoidance style (and look like camouflaged or distorted forms of the everyday pronouns), and the secret language Damin, used by initiated men of the Lardil tribe on Mornington Island, which substitutes the complex pronominal system of everyday Lardil by just two forms, representing 'ego' and 'other'. The secret language of shopkeepers in the German town of Breyell in Westphalia was reported by Kluge (1901) to have 1SG *minotes* and 2SG *zinotes*, and the secret vocabulary of the Gurbet peripatetics in Iran has 1SG *xukī-m*, 2SG *xukī-t*, etc.

6 Gardani (in press) provides a literature-based survey of borrowed inflectional morphology, in which the overwhelming majority of cases involve the marking of plurality on nouns.

7 Cf. Dixon (2006, 2001), but see Bowern (2006), Evans (2005), Koch and Sutton (2008).

8 See also remark to this effect by Curnow (2001: 416).

9 Domari has an indefinite article -*ak* which corresponds to the indefinite article -*ek* in Northern Kurdish, though in this case it is possible that we are dealing with the outcome of an internal grammaticalisation process of the Domari numeral *ek* 'one', modelled on the Kurdish pattern.

10 Including both Christian-Orthodox ethnic Greeks and Greek-speaking Muslim Turks whose ancestors emigrated to Turkey from Greek territories after the establishment of the Turkish Republic in 1922.

9   Converging structures: pattern replication

1 Common transliteration conventions in Romani linguistics use {c}for [ts]; but Sinti is frequently written in a system based on or heavily oriented towards German orthography.

2 Such indirect influence of contact is not necessarily limited to language attrition. Colloquial Hebrew, with an expanding number of native speakers, is undergoing rapid paradigm levelling and reduction as a result of speaker insecurity due to the absence of a model generation of native speakers (see Matras and Schiff 2005).

3 See Haspelmath (1998: 318), and for a usage-based explanation Haspelmath (1999).

4 'Double case' or 'suffixaufnahme'; cf. Payne (1995), Koptjevskaja-Tamm (2000).

5 Zuckermann (2003) mentions these and a few more well-known, well-attested, and frequently discussed cases of similar neologisms. The great majority of items listed in Zuckermann's overview tables (2003: 224–230) as examples of 'Phono-Semantic Matches' are, however, pure ghost-words, which may have been proposed by someone, somewhere, at some early stage in the history of the Hebrew language revivalist movement, but are not in contemporary use and have never reached any level of popular dissemination. Examples are *lo kemó tof* for 'locomotive', *karnéy báal* for 'carneval', *amá reká* (lit. 'empty nation') for 'America', *bo deá* (lit. 'author of a point of view') for *Buddha*, and dozens more.

6 Only in highly literary styles does one find usages such as *er war erfolgreicher als Beamter denn als Lehrer* 'he was more successful as a civil servant *than* as a teacher', and even here only for the sake of avoiding a double sequence of *als*, the normal particle that introduces the object of comparison; the child will have had no access to such usages.

7 Reinforced, quite possibly, by a tacit awareness on the part of the child of English–German functional near-equivalents such as *the-der*, *that-das*, *there-da* as well as *then-dann*.

8 Bulut (2006) reports on the replication of the Iranian postposed relative clause, introduced by the relativiser *ki/kê*, in Turkic dialects of western Iran, in contact with Kurdish and Persian. Interestingly, the pattern had been prevalent in Old Anatolian dialects of Turkish, under the influence of Persian and in the written form especially under the influence of the Persian literary language, but has largely retreated from the Anatolian varieties since the decline of Ottoman Turkish and its close orientation toward Persian literary sources.

9 Further evidence for such an extension comes from the shape of the attributive constructions with feminine nouns, which take the overt construct ending *-t* that in other Arabic dialects is reserved for nominal attribution (possession): *jazīr-at l-xaḍra* [island-F.CONS DEF-green] 'The green island'.

10 The notation here reflects Palestinian Arabic forms.

11 TOP.NON.A/S = topical non-subject; REM.P.VIS = remote past visual.

12 European Science Foundation project on the Typology of European Languages, 1990–1995; project volumes published in the series Empirical Approaches to Language Typology, Mouton de Gruyter publishers, Berlin.

13 This is not just limited to the Balkan dialects of Romani, as some people assume. Romani is, as a whole, a Balkanised language and even dispersed dialects continue to show Balkan features.

10   Contact languages

1 In the exceptional case of Israeli Hebrew, there is indeed no relation at all between the many languages of the parent generation comprising emigrants to Palestine from Europe and the Middle East, and the Hebrew adopted by the young generation; however, the acquisition of Hebrew was guided by the presence of a written tradition of Hebrew, including the modern-secular use of Hebrew in nineteenth-century press and literature (cf. Morag 1993, Nahir 1998).

2 Henceforth I shall be using 'creole' as a cover-term, assuming that creoles derive from a stage of pidginisation and that any characteristic grammatical patterns are the outcome of processes of expansion and creolisation; cf. also McWhorter (1998, 2005) on the 'creole prototype'.

3 Data recorded by Asmaa al-Baluchi (2005).

4 A noteworthy exception is the partly grammaticalised forms *yumi* 'we (inclusive')', *mipela* 'we (exclusive)', etc. in Tok Pisin, which arise through the need to replicate the pattern of an inclusive–exclusive semantic opposition in the substrate and contact languages.

5 An illustrative discussion of the differentiated effect of superstrate contact on related Portuguese-based pidgins in India is provided by Clements and Koontz-Garboden (2002).

6 There are differences between the two notions. Discussing Media Lengua, Muysken (1981) regards relexification as a wholesale substitution of the lexical inventory on the basis of a word-matching procedure. 'Lexical re-orientation' as discussed in Matras (2000a) is broader, and allows equally for the recruitment of a smaller inventory of lexemes for special effects or for cryptolectal purposes (disguise of meaning). It is not limited to a one-to-one word-matching process, but allows lexical creativity within the recruited component, as in Lekoudesch *schocha majim* 'coffee', literally 'black water', drawing on Hebrew lexicon.

7 Both languages allow creative word-formation through composition: Lekoudesch *Kassirrosch* 'pig-head' (Hebr. *rōš* 'head', *xazīr* 'pig'), *Schochamajim lou Kuhlef* 'black coffee' (Hebr. *šaxōr* 'black', *majim* 'water', *lō* 'no', *xalav* 'milk'); Jenisch *Dschukelmass* 'dog-meat' (Romani *džukel* 'dog', *mas* 'meat').

8 The last speakers, it appeared, were recorded in the 1950s (cf. Tipler 1957).

9 All examples cited here were recorded from speakers and recordings are archived in the Romani Project at the University of Manchester.

10 See also Bakker (1998) for a similarly argued distinction between Para-Romani languages as mixed languages, and secret lexicons.

11 See Matras (2000a) and (2003) for a similar point.

References

Abutalebi, J., Cappa, S. F., and Perani, D. 2001. The bilingual brain as revealed by functional neuroimaging. *Bilingualism: Language and Cognition* 4, 179–190.

Adamson, L. and Smith, N. 1995. Sranan. In: Muysken, P. and Smith, N. eds. *Substrata versus univerals in creole genesis*. Amsterdam: John Benjamins. 219–232.

Aikhenvald, A. Y. and Dixon, R. M. W. eds. 2001. *Areal diffuson and genetic inheritence: problems in comparative linguistics*. Oxford: Oxford University Press.

Aikhenvald, A. Y. and Dixon, R. M. W. eds. 2006. *Grammars in contact. A cross-linguistic typology*. Oxford: Oxford University Press.

Aikhenvald, A. Y. 2001. Language contact and language change in Amazonia. In: Blake, B. J. and Burridge, K. eds. *Historical linguistics 2001. Selected papers from the 15th International Conference on Historical Linguistics, Melbourne 13–17 August 2001.* 1–20.

Aikhenvald, A. Y. 2002. *Language contact in Amazonia*. Oxford: Oxford University Press.

Aikhenvald, A. Y. 2003. Mechanisms of change in areal diffusion: new morphology and language contact. *Journal of Linguistics* 39, 1–29.

Aikhenvald, A. Y. 2006. Grammars in contact: A cross-linguistic perspective. In: Aikhenvald, A. Y. and Dixon, R. M. W. eds. 1–66.

Aikhenvald, A. Y. 2007a. Language contact along the Sepik River, Papua New Guinea. Paper presented at the Workshop on Language Contact along Rivers, Research Centre for Linguistics Typology, La Trobe University, November 2007.

Aikhenvald, A. Y. 2007b. Multilingual fieldwork and emergent grammars. *Proceedings of the 33rd annual meeting of the Berkeley Linguistics Society*. Berkeley: Berkeley Linguistics Society.

Albert, M. L. and Obler, L. K. 1978. *The bilingual brain*. New York: Academic Press.

Alves, M. 2007. Sino-Vietnamese grammatical borrowing: An overview. In: Matras, Y. and Sakel, J. eds. 343–361.

Ameka, F. K. 2006. Grammars in contact in the Volta basin (West Africa): On contact-induced grammatical change in Likpe. In: Aikhenvald, A. Y. and Dixon, R. M. W. eds. 114–142.

Ameka, F. K. 2007. Grammatical borrowing in Likpe (Sɛkpɛlé). In: Matras, Y. and Sakel, J. eds. 107–122.

Anders, K. 1993. *Einflüsse der russischen Sprache bei deutschsprachigen Aussiedlern.* (Arbeiten zur Mehrsprachigkeit 44.) Hamburg: Germanisches Seminar.

Anderson, G. D. S. 2006. Towards a typology of the Siberian linguistic area. In: Matras, Y., McMahon, A., and Vincent, N. eds. 266–300.

Appel, R. and Muysken, P. 1987. *Language contact and bilingualism*. London: Edward Arnold.

Arends, J. and Bruyn, A. 1995. Gradualist and developmental hypotheses. In: Arends, J., Muysken, P., and Smith, N. eds. 111–120.

Arends, J. 1993. Towards a gradualist model of creolization. In: Byrne, F. and Holm, J. eds. *Atlantic meets Pacific. A global view of pidginization and creolization*. Amsterdam: John Benjamins. 371–380.

Arends, J., Kouwenberg, S., and Smith, N. 1995. Theories focusing on the non-European input. In: Arends, J., Muysken, P., and Smith, N. eds. 99–109.

Arends, J., Muysken, P., and Smith, N. eds. 1995. *Pidgins and creoles. An introduction*. Amsterdam: John Benjamins.

Auer, P. 1984. *Bilingual conversation*. Amsterdam: John Benjamins.

Auer, P. 1995. The pragmatics of code-switching: a sequential approach. In: Milroy, L. and Muysken, P. eds. 115–35.

Auer, P. 1999. From codeswitching via language mixing to fused lects: toward a dynamic typology of bilingual speech. *International Journal of Bilingualism* 3, 309–332.

Auer, P. ed. 1998. *Code-switching in conversation*. London: Routledge.

Backus, A. 1996. *Two in one. Bilingual speech of Turkish immigrants in the Netherlands*. Tilburg: Tilburg University Press.

Backus, A. 2003. Can a mixed language be conventionalized alternational codeswitching? In: Matras, Y. and Bakker, P. eds. 237–270.

Baghbidi, H. R. 2003. The Zargari language. An endangered European Romani in Iran. *Romani Studies* 5/13, 123–148.

Bakker, P. and Mous, M. 1994. Introduction. In: Bakker, P. and Mous, M. eds. 1–11.

Bakker, P. and Mous, M. eds. 1994. *Mixed languages. 15 case studies in language intertwining*. Amsterdam: IFOTT.

Bakker, P. and Muysken, P. 1995. Mixed languages and language intertwining. In: Arends, J., Muysken, P., and Smith, N. eds. 41–52.

Bakker, P. and Papen, R. A. 1997. Michif. In: Thomason, S. G. ed. 365–363.

Bakker, P. and van der Voort, H. 1991. Para-Romani languages. An overview and some speculations on their genesis. In: Bakker, P. and Cortiade, M. eds. *In the margin of Romani. Gypsy languages in contact*. Amsterdam: Institute for General Linguistics. 16–44.

Bakker, P. 1987. A Basque nautical pidgin: A missing link in the history of *Fu*. *Journal of Pidgin and Creole Languages* 2, 1–30.

Bakker, P. 1989. 'The language of the coast tribes is half-Basque'. A Basque-Amerindian pidgin in use between Europeans and Native Americans in North America ca. 1540–ca. 1640. *Anthropological Linguistics* 31, 117–147.

Bakker, P. 1994. Michif, the Cree-French mixed language of the Métis buffalo hunters in Canada. In: Bakker, P. and Mous, M. eds. 13–33.

Bakker, P. 1995. Pidgins. In: Arends, J., Muysken, P., and Smith, N. eds. 25–39.

Bakker, P. 1996. Language intertwining and convergence: typological aspects of genesis of mixed languages. *Sprachtypologie und Universalienforschung* 49, 9–20.

Bakker, P. 1997a. *A language of our own. The genesis of Michif – the mixed Cree-French language of the Canadian Métis*. New York: Oxford University Press.

Bakker, P. 1997b. Athematic morphology in Romani: The borrowing of a borrowing pattern. In: Matras, Y., Bakker, P., and Kyuchukov, H. eds. *The typology and dialectology of Romani*. Amsterdam: John Benjamins. 1–21.

Bakker, P. 1998. Pararomani languages and secret languages. In: Matras, Y. ed. 69–96.

Bakker, P. 2000a. Convergence intertwining: An alternative way towards the genesis of mixed languages. In: Gilbers, D. G., Nerbonne, J., and Schaeken, J. eds. 29–35.

Bakker, P. 2000b. Rapid language change: Creolization, intertwining, convergence. In: Renfrew, C., McMahon, A., and Trask, R. L. eds. 585–620.

Bakker, P. 2002. An Early vocabulary of British Romani (1616): A linguistic analysis. *Romani Studies* 5/12, 75–101.

Bakker, P. 2003. Mixed languages as autonomous systems. In: Matras, Y. and Bakker, P. eds. 107–150.

Bakker, P. 2006. The Sri Lanka Sprachbund: The newcomers Portuguese and Malay. In: Matras, Y., McMahon, A., and Vincent, N. eds. 135–159.

Bakker, P., Post, M., and van der Voort, H. 1995. TMA particles and auxiliaries. In: Arends, J., Muysken, P., and Smith, N. eds. 247–258.

Bakker, P., Smith, N., and Veenstra, T. 1995. Saramaccan. In: Muysken, P. and Smith, N. ed. *Substrata versus univerals in creole genesis*. Amsterdam: John Benjamins. 165–178.

Bao, Z. 2005. The aspectual system of Singapore English and the systemic substratist explanation. *Journal of Linguistics* 41, 237–267.

Bauer, E. B., Hall, J. K., and Kruth, K. 2002. The pragmatic role of codeswitches in play contexts. *International Journal of Bilingualism* 6, 53–74.

Beck, D. 2000. Bella Coola and North Wakashan: Convergence and diversity in the Northwest Coast Sprachbund. In: Gilbers, D. G., Nerbonne, J., and Schaeken, J. eds. 37–53.

Bentahila, A. and Davies, E. E. 1983. The syntax of Arabic-French code-switching. *Lingua* 59, 301–330.

Bentahila, A. and Davies, E. E. 1995. Patterns of code-switching and patterns of language contact. *Lingua* 96, 75–93.

Berk-Seligson, S. 1986. Linguistic constraints on intra-sentential code-switching: A study of Spanish/Hebrew bilingualism. *Language in Society* 15, 313–348.

Berlin, B. and Kay, P. 1969. *Basic color terms: their universality and evolution*. Berkeley: University of California Press.

Bhatia, T. K. and Ritchie, W. C. 1999. The bilingual child. In: Ritchie, W. C. and Bhatia, T. K. eds. *Handbook of child language acquisition*. San Diego: Academic Press. 569–641.

Bhatia, T. K. and Ritchie, W. C. eds. 2004. *The handbook of bilingualism*. Oxford: Blackwell.

Bickerton, D. 1981. *Roots of language*. Ann Arbor: Karoma.

Bickerton, D. 1984. The Language Bioprogram hypothesis. *Behavioral and Brain Sciences* 7, 173–222.

Biggam, C. P. 1997. *Blue in Old English. An interdisciplinary semantic study*. Amsterdam: Rodopi.

Bisang, W. 1996. Areal typology and grammaticalization: processes of grammaticalization based on nouns and verbs in East and Mainland South East Asian languages. *Studies in Language* 20, 519–597.

Bisang, W. 1998. Grammaticalisation and language contact, constructions and positions. In: Giacalone Ramat, A. and Hopper, P. J. eds. *The limits of grammaticalization*. Amsterdam: Benjamins. 13–58.

Bisang, W. 2006. Linguistic area, language contact, and typology: Some implications from the case of Ethiopia as a linguistic area. In: Matras, Y., McMahon, A., and Vincent, N. eds. 75–98.

Blakemore, D. 2002. *Relevance and linguistic meaning. The semantics and pragmatics of discourse markers*. Cambridge: Cambridge University Press.

Blom, J. P. and Gumperz, J. 1972. Social meaning in structure: Code-switching in Norway. In: Gumperz, J. and Hymes, D. eds. *Directions in sociolinguistics*. New York: Holt, Rinehart and Winston. 409–434.

Bloom, P. 2000. *How children learn the meaning of words*. Cambridge, MA: MIT Press.

Bolonyai, A. 1998. In-between languages: language shift/maintenance in childhood bilingualism. *International Journal of Bilingualism* 2, 21–43.

Boretzky, N. and Igla, B. 1994. Romani mixed dialects. In: Bakker, P. and Mous, M. eds. 35–68.

Boretzky, N. 1983. *Kreolsprachen, Substrate und Sprachwandel*. Wiesbaden: Harrassowitz.

Borg, A. and Azzopardi-Alexander, M. 1997. *Maltese*. London: Routledge.

Bořkovcová, M. 2006. Romský etnolekt češtiny. Případová studie. Prague: Signeta.

Bowern, C. 2006. Another look at Australia as a linguistic area. In: Matras, Y., McMahon, A., and Vincent, N. eds. 244–265.

Brody, J. 1987. Particles borrowed from Spanish as discourse markers in Mayan languages. *Anthropological Linguistics* 29, 507–532.

Brody, J. 1995. Lending the 'Unborrowable': Spanish discourse markers in indigenous American languages. In: Silva-Corvalán, C. ed. *Spanish in four continents. Studies in language contact and bilingualism*. Washington DC: Georgetown University Press. 132–147.

Broersma, M. and De Bot, K. 2006. Triggered codeswtiching: A corpus-based evaluation of the original triggering hypothesis and a new alternative. *Bilingualism: Language and Cognition* 9, 1–13.

Brown, C. H. 1999. *Lexical acculturation in Native American languages*. New York: Oxford University Press.

Bruyn, A. 1996. On identifying instances of grammaticalization in Creole languages. In: Baker, P. and Syea, A. eds. *Changing meanings, changing functions. Papers relating to grammaticalization in contact languages*. London: University of Westminster Press. 29–46

Bühler, K. 1934 [1982]. *Sprachtheorie*. Stuttgart: Fischer.

Bulut, C. 2006. Syntactic traces of Turkic-Iranian contiguity. An areal survey of contact-induced shift in patterns of relativzation. In: Johanson, L. and Bulut, Ch. eds. *Turkic-Iranian contact areas. Historical and linguistic aspects*. Wiesbaden: Harrassowitz. 165–208.

Burridge, K. 2006. Language contact and convergence in Pennsylvania German. In: Aikhenvald, A. Y. and Dixon, R. M. W. eds. 179–200.

Campbell, L. 1993. On proposed universals of grammatical borrowing. In: Aertsen, H. and Jeffers, R. J. eds. *Historical linguistics 1989*. Amsterdam: John Benjamins. 91–109.

Campbell, L. 1997. Amerind personal pronouns: A second opinion. *Language* 73, 339–351.

Campbell, L. 2006. Areal linguistics: A closer scrutiny. In: Matras, Y., McMahon, A., and Vincent, N. eds. 1–31.

Campbell, L., Kaufman, T., and Smith-Stark, Th. C. 1986. Meso-America as a linguistic area. *Language* 62, 530–570.

Carlin, E. B. 2006. Feeling the need. The borrowing of Cariban functional categories into Mawayana (Arawak). In: Aikhenvald, A. Y. and Dixon, R. M. W. eds. 313–332.

Carroll, J. 1981. Twenty-five years of research on foreign language aptitude. In: Diller, K. ed. *Individual differences in language ability and language behavior*. New York: Academic Press. 83–118.

Carroll, M. and Lambert, M. 2003. Information structure in narratives and the role of grammaticised knowledge: A study of adult French and German learners of English. In: Dimroth, C. and Starren, M. eds. *Information structure and the dynamics of language acquisition*. Amsterdam: Benjamins. 267–289.

Chamoreau, C. 2007. Grammatical borrowing in Purepecha. In: Matras, Y. and Sakel, J. eds. 465–480.

Chaudenson, R. 1992. *Des îles, des hommes, des langues*. Paris: L'Harmattan.

Chen, H. 2007. Code-switching in conversation: a case study from Taiwan. Unpublished PhD. Dissertation, University of Manchester.

Christodoulou, I. 1991. *Greek outside Greece. Language use by Greek-Cypriots in Britain*. Nicosia: Diaspora Books.

Chyet, M. 1995. Neo-Aramaic and Kurdish – an interdisciplinary consideration of their influence on each other. In: Izre'el, S. and Drory, R. eds. *Israel Oriental Studies XV – Language and culture in the Near East*. Leiden: E. J. Brill. 219–252.

Clahsen, H. and Felsen, C. 2006. How native-like is non-native language processing? *Trends in Cognitive Sciences* 10, 564–570.

Clements, J. C. and Koontz-Garboden, A. J. 2002. Two Indo-Portuguese creoles in contrast. *Journal of Pidgin and Creole Languages* 17, 191–236.

Clyne, M. and Kipp, S. 2006a. Australia's community languages. *International Journal for the Sociology of Language* 180, 7–21.

Clyne, M. and Kipp, S. 2006b. *Tiles in the multilingual mosaic. Macedonian, Filipino and Somali in Melbourne*. Canberra: ANU (Pacific Linguistics).

Clyne, M. 1967. *Transference and triggering*. The Hague: Nijhoff.

Clyne, M. 1968. Zum Pidgin-Deutsch der Gastarbeiter. *Zeitschrift für Mundartforschung* 35, 130–139.

Clyne, M. 1987. Constraints on code switching: How universal are they? *Linguistics* 25, 739–764.

Clyne, M. 2003. *Dynamics of language contact*. Cambridge: Cambridge University Press.

Clyne, M. ed. 1982. Foreigner Talk. *International Journal of the Sociology of Language* 28.

Coleman, W. D. 1981. From Bill 22 to Bill 101: The politics of language under the Parti Québécois. *Canadian Journal of Political Science/Révue canadienne de science politique* 14, 459–485.

Comeau, L., Genesee, F., and Lapaquette, L. 2003. The Modeling Hypothesis and child bilingual codemixing. *International Journal of Bilingualism* 7, 113–126.

Comrie, B. 1991. Comment: Yiddish is Slavic. In: Fishman, J. ed. *Yiddish – the fifteenth Slavic language (= International Journal for the Sociology of Language* 91). Berlin: Mouton de Gruyter. 151–156.

Comrie, B. 2000. Language contact, lexical borrowing, and semantic fields. In: Gilbers, D. G., Nerbonne, J., and Schaeken, J. eds. 73–86.

Comrie, B. 2004. Prolegomena to the study of loan words in Tsezic languages. Paper presented at the Loan Word Typology Workshop, Max-Planck-Institute for Evolutionary Anthropology, Leipzig, 1–2 May 2004.

Costa, A. and Caramazza, A. 1999. Is lexical selection in bilingual speech production language-specific? Further evidence from Spanish-English and English-Spanish bilinguals. *Bilingualism: Language and Cognition* 2, 231–244.

Costa, A. 2004. Speech production in bilinguals. In: Bhatia, T. J. and Ritchie, W. C. eds. 201–223.

Crass, J. 2007. Grammatical borrowing in K'abeena. In: Matras, Y. and Sakel, J. eds. 91–105.

Croft, W. 2000. *Explaining language change: An evolutionary approach.* Harlow, Essex: Longman.

Croft, W. 2001. *Radical construction grammar. Syntactic theory in typological perspective.* Oxford: Oxford University Press.

Croft, W. 2003. Mixed languages and acts of identity: An evolutionary approach. In: Matras, Y. and Bakker, P. eds. 41–72.

Crystal, D. 2000. *Language death.* Cambridge: Cambridge University Press.

Curnow, T. J. 2001. What language features can be 'borrowed'? In: Aikhenvald, A. Y. and Dixon, R. M. W. eds. 2001. 412–436.

Dahl, Ö. and Koptjevskaja-Tamm, M. eds. 2001. *The Circum-Baltic languages: typology and contact.* Vol. I & II. Amsterdam: John Benjamins.

Dal Negro, Slivia. 2005. Lingue in contatto: Il caso speciale dei segnali discorsivi. In: Banti, G., Marra, A., and Vineis, E. eds. *Atti del 4° congresso di studi dell'Associazione Italiana di Linguistica Applicata.* Perugia: Guerra Edizioni. 73–88.

Dawkins, R. M. 1916. *Modern Greek in Asia Minor.* Cambridge: Cambridge University Press.

De Bot, K., Lowie, W., and Verspoor, M. 2007. A dynamic systems theory approach to second language acquisition. *Bilingualism: Language and Cognition* 10, 7–21.

De Camp, D. 1971. Towards a generative analysis of post-creole speech continuum. In: Hymes, D. ed. 349–370.

De Houwer, A. 1990. *The acquisition of two languages from birth: A case study.* Cambridge: Cambridge University Press.

De Rooij, V. A. 1996. *Cohesion through contrast: discourse structure in Shaba Swahili/French conversations.* Amsterdam: IFOTT.

De Rooij, V. A. 2000. French discourse markers in Shaba Swahili conversations. *International Journal of Bilingualism,* 4, 447–468.

Deuchar, M. and Quay, S. 1998. One vs. two systems in early bilingual syntax: Two versions of the question. *Bilingualism: Language and Cognition* 1, 231–143.

Deuchar, M. and Quay, S. 2000. *Bilingual acquisition. Theoretical implications of a case study.* Oxford: Oxford University Press.

Deuchar, M. 1999. Are function words non-language-specific in early bilingual two-word utterances? *Bilingualism: Language and Cognition* 2, 23–34.

Dimmendaal, G. J. 2001. Areal diffusion versus genetic inheritance: an African perspective. In: Aikhenvald, A. Y. and Dixon, R. M. W. eds. 2001. 358–392.

Dimroth, C. 2007. Zweitspracherwerb bei Kindern und Jugendlichen. Gemeinsamkeiten und Unterschiede. In: Anstatt, T. ed. *Mehrsprachigkeit bei Kindern und Erwachsenen*. Tübingen: Narr-Francke. 115–137.

Dixon, R. M. W. 1980. *The languages of Australia*. Cambridge: Cambridge University Press.

Dixon, R. M. W. 2001. The Australian linguistic area. In: Aikhenvald, A. Y. and Dixon, R. M. W. eds. 64–104.

Dixon, R. M. W. 2002. *Australian languages, their nature and development*. Cambridge: Cambridge University Press.

Dixon, R. M. W. 2006. Grammatical diffusion in Australia: Free and bound pronouns. In: Aikhenvald, A. Y. and Dixon, R. M. W. eds. 67–93.

Donakey, A. 2007. Language planning and language policy in Manchester. Unpublished MA dissertation, University of Manchester.

Döpke, S. 1992. *One parent one language*. Amsterdam: John Benjamins.

Dorian, N. 1981. *Language death: The life cycle of a Scottish Gaelic dialect*. Philadelphia: University of Pennsylvania Press.

Dutton, T. 1997. Hiri Motu. In: Thomason, S. G. ed. 9–41.

Ehlich, K. and Rehbein, J. 1986. *Muster und Institution. Untersuchungen zur schulischen Kommunikation*. Tübingen: Narr.

Ehlich, K. 1986. *Interjektionen*. Tübingen: Niemeyer.

Ehlich, K. 2007. *Sprache und sprachliches Handeln*. Berlin: De Gruyter.

Eloeva, F. A., and Rusakov, A. J. 1990. *Problemy jazykovoj interferencii (cyganskie dialekty Evropy): Učebnoe posobie*. Leningrad: Leningradskij gosudarstvennyj universitet.

Elšík, V. and Matras, Y. 2006. *Markedness and language change: The Romani sample*. Berlin: Mouton de Gruyter.

Elšík, V. and Matras, Y. 2008. Modality in Romani. In: Hansen, B., de Haan, F., and van der Auwera, J. eds. *Modality in European languages*. Berlin: Mouton de Guyter.

Elšík, V. 2007. Grammatical borrowing in Hungarian Rumungro. In: Matras, Y. and Sakel, J. eds. 261–282.

Elšík, V. In press. Loanwords in Selice Romani, and Indo-Aryan language of Slovakia. In: Haspelmath, M. and Tadmor, U. eds. *Loanword typology*. Berlin: Mouton de Gruyter.

Emeneau, M. B. 1956. India as a linguistic area. *Language* 32, 3–16.

Enfield, N. J. 2003. *Linguistic epidemiology: semantics and grammar of language. Contact in mainland Southeast Asia*. London: Routledge Curzon.

Epps, P. 2001. The Vaupés melting pot: Tucanoan influence on Hup. In: Aikhenvald, A. Y. and Dixon, R. M. W. eds. 267–289.

Epps, P. 2006. The Vaupés melting pot: Tucanoan influence on Hup. In: Aikhenvald, A. Y. and Dixon, R. M. W. eds. 237–266.

Epps, P. 2007. Grammatical borrowing in Hup. In: Matras, Y. and Sakel, J. eds. 551–565.

Ervin, S. and Osgood, C. 1954. Second language learning and bilingualism. *Journal of Abnormal and Social Psychology Supplement* 49, 139–146.

Estrada Fernández, S. and Guerrero, L. 2007. Grammatical borrowing in Yaqui. In: Matras, Y. and Sakel, J. eds. 419–433.

Evans, N. 2005. Australian languages reconsidered: A review of Dixon (2002). *Oceanic Linguistics* 44, 242–286.

Extra, G. and Yağmur, K. eds. 2004. *Urban multilingualism in Europe. Immigrant minority languages at home and school.* Clevedon: Multilingual Matters.

Ferguson, C. A. 1970. The Ethiopian language area. *Journal of Ethiopian Studies* 8, 67–80.

Ferguson, C.A. 1977. Simplified registers, broken language and Gastarbeiterdeutsch. In: Molony, C., Zobl, H., and Stölting, W. eds. *Deutsch im Kontakt mit anderen Sprachen.* Kronberg: Scriptor. 25–39.

Field, F. W. 2002. *Linguistic borrowing in bilingual contexts.* Amsterdam: John Benjamins.

Filiputti, D., Tavano, A., Vorano, L., De Luca, G., and Fabbro, F. 2002. Nonparallel recovery of languages in a quadrilingual aphasic patient. *International Journal of Bilingualism* 6, 395–410.

Fischer, S. R. 2007. Grammatical borrowing in Rapanui. In: Matras, Y. and Sakel, J. eds. 387–402.

Fishman, J. 1964. Language maintenance and language shift as a field of inquiry. *Linguistics* 9, 32–70.

Fishman, J. 1965. Who speaks what language to whom and when? *La Linguistique* 2, 67–87.

Fishman, J. 1967. Bilingualism with and without diglossia. Diglossia with and without bilingualism. *Journal of Social Issues* 23, 29–38.

Foley, W. A. 1986. *The Papuan languages of New Guinea.* Cambridge: Cambridge University Press.

Forman, M. L. 1972. Zamboangueño texts with grammatical analysis: A study of Philippine Creole Spanish. PhD dissertation, Cornell University.

Frake, C. O. 1971. Lexical origins and semantic structure in Philippine Creole Spanish. In: Hymes, D. ed. 223–242.

Frank, I. and Poulin-Dubois, D. 2002. Young monolingual and bilingual responses to violation of the Mutual Exclusivity Principle. *International Journal of Bilingualism* 6, 125–146.

Fraser, B. 1990. An approach to discourse markers. *Journal of Pragmatics* 14, 383–395.

Friederici, A. 2001. Syntactic, prosodic, and semantic processes in the brain: Evidence from event-related neuroimaging. *Journal of Psycholinguistic Research* 30, 237–250.

Friedman, V. A. 1991. Case in Romani: old grammar in new affixes. *Journal of the Gypsy Lore Society* 5/1, 85–102.

Friedman, V. A. 2003. *Turkish in Macedonia and beyond: Studies in contact, typology, and other phenomena in the Balkans and the Caucasus.* Wiesbaden: Harrassowitz.

Fuller, J. 2001. The principle of pragmatic detachability in borrowing: English-origin discourse markers in Pennsylvania German. *Linguistics* 29, 351–369.

Gal, S. 1979. *Language shift: Social determination of linguistic change in bilingual Austria.* New York: Academic Press.

Garafanga, J. and Torras, M.-C. 2002. Interactional otherness: Towards a redefinition of codeswitching. *International Journal of Bilingualism* 6, 1–22.

Garcia, O. and Fishman, J. A. 2002. *The multilingual apple. Languages in New York City*. Berlin: Mouton de Gruyter.

Gardani, F. In press. *Borrowing of inflectional morphemes in language contact*. Frankfurt: Peter Lang.

Gardner-Chloros, P., Charles, R., and Cheshire, J. 2000. Parallel patterns? A comparison of monolingual speech and bilingual codeswitching discourse. *Journal of Pragmatics* 32, 1305–1341.

Gardner-Chloros, P. 1991. *Language selection and switching in Strasbourg*. New York: Oxford University Press.

Gilbers, D., Nerbonne, J., and Schaeken, J. eds. 2000. *Languages in contact*. Amsterdam: Rodopi.

Givón, T. 1979. From discourse to syntax: Grammar as a processing strategy. In: Givón, T. ed. *Discourse and syntax*. New York: Academic Press. 81–111.

Givón, T. 1982. Tense-aspect modality: The Creole proto-type and beyond. In: Hopper, P. J. ed. *Tense-aspect: between semantics and pragmatics*. Amsterdam: John Benjamins. 115–163.

Givón, T. 1984. *Syntax: A functional-typological introduction. Vol. I*. Amsterdam: John Benjamins.

Givón, T. 1990. *Syntax: A functional-typological introduction. Vol. II*. Amsterdam: John Benjamins.

Goddard, I. 1997. Pidgin Delaware. In: Thomason, S. G. ed. 43–98.

Goglia, F. 2006. Communicative strategies in the Italian of Igbo-Nigerian immigrants in Padova (Italy): a contact linguistic approach. PhD dissertation, University of Manchester.

Gołąb, Z. 1956. The concept of isogrammatism. *Buletin Polskiego Towarzystwa Jezykoz-nawczego* 15, 1–12.

Gołąb, Z. 1959. Some Arumanian-Macedonian isogrammatisms and the social background of their development. *Word* 15, 415–435.

Goldberg, A. E. 1995. *Constructions: A construction grammar approach to argument structure*. Chicago: Chicago University Press.

Gollan, T. H. and Silverberg, N. B. 2001. Tip-of-the-tongue states in Hebrew-English bilinguals. *Bilingualism: Language and Cognition* 4, 63–83.

Golovko, E. V., and Vakhtin, N. 1990. Aleut in contact: the CIA Enigma. *Acta Linguistica Hafniensia* 22, 97–125.

Golovko, E. V. 1994. Copper Island Aleut. In: Bakker, P. and Mous, M. eds. 113–121.

Golovko, E. V. 1996. A case of nongenetic development in the Arctic area: The contribution of Aleut and Russian to the formation of Copper Island Aleut. In: Jahr, E. H. and Broch, I. eds. 63–77.

Golovko, E. V. 2003. Language contact and group identity: The role of 'folk' linguistic engineering. In: Matras, Y. and Bakker, P. eds. 177–207.

Goodman, M. 1987. The Portuguese element in the American creoles. In: Gilbert, G. G. ed. *Pidgin and creole languages. Essays in memory of John E. Reinecke*. Honolulu: University of Hawaii Press. 361–405.

Goral, M., Levy, E. S., and Obler, L. K. 2002. Neurolinguistic aspects of bilingualism. *International Journal of Bilingualism* 6, 411–440.

Gordon, P. 2004. Numerical cognition without words: Evidence from Amazonia. *Science* 306, 496–499.

Green, D. and Price, C. 2001. Functional imaging in the study of recovery patterns in bilingual aphasia. *Bilingualism: Language and Cognition* 4, 191–201.

Green, D. 1998. Mental control of the bilingual lexico-semantic system. *Bilingualism: Language and Cognition* 1, 67–81.

Greenberg, J. H. 1959. Africa as a linguistic area. In: Bascom, W. and Hertovits, W. eds. *Continuity and change in African languages*. Chicago: Chicago University Press. 15–27.

Greenberg, J. H. 1999. Are there mixed languages? In: Fleischman, L. S. *et al.* eds. *Essays in poetics, literary history and linguistics presented to Viacheslav Vsevolodovich Ivanov on the occasion of his seventieth birthday*. Moscow: OGI. 626–633.

Greenberg, J. H. ed. 1966. *Universals of language*. Cambridge, MA: MIT Press.

Grenoble, L. 2000. Morphosyntactic change: The impact of Russian on Evenki. In: Gilbers, D. G., Nerbonne, J., and Schaeken, J. eds. 105–120.

Grosjean, F. 1982. *Life with two languages: An introduction to bilingualism*. Cambridge, MA: Harvard University Press.

Grosjean, F. 1989. Neurolinguists beware! The bilingual is not two monolinguals in one person. *Brain and Language* 36, 3–15.

Grosjean, F. 1998. Studying bilinguals: Methodological and conceptual issues. *Bilingualism: Language and cognition* 1, 131–149.

Grosjean, F. 2001. The bilingual's language modes. In: Nicol, J. L. ed. *One mind, two languages. Bilingual language processing*. Oxford: Blackwell. 1–22.

Grosjean, F. 2004. Studying bilinguals: Methodological and conceptual issues. In: Bhatia, T. J. and Ritchie, W. C. eds. 32–63.

Güldemann, T. 2006. Structural isoglosses between Khoekhoe and Tuu: The Cape as a linguistic area. In: Matras, Y., McMahon, A., and Vincent, N. eds. 99–134.

Gumperz, J. 1982. *Discourse strategies*. Cambridge: Cambridge University Press.

Gut, Ulrike. 2000. *Bilingual acquisition of intonation. A study of children speaking German and English*. Tübingen: Niemeyer.

Haase, M. 1991. *Sprachkontakt und Sprachwandel im Baskenland. Die Einflüsse des Gaskognischen und Französischen auf das Baskische*. Hamburg: Buske.

Hackert, S. 2004. *Urban Bahamian Creole. System and variation*. Amsterdam: John Benjamins.

Haig, G. 2001. Linguistic diffusion in present-day East Anatolia: From top to bottom. In: Aikhenvald, A. Y. and Dixon, R. M. W. eds. 195–224.

Hajek, J. 2006. Language contact and convergence in East Timor. In: Aikhenvald, A. Y. and Dixon, R. M. W. eds. 161–178.

Hall, R. A. 1962. The life cycle of pidgin languages. *Lingua* 11, 151–156.

Hall, R. A. 1966. *Pidgin and creole languages*. Ithaca: Cornell University Press.

Halwachs, D. W. 2005. Roma and Romani in Austria. *Romani Studies* 5/15, 145–173.

Hamers, J. and Blanc, M. 2000 (second edition). *Bilinguality and bilingualism*. Cambridge: Cambridge University Press.

Hancock, I. F. 1986. The domestic hypothesis, diffusion and componentiality: An account of Anglophone creole origins. In: Muysken, P. and Smith, N. ed. *Substrata versus univerals in creole genesis*. Amsterdam: John Benjamins. 71–102.

Harris, A. and Campbell, L. 1995. *Historical syntax in cross-linguistic perspective*. Cambridge: Cambridge University Press.

Haspelmath, M. 1997. *Indefinite pronouns*. Oxford: Oxford University Press.

Haspelmath, M. 1998. Does grammaticalization need reanalysis? *Studies in Language* 22, 315–351.

Haspelmath, M. 1999. Why is grammaticalization irreversible? *Linguistics* 37, 1043–1068.

Haspelmath, M., Dryer, M., Gil, D., and Comrie, B. eds. 2005. *The world atlas of language structures*. Oxford: Oxford University Press.

Haugen, E. 1950. The analysis of linguistic borrowing. *Language* 26, 210–231.

Haugen, E. 1953 [1969]. *The Norwegian language in the Americas: A study in bilingual behavior*. Bloomington: Indiana University Press.

Hayward, R. and Orwin, M. 1991. The prefix conjugation in Qafar-Saho: The survival and revival of a paradigm – Part 1. *African Languages and Cultures* 4, 157–176.

Heath, J. 1978. *Linguistic diffusion in Arnhem Land*. Canberra: Australian Institute for Aboriginal Studies.

Heath, J. 1984. Language contact and language change. *Annual Review of Anthropology* 13, 367–384.

Heidelberg Project (Heidelberger Forschungsprojekt 'Pidgin-Deutsch'). 1975. *Sprache und Kommunikation ausländischer Arbeiter*. Kronberg: Scriptor.

Heine, B. and Kuteva, T. 2003. On contact-induced grammaticalization. *Studies in Language* 27, 529–72.

Heine, B. and Kuteva, T. 2005. *Language contact and grammatical change*. Cambridge: Cambridge University Press.

Heine, B. and Kuteva, T. 2006. *The changing languages of Europe*. Oxford: Oxford University Press.

Heine, B. and Miyashita, H. 2008. Accounting for a functional category: German *drohen* 'to threaten'. *Language Sciences* 30, 53–101.

Heine, B. 1969. Zur Frage der Sprachmischung in Afrika. *Zeitschrift der Deutschen Morgenländischen Gesellschaft*, Supplementa I/3, 1104–1112.

Heine, B. 2005a. On contact-induced syntactic change. *Sprachtypologie und Universalienforschung* 58, 60–74.

Heine, B. 2005b. On reflexive forms in creoles. *Lingua* 115, 201–257.

Heine, B., Claudi, U., and Hünnemeyer, F. 1991. *Grammaticalization: A conceptual framework*. Chicago: University of Chicago Press.

Hekking, E. and Bakker, D. 2007. The case of Otomi: A contribution to grammatical borrowing in cross-linguistic perspective. In: Matras, Y. and Sakel, J. eds. 435–464.

Herkenrath, A., Karakoç, B., and Rehbein, J. 2002. Interrogative elements as subordinators in Turkish – aspects of Turkish-German bilingual children's language use. Working Papers in Multilingualism 44. Hamburg: Sonderforschungsbereich Mehrsprachigkeit.

Hermans, D., Bongearts, T., De Bot, K., and Scheruder, R. 1998. Producing words in a foreign language: Can speakers prevent interference from their first language? *Bilingualism: Language and Cognition* 1, 213–229.

Hickey, R. 2006. Contact, shift and language change. Irish English and South African Indian English. In: Tristram, H. L. C. ed. *Celtic Englishes IV*. Potsdam: University Press. 234–258.

Hinrichs, U. 1999. Die sogenannten 'Balkanismen' als Problem der Südosteuropa-Linguistik und der Allgemeinen Sprachwissenschaft. In: Hinrichs, U. ed. *Handbuch der Südosteuropa-Linguistik.* Wiesbaden: Harrassowitz. 429–462.

Hlavac, J. 2006. Bilingual discourse markers: Evidence from Croatian-English code-switching. *Journal of Pragmatics* 38, 1870–1900.

Ho-Dac, Tuc. 2002. *Vietnamese-English bilingualism. Patterns of code-switching.* London: Routledge.

Hoffmann, C. 1991. *An introduction to bilingualism.* London: Longman.

Höhlig, M. 1997. *Kontaktbedingter Sprachwandel in der adygeischen Umgangssprache im Kaukasus und in der Türkei.* Munich: Lincom Europa.

Holm, J. 1988–89. *Pidgins and creoles.* Cambridge: Cambridge University Press.

Holm, J. 2000. *An introduction to pidgins and creoles.* Cambridge: Cambridge University Press.

Holzinger, D. 1993. *Das Rómanes: Grammatik und Diskursanalyse der Sprache der Sinte.* (= Innsbrucker Beiträge zur Kulturwissenschaft, 85.) Innsbruck: Verlag des Instituts für Sprachwissenschaft der Universität Innsbruck.

Hopper, P. J. and Traugott, E. C. 1993. *Grammaticalization.* Cambridge: Cambridge University Press.

Houtzagers, P. 2000. Effects of language contact as a source of (non)information: The historical reconstruction of Burgenland Kajkavian. In: Gilbers, D. G., Nerbonne, J., and Schaeken, J. eds. 157–164.

Huttar, G. 2002. Borrowing of verbs versus nouns. [Discussion summary.] Linguist List 13.588 (www.linguistlist.org/issues/13/13–588.html).

Huttar, G. L. and Velantie, F. J. 1997. Ndyuka-Trio Pidgin. In: Thomason, S. G. ed. 99–124.

Hyltenstam, K. and Abrahamsson, N. 2003. Maturational constraints in SLA. In: Doughty, C. J. and Long, M. H. eds. *The handbook of second language acquisition.* Oxford: Blackwell. 539–588.

Hymes, D. 1974. *Foundations in sociolinguistics: An ethnographic approach.* Philadelphia: University of Pennsylvania Press.

Hymes, D. ed. 1971. *Pidginization and creolization of languages.* Cambridge: Cambridge University Press.

Igla, B. 1996. *Das Romani von Ajia Varvara. Deskriptive und historisch-vergleichende Darstellung eines Zigeunerdialekts.* Wiesbaden: Harrassowitz.

Ijabla, E., Obler, L. K., and Changappa, S. 2004. Bilingual aphasia. In: Bhatia, T. J. and Ritchie, W. C. eds. 71–89.

Iwasaki, S. and Horie, P. I. 2000. Creating speech register in Thai conversation. *Language in Society* 29, 519–554.

Jahr, E. H. and Broch, I. eds. 1996. *Language contact in the arctic.* Berlin: Mouton.

Jahr, E. H. 1996. On the pidgin status of Russenorsk. In: Jahr, E. H. and Broch, I. eds. 107–122.

Jake, J. L. and Myers-Scotton, C. 1997. Relating interlanguage to code-switching: the composite matrix language. *Proceedings of Boston University Conference on Language Development* 21, 319–330.

Jake, J. L. 1998. Constructing interlanguage: building a composite matrix language. *Linguistics* 36, 333–382.

Jendraschek, G. 2006. Basque in contact with Romance languages. In: Aikhenvald, A. Y. and Dixon, R. M. W. eds. 143–162.

Jensen, A. and Canger, U. 2007. Grammatical borrowing in Nahuatl. In: Matras, Y. and Sakel, J. eds. 403–418.

Johanson, L. 2002. *Structural factors in Turkic language contacts*. Richmond: Curzon.

Johnson, C. E. and Wilson, I. L. 2002. Phonetic evidence for early language differentiation: Research issues and some preliminary data. *International Journal of Bilingualism* 6, 271–289.

Joseph, B. 1983. *The synchrony and diachrony of the Balkan infinitive*. Cambridge: Cambridge University Press.

Kainz, F. 1960. Speech pathology I: Aphasic speech. In: Paradis, M. *Readings on aphasia in bilinguals and polyglots*. Montreal: Didier.

Kaplan, R. B. and Baldauf, R. B. 1997. *Language planning from practice to theory*. Clevedon: Multilingual Matters.

Kapp, D. B. 2004. Basic colour terms in South Dravidian tribal languages. *Indo-Iranian Journal* 47, 193–201.

Keesing, R. M. 1988. *Melanesian Pidgin and the Oceanic substrate*. Stanford: Stanford University Press.

Keesing, R. M. 1991. Substrates, calquing and grammaticalization in Melanesian Pidgin. In: Traugott, E. C. and Heine, B. eds. 1991. *Approaches to grammaticalization –* Vol. 1: *Focus on theoretical and methodological issues*. Amsterdam: John Benjamins. 315–342.

Khan, G. 2004. *The Jewish Neo-Aramaic dialect of Sulemaniyya and Ḥalabja*. Leiden: Brill.

Khasanova, M. 2000. The lower Amur languages in contact with Russian. In: Gilbers, D. G., Nerbonne, J., and Schaeken, J. eds. 179–185.

Klein, W. and Dittmar, N. 1979. *Developing grammars. The acquisition of German syntax by foreign workers*. Berlin/Heidelberg/New York: Springer.

Klein, W. 1986. *Second language acquisition*. Cambridge: Cambridge University Press.

Klepsch, A. 1996. Das Lachoudische: Eine jiddische Sondersprache in Franken. In: Siewert, K. ed. 81–93.

Kluge, F. 1901. *Rotwelsch. Quellen und Wortschatz der Gaunersprache*. Strassburg: Trübner.

König, E. 1991. *The meaning of focus particles. A comparative perspective*. London: Routledge.

Koch, H. (with Sutton, P.) 2008. Australian languages: A singular vision. (Review article on R. M. W. Dixon's *Australian languages: their nature and development*. Cambridge University Press, 2002.) *Journal of Linguistics* 44, 471–504.

Köppe, R. 1996. Language differentiation in bilingual children: the development of grammatical and pragmatic competence. *Linguistics* 34, 927–954.

Koptjevskaja-Tamm, M. 2000. Romani genitives in cross-linguistic perspective. In: Elšík, V. and Matras, Y. eds. *Grammatical relations in Romani: The noun phrase*. Amsterdam: John Benjamins. 123–149.

Koptjevskaja-Tamm, M. 2006. The circle that won't come full: Two potential isoglosses in the Circum-Baltic area. In: Matras, Y., McMahon, A., and Vincent, N. eds. 182–226.

Kossmann, M. 2007. Grammatical borrowing in Tasawaq. In: Matras, Y. and Sakel, J. eds. 75–89.

Kouwenberg, S. and LaCharité, D. 2004. *Journal of Pidgin and Creole Languages* 19, 285–331.

Kouwenberg, S. and Muysken, P. 1995. Papiamento. In: Arends, J., Muysken, P., and Smith, N. eds. 205–218.

Kouwenberg, S. 1994. *A grammar of Berbice Dutch Creole*. Berlin: Mouton de Gruyter.

Krier, F. 1980. Lehnwort und Fremdwort im Maltesischen. *Folia Linguistics* 14, 179–184.

Kroll, J. F. and Dussias, P. E. 2004. The comprehension of words and sentences in two languages. In: Bhatia, T. J. and Ritchie, W. C. eds. 169–200.

Kroll, J. F. and Stewart, E. 1994. Category interference in translation and picture naming: evidence and asymmetric connection between bilingual memory representations. *Journal of Memory and Language* 33, 149–174.

Kroll, J. F. and Sunderman, G. 2003. Cognitive processes in second language learners and bilinguals: The development of lexical and conceptual representations. In: Doughty, C. J. and Long, M. H. eds. *The handbook of second language acquisition*. Oxford: Blackwell. 104–129.

Kroll, J. F., Bobb, S. C., and Wodniecka, Z. 2006. Language selectivity is the exception, not the rule: Arguments against a fixed locus of language selection in bilingual speech. *Bilingualism: Language and Cognition* 9, 119–135.

Labov, W. 1972a. *Language in the inner city. Studies in Black English Vernacular.* Philadelphia: University of Pennsylvania Press.

Labov, W. 1972b. *Sociolinguistic patterns*. Philadelphia: University of Pennsylvania Press.

Labov, W. 1994. *Principles of linguistic change. Volume I: Internal factors*. Oxford: Basil Blackwell

Ladstätter, O. and Tietze, A. 1994. *Die Abdal (Äynu) in Xinjiang*. Wien: Verlag der Österreichischen Akademie der Wissenschaften.

Lambert, W., Havelka, E., and Crosby, C. 1958. The influence of language acquisition contexts on bilingualism. *Journal of Abnormal and Social Psychology* 56, 77–82.

Lanvers, U. 2001. Language alternation in infant bilinguals: A developmental to codeswitching. *International Journal of Bilingualism* 5, 437–464.

Lanza, E. 1997. *Language mixing in infant bilingualism. A sociolinguistic perspective*. Oxford: Clarendon.

Larsen-Freeman, D. and Long, M. H. 1991. *An introduction to second language acquisition research*. London: Longman.

Lefebvre, C. 1993. The role of relexification and syntactic reanalysis in Haitian Creole: methodological aspects of a research program. In: Mufwene, S. ed. *Africanisms in Afro-American language varieties*. Athens, GA: University of Georgia Press. 254–279.

Lefebvre, C. 1998. *Creole genesis and the acquisition of grammar: the case of Haitian Creole*. Cambridge: Cambridge University Press.

Lefebvre, C. 2004. Coordinating constructions in Fongbe with reference to Haitian Creole. In: Haspelmath, M. ed. *Coordinating constructions*. Amsterdam: John Benjamins. 123–164.

Leopold, W. F. 1949. *Speech development of a bilingual child: Volume 3*. New York: AMS Press.

Levelt, W., Roelofs, A., and Meyer, A. S. 1999. A theory of lexical access in speech production. *Behavioral and Brain Sciences* 22, 1–75.

Levin, S. 1995. *Semitic and Indo-European: the principal etymologies*. Amsterdam: John Benjamins.

Li Wei and Milroy, L. 1995. Conversational codeswitching in a Chinese community in Britain: a sequential analysis. *Journal of Pragmatics* 23, 281–299.

Li Wei. 1998. The 'why' and 'how' questions in the analysis of conversational code-switching. In: Auer, P. ed. 156–179.

Li Wei. 2002. 'What do you want me to say?' On the conversation analysis approach to bilingual interaction. *Language in Society* 31, 159–180.

Li Wei. 2005. How can you tell? Towards a commonsense explanation of conversational code-switching. *Journal of Pragmatics* 37, 375–389.

Lindholm, J. J. and Padilla, A. M. 1978. Language mixing in bilingual children. *Journal of Child Language* 5, 327–335.

Lipski, J. M. 1992. New thoughts on the origins of Zamboangueño (Philippine Creole Spanish). *Language Sciences* 14, 197–231.

Lo, Y. S. 2007. Cantonese-English code-switching in the Manchester Chinese immigrant community. Unpublished PhD dissertation, University of Manchester.

Long, M. H. 2003. Stabilization and fossilization in interlangauge development. In: Doughty, C. J. and Long, Michael H. eds. *The handbook of second language acquisition*. Oxford: Blackwell. 487–535.

Lötzsch, R. 1996. Interferenzbedingte grammatische Konvergenzen und Divergenzen zwischen Sorbisch und Jiddisch. *Sprachtypologie und Universalienforschung* 49, 50–59.

Loveday, L. 1996. *Language contact in Japan. A socio-linguistic history*. Oxford: Clarendon Press.

Macalister, R. A. S. 1914. *The language of the Nawar of Zutt, the nomad smiths of Palestine*. (Gypsy Lore Society Monographs 3.) London: Edinburgh University Press.

Macswan, J. 2000. The architecture of the bilingual language faculty: evidence from intrasentential code switching. *Bilingualism: Language and Cognition* 3, 37–54.

Maschler, Y. 1994. Metalanguaging and discourse markers in bilingual conversation. *Language in Society* 23, 325–366.

Maschler, Y. 1997. Emergent bilingual grammar: The case of contrast. *Journal of Pragmatics* 28, 279–313.

Maschler, Y. 1998. On the transition from codeswitching to a mixed code. In: Auer, P. ed. 125–149.

Maschler, Y. 2000. Towards fused lects: discourse markers in Hebrew-English bilingual conversation twelve years later. *International Journal of Bilingualism* 4, 529–561.

Masica, C. 1976. *Defining a Linguistic Area: South Asia*. Chicago: Chicago University Press.

Masica, C. 1991. *The Indo-Aryan languages*. Cambridge: Cambridge University Press.

Masica, C. 2001. The definition and significance of linguistic areas: methods, pitfalls, and possibilities (with special reference to the validity of South Asia as a linguistic area). In: Singh, R., Bhaskararao, P., and Subbarao, K. V. eds. *The yearbook of South Asian languages and linguistics 2001. Tokyo symposium on South Asian languages: Contact, convergence and typology*. New Delhi: Sage. 205–267.

Masliyah, S. 1996. Four Turkish suffixes in Iraqi Arabic: *-li, -lik, -siz* and *−çi*. *Journal of Semitic Studies* 41, 291–300.

Matisoff, J. A. 2001. Genetic versus contact relationship: Prosodic diffusibility in south-East Asian languages. In: Aikhenvald, A. Y. and Dixon, R. M. W. eds. 291–327.

Matras, Y. and Bakker, P. 2003. The study of mixed languages. In: Matras, Y. and Bakker, P. eds. 1–20.

Matras, Y. and Bakker, P. eds. 2003. *The mixed language debate. Theoretical and empirical advances.* Berlin: Mouton de Gruyter.

Matras, Y. and Bührig, K. eds. 1999. *Sprachtheorie und sprachliches Handeln. Festschrift für Jochen Rehbein.* Tübingen: Stauffenburg.

Matras, Y. and Sakel, J. 2007a. Investigating the mechanisms of pattern-replication in language convergence. *Studies in Language* 31, 829–865.

Matras, Y. and Sakel, J. 2007b. Introduction. In: Matras, Y. and Sakel, J. eds. 1–13.

Matras, Y. and Sakel, J. eds. 2007. *Grammatical borrowing in cross-linguistic perspective.* Berlin: Mouton de Gruyter.

Matras, Y. and Sasse, H.-J. eds. 1995. *Verb-subject order and theticity in European languages.* (Special issue of *Sprachtypologie und Universalienforschung* 48, 1–2.) Berlin: Akademie.

Matras, Y. and Schiff, L. 2005. Spoken Israeli Hebrew revisited: Structures and variation. In: *Studia Semitica. Journal of Semitic Studies Jubilee Volume.* (*Journal of Semitic Studies Supplement* 16), 145–193.

Matras, Y. and Shabibi, M. 2007. Grammatical borrowing in Khuzistani Arabic. In: Matras, Y. and Sakel, J. eds. 137–149.

Matras, Y. and Tufan, Ş. 2007. Grammatical borrowing in Macedonian Turkish. In: Matras, Y. and Sakel, J. eds. 215–227.

Matras, Y. 1988. *Lekoudesch: Integration jiddischer Wörter in die Mundart von Rexingen bei Horb. Mit vergleichbarem Material aus Buttenhausen bei Münsingen.* [Arbeiten zur Mehrsprachigkeit 33/1988.] Hamburg: Germanisches Seminar.

Matras, Y. 1991. Zur Rekonstruktion des jüdisch-deutschen Wortschatzes in den Mundarten ehemaliger "Judendörfer" in Südwestdeutschland. *Zeitschrift für Dialektologie und Linguistik* 58, 267–293.

Matras, Y. 1994. *Untersuchungen zu Grammatik und Diskurs des Romanes – Dialekt der Kelderaša/Lovara.* Wiesbaden: Harrassowitz.

Matras, Y. 1996a. Sondersprachliche Hebraismen. Am Beispiel der südwestdeutschen Viehhändlersprache. In: Siewert, K. ed. 43–58.

Matras, Y. 1996b. Prozedurale Fusion: Grammatische Interferenzschichten im Romanes. *Sprachtypologie und Universalienforschung* 49, 60–78.

Matras, Y. 1998a. Utterance modifiers and universals of grammatical borrowing. *Linguistics* 36, 281–331.

Matras, Y. 1998b. Convergent development, grammaticalization, and the problem of 'mutual isomorphism'. In: Boeder, W., Schroeder, Ch., and Wagner, K.-H. eds. *Sprache in Raum und Zeit.* Tübingen: Narr. 89–103.

Matras, Y. 1998c. Para-Romani revisited. In: Matras, Y. ed. 1–27.

Matras, Y. 1998d. Convergence vs. fusion in linguistic areas. Paper presented at the *Annual Meeting of the Deutsche Gesellschaft für Sprachwissenschaft*, Halle, 5–7 March 1998.

Matras, Y. 1998e. The Romani element in Jenisch and Rotwelsch. In: Matras, Y. ed. 193–230.

Matras, Y. 1999a. The state of present-day Domari in Jerusalem. *Mediterranean Language Review* 11, 1–58.

Matras, Y. 1999b. The speech of the Polska Roma: Some highlighted features and their implications for Romani dialectology. *Journal of the Gypsy Lore Society* 5/9, 1–28.

Matras, Y. 2000a. Mixed Languages: A functional-communicative approach. *Bilingualism: Language and Cognition* 3, 79–99.

Matras, Y. 2000b. Fusion and the cognitive basis for bilingual discourse markers. *International Journal of Bilingualism* 4, 505–528.

Matras, Y. 2000c. How predictable is contact-induced change in grammar? In: Renfrew, C., McMahon, A., and Trask, R. L. eds. 563–583.

Matras, Y. 2002. *Romani: A linguistic introduction.* Cambridge: Cambridge University Press.

Matras, Y. 2003. Mixed languages: re-examining the structural prototype. In: Matras, Y. and Bakker, P. eds. 151–175.

Matras, Y. 2004a. Layers of convergent syntax in Macedonian Turkish. *Mediterranean Language Review* 15, 63–86.

Matras, Y. 2004b. Romacilikanes: The Romani dialect of Parakalamos. *Romani Studies* 5/14, 59–109.

Matras, Y. 2005a. The full extent of fusion: A test case for connectivity and language contact. In: Bisang, W., Bierschenk, T., Kreikenbom, D., and Verhoeven, U. eds. *Kulturelle und sprachliche Kontakte: Prozesse des Wandels in historischen Spannungsfeldern Nordostafrikas/Westasiens. Akten zum 2. Symposium des SFB 295.* Würzburg: Ergon Verlag. 241–255.

Matras, Y. 2005b. Language contact, language endangerment, and the role of the 'salvation linguist'. In: Austin, P. K. ed. *Language documentation and description*, Volume 3. London: Hans Rausing Endangered Languages Project. 225–251.

Matras, Y. 2007a. Contact, connectivity and language evolution. In: Rehbein, J., Hohenstein, C., and Pietsch, L. eds. *Connectivity in grammar and discourse.* Amsterdam: John Benjamins. 51–74.

Matras, Y. 2007b. The borrowability of grammatical categories. In: Matras, Y. and Sakel, J. eds. 31–74.

Matras, Y. 2007c. Grammatical borrowing in Domari. In: Matras, Y. and Sakel, J. eds. 151–164.

Matras, Y. ed. 1998. *The Romani element in non-standard speech.* Wiesbaden: Harrassowitz.

Matras, Y., Gardner, H., Jones, C., and Schulman, V. 2007. Angloromani: A different kind of language? *Anthropological Linguistics* 49, 142–164.

Matras, Y., McMahon, A., and Vincent, N. eds. 2006. *Linguistic areas. Convergence in historical and typological perspective.* Houndmills: Palgrave.

Maurais, J. 2003. Towards a new global linguistic order? In: Maurais, J. and Morris, M. A. eds. *Languages in a globalising world.* Cambridge: Cambridge University Press. 13–36.

McConvell, P. and Meakins, F. 2005. Gurindji Kriol: A mixed language emerges from code-switching. *Australian Journal of Linguistics* 25, 9–30.

McConvell, P. 2002. Mix-im-up speech and emergent mixed languages in indigenous Australia. *Texas Linguistic Forum* 44, 328–349.

McMahon, A. 2005. Heads I win, tails you lose. In: Carr, P., Durand, J., and Eden, C. eds. *Headhood. elements, specification and contrastivity*. Amsterdam: John Benjamins. 255–275.

McWhorter, J. H. 1997. *Towards a new model of creole genesis*. New York: Peter Lang.

McWhorter, J. H. 1998. Identifying the creole prototype: vindicating a typological class. *Language* 74, 788–818.

McWhorter, J. H. 2000. *The missing Spanish creoles. Recovering the birth of plantation contact languages*. Berkeley: University of California Press.

McWhorter, J. H. 2005. *Defining creole*. Oxford: Oxford University Press.

Meeuwis, M. and Blommaert, J. 1998. A monolectal view of code-switching: Layered code-switching among Zairians in Belgium. In: Auer, P. ed. 76–98.

Meisel, J. M. 1975. Ausländerdeutsch und Deutsch ausländischer Arbeiter. Zur möglichen Entstehung eines Pidgin in der BRD. *Zeitschrift für Literaturwissenschaft und Linguistik* 18, 9–53.

Meisel, J. M. 1989. Early differentiation of languages in bilingual children. In: Hyltenstam, K. and Obler, L. eds. *Bilingualism across the lifespan: Aspects of acquisition, maturity and loss*. Cambridge: Cambridge University Press. 13–40.

Meisel, J. M. 2001. The simultaneous acquisition of two first languages: Early differentiation and subsequent development of grammars. In: Cenoz, J. and Genesee, F. eds. *Trends in bilingual acquisition*. Amsterdam: John Benjamins. 11–41.

Meisinger, O. 1902. Lotekhôlisch. Ein Beitrag zur Kenntnis der fränkischen Händlersprache. *Zeitschrift für hochdeutsche Mundarten* 3, 121–127.

Migge, B. and Smith, N. 2007. Substrate influence in creole formation. *Journal of Pidgin and Creole Languages* 22, 1–15.

Migge, B. and Winford, D. 2007. Substrate influence on the emergence of the TMA systems of the Surinamese creoles. *Journal of Pidgin and Creole Languages* 22, 73–99.

Migge, B. 2003. *Creole formation as language contact. The case of the Suriname Creoles*. Amsterdam: John Benjamins.

Milroy, L. and Muysken, P. eds. 1995. *One speaker, two languages. Cross-disciplinary perspectives on code-switching*. Cambridge: Cambridge University Press.

Minett, J. W. and Wang, S.-Y. 2003. On detecting borrowing. Distance-based and character-based approaches. *Diachronica* 20, 289–330.

Mithun, M. 2004. Typology and diachrony: How stable is the grammar of argument structure? Keynote paper presented at annual meeting of the LAGB, Roehampton, September 2004.

Moormann, J. 1920. 'Louter Lekoris'. Een levende geheimtaal. *Tijdschrift voor taal en letteren* 8, 235–239, 306–333.

Moormann, J. 1922. Losche Nekôdesch. Een Limburgsche geheimtaal. *Tijdschrift voor taal en letteren* 10, 26–43, 68–87.

Morag, Sh. 1993. The emergence of Modern Hebrew: Some sociolinguistic perspectives. In: Glinert, L. ed. *Hebrew in Ashkenaz; A language in exile*. New York/Oxford: Oxford University Press. 208–221.

Moravcsik, E. 1975. Verb borrowing. *Wiener Linguistische Gazette* 8, 3–30.

Moravcsik, E. 1978. Universals of language contact. In: Greenberg, J. H. ed. *Universals of human language*. Stanford: Stanford University Press. 94–122.

Mous, M. 2003a. *The making of a mixed language. The case of Ma'a/Mbugu.* Amsterdam: John Benjamins.

Mous, M. 2003b. The linguistic properties of lexical manipulation and its relevance for Ma'á. In: Matras, Y. and Bakker, P. eds. 209–235.

Mufwene, S. S. 1996. The founder principle in creole genesis. *Diachronica* 13, 83–134.

Mufwene, S. S. 1997a. Jargons, pidgins, creoles, and koines: what are they? In: Spears, A. K. and Winford, D. eds. *The structure and status of pidgins and creoles.* Amsterdam: John Benjamins. 35–70.

Mufwene, S. S. 1997b. Kitúba. In: Thomason, S. G. ed. 173–208.

Mufwene, S. S. 2001. *The ecology of language evolution.* Cambridge: Cambridge University Press.

Mühlhäusler, P. 1977. Bemerkungen zum "Pidgin Deutsch" von Neuguinea. In: Molony, C. *et al.* eds. *German in contact with other languages.* Kronberg: Scriptor. 58–70.

Mühlhäusler, P. 1986. *Pidgin and creole linguistics.* Oxford: Blackwell.

Mühlhäusler, P. 2001. Die deutsche Sprache im Pazifik. In: Hiery, H. J. ed. *Die deutsche Südsee 1884 – 1914: ein Handbuch.* Paderborn: Verlag Ferdinand Schöningh. 239–260.

Müller, N. 1998. Transfer in bilingual first language acquisition. *Bilingualism: Language and Cognition* 1, 151–171.

Muysken, P. and Smith, N. 1995. The study of pidgin and creole languages. In: Arends, J., Muysken, P., and Smith, N. eds. 3–14.

Muysken, P. and Veenstra, T. 1995. Serial verbs. In: Arends, J., Muysken, P., and Smith, N. eds. 289–315.

Muysken, P. 1981. Halfway between Quechua and Spanish: the case for relexification. In: Highfield, A. and Valdman, A. eds. *Historicity and variation in Creole studies.* Ann Arbor: Karoma. 52–78.

Muysken, P. 1997. Media Lengua. In: Thomason, S. G. ed. 365–426.

Muysken, P. 2000a. *Bilingual speech. A typology of code-mixing.* Cambridge: Cambridge University Press.

Muysken, P. 2000b. From linguistic areas to areal linguistics: A research proposal. In: Gilbers, D.G., Nerbonne, J., and Schaeken, J. eds. 263–275.

Myers-Scotton, C. and Bolonyai, A. 2001. Calculating speakers: Codeswitching in a rational choice model. *Language in Society* 30, 1–28.

Myers-Scotton, C. and Jake, J. 2000. Four types of morpheme: Evidence from aphasia, codeswitching, and second language acquisition. *Linguistics* 38, 1053–1100.

Myers-Scotton, C. 1992. Codeswitching as a mechanism of deep borrowing, language shift, and language death. In: Brenzinger, M. ed. *Language death. Factual and theoretical explorations with special reference to East Africa.* Berlin: Mouton de Gruyter. 31–58.

Myers-Scotton, C. 1993a. *Social motivations for codeswitching. Evidence from Africa.* Oxford: Oxford University Press.

Myers-Scotton, C. 1993b. *Duelling languages. Grammatical structure in codeswitching.* Oxford: Oxford University Press.

Myers-Scotton, C. 1998. A way to dusty death: the Matrix Language turnover hypothesis. In: Grenoble, L. A. and Whaley, L. J. eds. *Endangered languages: language loss and community response.* Cambridge: Cambridge University Press. 289–316.

Myers-Scotton, C. 2002a. Frequency and intentionality in (un)marked choices in codeswitching: 'This is a 24-hour country'. *International Journal of Bilingualism* 6, 205–219.

Myers-Scotton, C. 2002b. *Contact Linguistics*. Oxford: Oxford University Press.

Myers-Scotton, C. 2003. What lies beneath: Split (mixed) languages as contact phenomena. In: Matras, Y. and Bakker, P. eds. 73–106.

Myers-Scotton, C. 2006. *Multiple voices: an introduction to bilingualism*. Oxford: Blackwell Publishing.

Nahir, M. 1998. Micro language planning and the revival of Hebrew: A schematic framework. *Language in Society* 27, 335–357.

Nau, Nicole. 1995. *Möglichkeiten und Mechanismen kontaktbewegten Sprachwandels – unter besonderer Berücksichtigung des Finnischen*. Munich: Lincom.

Nelde, P. H. 1993. Contact or conflict? Observations on the dynamics and vitality of European languages. In: Jahr, E. H. ed. *Language conflict and language planning*. Berlin: Mouton de Gruyter. 165–177.

Nettle, D. and Romaine, S. 2000. *Vanishing voices. The extinction of the world's languages*. Oxford: Oxford University Press.

Nichols, J. and Peterson, D. A. 1996. The Amerind personal pronouns. *Language* 72, 336–371.

Nichols, J. and Peterson, D. A. 1998. Amerind personal pronouns: A reply to Campbell. *Language* 74, 605–614.

Nichols, J. 1992. *Linguistic diversity in space and time*. Chicago: Chicago University Press.

Nicoladis, E. 1998. First clues to the existence of two input languages: Pragmatic and lexical differentiation in a bilingual child. *Bilingualism: Language and Cognition* 1, 105–116.

Nortier, J. 1990. *Dutch/Moroccan Arabic code-switching among young Moroccans in the Netherlands*. Dordrecht: Foris.

Nortier, J. 1995. Code-switching in Moroccan Arabic/Dutch versus Moroccan Arabic/French language contact. *International Journal of the Sociology of Language* 112, 81–95.

O'Grady, G. N. and Hale, K. 2004. The coherence and distinctiveness of the Pama-Nyungan language family within the Australian linguistic phylum. In: Bowern, C. and Koch, H. eds. *Australian languages: Classification and the comparative method*. Amsterdam: John Benjamins. 69–92.

O'Neil, S. 2006. Mythic and poetic dimensions of speech in Northwestern California: From cultural vocabulary to linguistic relativity. *Anthropological Linguistics* 48, 305–334.

O'Shannessy, C. 2005. Light Walpiri: A new language. *Australian Journal of Linguistics* 25, 31–57.

Ogura, M. and Wang, S.-Y. 1996. Evolution theory and lexical diffusion. In: Fisiak, J. and Krygier, M. eds. *Advances in English historical linguistics*. Berlin: Mouton de Gruyter. 293–314.

Olshtain, E. and Blum-Kulka, S. 1989. Happy Hebrish: Mixing and switching in American-Israeli family interactions. In: Gass, S., Madden, C., Preston, D., and Selinker, L. eds. *Variation in second language acquisition. Volume I: Discourse and pragmatics*. Clevedon: Multilingual Matters. 59–83.

Osman, M. F. 2006. Language choice among Arabic-English bilinguals in Manchester. Unpublished MA dissertation, University of Manchester.

Owens, J. 1997. Arabic-based pidgins and creoles. In: Thomason, S. G. ed. 125–172.

Paradis, J. 2001. Do bilingual two-year-olds have separate phonological systems? *International Journal of Bilingualism* 5, 19–38.

Paradis, M. 1990. Language lateralisation in bilinguals. Enough already! *Brain and Language* 39, 576–586.

Paradis, M. 2004. *A neurolinguistic theory of bilingualism*. Amsterdam: John Benjamins.

Paradis, M. ed. 1995. *Aspects of bilingual aphasia*. Oxford: Pergamon.

Pasch, H. 1997. Sango. In: Thomason, S. G. ed. 209–270.

Patrick, P. L. 1999. *Urban Jamaican Creole. Variation in the mesolect*. Amsterdam: John Benjamins.

Payne, J. R. 1995. Inflecting postpositions in Indic and Kashmiri. In: Plank, F. ed. *Double case. Agreement by Suffixaufnahme*. New York: Oxford University Press. 283–298.

Pearson, B. Z., Fernández, Sl. C., and Oller, D. K. 1993. Lexical development in bilingual infants and toddlers: Comparison to monolingual norms. *Language Learning* 43, 93–120.

Pfaff, C. 1979. Constraints on language mixing: intrasentential code-switching and borrowing in Spanish/English. *Language* 55, 291–318.

Pienemann, M. 1998. *Language processing and second language development*. Amsterdam: John Benjamins.

Pitrès, A. 1895. Etude sur l'aphasie chez les polyglottes. *Revue de Medecine* 15, 873–899.

Plag, I. 2002. On the role of grammaticalization in creolization. A reassessment. In: Gilbert, G. G. ed. *Pidgin and creole linguistics in the 21st century. Essays at millennium's end*. New York: Lang. 229–246.

Poplack, S. 1980. Sometimes I'll start a sentence in Spanish y termino en español. *Linguistics* 18, 581–618.

Poplack, S. 1981. Syntactic structure and social function of code-switching. In: Duran, R. ed. *Latino language and communicative behavior*. Norwood: Ablex. 169–184.

Poplack, S., Sankoff, D., and Miller, C. 1988. The social correlates and linguistic processes of lexical borrowing and assimilation. *Linguistics* 26, 47–104.

Poulisse, N. 1999. *Slips of the tongue. Speech errors in first and second language production*. Amsterdam: John Benjamins.

Queen, R. M. 2001. Bilingual intonation patterns: Evidence of language change from Turkish-German bilingual children. *Language in Society* 30, 55–80.

Ramat, P. and Roma, E. eds. 2007. *Europe and the Mediterranean as linguistic areas. Convergencies from a historical and typological perspective*. Amsterdam: John Benjamins.

Ramat, P. and Stolz, T. eds. 2002. *Mediterranean languages. Papers from the MEDTYP workshop, Tirrenia, June 2000*. Bochum: Brockmeyer.

Rebuck, M. 2002. The function of English loanwords in Japanese. *NUCB Journal of Language, Culture and Communication* 4, 53–64.

Redlinger, W. and Park, T.-Z. 1980. Language mixing in young bilingual children. *Journal of Child Language* 7, 337–352.

Reershemius, G. 2002. Bilingualismus oder Sprachverlust? Zur Lage und zur aktiven Verwendung des Niederdeutschen in Ostfriesland am Beispiel einer Dorfgemeinschaft. *Zeitschrift für Dialektologie und Linguistik* 69, 163–181.

Rehbein, J. 1977. *Kompexes Handeln. Elemente zur Handlungstheorie der Sprache.* Stuttgart: Metzler.

Rehbein, J. 1979. Sprechhandlungsaugmente. Zur Organisation der Hörersteuerung. In: Weydt, H. ed. *Die Partikeln der deutschen Sprache.* Berlin: De Gruyter. 58–74.

Rendón, J. G. 2007a. Grammatical borrowing in Imbabura Quechua (Ecuador). In: Matras, Y. and Sakel, J. eds. 481–521.

Rendón, J. G. 2007b. Grammatical borrowing in Paraguayan Guarani. In: Matras, Y. and Sakel, J. eds. 523–550.

Renfrew, C., McMahon, A., and Trask, R. L. eds. 2000. *Time depth in historical linguistics. Vol. 2.* Cambridge: McDonald Institute for Archeological Research.

Ribot, T. 1881. *Les maladies de la mémoire.* Paris: Baillère.

Rießler, M. 2007. Grammatical borrowing in Kildin Saami. In: Matras, Y. and Sakel, J. eds. 229–244.

Rijkhoff, J., Bakker, D., Hengeveld, K., and Kahrel, P. 1993. A method of language sampling. *Studies in Language* 17, 169–203.

Robinson, P. 2003. Attention and memory during SLA. In: Doughty, C. J. and Long, M. H. eds. *The handbook of second language acquisition.* Oxford: Blackwell. 631–678.

Romaine, S. 1995. *Bilingualism* (second edition). Oxford: Blackwell.

Ronjat, J. 1913. *Le developpement du langage observé chez un enfant bilingue.* Paris: Champion.

Ross, M. 1996. Contact-induced change and the Comparative Method. In: Durie, M. and Ross, M. eds. *The comparative method reviewed.* Oxford: Oxford University Press. 180–217.

Ross, M. 2001. Contact-induced change in Oceanic languages in north-west Melanesia. In: Aikhenvald, A. Y. and Dixon, R.M.W. eds. 134–166.

Rozencvejg, V. J. 1976. *Linguistic interference and convergent change.* The Hague: Mouton.

Rudolph, E. 1996. *Adversative and concessive relations and their expressions in English, German, Spanish, Portugese on sentence and text level.* Berlin: De Gruyter.

Sacks, H., Schegloff, E. A., and Jefferson, G. 1974. A simplest systematics for the organization of turn-taking in conversation. *Language* 50, 696–735.

Sakel, J. and Matras, Y. 2008. Modelling contact-induced change in grammar. In: Stolz, T., Bakker, D., and Salas Palomo, R. eds. *Aspects of language contact. New theoretical, methodological and empirical findings with special focus on Romanisation processes.* Berlin: Mouton de Gruyter. 63–87.

Sakel, J. 2007a. Language contact between Spanish and Mosetén: A study of grammatical integration. *International Journal of Bilingualism* 11, 25–53.

Sakel, J. 2007b. Language contact and recursion: the case of Pirahã. Paper presented at the international workshop 'Variations et Changements morphosyntaxiques en situation de contacts de langues', Ministère de la Recherche, Paris, 20–24 September 2007.

Sakel, J. 2007c. Mosetén borrowing from Spanish. In: Matras, Y. and Sakel, J. eds. 567–580.

Salmons, J. 1990. Bilingual discourse marking: code switching, borrowing, and convergence in some German-American dialects. *Linguistics* 28, 453–480.

Samely, U. 1991. *Kedang (Eastern Indonesia). Some aspects of its grammar.* Hamburg: Buske.

Sandefur, J. R. 1979. *An Australian creole in the Northern Territory: A description of Ngukurr-Bamyili dialects (Part 1)*. Darwin: Summer Institute of Linguistics, Australian Aborigines Branch.

Sandfeld, K. 1930. *Linguistique balkanique: problèmes et resultants*. Paris: C. Klincksieck.

Sankoff, D. and Poplack, S. 1981. A formal grammar of code-switching. *Papers in Linguistics* 14, 3–46.

Sankoff, D. 1998. A formal production-based explanation of the facts of code-switching. *Bilingualism: Language and Cognition* 1, 39–50.

Sankoff, G. 1990. The grammaticalisation of tense and aspect in Tok Pisin and Sranan. *Language Variation and Change* 2, 295–312.

Savić, J. M. 1995. Structural convergence and language change: Evidence from Serbian/English code-switching. *Language in Society* 24, 475–492.

Saville-Troike, M. 1989. *The ethnography of communication: An introduction*. Oxford: Blackwell.

Scheuermann, U. 2001. Friesische Relikte im ostfriesischen Niederdeutsch. In: Muske, H. H. ed. *Handbuch des Friesischen*. Tübingen: Niemeyer. 443–448.

Schiffrin, D. 1987. *Discourse markers*. Cambridge: Cambridge University Press.

Schirmer, A., Alter, K., Kotz, S., and Friederici, A. 2001. Lateralization of prosody during language production: A lesion study. *Brain and Language* 76, 1–17.

Schultze-Berndt, E. 2000. *Simple and complex verbs in Jaminjung. A study of event categorisation in an Australian language*. Nijmegen: MPI.

Schultze-Berndt, E. 2007. Recent grammatical borrowing into an Australian Aboriginal language: The case of Jaminjung and Kriol. In: Matras, Y. and Sakel, J. eds. 363–386.

Sebba, M. 1997. *Contact languages*. Houndmills: Macmillan.

Selinker, L. 1972. Interlanguage. *International Review of Applied Linguistics* 10, 209–231.

Shabibi, M. 2006. Contact-induced grammatical change in Khuzestani Arabic. Unpublished PhD dissertation, University of Manchester.

Sharewood Smith, M. 1991. Language modules and bilingual processing. In: Bialystok, E. ed. *Language processing in bilingual children*. Cambridge: Cambridge University Press. 10–24.

Siewert, K. ed. 1996. *Rotwelschdialekte*. Wiesbaden: Harrassowitz.

Siewierska, A. 2004. *Person*. Cambridge: Cambridge University Press.

Silva-Corvalán, C. 1994. *Language contact and change. Spanish in Los Angeles*. Oxford: Clarendon Press.

Simango, S. R. 'My Madame is fine': The adaptation of English loans in Chichewa. *Journal of Multilingual and Multicultural Development* 21, 487–507.

Skutnabb-Kangas, T. and Phillipson, R. 1995. Linguistic human rights, past and present. In: Skutnabb-Kangas, T. and Phillipson, R. eds. 71–110.

Skutnabb-Kangas, T. and Phillipson, R. eds. 1995. *Linguistic human rights. Overcoming linguistic discrimination*. Berlin: Mouton de Gruyter.

Smith, N. 1995. An annotated list of creoles, pidgins, and mixed languages. In: Arends, J., Muysken, P., and Smith, N. eds. 331–374.

Smith, N. 1998. Complex personal pronouns in the secret languages of nomadic castes. In: Bruyn, A. and Arends, J. eds. *Mengelwerk voor Muysken*. Amsterdam: Institute for General Linguistics. 44–49.

Solta, G. R. 1980. *Einfuhrung in die Balkanlinguistik mit besonderer Berucksichtigung des Substrats und des Balkanlateinischen*. Darmstadt: Wissenschaftliche Buchgesellschaft.

Sperber, D. and Wilson, D. 1986. *Relevance. Communication and cognition*. Oxford: Blackwell.

Stewart, W. 1962. Creole languages in the Caribbean. In: Rice, F. A. ed. *Study of the role of second languages in Asia, Africa and Latin America*. Washington: Center for Applied Linguistics. 34–53.

Stolz, C. and Stolz, T. 1996. Funktionswortentlehnung in Mesoamerika. Spanisch-amerindischer Sprachkontakt Hispanoindiana II. *Sprachtypologie und Universalienforschung* 49, 86–123.

Stolz, C. and Stolz, T. 1997. Universelle Hispanismen? Von Manila über Lima bis Mexiko und zurück: Muster bei der Entlehnung spanischer Funktionswörter in die indigenen Sprachen Amerikas und Austronesiens. *Orbis* 39, 1–77.

Stolz, C. and Stolz, T. 2001. Hispanicised comparative constructions in Indigenous languages of Austronesia and the Americas. In: Zimmermann, K. and Stolz, T. eds. *Lo propio y lo ajeno en las lenguas austronésicas amerindias*. Madrid: Iberoamericana. 35–56.

Stolz, T. 1991. *Sprachbund im Baltikum? Estnisch und Lettisch im Zentrum eine sprachlichen Konvergenzlandschaft*. Bochum: Brockmeyer.

Stolz, T. 1996. Grammatical Hispanisms in Amerindian and Austronesian languages. The other kind of Transpacific isoglosses. *Amerindia* 21, 137–160.

Stolz, T. 2003. Not quite the right mixture: Chamorro and Malti as candidates for the status of mixed language: In: Matras, Y. and Bakker, P. eds. 271–315.

Stolz, T. 2006. All or nothing. In: Matras, Y., McMahon, A., and Vincent, N. eds. 32–50.

Stolz, T. 2007. Allora. On the recurrence of function-word borrowing in contact situations with Italian as donor language. In: Rehbein, J., Hohenstein, C., and Pietsch, L. eds., *Connectivity in grammar and discourse*. Amsterdam: John Benjamins. 75–99.

Storch, A. 2006. How long do linguistic areas last? Western Nilotic grammars in contact. In: Aikhenvald, A. Y. and Dixon, R. M. W. eds. 2006. 94–113.

Stroud, C. 2007. Multilingualism in ex-colonial countries. In: Auer, P. and Li Wei. eds. *Handbook of multilingualism and multilingual communication*. Berlin: Mouton de Gruyter. 509–538.

Swadesh, M. 1952. Lexicostatistic dating of prehistoric ethnic contacts. *Proceedings of the American Philosophical Society* 96, 452–463.

Sweeney, D. 2007. A sociolinguistic study of Irish in a community in the North West of Ireland. Unpublished BA dissertation, University of Manchester.

Tadmor, U. 2004. Function loanwords in Malay-Indonesian (and some other Southeast Asian languages). Paper presented a the Loan Word Typology Workshop, Max-Planck-Institute for Evolutionary Anthropology, Leipzig, 1–2 May 2004.

Tadmor, U. 2007. Grammatical borrowing in Indonesian. In: Matras, Y. and Sakel, J. eds. 301–328.

Tenser, A. 2008. *The Northeastern dialects of Romani*. Unpublished PhD dissertation, University of Manchester.

Thai, B. D. 2007. Preliminary observations on a 'Migrant Vietnamese'. Working Paper, The Australian National University.

Thomason, S. G. and Everett, D.L. 2001. Pronoun borrowing. In: Chang, Ch. *et al.* eds. *Proceedings of the twenty seventh annual meeting of the Berkeley Linguistics Society.* Berkeley: Berkeley Linguistics Society. 301–315.

Thomason, S. G. and Kaufman, T. 1988. *Language contact, creolization and genetic linguistics.* Berkeley: University of California Press.

Thomason, S. G. 1983. Chinook Jargon in areal and historical context. *Language* 59, 820–870.

Thomason, S. G. 1995. Language mixture: ordinary processes, extraordinary results. In: Silva-Corvalán, C. ed. *Spanish in four continents. Studies in language contact and bilingualism.* Washington DC: Georgetown University Press. 15–33.

Thomason, S. G. 1997a. Ma'a (Mbugu). In: Thomason, S. G. ed. 469–487.

Thomason, S. G. 1997b. Mednyj Aleut. In: Thomason, S. G. ed. 449–468.

Thomason, S. G. 1997c. A typology of contact languages. In: Spears, A. A. and Winford, D. eds. *The structure and status of pidgins and creoles.* Amsterdam: John Benjamins. 71–88.

Thomason, S. G. 1997d. On mechanisms of interference. In: Eliasson, S. and Jahr, E. H. eds. *Language and its ecology. Essays in memory of Einar Haugen.* Berlin: Mouton. 181–207.

Thomason, S. G. 1997e. Introduction. In: Thomason, S. G. ed. 1–7.

Thomason, S. G. 1999. Speakers' choices in language change. *Studies in the Linguistic Sciences* 29, 19–43.

Thomason, S. G. 2000. Linguistic areas and language history. In: Gilbers, D. G., Nerbonne, J., and Schaeken, J. eds. 311–327.

Thomason, S. G. 2001. *Language contact. An introduction.* Edinburgh: Edinburgh University Press.

Thomason, S. G. ed. 1997. *Contact languages: A wider perspective.* Amsterdam: John Benjamins.

Tipler, D. 1957. Specimens of Modern Welsh Romani. *Journal of the Gypsy Lore Society* 3/36, 9–24.

Tomasello, M. 1999. *The cultural origins of human cognition.* Cambridge, MA: Harvard University Press.

Topping, D. M. 1973. *Chamorro reference grammar.* Honolulu: University of Hawaii Press.

Torres, L. 2002. Bilingual discourse markers in Puerto Rican Spanish. *Language in Society* 31, 65–83.

Trubetzkoy, N. S. 1928. Proposition 16. *Acts of the First International Congress of Linguists,* Leiden. 17–18.

Tsunoda, T. 2005. *Language endangerment and language revitalization.* Berlin: Mouton de Gruyter.

Tufan, S. 2008. Language convergence in Gostivar Turkish. Unpublished PhD dissertation, University of Manchester.

Turi, J.-G. 1995. Typology of language legislation. In: Skutnabb-Kangas, T. and Phillipson, R. eds. 111–120.

Ullman, M. T. 2001. The neural basis of lexicon and grammar in first and second language: the declarative/procedural model. *Bilingualism: Language and Cognition* 4, 105–122.

Vaid, J. 1984. Visual, phonetic and semantic processing in early and late bilinguals. In: Paradis, M. and Lebrun, Y. eds. *Early bilingualism and child development*. Lisse: Swets & Zeitlinger. 175–191.

Vakhtin, N. 1998. Copper Island Aleut: a case of languages 'resurrection'. In: Grenoble, L. A. and Whaley, L. J. eds. *Endangered languages: language loss and community response*. Cambridge: Cambridge University Press. 317–327.

van den Heuvel, W. 2007. Grammatical borrowing in Biak. In: Matras, Y. and Sakel, J. eds. 329–342.

van der Auwera, J. 1998. Phasal adverbials in the languages of Europe. In: van der Auwera, J. and Ó Baoill, B. eds. *Adverbial constructions in the languages of Europe*, Berlin: Mouton de Gruyter. 25–145

van der Voort, H. 2000. A grammar of Kwaza. Unpublished PhD thesis, University of Amsterdam.

van Hout, R. and Muysken, P. 1994. Modelling lexical borrowability. *Language Variation and Change* 6, 39–62.

Verhaar, J. W. M. 1995. *Toward a reference grammar of Tok Pisin. An experiment in corpus linguistics*. Honolulu: University of Hawai'i Press.

Véronique, Daniel. 2003. Iconicity and finiteness in the development of early grammar in French as L2 and in French-based creoles. In: Giacalone Ramat, A. ed. *Typology and second language acquisition*. Berlin: Mouton. 221–266.

Vihman, M. 1985. Language differentiation by the bilingual child. *Journal of Child Language* 12, 297–324.

Volterra, V. and Taeschner, T. 1978. The acquisition and development of language by bilingual children. *Journal of Child Language* 5, 311–326.

Voorhoeve, C. L. 1994. Contact-induced change in the non-Austronesian languages in the north Moluccas, Indonesia. In: Dutton, T. and Darrel, T. T. eds. *Language contact and language change in the Austronesian world*. Berlin: Mouton de Gruyter. 649–674.

Wallace, S. 1983. Pronouns in contact. In: Agard, B., Kelley, G., Makkai, A., and Becker Makkai, V. eds. *Essays in honor of Charles F. Hockett*. Berlin: Mouton de Gruyter. 573–589.

Weinreich, U. 1953. *Languages in contact*. The Hague: Mouton.

Weinreich, U. 1958. On the compatibility of genetic relationship and convergent development. *Word* 14, 374–379.

Wellens, I. 2005. *The Nubi language of Uganda*. Leiden: Brill.

Wexler, P. 1990. *The schizoid nature of Modern Hebrew. A Slavic language in search of a Semitic past*. Wiesbaden: Harrassowitz.

Whinnom, K. 1965. The origins of the European-based creoles and pidgins. *Orbis* 14, 509–527.

White, L. 2003. Fossilization in steady state L2 grammars: Persistent problems with inflectional morphology. *Bilingualism: Language and Cognition* 6, 129–141.

Wichmann, S. and Wohlgemuth, J. 2008. Loan verbs in a typological perspective. In: Stolz, T., Bakker, D., and Salas Palomo, R. eds. *Aspects of language contact. New theoretical, methodological and empirical findings with special focus on Romanisation processes*. Berlin: Mouton de Gruyter. 89–121.

Williams, G. 2005. *Sustaining language diversity in Europe. Evidence from the Euromosaic project.* Houndmills: Palgrave Macmillan.

Winford, D. 2003. *An introduction to contact linguistics.* Oxford: Blackwell.

Winford, D. 2006. Revisiting relexification in creole formation. In: Thornburg, L. L. and Fuller, J. M. eds. *Studies in contact linguistics. Essays in honor of Glenn G. Gilbert.* New York: Peter Lang. 231–252.

Winter, W. 1973. Areal linguistics. In: Sebeok, T. A. ed. *Current trends in linguistics* Vol. 11. The Hague: Mouton. 35–147.

Zuckermann, G. 2003. *Language contact and lexical enrichment in Israeli Hebrew.* London: Palgrave Macmillan.

Author index

Language index

Subject index

addressee, 12, 14, 17, 27, 42, 43, 44, 45, 53, 93, 116
adjective, derivation, 190
adjective, inflection, 189
agentive, 30, 58, 181, 209, 210, 269
agglutinative morphology, 245
agreement, 24, 27, 58, 73, 82, 88, 132, 137, 188, 189, 190, 245, 248, 254, 255, 260, 261, 270, 283, 296, 303
aktionsart, 30, 211, 212, 235
Algeria, 49
Amazon, 48, 49, 59, 147, 179, 235, 271, 280
Amazonia, 220
Anatolia, 192, 200, 249, 251, 262, 267, 270, 271, 294
Angola, 285
aphasia, 7, 87, 88, 89, 91, 132, 308, 317
Arctic, 278
Arnhem Land, 48, 195, 197, 215, 250, 271
Aruba, 280
aspect, 4, 20, 76, 93, 116, 120, 132, 146, 162, 174, 177, 178, 179, 184, 185, 204, 208, 209, 211, 212, 213, 216, 236, 237, 258, 260, 262, 266, 270, 271, 282, 285, 307
Athens, 194
attributive construction, 189, 254, 256, 321
Australia, 44, 48, 57, 76, 138, 197, 205, 215, 216, 250, 268, 271, 275, 279, 282, 300, 301, 320
Austria, 55, 197, 271, 291

Balkans, 163, 183, 196, 197, 203, 210, 248, 249, 250, 251, 252, 265, 266, 267, 269, 320
Beijing, 111
Belgium, 46, 48, 55, 127
Belize, 279
Benin, 285
bilingual mode, 90, 91, 95, 101, 104, 105, 108, 109, 111, 112, 127, 134, 140, 145, 147, 151, 165, 183, 193, 194, 206, 312
Black Forest, 293
Bonaire, 280
bound morphemes, 129, 155
Brazil, 49
Britain, 97, 122, 151, 231, 295
British Isles, 295

Brussels, 55
Bulgaria, 183, 184, 185, 196, 213, 257, 319
Burgenland, 189, 197, 271

California, 220, 235
Canada, 44, 47, 54, 55
Cape Verde, 280
Cappadocia, 262
Caribbean, 279, 281, 284, 285
Carinthia, 55
case marker, 216, 218, 262, 264
Caucasus, 180, 192, 194, 267, 275
Central African Republic, 280
Central America, 138, 158, 190, 194, 200, 279
China, 284
Circum-Baltic region, 268
classifier, 174, 218, 279
clitic, 157
colonial settings, 48, 58, 199
colour terms, 187, 188
Columbia, 280
Commander Islands, 298
comparative, 59, 73, 99, 113, 154, 157, 159, 161, 173, 190, 191, 266, 268, 269, 277, 306
complementation, 162, 196, 244, 245, 248, 250
compound bilingual, 87
concord markers, *see* person concord markers, 184, 261
conditional (particle), 18, 19, 162
conjunction, 18, 20, 27, 80, 83, 96, 97, 137, 180, 181, 240, 282, 290
content morphemes, 132, 300
contrast, 2, 7, 15, 20, 22, 37, 43, 45, 47, 55, 60, 61, 64, 65, 69, 72, 83, 84, 89, 99, 101, 106, 109, 111, 113, 115, 116, 117, 118, 120, 121, 122, 126, 127, 132, 143, 151, 152, 159, 162, 169, 187, 189, 190, 194, 195, 200, 212, 213, 215, 228, 230, 244, 250, 251, 255, 256, 269, 271, 278, 289, 305, 309, 316, 318, 319, 320
convergence, 5, 8, 40, 59, 139, 158, 196, 223, 224, 225, 226, 229, 230, 232, 236, 244, 246, 249, 250, 251, 256, 258, 259, 260, 262, 263, 264, 266, 267, 268, 271, 272, 276, 310
coordinate bilingual, 87
Copper Island, 291, 298, 299, 300, 302, 305